GREEK BUDDHA

GREEK BUDDHA

Pyrrho's Encounter with Early Buddhism in Central Asia

CHRISTOPHER I. BECKWITH

PRINCETON UNIVERSITY PRESS
PRINCETON AND OXFORD

Published by Princeton University Press, 41 William Street,
Princeton, New Jersey 08540
In the United Kingdom: Princeton University Press,
6 Oxford Street, Woodstock, Oxfordshire OX20 1TW

press.princeton.edu

Library of Congress Cataloging-in-Publication Data
Beckwith, Christopher I., 1945–
Greek Buddha : Pyrrho's encounter with early
Buddhism in Central Asia / Christopher I. Beckwith.
pages cm
Includes bibliographical references and index.
ISBN 978-0-691-16644-5 (hardback)
1. Pyrrhon, of Elis. 2. Buddhism—History—To ca. 100 A.D.
3. Buddhism—Influence. 4. Buddhism and philosophy. I. Title.
B613.B43 2015
186'.1—dc23
2014044329

British Library Cataloging-in-Publication Data is available

This book has been composed in Charis

Printed on acid-free paper. ∞

Printed in the United States of America

3 5 7 9 10 8 6 4 2

Contents

Preface

In the past few decades a quiet revolution has been under way in the study of the earliest Buddhism. Its beginnings lay in the discoveries of John Marshall, the archaeologist who excavated the great ancient city of eastern Gandhāra, Taxila (near what is now Rawalpindi), and published his results in 1951. The evidence was incontrovertible: the Buddhist monastery, the *vihāra*, with its highly distinctive architectural plan, appeared there fully formed in the first century AD, and had been preceded by the *ārāma*, a crude temporary shelter that was also found there.[1] Marshall openly stated that organized Buddhist monasticism accompanied the appearance of monasteries then—in the Saka-Kushan period—and had not existed before that time. This partly corresponded to the traditional trajectory of the development of Buddhism, but in delaying the appearance of monasticism for an entire half millennium after the Buddha, it challenged practically everything else in the traditional account of Early Buddhism. Most scholars paid no attention whatsoever to this. However, eventually others noticed additional problems, particularly contradictions in the canonical texts themselves that challenged many fundamental beliefs about the early development of the religion. André Bareau, Johannes Bronkhorst, Luis Gómez, Gregory Schopen, and others challenged many of these traditional beliefs in studies of the canonical texts viewed in the context of other material—archaeological excavations (of which there were and are precious few), material in non-Buddhist texts, and so forth. Their discoveries have overthrown so many of the traditional ideas that, as so often in scholarship, those who follow the traditional view have felt compelled to fight back. But the new views on Buddhism are themselves not free of

[1] See now Beckwith (2014).

traditional notions, and these have prevented a comprehensive, principled account of Early Buddhism from developing.

The most important single error made by almost everyone in Buddhist studies is methodological and theoretical in nature. In all scholarly fields, it is absolutely imperative that theories be based on the data, but in Buddhist studies, as in other fields like it, even dated, "provenanced" archaeological and historical source material that controverts the traditional view of Early Buddhism has been rejected because it does not agree with that traditional view, and even worse, because it does not agree with the traditional view of the entire world of early India, including beliefs about Brahmanism and other sects that are thought to have existed at that time, again based not on hard data but on the same late traditional accounts. Some of these beliefs remain largely or completely unchallenged, notably:

- the belief that Śramaṇas existed before the Buddha, so he became a Śramaṇa like many other Śramaṇas
- the belief that there were Śramaṇas besides Early Buddhists, including Jains and Ājīvikas, whose sects were as old or older than Buddhism, and the Buddha even knew some of their founders personally
- that, despite the name Śramaṇa, and despite the work of Marshall, Bareau, and Schopen, the Early Buddhists were "monks" and lived in "monasteries" with a monastic rule, the Vinaya
- that, despite the scholarship of Bronkhorst, the Upanishads and other Brahmanist texts are very ancient, so old that they precede Buddhism, so the Buddha was influenced by their ideas
- that the dated Greek eyewitness reports on religious-philosophical practitioners in late fourth century BC India do not tally with the traditional Indian accounts written a half millennium or more later, so the Greek reports must be wrong and must be ignored
- perhaps most grievously, the belief that *all* stone inscriptions in the early Brahmi script of the Mauryan period were erected by "Aśoka", the traditional grandson of the Mauryan Dynasty's historical founder, Candragupta, and whatever any of those inscriptions say is therefore evidence about what went on during (or before) the time he is thought to have lived
- we "know" what problematic terms (such as Sanskrit *duḥkha* ~ Pali *dukkha*) mean, despite the fact that their meaning is actually contested by scholars, the modern and traditional dictionaries do not

agree on their etymologies or what they "really" mean, and the texts do not agree either[2]

These and other stubborn unexamined beliefs have adversely affected the work of even the most insightful scholars of Buddhism. Yet no contemporaneous or near-contemporaneous hard evidence of any kind affirms such beliefs. Moreover, it is bad enough that such ideas have caused so much damage for so long within Indology, but the resulting misinformation has inflicted damage in other fields as well, including ancient Greek and Chinese philosophy, where the traditional construct has been used as the basis, once again, for rejecting the hard data, forcing scholars in those fields to attempt to explain away what seems to be obvious Indian Buddhist influence. This then helps maintain the traditional fiction of three totally unrelated peoples and traditions as "cultural islands" that had absolutely no contact of any kind with each other until much later times, as used to be unquestioned belief as recently as Karl Jaspers's famous book on the Axial Age,[3] and continues, by and large, among those who follow in his footsteps.

Setting aside the traditional beliefs mentioned above, and much other folklore, what hard data might be found on the topic at hand? What sort of picture can we construct based *primarily* on the hard data rather than on the traditional views? In the present book I present a scientific approach, to the extent that I have been able to do so and have not been mislead by my own unrecognized "views".

It is important to note that this book is *not* a comparison of anything. It is also most definitely not a critique or biobibliographic survey of earlier research. Such a study would be great to have (and in fact, an excellent bibliography on Pyrrhonism was published by Richard Bett in 2010), but I have cited only what I thought necessary to cite or what I was able to find myself, with a strong preference for primary sources.[4]

[2] Some of these problems are discussed in Chapter Three. See Appendix C for further details.

[3] Jaspers (1949; English translation 1953). I should stress, however, that Jaspers's book is nevertheless very insightful and is still worth reading today.

[4] I have also paid some attention to recent traditional interpretations of "Early" Buddhism, and have in several instances cited them for Normative Buddhist reflections of actual Early Buddhist thought.

I have attempted to solve several major problems in the history of thought. The most important of these problems involves the source of Pyrrho's teachings. I would like to call it philosophy, and I have sinned—sometimes willfully—by doing so when I talk about Early Pyrrhonism's more "philosophical" aspects, but in general to call it *philosophy* in a modern language is to seriously mislabel it. The same would be true if I called it *religion*. It was to some extent both, and to some extent neither, and it was *science*, too.

I first spent a great deal of time reexamining and rethinking the Greek testimonies of Pyrrho's thought, and in 2011 finally published a long article on the topic in *Elenchos* (reprinted with minor revisions in Appendix A). I then looked into the studies which claim—in accord with statements of ancient authors—that Pyrrho acquired his unusual way of thought in India. I also read studies that claimed the exact opposite—that he did not learn anything at all of major importance for his thought there—and other arguments which essentially claim that Indian philosophy is basically Greek in origin. That forced me to investigate Early Buddhism in depth, with the result that I discovered the above problems, among others, and my study became much longer and more involved than I had expected.

My research set out to determine whether Indian thought—particularly Buddhism—had influenced Pyrrho's thought. It ended up delving very deeply into the problem of identifying genuine Early Buddhism: the teachings and practices of the Buddha himself, and of his followers for the first century or two after his death. As mentioned above, in my view all scholarship, regardless of its subject matter, should follow the dictum "theories must accord with the data", with the corollary that the earliest hard data must always be ranked higher in value than other data. In addition, theories and scholarly arguments must be based on rational, logical thought. These are among the core principles of scientific work in general, and I have done my best to follow them.

One of the anonymous reviewers of the manuscript of this book has different ideas about how I should have proceeded. He says, "A strong case could be made that even relatively specific features of the history of philosophy such as the Problem of the Criterion (relative, that is, to the general phenomenon of skepticism) could be explained as a generic motif rather than, so to speak, as a patented idea". He contends that "two figures saying similar, or even identical, things in different parts of the world is never enough to establish direct influence."

This is a problematic claim with respect to philosophy and religious studies. The field of biblical studies is founded on the ability and necessity to do text criticism. It is purely *because* textual near identity is recognizable that textual scholars can identify interpolations, university teachers can recognize plagiarization—even cross-linguistic plagiarization[5]—and so on. Is it really conceivable that, for example, the famous statement of Protagoras, "Man is the measure of all things", is unrelated to the Greek original, or is not recognizable? The ancient Greek πάντων χρημάτων μέτρον ἐστὶν ἄνθρωπος has *exactly* the same meaning as the modern Chinese translation, 人是萬物的尺度, the modern Russian translation, Человек есть мера всех вещей, and so on. Assuming it is correctly translated, the quotation is famous, easily recognizable, and not liable to be confused with any other, whatever the language, despite its brevity. But why? It is the *highly distinctive content* of the text that makes it easily identifiable. Translation converts the *meaning* expressed from one language to another. It does not do it perfectly because with perfect identity no translation occurs—the texts are identical. The reviewer's assertion denies the possibility of communication by language even in the same language (not to speak of the possibility of understanding, say, a German translation of an English textbook, or vice versa, as students manage to do every day), and the necessity of intelligibility assumed by the very existence of the field of linguistic typology.

Aristotle talks about exactly this topic in his *Metaphysics*. For example, no doubt many ancient Greeks, Indians, and Chinese said, "It's a nice day today," and proceeded to take a walk somewhere to enjoy the fine weather. Many people everywhere do that, and my wife is liable to say the same thing to me when it is warm and sunny. So it is easy for us to imagine that countless Greeks, Indians, and Chinese have said the same thing. But to paraphrase Aristotle again, we can hardly imagine that anyone in ancient India or China could then have said, "Let's walk to the Odeon in Athens!"

[5] A student in one of my classes recently was guilty of such plagiarization in her paper and admitted it—"Well, not *all* of it," she said to me in her native language.

The reviewer instead compares the historical appearance of Pyrrhonism to that of "the widespread phenomenon of world-denying mendicants or for that matter cultural motifs of lycanthropy, unicorns, or night-walking." He proposes that "pan-Eurasian social dynamics could be enough to explain the independent appearance of philosophical theories that deny the attainability of certain knowledge and that reject all positive doctrine."[6] Yet Pyrrho's declaration in the Aristocles passage has challenged not only the manuscript reviewer but a century of scholars, who have not been able to explain it no matter what approach they have adopted, thus demonstrating both how unique it is and how difficult it has been for anyone to deal with it. This is only one part of the actual, *complex* problem that needs to be discussed and explained.

Another of the reviewers of the manuscript of this book suggests that I should discuss the controversial issue of the date of the foundation of Jainism, its relationship to Buddhism, and so on, in greater detail. I strongly agree that it would be great to have a careful, historically sound study of this topic, and I have long encouraged other scholars to undertake one. So far, however, Indologists, including Buddhologists, have not examined the Jain dating issue carefully and thoroughly from a historical point of view, and no such comprehensive study yet exists, though the issue is mentioned by a number of scholars, including Mette (1995), who though evidently pro-Jain concludes that Buddhism seems to be in all respects earlier than Jainism. The earliest incontestable hard evidence for the existence of Jainism is not earlier than the Saka-Kushan period (first century BC to third century AD), about a half millennium after the Buddha, as shown by the fact that none of the explicitly identified and datable Jain material listed in Ghosh's authoritative register of Indian archaeological sites is earlier than the Saka-Kushan period, the earliest being caves dated (generously) to ca. 100 BC to AD 200.[7] My approach in the book is to base all of my main arguments on hard

[6] This is the view of dogmatic Academic Scepticism, *not* Pyrrhonism.

[7] Ghosh (1990: 2:446a). A figurine mentioned by B. Lal is called the "earliest Jain figure found so far", and is dated to "ca." fourth to third centuries BC (Ghosh 1990: 2:32a), but this is of course untenable, since there are no known statues of religious figures from *any* sect before the Saka-Kushan period. Ghosh's index lists ten sites with Jain artifacts (mostly medieval), but by contrast about ninety sites with Buddhist materials, many of them substantial and dated to the last three centuries BC. For Mathura, which is today an important Jain site, Ghosh lists no Jain artifacts at all from archaeological work.

data—inscriptions, datable manuscripts, other dated texts, and archaeological reports. I do not allow traditional belief to determine anything in the book, so I have necessarily left the topic out, other than to mention it briefly in a few places, with relevant citations. Here I quote a century-old summary that remains the received view:

> Jainism bears a striking resemblance to Buddhism in its monastic system, its ethical teachings, its sacred texts, and in the story of its founder. This closeness of resemblance has led not a few scholars—such as Lassen, Weber, Wilson, Tiele, Barth—to look upon Jainism as an offshoot of Buddhism and to place its origin some centuries later than the time of Buddha. But the prevailing view today—that of Bühler, Jacobi, Hopkins, and others—is that Jainism in its origin is independent of Buddhism and, perhaps, is the more ancient of the two. The many points of similarity between the two sects are explained by the indebtedness of both to a common source, namely the teachings and practices of ascetic, monastic Brahminism.

However, he then comments, "The canon of the White-robed Sect consists of forty-five Agamas, or sacred texts, in the Prakrit tongue. Jacobi, who has translated some of these texts in the 'Sacred Books of the East', is of the opinion that they cannot be older than 300 B.C.[8] According to Jainist tradition, they were preceded by an ancient canon of fourteen so-called Purvas, which have totally disappeared . . .".[9] With regard to the idea that any kind of monasticism, least of all Brahmanist asceticism, could be the "common source", it may be noted that monasteries per se in India cannot be dated earlier than the first century AD, when they first appear in Taxila; they were introduced from Central Asia, where Jainism was and is unknown.[10] Finally, my discussion here, and throughout this book, is concerned only with issues of *historical* accuracy. In my opinion, all great religions have much that is admirable in them, however old or new they may be.

I would like to emphasize that this book does not belong to any existing view, school, or field, as far as I am aware, so that it does not subscribe to any tradition walled off from the rest of intellectual life.

[8] This date is far too early. The oldest written texts in any Indian language are the Major Inscriptions of the Mauryas, which are dated to the first half of the third century BC and do not mention Jainism; see Chapter Three and Appendix C.

[9] Aiken (1910).

[10] Beckwith (2014).

It therefore has no gatekeepers, clad in the traditional metaphorical chain-mail armor and bearing the traditional metaphorical halberd, proclaiming threats to their perceived enemies in archaic languages, dedicated to keeping new knowledge out and stamping out all possible threats to those inside its walls so that the residents can safely continue their traditional beliefs without the necessity of thinking about them. The book is also inevitably imperfect, though I have tried to make it as correct as I could, despite the limitations of my own imperfections. So I hope it is not the "last word" on the many topics it covers, but only the "first word". My goal throughout has been exclusively to examine the evidence as carefully and precisely as possible, and to draw reasonable conclusions based on it—while of course considering other studies that shed light on the problems or in some cases argue for a different interpretation. This sounds like a rather un-Pyrrhonian enterprise, but ultimately, and somewhat unexpectedly, it is what Pyrrhonism is all about.

Acknowledgements

Although for me this book represents almost entirely new research on new ideas, it can also be said to go back to around 1967, when I was an undergraduate major in Chinese at Ohio State University and took a general philosophy survey class. The professor, Everett John Nelson, devoted one lecture to what I remember as "Classical Scepticism". I liked very much what I heard, and immediately went out and read the works of Sextus Empiricus in translation. Shortly after I took that course, I took Professor William Lyell's class in Chinese philosophy, and wrote a term paper for it in which I compared the ideas of Laotzu in the *Tao Te Ching* to the ideas of Sextus Empiricus. It never occurred to me then that the similarities I perceived had a foundation in anything historical—partly because at the time I had a strong dislike for history in the usual sense. My two minor interests in Pyrrhonism and Early Taoism remained just that for the following decades, until by chance synergy happened and I found myself working on elements of both for one or another research project, and ended up, to my surprise, confirming the underlying perception in my long-ago undergraduate term paper.

At that point I had the opportunity to spend over a year in 2011–2012 as a visiting research fellow in the Käte Hamburger Kolleg "History of Religions between Europe and Asia", at the Ruhr University in Bochum, Germany. There I was faced with a challenging, high-level research program involving regular colloquia, research group meetings, and, especially, workshops and conferences. After being quickly drafted to give papers in half a dozen workshops, I realized that I would not be able to write my planned book there unless my papers were on topics related to the book. When, half a year later, that decision finally began taking hold, I found myself investigating the problems of my topic in unexpected ways, mostly because of the need to accommodate myself to the particular theoretical approach of the given workshop or conference in which I was to present my paper. It was not easy for me to reorient myself in this way, but somehow I eventually managed, at least in part, so that to a certain extent I looked at the sources with new eyes and thought about them with a new mind. This turned out to be extremely fruitful, as it led me to discover things that I had never noticed before, and that nobody else had noticed either, as far as I know. It is partly for this reason that, I hope, this book makes a contribution to the solution of some major problems in philosophy, religious studies, and intellectual history in general.

I must therefore first thank Professor Everett John Nelson and Professor William Lyell for trying to teach me philosophy many decades ago when I was an undergraduate student at Ohio State, and for eventually succeeding—to my own amazement—in stimulating a genuine interest in the subject, as well as Professor Helmut Hoffmann, my doctoral advisor, who taught me much about Buddhism and scholarship in general.

I especially thank my friend and colleague Michael L. Walter, with whom I have had countless amiable and enlightening discussions about the history of Buddhism, including many points covered in this book. Without his kindness, assistance, and critical mind I would never have begun it.

I am also deeply indebted to Cynthia King for her very helpful comments on things Greek from beginning to end of this project, as well as for reading and offering numerous corrections and suggestions on an early draft of the manuscript; to Georgios Halkias for his unwavering support and also for his insightful comments on and corrections to the manuscript;[1] to Gregory Schopen for reading the manuscript and

[1] Regarding this book's main title, *Greek Buddha*, my colleague Georgios Halkias kindly informs me (shortly before I sent the manuscript to the press) that "the same title was used by Nikos Dimou, *O Ellina Boudas*, Athens: Nefeli Press, 1984. It is a study on Pyrrho and the influences of Hellenism on Buddhism." He also notes that the term appears to have been coined "by F. Nietzsche somewhere in his writings, again in reference to Pyrrho." A quick Internet search reveals that the term also has been used to refer to Heraclitus, and for many other purposes. I hope my own usage does not mislead anyone into thinking that it has anything to do with earlier usages. The title *Greek Buddha* occurred to me several years ago without my having the slightest knowledge of the fact that it had previously been used by anyone else in any language.

offering helpful comments; and to the three anonymous reviewers of the manuscript, whose observations led me to clarify many things.

I am also grateful for the above-noted fellowship awarded to me by the Käte Hamburger Kolleg at the Ruhr-Universität Bochum, where I wrote the first actual rough draft manuscript. For doing their very best to make my stay in Bochum enjoyable and productive, and for their input with respect to various parts of the book when they were still research papers, I am much indebted to Volkhard Krech, director of the Käte Hamburger Kolleg; Nikolas Jaspert, director of the research group to which I belonged within the Kolleg; Roman Höritsch and the other staff members; and among the other members of the Kolleg at that time, especially Anna Akasoy, Sven Bretfeld, Alexandra Cuffel, Licia Di Giacinto, Adam Knobler, Hans Martin Krämer, Carmen Meinert, Zara Pogossian, Jessie Pons, Peter Wick, Michael Willis, and Sven Wortmann.

In addition, I would like to thank Stefan Baums, Joel Brereton, Johannes Bronkhorst, E. Bruce Brooks, Michael Butcher, Jamsheed Choksy, Baohai Dang, Max Deeg, Michael Dunn, Andrew Glass, Luis Gómez, Kyle Grothoff, Jens-Uwe Hartmann, Anya King, Boram Lee, Natalia Murataeva, Richard Nance, Jan Nattier, Patrick Olivelle, Andrew Shimunek, Raphael Squiley, and all others who answered questions, commented on this book or parts of it in their various incarnations, or argued points with me.

For his unwavering enthusiasm and support for this book from its very inception, I am deeply grateful to Rob Tempio, my editor at Princeton University Press. I would also like to thank everyone else involved in the production of this book.

As always I thank my wife, Inna, for encouraging me to begin, continue, and finish the book, and for helping me in countless ways throughout. I could not have done it without her.

Despite all of the valuable help of different kinds from family, friends, and colleagues, I have sometimes ignored their advice for one reason or another, or in some cases I might have misunderstood it, but in any case I am, as always, responsible for any errors that might remain.

I never imagined that I would write a book on Greek philosophy, even marginally—or on any kind of philosophy or religion—despite my admiration for ancient Greek thought in general. I have no idea how my son became interested in ancient Greek astronomy, which he took up in the early years of elementary school when he was no more than seven or eight years old and lugged the library's huge copy of the translation of Ptolemy's *Almagest* there to read during recess. But I like to think that there is a connection between us in our interest in things Greek, and I hope that he will have the chance to follow it up again some day. I dedicate this book, with all my love, to *Didi* my son, Lee Beckwith.

On Transcription, Transliteration, and Texts

Chinese

I follow the traditional modified Wade-Giles system used by many scholars—for example, *Tao Te Ching,* Chuang Chou—except for proper names or derived words that have established traditional Anglicized forms, such as Confucius, Laotzu, Taoism, Peking, and so on. Only when citing Mandarin pronunciation per se do I use the Pinyin system with tone marks. Unfortunately, *there are no true critical editions of any Chinese texts.* I have done the best I could with what there is.

Greek

I follow convention as much as possible. I use the traditional transliteration system, with *y* rather than *u* for Greek υ upsilon except in the digraph ου, which is transliterated as *ou,* though transcribed as *u* in Latinized Greek. In general I have attempted to preserve recognizability for words that have been borrowed into English, such as *mythos* (rather than *muthos*) ‘word, story, fiction, myth’. For texts, in the most important cases I have consulted several editions, particularly the critical edition of Eusebius by Mras, the edition of fragments of Early Pyrrhonism by Decleva Caizzi, and the recent critical edition of Strabo by Radt. For other Greek works I have usually relied on the Loeb Library series.

Indic

I generally follow traditional Indological practice in converting the often divergent Prakrit dialect spellings to Sanskrit, though Pali text titles are cited in Pali, and other Prakrit forms verbatim. The respective standard transcription systems are followed, except in transcription of forms from early inscriptions. When Indic words, including proper names, have become loanwords in English, even if only in Buddhological publications, I have normally adopted the usual spellings sans diacritics, italicization, or recognition of morphophonological variations in the original, for example the words *dharma, karma, Madhyamika, Mahayana, samsara.* I have converted all variant transcriptions of *anusvāra* to *ṃ* without comment except in proper names in which *ṅ* has become customary (e.g., Kaliṅga). For texts of the early Indian inscriptions, I have mainly relied on my own reading of the rubbings and photographs that are clear enough for me to read.

Abbreviations

Bax.:	Baxter 1992.
CTP:	*Chinese Text Project*, http://ctext.org/.
D.L.:	Diogenes Laertius, ed. Hicks (Loeb) 1925, or via Perseus.
Enquiry:	Hume 1758.
Herodotus:	*Herodotus*, ed. Godley (Loeb) 1926, or via Perseus.
LSJ:	Liddell, Scott, Jones, *Greek-English Lexicon* 1968, or via Perseus.
MChi:	Middle Chinese.
MSC:	Modern Standard Chinese (Mandarin).
OChi:	Old Chinese.
Perseus:	Perseus Digital Library, http://www.perseus.tufts.edu/hopper/.
Praep. evang.:	Eusebius, *Praeparatio Evangelica*, ed. Mras 1983.
Pul.:	Pulleyblank 1991.
Strabo:	*Geography*, ed. Radt 2002–2011, or via Perseus.
TLG:	*Thesaurus Linguae Graecae*, http://www.tlg.uci.edu/.

GREEK BUDDHA

PROLOGUE

Scythian Philosophy

PYRRHO, THE PERSIAN EMPIRE, AND INDIA

In the eighth century BC, Scythian warriors pursuing the Cimmerians rode south out of the steppes into the Near East in the area of northern Iran. They defeated the Cimmerians in the 630s and in the process conquered the powerful nation of the Medes, their Iranic ethnolinguistic relatives. As allies of the Assyrians, the Scythians fought across the Levant as far as Egypt. When they were defeated by the Medes in about 585 BC, they withdrew to the north and established themselves in the North Caucasus Steppe and the Pontic Steppe north of the Black Sea. They and their relatives built a huge empire stretching across Central Eurasia as far as China, including most of urbanized Central Asia, and grew fabulously rich on trade.[1]

The Scythians and other North Iranic speakers thus dominated Central Eurasia at the same time that their southern relatives, the Medes and Persians, formed a vast empire based in the area of what is now western Iran and Iraq. Though the Scythians were increasingly fragmented, and were probably weakened by the Persian capture of the prosperous and populous Central Asian countries of Bactria, Sogdiana, and others, they and other North Iranic–speaking relatives—including

[1] Beckwith (2009: 61–62). The present chapter is an essay mainly intended to present some of the background and basic themes of this book. For citations, texts, and detailed discussion of most arguments presented, please see the numbered chapters and the appendixes.

their eastern branch, the Sakas—continued to rule much of Central Eurasia for many centuries.[2]

To their south the prophet Zoroaster "reformed" the traditional religion of Media, Mazdaism, evidently around the time of Cyrus the Great, who was half Mede and half Persian. Although the Scythians never adopted Zoroastrianism, they too were interested in religion and philosophy. We know of not one but two great Scythian philosophers, and both still have much to teach us.

Anacharsis the Scythian

Anacharsis was the brother of Caduida, king of the Scythians. He spoke Greek because his mother was a Greek.[3] In about the forty-seventh Olympiad (592–589 BC), the age of Solon, he travelled to Greece and became well known for his astute, pithy remarks and wise sayings. Of the very brief quotations that are thought to go back to Anacharsis himself, many consist of observations on the opposite character of this or that cultural element among the Greeks as contrasted with the same element among the Scythians. For example, "He said he wondered why among the Greeks the experts contend, but the non-experts decide."[4] The Greeks regularly quoted this and other pithy sayings of Anacharsis, which taken together are unlike those of any other known figure, Greek or foreign, in ancient Greek literature. Though he was considered to be a Scythian, the Greeks liked him, and he was counted as one of the Seven Sages of Antiquity in Greek philosophy. His own literary

[2] On the names of the Scythian peoples, see Szemerényi (1980); cf. Beckwith (2009: 377–380), where it is shown that the name *Saka* is an eastern Scythian dialect form of the same word that gave us the name "Scythian".

[3] Diogenes Laertius I, 8.103 (Hicks 1925: 1:106–107). Alekseyev (2005: 40) says he was the brother of Saulius, son of Gnurus.

[4] Diogenes Laertius I, 8.103 (Hicks 1925: 1:106–107): "θαυμάζειν δὲ ἔφη πῶς παρὰ τοῖς Ἕλλησιν ἀγωνίζονται μὲν οἱ τεχνῖται, κρίνουσι δὲ οἱ μὴ τεχνῖται." There are several versions of this saying. Kindstrand (1981: 119, 150–151) prefers a political context, based on Plutarch's version, but a generic comment seems most likely in view of the usual presentation of Anacharsis in the earliest sayings attributed to him. This particular saying is also directly comparable to the following quotation on the Criterion attributed to him by Sextus Empiricus (cf. Kindstrand 1981: 49), which seems quite likely to have been modeled on this evidently genuine short saying. See now Griffith (2013) on judging between contending experts in Aristophanes' *Frogs* and in ancient Greek culture in general.

works are lost, but his fame was such that other writers used him as a stock character in their own compositions.[5i]

Sextus Empiricus, in his *Against the Logicians*, quotes an otherwise unknown work attributed to Anacharsis, on the Problem of the Criterion:

> Who judges something skillfully? Is it the ordinary person or the skilled person? We would not say it is the ordinary person. For he is defective in his knowledge of the peculiarities of skills. The blind person does not grasp the workings of sight, nor the deaf person those of hearing. And so, too, the unskilled person does not have a sharp eye when it comes to the apprehension of what has been achieved through skill, since if we actually back this person in his judgment on some matter of skill, there will be no difference between skill and lack of skill, which is absurd. So the ordinary person is not a judge of the peculiarities of skills. It remains, then, to say that it is the skilled person—which is again unbelievable. For one judges either a person with the same pursuits as oneself, or a person with different pursuits. But one is not capable of judging someone with different pursuits; for one is familiar with one's own skill, but as far as someone else's skill is concerned one's status is that of an ordinary person. Yet neither one can certify a person with the same pursuits as oneself. For this was the very issue we were examining: who is to be the judge of these people, who are of identical ability as regards the same skill. Besides, if one person judges the other, the same thing will become both judging and judged, trustworthy and untrustworthy. For in so far as the other person has the same pursuits as the one being judged, he will be untrustworthy since he too is being judged, while in so far as he is judging he will be trustworthy. But it is not possible for the same thing to be both judging and judged, trustworthy and untrustworthy; therefore there is no one who judges skillfully. For this reason there is not a criterion either. For some criteria are skilled and some are ordinary; but neither do the ordinary ones judge (just as the ordinary person does not), nor do the skilled ones (just as the skilled person does not), for the reasons stated earlier. Therefore nothing is a criterion.[6]

[5] On the origin and fate of Anacharsis, see Endnote i.

[6] Sextus Empiricus, *Adversus mathematicos* VII, 1, 55–59, translation by Bett (2005: 13–14), courtesy Cambridge University Press, section numbers omitted. For explanation of the traditional mistaken title (*Adversus mathematicos*) of this and other works by Sextus, see Bett (2005: x-xii). The passage begins with the comment by Sextus, "Anacharsis the Scythian, they say, does away with the apprehension that is capable of judging every skill, and strenuously criticizes the Greeks for holding on to it."

The focus of the text is the Problem of the Criterion, which is acknowledged not to have existed in Greek philosophy before the time of Pyrrho,[7] so it is clear that it cannot be an authentic work of Anacharsis, as scholars have already determined on other grounds.[8] Nevertheless, it is modeled directly on the above brief, genuine quotation of Anacharsis himself on the same topic—the problem of judging or deciding—and other genuine quotations similar in nature.

The argument is also strikingly close to the second part of the argument about the Problem of the Criterion in the *Chuangtzu*. Exactly as in the genuine saying of Anacharsis and in the argument attributed to him by Sextus Empiricus, the Chinese argument specifically concerns the ability to decide which of two contending individuals is right:

> If you defeat me, I do not defeat you, are you then right, and I am not? If I defeat you, you do not defeat me, am I then right, you are not? Is one of us right, one of us wrong? Or are both of us right, both of us wrong? If you and I cannot figure it out, then everyone will be mystified by it. Who shall we get to decide who is right? We could get someone who agrees with you to decide who is right, but since he agrees with you, how could he decide it aright? We could get someone who agrees with me to decide who is right, but since he agrees with me, how can he decide it aright? Therefore, neither I nor you nor anyone else can figure it out.[9]

The first part of the argument is structured as a tetralemma.[10]

[7] See Chapter One and Appendix A.

[8] Kindstrand (1981).

[9] 既使我與若辯矣，若勝我，我不若勝，若果是也? 我果非也邪? 我勝若，若不吾勝，我果是也？而果非也邪？其或是也，其或非也邪？其俱是也，其俱非也邪? 我與若不能相知也，則人固受其黮闇。吾誰使正之? 使同乎若者正之，既與若同矣，惡能正之！使同乎我者正之，既同乎我矣，惡能正之！使異乎我與若者正之，既異乎我與若矣，惡能正之！使同乎我與若者正之，既同乎我與若矣，惡能正之！然則我與若與人俱不能相知也，而待彼也邪? (*Chuangtzu* 2; text from *CTP*). The introductory remark, 既使我與若辯矣 "Since (someone) has made me argue with you," undoubtedly refers to Confucius; the last remark, 而待彼也邪 "So we're waiting for *him*?", is also probably a sarcastic reference to Confucius, who is criticized mercilessly in the immediately preceding passage. These remarks are outside the argument itself. Cf. the translations by Graham (1981: 60) and Watson (1968: 48). I am indebted to Boram Lee and E. Bruce Brooks for a helpful discussion of this passage on the Warring States Workshop online forum.

[10] On the tetralemma, see Chapter One and Appendix A. This one is a rather complex example, and is followed by a short conclusion: "If you and I cannot figure it out, then everyone will be mystified by it."

The explanation for the similarity of these two passages could well be that the author of the "Anacharsis" quotation given by Sextus Empiricus had heard just such an argument, directly or indirectly, from a Scythian. This would have been a simple matter during the Classical Age because many Scythians then lived in Athens, where a number of them even served as the city's police force. If it was a stock Scythian story, an eastern Scythian—a Saka—could have transmitted a version of it to the Chinese, so that it ended up in the *Chuangtzu*, which is full of stories and arguments of a similar character.

Whatever the explanation, the explicit Greek connection of this story with a Scythian philosopher known for pithy sayings having a clever argument structure clearly indicates that it is the kind of thing Scythians were *expected* to say. In view of the Chinese testimony, it seems likely that it was something that some Scythians actually did say.

Gautama Buddha, the Scythian Sage

The dates of Gautama Buddha are not recorded in any reliable historical source, and the traditional dates are calculated on unbelievable lineages including round numbers such as one hundred, so they are not reliable either, as noted already by Fleet, Hultzsch, and many others.[11] His personal name, Gautama, is evidently earliest recorded in the *Chuangtzu*, a Chinese work from the late fourth to third centuries BC.[12] His epithet *Śākamuni* (later Sanskritized as *Śākyamuni*), 'Sage of the Scythians ("Sakas")', is unattested in the genuine Mauryan inscriptions[13] or the Pali Canon.[14] It is earliest attested, as *Śakamuni*, in the Gāndhārī Prakrit texts, which date to the first centuries AD (or possibly even the

[11] Fleet, in *JRAS* 1909: 333, 335, cited in Hultzsch (1925: xxxiii). Scholars' continued insistence on following such dates anyway led to a 1988 conference devoted specifically to reconsideration of the dates of the Buddha, which however largely continued to take the fanciful, ahistorical, traditional accounts as if they were actual historical accounts, with the significant exceptions of the papers by Härtel (1995) and Bareau (1995).

[12] See Chapter Three.

[13] See Chapter Two and Appendix C.

[14] However, it has been demonstrated that the caretakers of the Pali tradition systematically expunged references to various ideas and practices to which they objected, especially things thought to be non-Indian (Sven Bretfeld, p.c., 2012).

late first century BC).[15] It is thus arguable that the epithet could have been applied to the Buddha during the Śāka (Saka or "Indo-Scythian") Dynasty—which dominated northwestern India on and off from approximately the first century BC, continuing into the early centuries AD as satraps or "vassals" under the Kushans—and that the reason for it was strong support for Buddhism by the Sakas, Indo-Parthians, and Kushans.

However, it must be noted that the Buddha is the only Indian holy man before early modern times who bears an epithet explicitly identifying him as a non-Indian, a foreigner. It would have been unthinkably odd for an Indian saint to be given a foreign epithet if he was not actually a foreigner. Moreover, the Scythians-Sakas are well attested in Greek and Persian historical sources before even the traditional "high" date of the Buddha, so the epithet should presumably have been applied to him already in Central Asia proper or its eastern extension into India—eastern Gandhāra. There are also very strong arguments—including basic "doctrinal" ones—indicating that Buddhism had fundamental foreign connections from the very beginning, as shown below. It is at any rate certain that Buddha has been identified as *Śākamuni* ~ *Śākyamuni* "Sage of the Scythians" in all varieties of Buddhism from the beginning of the recorded Buddhist tradition to the present, and that much of what is thought to be known about him can be identified specifically with things Scythian.[16]

Moreover, it must not be overlooked that we have no concrete *datable* evidence that any other wandering ascetics preceded the Buddha. The Scythians were nomads (from Greek νομάδες 'wanderers in search of pasture, pastoralists') who lived in the wilderness, and it is thus quite likely that Gautama himself introduced wandering asceticism to India, just as the Scythians had earlier invented mounted steppe nomadism.[17]

[15] Baums and Glass (2010), a work in progress, when checked in July 2013, included three occurrences, each in a different manuscript. It also occurs in Sanskrit in much later texts from Gandhāra, as well as once, in a fifth-century AD Bactrian Buddhist text, as σαοκομανο *saokomano*, without the characteristic *-y-* of the Sanskritized form of the name (Sims-Williams 2010: 73).

[16] Walter (2012). The tradition by which Buddha was from a local Nepalese *Śākya* "clan" in the area of Lumbini is full of chronological and other insuperable problems, as shown by Bareau (1987); it is a very late development.

[17] Beckwith (2009: 58ff.). Considering the mostly Anatolian origins of Greek philosophy, and the long domination of that region by the Medes and Persians, it must be wondered if the peripatetic tradition in Greek philosophy also reflects the Iranic penchant for wandering.

One way or the other, it would seem that the Buddha's teachings were unprecedented mainly because they opposed new foreign ideas—the Early Zoroastrian ideas of good and bad karma, rebirth in Heaven (for those who were good), absolute Truth versus the Lie, and so on—which were previously unknown in "India proper". He did this because he himself was foreign, and people actually understood and accepted that by calling him *Śākamuni*.

Buddha therefore must have lived after the introduction of Zoroastrianism in 519/518 BC, when the Achaemenid ruler Darius I invaded and conquered several Central Asian countries and then continued to the east, where he conquered Gandhāra and Sindh, which were Indic-speaking, in about 517/516 BC.[18] In the process of firming up his rule over the new territories, he stationed subordinate feudal lords, or *satraps*, over them, and some of the army was garrisoned there. Darius had come from conquering much of Central Asia proper, including Bactria and Arachosia, as well as the Sakā Tigraxaudā 'the Scythians wearing pointed hats', a nation of Scythians whose king, Skunkha, he captured[19] and is portrayed in a captioned relief accompanying the Behistun Inscription. From then on Scythians formed the backbone of the imperial forces together with the Medes and Persians,[20] so some of the soldiers in the Indian campaign must have been Scythians, that is, Śākas. Herodotus details the dress and equipment of the Central Asian and Indian troops, who are listed by nation including, among others, Bactrians, Sakas ("that is, Scythians"), Indians (*Indoi*), Arians (more correctly Hareians,[21] neighbors of the Bactrians), Parthians, Khwarizmians, Sogdians, and Gandhārans.[22]

Gandhāra became an important part of the empire. It is regularly included in the lists of provinces from the beginning of Darius's reign on to the end of the empire along with Bactria, Arachosia, the Sakas,

[18] Shahbazi (1994). Although the *exact* date of his invasion of Gandhāra and Sindh is unknown, it probably happened shortly after his Central Asian campaign, so around 517 (Briant 1996: 153). In any case, there is no doubt about the conquest of the region during the early part of his reign (Kuhrt 2007: 182, 188–189). See also the extensive complementary treatment in the Epilogue of the present book.

[19] Kuhrt (2007: 157n122, 150, figure 5.3).

[20] Briant (1996: 50).

[21] Herat, in modern northwestern Afghanistan, preserves the ancestral name of the region, Old Persian *Haraiva*.

[22] Herodotus VII, 64.1 to VII, 66.1.

and other neighboring realms.[23] There was a Persian satrap in Taxila, and official travellers went frequently between the Persian capital and one or another provincial locality in India,[24] as attested by accounts preserved in the Persepolis Fortification Tablets, which detail the payments in kind to the travellers.[25] Moreover, "the Indians", one of the twenty financial districts of the Persian Empire recorded by Herodotus, paid by far the greatest sum in "tribute".[26] The Achaemenid influence in Gandhāra was strong and long-lasting.[27]

The conquest by Darius introduced the Persians' new religion, reformed Mazdaism, or Early Zoroastrianism,[28] a strongly monotheistic faith with a creator God, Ahura Mazda, and with ideas of absolute Truth (Avestan *aša*, Old Persian *arta*) versus 'the Lie' (*druj*), and of an accumulation of Good and Bad deeds—that is, "karma"—which determined whether a person would be rewarded by "rebirth" in Heaven. These ideas are all found in the Gāthās, the oldest part of the Avesta, which are attributed to Zoroaster himself, and all are expressed openly and repeatedly in the Old Persian royal inscriptions as well. Essentially the same ideas occur in the Major Inscriptions of the Mauryas in the third century BC in India.[29] The traditional view[30] is that the Buddha reinterpreted existing Indian ideas found in the Upanishads, but the Upanishads in question cannot be dated to a period earlier than the Buddha, as shown by Bronkhorst[31] and discussed below. Just as Early Buddhism cannot be expected to be similar to the Normative Buddhism of a half millennium or more later, so Early Brahmanism cannot be

[23] Briant (1996: 50).

[24] Briant (1996: 777, 370).

[25] Meadows (2005: 186).

[26] Meadows (2005: 183).

[27] Briant (1996: 778).

[28] I call it "Early Zoroastrianism" because it did not exist for very long in its pristine state, but also because it was very different from fully developed Late Zoroastrianism (one could call it "Normative Zoroastrianism", following the terminology developed in this book for Buddhism). Soudavar (2010: 119), emphasis added, remarks, "Zoroastrianism *as we now know* [*it*], with its complicated rituals and canonical laws, had not enough time to develop between the lifetime of its prophet and the advent of Darius in the year 522 BC."

[29] See Chapters Two and Three.

[30] E.g., Gombrich (1996: 51).

[31] Bronkhorst (1986).

expected to be similar to Late Brahmanism (not to speak of Hinduism), attested even later. "Zoroaster was . . . the first to teach the doctrines of . . . Heaven and Hell, the future resurrection of the body . . . , and life everlasting for the reunited soul and body",[32] and Early Zoroastrianism was the faith of the ruling nation of the Persian Empire. Both Early Buddhism and Early Brahmanism are the direct outcome of the introduction of Zoroastrianism into eastern Gandhāra by Darius I. Early Buddhism resulted from the Buddha's rejection of the basic principles of Early Zoroastrianism, while Early Brahmanism represents the acceptance of those principles. Over time, Buddhism would accept more and more of the rejected principles.

Darius also sponsored the creation of a completely new writing system—Old Persian cuneiform script, which is partly modeled on Aramaic script, one of the main administrative scripts of the Persian Empire—and the practice of erecting monumental inscriptions.[33] In the great Behistun Inscription at the top of Mount Bagastana,[34] Darius I repeats over and over how he achieved what he did because the early Achaemenids' monotheistic God of Heaven, *Ahura Mazda* 'Lord Wisdom', helped him. He insists that what he did was True, it was not a Lie, and repeatedly says that those who opposed him "lied". *Druj* 'the Lie' made them rebel and deceive the people, they were "lie-followers", and so on. The obsessive repetition of this litany throughout the inscriptions is striking. Anyone familiar with these basic Zoroastrian concepts could hardly contend that Darius was not an Early Zoroastrian. He could not have been anything else.

While, not surprisingly, the ordinary generic human contrast between truth and falsehood is found in the Vedas, the specifically Early Zoroastrian form of the ideas, including the result of following one or the other path, is completely alien to them. In the early Vedic religion, ritually correct performance of blood sacrifices was believed

[32] Boyce (1979: 29).

[33] In addition, he built imperial roads with rest houses provisioned for travellers. These three actions were prominently imitated by the early rulers of the Mauryan Empire in India, the northwestern part of which had been part of the Persian Empire until Alexander's conquest.

[34] This is the ancient name, which means 'place of gods' (Razmjou 2005: 153) or 'the place of God'.

to be rewarded in this life, but the reward had nothing to do with one's virtuous actions or one's future in the afterlife. These ideas thus seem to have been introduced by the Achaemenid Persians into eastern Gandhāra and Sindh, the western limits of the ancient Indic world and southeastern limits of the Central Asian world, just as they were introduced into Near Eastern parts of the vast Persian Empire. In fact, Early Zoroastrianism is attested in Achaemenid Central Asia and India in the earliest Persian imperial written documents from the region.[35ii]

These specific "absolutist" or "perfectionist" ideas are firmly *rejected* by the Buddha in his earliest attested teachings, as shown in Chapter One. In short, the Buddha reacted primarily (if at all) not against Brahmanism,[36] but against Early Zoroastrianism. At the lower end of the chronological scale, the Buddha must have lived before the visit of the two best known and attested Greek visitors of the late fourth century, Pyrrho of Elis, who was in Bactria, Gandhāra, and Sindh from 330 to 325 BC with Alexander the Great and learned an early form of Buddhism there, and two decades later the ambassador Megasthenes, who travelled from Alexandria in Arachosia (now Kandahar) to Gandhāra and Magadha in 305–304 BC and recorded his observations on Indian beliefs, including Early Buddhism and Early Brahmanism, in his *Indica*.[37]

The word *bodhi* 'enlightenment', literally 'awakening', is first attested in the Eighth Rock Edict of the Mauryan ruler Devānāṃpriya Priyadarśi (fl. 272–261 BC), who says that in the tenth year after his coronation he went to Saṃbodhi—now known as Bodhgayā (located about fifty miles south of Patna, ancient Pāṭaliputra)—where according to tradition the Buddha achieved enlightenment under the Bodhi Tree. The ruler says that after this visit he began to preach the *Dharma*

[35] Benveniste et al. (1958: 4), based on two inscriptions in Aramaic. Cf. Bronkhorst (2007: 358), who remarks, "In the middle of the third century BC, it was Mazdaism, rather than Brahmanism, which predominated in the region between Kandahar and Taxila". For Bronkhorst's views on Brahmanism and early Magadha, see Endnote ii.

[36] Cf. Bronkhorst (1986; 2011: 1–4), q.v. the preceding note. From his discussion it is clear that even the earliest attested Brahmanist texts reflect the influence of Buddhism, so it would seem that the acceptance of Early Zoroastrian ideas in Gandhāra happened later than the Buddhist rejection of them, but before the Alexander historians and Megasthenes got there in the late fourth century BC.

[37] See Chapter Two for a detailed study of the relevant fragments of his book preserved in Strabo's *Geography*.

around his empire.[38] The inscription thus can only refer to the ruler's acceptance of a form of the *Early* Buddhist Dharma—not the more familiar Normative Buddhism, which is attested several centuries later. The inscription also establishes that reverence for the Buddha existed by this time at Bodhgayā, in Magadha.[39]

The dates of Darius's conquest of Gandhāra and Sindh (ca. 517 BC), and the late fourth century—marked by the visit of Alexander (330–325 BC) along with his courtier Pyrrho, followed by Megasthenes two decades later—are the chronological limits bracketing the enlightenment-to-death career of Gautama Buddha. It is possible to further narrow this down to some extent.

The shock of the introduction of new, alien religious ideas in the traditionally non-Persian, non-Zoroastrian environment of Central Asia, eastern Gandhāra, and Sindh must have happened fairly soon after Darius's conquest and the establishment of his satrapies, when the satraps were undoubtedly still ethnically Persian and strongly Zoroastrian, and would have needed the ministrations of their priests. That would place the most likely time for the Buddha's period of asceticism and enlightenment within the first fifty years or so of Persian rule, meaning ca. 515 to ca. 465 BC, and his death after another forty years or so—following the dubious tradition that he lived eighty years[40]—making the latest date for his death ca. 425 BC. This chronology would also leave enough time for Early Buddhism to spread from Magadha (the region where Saṃbodhi, or Bodhgayā, is located)—assuming it was first preached there by the Buddha—northwestward into western Gandhāra, Bactria, and beyond, and (as shown in Chapter Three), for his name *Gautama* and some of his ideas and practices to travel all the way to China and become popular no later than the Guodian tomb's end date (terminus ante quem) of 278 BC. Among the things that the scenario presented here explains are the striking alienness of Buddhism

[38] Kalsi VIII, 22–23 (Hultzsch 1925: 36–37). Cf. Chapter Three.

[39] This makes it likely that the comment in Megasthenes' account about the Śramaṇas interceding between the kings and 'the divine one' also refers to reverence for the Buddha. See Chapter Two.

[40] His traditional life span is undoubtedly fictitious, as 8, 80, 108, etc. are holy numbers in later, Normative Buddhism.

in India proper,[41] its earliness in Gandhāra and Bactria,[42] and the difficulty of showing that the Buddha was originally from Magadha.

This brings up the problem of the Buddha's birthplace. Not only are his dates only very generally definable, his specific homeland is unknown as well. Despite widespread popular belief in the story that he came from Lumbini in what is now Nepal, all of the evidence is very late and highly suspect from beginning to end. Bareau has carefully analyzed the Lumbini birth story and shown it to be a late fabrication.[43] There are reasons to put the Buddha's teaching period—most of his life, according to the traditional accounts—somewhere in northern India, in a region affected by the monsoons. In particular, the eventual development of the primitive *ārāma*, the temporary seasonal shelter of the Buddha's lifetime, into the *saṃghārāma* (an *ārāma* specifically for Buddhist monks)[44]—the received historical trajectory, based on tradition, the "early" sutras, and archaeological data[45]—actually *requires* an original location in the monsoon zone. That is to say, if *ārāmas* were necessary,

[41] Independently mentioned to me by Michael L. Walter (p.c., 2010) and Michael Willis (p.c., 2012).

[42] This is one of several problems with Bronkhorst's "Magadha" theory of the *origin* of Buddhism. Though he points out that Gandhāra is one of the earliest regions in which Buddhism is attested (Bronkhorst 2011: 20–21), it is actually attested there far earlier than anywhere else; cf. above.

[43] Bareau (1987). The lone piece of evidence impelling scholars to accept the Lumbini story has been the Lumbini Inscription, which most scholars believe was erected by Aśoka. However, the inscription itself actually reveals that it is not by Aśoka, and all indications are that it is a late forgery, possibly even a modern one. See Appendix C.

[44] This is the traditional understanding. Later, in the Kushan period, the fully developed monastery (eventually called the *vihāra*) was introduced from Central Asia, as known from the excavations at Taxila (Marshall 1951). The idea of the "monastery" must have developed slowly within Buddhism—no other religious or philosophical system anywhere is known to have developed it earlier. It clearly cannot be dated until well after the time of Megasthenes' account, which mentions explicitly where the *śramaṇas* lived but says nothing about monasteries or anything similar. The earliest identifiable group living centers, even if they were *saṃghārāmas* (unlikely, since the stories about them are clearly ahistorical), are primitive affairs that can hardly be called "monasteries", as pointed out by Schopen (2004: 219; 2007: 61; cf. Bronkhorst 2011), partly on the basis of the early donative inscriptions at Sāñcī, which—unlike later donative inscriptions—do not mention *vihāras*, indicating that the monks lived in villages. It is now clear that fully developed organized monasticism must have come first, and preceded any *saṃghārāmas*, but it developed in Central Asia, whence it was introduced to India and China in the Kushan period (Beckwith 2014; forthcoming-a). Cf. Chapter Two.

[45] Dutt (1962); see Chapter Two and the discussion in Beckwith (2012c).

then monsoons were necessary too, meaning Early Buddhism must have developed in a monsoon zone region of early India. However, that could be almost anywhere from the upper Indus River in the west—including ancient eastern Gandhāra—to the mouths of the Ganges in the east.

Of course, actual Early Buddhism (i.e., Pre-Normative Buddhism) did not entirely disappear in later times, and constitutes a significant element in the teachings and practices shared by most followers of Normative Buddhism and thus by most Buddhist schools or sects known from the Saka-Kushan period down to modern times. At the early end of the spectrum, the doctrinal content of the Gāndhārī documents dating to the early Normative period agrees closely with the doctrinal content of what are believed to be the earliest texts of the Pali Canon,[46] with the main exception that some Mahayana texts have been found among the materials from Gandhāra.[47] However, one may safely assume that the Buddha must have passed away well before 325 to 304 BC, the dates for the appearance of the earliest hard evidence on the existence of Buddhism or elements of Buddhism. This is still *three centuries* before even the earliest Gāndhārī texts and the traditional (high) date of the Pali Canon. Despite widespread belief that the latter collections of material, both of which are from the Saka-Kushan period or later, represent "Early Buddhism", the work of many scholars has shown that even by internal evidence alone it must be already quite far removed from the *earliest* Buddhism—the teachings and practices of the followers of the Buddha himself and the next few generations after him, up to the mid-third century BC—which is referred to in this book as Early Buddhism.

Pyrrho's Journey to Gandhāra and Back Again

In or about the year 334 BC, Pyrrho of Elis (ca. 355–ca. 265 BC)[48] met Alexander the Great and joined the Macedonian conqueror's

[46] Stefan Baums (p.c., 2012); I am of course responsible for any misunderstanding about this.

[47] For some of the best-preserved examples, see Braarvig and Liland (2010). Most are however in Sanskrit and from about the fourth to the sixth century AD, approximately a millennium after the Buddha.

[48] He was actually from Petra, a small town near Elis (Pausanias VI, 24, 5; cf. Conche 1994: 16). It is not recorded when he—supposedly already with his teacher Anaxarchus

entourage. It is unlikely that Pyrrho was over thirty years old when he left on his trip, as the usual chronologies suggest.[49] Pyrrho had been a painter, and was—or more likely became on the trip—a student of the philosopher and musician[50] Anaxarchus (killed ca. 320 BC). Alexander himself was only twenty-six years old when he left Persia to invade the East, and most of his companions were equally young or younger, as they needed to be to survive the rigors of the campaign. Anaxarchus was famously close to Alexander,[51] and they interacted personally in such a way that it is difficult to believe he was over fifty years old at the time—*twice* as old as Alexander. If it is assumed that Anaxarchus was closer to Alexander in age, and thus ten to twenty years younger, Pyrrho, who receives attention in the sources mainly as his student rather than in his own right, must have been much younger still, perhaps twenty years old, at the time. It is significant that when Pyrrho is mentioned in India, he is shown to be naïve or impressionable; both are stereotypical characteristics of youth.[52]

(q.v. D.L. IX, 58–60; O'Keefe 2006)—joined Alexander's court. Conche (1994: 28–30) argues that Pyrrho most probably met Alexander in 332 BC, but as Clayman (2009: 16) remarks the meeting must have been no later than 334, when Alexander, his court, and the army crossed the Dardanelles. Cf. the following note.

[49] Scholars (e.g., Bett 2000: 1n1; Clayman 2009: 16) have generally accepted the estimate of von Fritz (1963: 90) that Pyrrho was born in ca. 365–360 and died in ca. 275–270 BC, based primarily on the assumption that he was about thirty years old when he joined Alexander's campaign to conquer the Persian Empire. He was a painter (Clayman 2009), but he was unmarried, and it was normal for Greek men to marry by the age of thirty. Although some sources suggest that he had previously studied with other teachers of philosophy, most of these comments are highly doubtful, especially the putative connection with the Megarians in Diogenes Laertius, q.v. Bett (2000: 1–2, 165–169). It is probable, as Clayman (2009) has suggested, that he learned philosophy from Anaxarchus and the other philosophers Alexander brought with him in his court. In that case, he should have been younger still at the beginning of the campaign, having been born closer to 355, and thus died closer to 265 BC. At any rate, even following von Fritz's dates and the tradition that he lived for almost ninety years, he would have lived some fifty more years after his return from the East and therefore "was very much alive when Timon left [Elis, to make a living as a travelling sophist], certainly not later than 276, but probably much earlier" (Clayman 2009: 16).

[50] So Plutarch, *De Alex. fort. virt.* 1, 331e.

[51] Arrian, *Anabasis* IV, 9–11; see Romm and Mensch (2005: 103–106).

[52] One of the big assumptions in the scholarly literature is that Pyrrho learned philosophy in Greece and was already a student of Anaxarchus when he joined Alexander's expedition. There is no good evidence for this, and some specific evidence against it. As

Toward the end of 330 BC Alexander and his followers reached Kāpiśa, a principality in what is now east-central Afghanistan. After campaigning in Central Asia, including the conquest of Bactria, Sogdiana, and western Gandhāra, they crossed the Hindu Kush into eastern Gandhāra, the southeasternmost corner of Central Asia and the northwesternmost part of India. They spent over two years there—spring 327 to fall 325—before leaving by land and by sea to return to the Near East.[53]

In their travels, Pyrrho and his teacher Anaxarchus met Iranic and Indic *philosophoi* "philosophical-religious practitioners".[54] At some time during Pyrrho's attachment to the court, he wrote a poem in praise of Alexander, who rewarded Pyrrho with a large sum of money—according to Plutarch, ten thousand gold coins.[55] Unfortunately, the poem is lost.

far as we know, Pyrrho was a painter when he joined Alexander's expedition, and also a poet—his one known written work was a poem, which is unfortunately lost. He spent a full decade as part of Alexander's court, which included prominent philosophers from different Greek schools, but also the famous Indian thinker Calanus, who according to Arrian had a good number of students among the Greeks for the last two years of their fellowship. It is thus quite likely that Pyrrho was influenced—even if only negatively—by other Greek thinkers, but it was as a member of Alexander's expeditionary court that he either learned Greek philosophy or perfected his knowledge of it. For discussion of the "smorgasbord" approach to analyzing Pyrrho's philosophy, see Appendix B.

[53] Bosworth (1988), Cawthorne (2004), Holt (1989).

[54] So in Megasthenes. Centuries later, Diogenes Laertius IX, 61 calls the thinkers Pyrrho met by their stereotypical Greek names, *Gymnosophistai* 'naked wise-men (specifically of India)' and *Magoi* 'Magi' (the stereotypical Greek term for 'Persian wise men'). The ancient Greek word *philosophos* (plural *philosophoi*) literally means 'those who love wisdom', and includes a rough approximation of the modern idea of a 'philosopher', but the Greek word equally meant 'religious teacher-practitioner'; it certainly does not mean the same thing as modern English *philosopher*. Moreover, on the more "philosophical" side of things, *philosophia* meant something more like 'science' than is the case with modern English *philosophy*. The nearly universal custom of using the modern loan cognate of an ancient Greek word as the equivalent of the ancient word has resulted in misrepresentation and misunderstanding of Antiquity by scholars as well as by laymen; cf. the examples discussed in Appendix A.

[55] Sextus Empiricus, *M* I.282: λέγεται γὰρ αὐτὸν καὶ ποίησιν εἰς τὸν Μακεδόνα Ἀλέξανδρον γράψαντα μυρίοις χρυσοῖς τετιμῆσθαι (Bury 1933, IV: 162–163); translated by Bury as "for Pyrrho himself, it is said, wrote a poem for Alexander of Macedon and was rewarded with thousands of gold pieces." Unlike Plutarch, who does not give the reason, Sextus explicitly says the coins were for the poem. For the Plutarch version, see the discussion of Narrative 1, Pyrrho in India, in Chapter One.

This incident is explicitly given as the explanation for Pyrrho's reaction to an event involving his teacher Anaxarchus. An Indian philosopher chastised Anaxarchus for pandering to kings—specifically implying Alexander—and this reminded Pyrrho of his own behavior in writing a poem in praise of the ruler and accepting money for it. As a result, Pyrrho "withdrew from the world and lived in solitude."[56] Diogenes Laertius also says that Pyrrho's encounter with the Iranic and Indian philosophers led him to develop his "most noble philosophy".[57]

Pyrrho undoubtedly returned to the Near East with the court and returned home no later than the death of Alexander in 323. Back in Greece he taught about ethics, specifically about the causes of *pathē* 'passion, suffering' and a way to be *apatheia* 'without passion, suffering', and thus achieve *ataraxia* 'undisturbedness, calm'. His new way of thinking and living focused on the logical point that our thought is circular and imperfect and therefore cannot tell us anything absolute about ethical matters.[58] He urges us therefore to have *no views*, and to have *no inclinations* for or against any interpretations or views on ethical matters. If we follow his path, says his student Timon, we will eventually achieve *apatheia* 'passionlessness' and then *ataraxia* 'undisturbedness, calm'.[59]

Pyrrho practiced his teachings for the rest of his long life. He was honored by the people of Elis, who erected a statue of him in the center of town and out of respect for him made *philosophoi* exempt from taxation.[60]

Did Pyrrho Learn Anything in Central Asia and India?

It has been argued by most Classicists that the thought of Pyrrho is completely Greek in origin, with the possible exception of a few very minor details that he might have picked up in India. However, upon

[56] D.L. IX, 63, trans. Hicks (1925: 2:477).

[57] D.L. IX, 61, trans. Hicks (1925: 2:475); cf. the discussion of this narrative in Chapter One.

[58] For the logic, see Chapter Four.

[59] See Chapter One and Appendix A.

[60] See the discussion and citations in Chapter One.

closer inspection of the ancient testimonies on Pyrrho and Timon,[61] and of other contemporaneous sources on the early Greek contact with the "philosophers" of Central Asia and India, it appears that there are far too many exceptions.

Most significantly, no one has been able to relate Pyrrho's thought, *as a system*, to any other European tradition. If Pyrrhonism were simply a pastiche of Greek philosophical tidbits—as most Classicists have in effect argued[62]—why would anyone have paid any attention to it, and how could it possibly have revolutionized Hellenistic philosophy, as it most certainly did? And if Pyrrho's thought were fundamentally Greek, or—as has also been argued—if *Indian* "philosophy" were fundamentally Greek,[63] it would not be possible to explain why the ancient witnesses marvel at his teachings and practices,[64] which they are mostly baffled by, though at the same time they express admiration for his incredible, unprecedented ethical achievements. Yet these and other attempts to explain Early Pyrrhonism—and to dismiss any connection with Buddhism—are based on fundamental misunderstandings of Pyrrho's teachings and, especially, of the Buddha's teachings attested in

[61] On distinguishing Pyrrho from Timon in works by Timon, see the discussion by Bett (2000: 6–12). It is clear from Aristocles' comments elsewhere in his chapter on Pyrrhonism as well as references by other writers that the Aristocles passage comes from Timon's *Pythō* (see Appendix A). Its introductory and concluding bits definitely are Timon's own work. Pyrrho's section is highly artificial and extremely carefully constructed, so it must reflect the artistic hand of Timon too, but its strikingly distinctive character and its consistency with other testimonies (pace Bett 2000), as shown in Chapter One, indicate it really does reflect Pyrrho's own thought. Nevertheless, it is probable that Pyrrho did not disagree with Timon, or vice versa, and that Timon simply expressed some things in his prefatory and concluding remarks that Pyrrho might have preferred to be left unsaid.

[62] On the smorgasbord approach to the history of thought, see Appendix B.

[63] This refers to the argument that the thought of Pyrrho derived from Greek tradition even if Pyrrho adopted it from the Buddhist thinkers he met in Central Asia and India, because their ideas are originally Greek. See Appendix B.

[64] An anonymous peer reviewer of the manuscript of this book notes, "But this does not mean that we have to postulate a non-Greek origin. The Cynics and the Cyrenaics were also regarded as extraordinary, and this does not lead people to postulate non-Greek origins for their ideas." However, we cannot rule out a non-Greek origin either. Bett (2000) shows that the unique, core teaching of Pyrrho—to reach *ataraxia* by having "no views"—is unprecedented in Greek thought. He also notes that Pyrrho's practice of a type of early yoga is best explained as an artifact of his Indian experience. See Chapter One.

the Early Buddhism of the late fourth century BC, as shown by the hard data, unlike the late, traditional, fantasy-filled picture that too many continue to think is "Early" Buddhism. Richard Bett has shown that the key distinctive point of Pyrrho's thought that is unprecedented in Greece and sets it apart from all other Greek philosophy is that having "no views" and choosing to "not decide" leads to the goal of undisturbedness, peace. He says that among Greek thinkers it belongs to Pyrrho and the Pyrrhonists alone.[65]

How can Pyrrho's teachings be briefly described *as a system*, then? All accounts agree that *ataraxia* "undisturbedness, calm", the telos or 'goal' for Pyrrho, is directly connected to the rest of his thought and practice, which constitutes a coherent, consistent system. We must ask then not only how it is connected to the rest of his thought but how it is to be achieved. Pyrrho and Timon tell us that *ataraxia* is achieved "indirectly," in a particular sequence, following a particular program of thought and practice connected to three important fundamental logical points, as a consequence of which one should have "*no views*" and "*not incline* (in either direction)" toward them—that is, one should "not decide".

Bett, like most other scholars, does not connect Pyrrho's philosophical-religious program to India. However, he does conclude that Pyrrho is unique in Greek thought in saying that having *no views* and *not deciding* leads to undisturbedness. This "thread running most consistently through the entire history of Pyrrhonism" is "a point that sets the Pyrrhonists apart from all other Greek philosophers". Whereas others "who adopt the goal of *ataraxia*, or some related form of tranquility, typically aspire to achieve this goal as a result of coming to understand the nature of things through painstaking enquiry, and being able to ascribe to them some set of definite characteristics", the Pyrrhonians renounce "any attempt at such understanding".[66] The idea that having no views leads to undisturbedness is a well-known Early Buddhist idea.[67]

[65] Bett (2000: 179, 219–221).

[66] Bett (2000: 220).

[67] Bett (2000) was apparently unaware of the scholarship on this; see the discussion and references in Chapter One.

Bett also suggests that an Indian origin best explains Pyrrho's practice of what appears to be yoga. In fact, it was specifically an early form of yoga that involved *not moving* for extended periods, and *enduring pain*, as described very well in the Alexander histories, in the testimonies on Pyrrho, and in the account of Megasthenes.[68] Furthermore, Diogenes Laertius, and many modern scholars, credit Pyrrho with introducing the Problem of the Criterion to European thought. They do not say it was introduced from India, but that is perhaps because of the way Pyrrho himself states the problem in the best ancient source for his thought that we have, the verbatim quotation by Eusebius of Aristocles' version of Timon's report of Pyrrho's own statement, analyzed in Chapter One alongside the parallel testimonies.[69] Despite the widely differing interpretations of Bett and other scholars interested in Pyrrho, these elements have been recognized by them as key features of his thought and practice. Any analysis of Early Pyrrhonism must therefore account for them in a principled way, as a part of a complete system: Early Pyrrhonism.

No specialist has been able to find a convincing systematic origin for Early Pyrrhonism in Greek thought, and no one has suggested looking to the Persians, Chaldeans, Egyptians, or Chinese, among many other conceivable distant alternatives. However, a few scholars have taken the ancient Greeks' own remarks to heart. Citing some of the salient features of *Late* Pyrrhonism, they have proposed that Pyrrho's Indian sojourn really did affect his thought, as Diogenes Laertius says it did based on contemporaneous accounts of Pyrrho's life and thought, which he quotes. A small number of articles published over the last century and a half discuss this issue, mostly comparing the Late Pyrrhonism of Sextus Empiricus with the late Buddhist Madhyamika system, which is thought to go back to the legendary sage Nāgārjuna (traditionally dated to about the second century AD).[70] They then conclude that the comparison was after all unwarranted because one can still explain the constituent elements of Pyrrhonism by picking and choosing from

[68] Bett (2000: 169–170). On the characteristics of early yoga, see Bronkhorst (1986); see further in Chapter One.

[69] For a close study of the Greek text, see Appendix A.

[70] For a partial bibliography of such comparative works, see Bett (2000, 2010a) and Kuzminski (2010).

the many ideas of ancient Greek philosophy. The ad hoc approach prevailed essentially unchallenged among Classicists up to the publication a few years ago of a monograph by Adrian Kuzminski, which presents a systematic comparison between Late Pyrrhonism and Madhyamika Buddhism.[71]

The hitherto noted similarities of Pyrrhonism to Buddhism are on the right track, including the similarity to Madhyamika, since it has already been pointed out long ago that the key elements of Madhyamika are firmly attested in early works preserved in the Pali Canon.[72] They are essential elements or logical corollaries of the basic teachings of the Buddha, as shown in Chapter One.

However, there is much more that can be said. In particular, it is important to compare Pyrrho's own thought with the thought of the Buddhism *of his own day* as much as possible. Despite a large literature arguing for a sharp divide between the Early and Late forms of Pyrrhonism, careful consideration reveals that Late Pyrrhonism hardly deviates *systemically* in any significant way from Early Pyrrhonism: the emphasis on *epochē* 'suspension of judgement' about matters of metaphysics, epistemology, and so on, derives directly from Pyrrho's explicit exhortation to have *no views* and to be *aklineis* 'uninclined'—to not make judgements about such things, or 'not decide'. Its connection with Late Pyrrhonism is explicit in a quotation of Timon's *Pythō*, where he states the attitude as "determining nothing and withholding assent."[73] Even the revived Neo-Pyrrhonism of David Hume captures many of the essential features of ancient Pyrrhonism, regardless of Hume's poor sources and their contamination by dogmatic Academic Scepticism.[74] As shown in Chapter Four, this is due in final analysis

[71] Kuzminski (2010); cf. his earlier article, Kuzminski (2007). I discovered his book and article after my work on Pyrrho was already far advanced. His approach is based mainly on comparing Late Pyrrhonism with the teachings of the fully developed Madhyamika school of late Normative Buddhism, so while philosophically interesting and important in its own right, it is in general not relevant to the present work.

[72] Gómez (1976). As shown in Chapter Two, the same elements are attested in the account of Megasthenes, dated to 305–304 BC.

[73] Diogenes Laertius IX, 76, translation by Bett (2000: 31); cf. Appendix A.

[74] One of the anonymous reviewers of the manuscript of this book misunderstood my use of the term "dogmatic" in connection with various philosophical views, in one instance taking it as a criticism of the view of Richard Bett. However, I have simply taken

to the coherence of Pyrrho's thought, which is in turn based on Early Buddhist thought.

This book shows not only that Pyrrho's complete package is similar to Early Buddhism, but also that the same significant parts and interconnections occur in the same way in both systems. The earliest sources on Early Pyrrhonism and Early Buddhism are examined closely, including in some cases determining what "Early" means.[75] They show that the close parallel between Early Pyrrhonism and Early (Pre-Normative) Buddhism is systemic and motivated by the same internal logic. Pyrrho's journey to Central Asia and India with Alexander thus had an outcome for the future of philosophy that has lasted down to the present.

---

over the ancient Sceptics' own terminology, using the term "dogmatic" as a way of distinguishing all other philosophical traditions from the true Pyrrhonian attitude, which is explicitly and literally "nondogmatic". I intend no criticism of any modern scholar by it.

[75] See the Epilogue for a point-by-point summary of what attested Early Buddhism was like in contrast to early Normative Buddhism.

CHAPTER 1

Pyrrho's Thought

BEYOND HUMANITY

A brief passage that derives ultimately from the lost dialogue *Pythō* 'Python'[1] by Timon of Phlius is accepted to be the single most important testimony for the thought of his teacher, Pyrrho.[2] Because it is preserved in a chapter of a history of philosophy by Aristocles of Messene (quoted verbatim in the *Preparation for the Gospel* by Eusebius), it is generally known as "the Aristocles passage". The text begins with Timon's short introduction, in which he says, "Whoever wants to be happy must consider these three [questions]: first, how are *pragmata* '(ethical) matters, affairs, topics' by nature? Secondly, what attitude should we adopt towards them? Thirdly, what will be the outcome for those who have this attitude?"[3] Then Timon quotes[4] Pyrrho's own revelation of the three negative characteristics of all *pragmata* 'matters, affairs, questions, topics'. The ethical meaning of the word *pragmata* is absolutely clear because other testimonies[5] show that it meant for Pyrrho exclusively ethical 'matters, affairs, topics'. Accordingly, the

[1] Based on remarks by Aristocles in his history of philosophy preserved by Eusebius; see Appendix A.

[2] See Appendix A for the Greek text, detailed point-by-point analysis, and full references.

[3] This is my slight revision of the translation by Long and Sedley (1987: 1:14–15). For their original and my commentary, see Appendix A.

[4] As normal in ancient Greek, this is done in *oratio obliqua* 'indirect discourse', so it is not necessarily exact, but unlike the English equivalent, *oratio obliqua* in Greek is explicitly marked grammatically *as a quotation*, even if indirect. Poetry, by contrast, is virtually always quoted verbatim. For further examples and discussion, see Chapter Two.

[5] Especially Narrative 5, "Pyrrho and the Dog", below in this chapter.

word will be so translated below, or given in Greek as *pragmata* (singular *pragma*).[6]

Following these prefatory remarks, Timon says, "Pyrrho himself declares that"[7]

> As for *pragmata* 'matters, questions, topics',[8] they are all *adiaphora* 'undifferentiated by a logical differentia' and *astathmēta* 'unstable, unbalanced, not measurable' and *anepikrita* 'unjudged, unfixed, undecidable'. Therefore, neither our sense-perceptions nor our 'views, theories, beliefs' (*doxai*) tell us the truth or lie [about *pragmata*]; so we certainly should not rely on them [to do it]. Rather, we should be *adoxastous* 'without views', *aklineis* 'uninclined [toward this side or that]', and *akradantous* 'unwavering [in our refusal to choose]', saying about every single one that it no more is than[9] it is not or it both is and is not or it neither is nor is not.[10]

To paraphrase, Pyrrho says that ethical matters or questions are not logically differentiated, they are unstable (or 'unassessed and unassessable by any measure'), and they are unjudged, not fixed (or, undecidable). Therefore, our inductive and deductive reasoning cannot tell us whether any ethical question is True or False, so we should not count

[6] *LSJ*'s primary definitions of the word *pragma* are: 'deed, act, thing, advantage, concern, affair, matter, matter in hand, question [i.e., subject, topic], fact, circumstances, state-affairs, fortunes, business ("esp[ecially] lawbusiness"), trouble, annoyance'. In the long entry in *LSJ* there is not a single glossed example of *pragma* (singular) ~ *pragmata* (plural) in the meaning of a physical object, such as a stone, a tree, a dog, etc. The sense "thing, concrete reality" listed in the *LSJ* entry does *not* in fact refer to "concrete physical things" at all, as one should expect, but only to abstract "subjects" or "objects". As I note in Appendix A, the English in *LSJ* is sometimes peculiar, probably because it was first published in the mid-nineteenth century. I also checked all linked source citations and read them; none use the word in a physical or metaphysical sense.

[7] There is no reflection of the word *pephyke* 'by nature, really' in Pyrrho's statement, despite most scholars' interpretations. It has been used to further the "metaphysical" interpretation of Pyrrho's statement, e.g., by Bett (2000). The word occurs only in Timon's introductory remarks, which Aristocles explicitly says are by Timon. In my 2011 article reprinted in Appendix A, I unthinkingly followed the usual interpretation. I would like to thank an anonymous reviewer of the manuscript for catching me on this. My translation here corrects this error.

[8] Literally, "Matters (*pragmata*) are *equally* . . .", i.e., "*All* matters are . . .".

[9] Literally "(it) no more *is* or (it) *is not*", making the symmetry complete. On the tetralemma, see below and the extended discussion in Appendix A.

[10] Eusebius, ed. K. Mras (1983: XIV 18:1–5); Chiesara (2001: 20–21); see Appendix A for the Greek text and commentary.

on them to tell us. Instead, we should have no views on ethical matters, we should not incline toward any choice with respect to ethical questions, and we should not waver in our avoidance of attempts to decide such matters, reciting the tetralemma formula—"It no more is than it is not or it both is and is not or it neither is nor is not"—in response to every single one of such ethical questions.

The Aristocles passage is crucially important, highly condensed, and not easy to understand, as attested to by the fact that its basic meaning has been disputed by scholars of Classical philosophy for the past century. It thus requires additional explanation.

To begin with, as the subject of Pyrrho's entire declaration, the meaning of *pragmata* is crucially important, so it needs a little further clarification.

The Greek word *pragma* (singular) ~ *pragmata* (plural) is largely abstract. In other words, it means 'something, things', but in the abstract logical sense of 'an object of our cogitation or disputation',[11] so translating *pragmata* as 'things'—in the same general abstract logical sense—is not wrong, but *things* in English are by default largely physical or metaphysical objects. As a result, scholars have let themselves be misled by that default meaning into misinterpreting Pyrrho's entire message. When helpful below, *pragmata* will be translated as "ethical things, matters (etc.)".

Moreover, it must be emphasized that Pyrrho sees *pragmata* as *disputed* matters.[12] If people agreed on *pragmata* or did not argue about them, they would not be characterizable as Pyrrho says. They would already be decided and no problem. Arguments about opposing or disputed "matters, topics" are ubiquitous in Greek philosophy, as for example in Plutarch, "They quarrel about whether the matter (*pragma*) is good or evil or white or not white."[13]

[11] I.e., in the sense of Tugendhat: "What is meant by 'objects' in philosophy has its basis in . . . what we mean by the word 'something'. . . . There is a class of linguistic expressions which are used to stand for an object; and here we can only say: to stand for something. These are the expressions which can function as the sentence-subject in so-called singular predicative statements and which in logic have also been called *singular terms* . . ." (Tugendhat 1982: 21–23), quoted in Laycock (2010).

[12] Cf. the usage of Aristotle in *Nicomachean Ethics* 1094b, where it occurs in the singular and means 'subject, topic (under discussion)'; v. *LSJ*, s.v. *pragma*.

[13] Plutarch *Adversus Colotem* (Stephanus 1109D7, from *TLG*): διαμάχονται περὶ τοῦ χρηστὸν ἢ πονηρὸν ἢ λευκὸν ἢ μὴ λευκὸν εἶναι τὸ πρᾶγμα.

Based evidently on the general scholarly unclarity about *pragmata,*[14] some have argued that the Aristocles passage represents a "dogmatic" metaphysical position, on account of which they conclude that Pyrrho could not be the founder of Pyrrhonism. This idea has been much criticized,[15] mainly because the ancient testimonies overwhelmingly say that the concern of Pyrrho is purely with ethics, and many modern scholars agree.[16] The very first significant word in his declaration is *adiaphora,* a logical term, which is followed by inference after inference. Pyrrho's way of skewering ethical issues is to use logic. How would using metaphysics for ethical problems make sense?[17] Pyrrho never, in this or any other testimony, talks about physical or metaphysical issues (though he is said to have criticized other philosophers who did talk about them), and in two testimonies—the Aristocles passage and the narrative about the dog[18]—he explicitly mentions *pragmata* and makes it very clear that he uses the word to refer to conflicting *ethical* "matters, affairs". In short, for Pyrrho, *pragmata* are always and only *ethical* 'topics, questions, matters, affairs' which people dispute or try to interpret with antilogies—opposed choices such as Good : Bad, or True : False.

Pyrrho's declaration may now be examined section by section.

The Three Characteristics

Pyrrho famously declares that all ethical "matters, questions" have three characteristics which, oddly, are all *negative,* so his statement is actually a declaration of what matters are *not.* That is, the positive equivalent of each negative term is what Pyrrho negates, so we must

[14] Scholars have given and discussed at length examples referring to hard physical objects, including "a tomato", "the earth", and "rocks" (Bett 2000: 23, 117–120), "the sun" and "an icy lake" (Thorsrud 2009: 21), etc.

[15] See the survey of previous studies in Appendix A. An anonymous reviewer of the manuscript of this book, like Bett, understands *pragmata* to mean physical or metaphysical "things". The reviewer notes, also like Bett, that scholars "who favor the 'metaphysical' reading of Pyrrho's thought . . . have had a hard time making their case to scholars of Greek philosophy".

[16] The anonymous reviewer who favors the metaphysical interpretation (see the previous note) agrees with this too.

[17] Cf. Stopper (1983) on the putative "zany inference" in the Aristocles passage.

[18] See below in this chapter.

base our understanding of the terms on their positive forms, which (unlike the negative ones) are all well attested in Classical Greek. His declaration is presented as the foundation of his teaching, and modern scholars' intensive analysis of the entire passage and the other ancient testimonies has confirmed that it is indeed the core of his thought:[19] it is inseparable from his practical indirect path, via *apatheia* 'passionlessness', to *ataraxia* 'undisturbedness, calm'. Because of its conciseness, the text requires interpretation based on the remaining part of the Aristocles passage, other material in Aristocles' chapter on Pyrrhonism, and other testimonies, including in particular those containing statements attributed directly to Pyrrho himself.

1. Adiaphora *'Without a Self-Identity'*

The first term, *adiaphora*, is the negative of *diaphora* 'differentiated by a logical differentia' and literally means 'undifferentiated by a logical differentia',[20] that is, 'without a logical self-identity': *pragmata* 'matters, affairs' do not come supplied with their own self-identifying differentiae or other categorizing criteria. For example, someone's expression of anger is not automatically identified for us by a "thought balloon" spelling out its genus (or superordinate category) "an emotion" and further differentiating it as a "bad" emotion, thus distinguishing it from "good" emotions (among other choices). In several testimonies Pyrrho denies that *pragmata* are in fact differentiated from their contrasting opposites, for example "the just" versus "the unjust", or "the truth" versus "a lie". People dispute *pragmata* as to whether they are good or bad, just or unjust, and so on, but any specific *pragma*, in order to be a subject of philosophical discussion at all, must necessarily be discrete

[19] See Bett (2000: 14–18) and Appendix A.

[20] A differentia is a kind of categorization that distinguishes a genus from a species, as explained by Aristotle (*Metaphysics* Δ 6 (1016a) 24–27, from Ross and Smith 1908): λέγεται δ' ἓν καὶ ὧν τὸ γένος ἓν διαφέρον ταῖς ἀντικειμέναις διαφοραῖς—καὶ ταῦτα λέγεται πάντα ἓν ὅτι τὸ γένος ἓν τὸ ὑποκείμενον ταῖς διαφοραῖς (οἷον ἵππος ἄνθρωπος κύων ἕν τι ὅτι πάντα ζῷα), translated by Apostle (1966:80) as "Also those things are called 'one' whose genus is one, although they differ by opposing differentiae; and all these are said to be one in view of the fact that the genus underlying the differentiae is one. For example, a horse and a man and a dog are one in this sense: they are all animals" (Apostle 1966: 80). I.e., "horse", "man", and "dog" all belong to the *genus* "animal", but are all distinct *species* that "differ by opposing differentiae".

and differentiated from other *pragmata* by a logical differentia. Because *pragmata* themselves do not actually have differentiae (as Timon says, "by nature"), *we ourselves* necessarily supply the differentiae. But that makes the entire process strictly circular and therefore logically invalid.[21]

A direct consequence of the teaching of *adiaphora* 'without a logical differentia, no self-identity' is the explicit denial of the validity of opposed categories, or "antilogies".

2. Astathmēta *'Unstable, Unbalanced, Not Measurable'*

The second term, *astathmēta*, is an adjective from the stem *sta-* 'stand' with the negative prefix *a-*, literally meaning 'not standing'. The word is based on the noun *stathmos* 'standing place, stable; a balance-beam, measuring scale'. For example, Aristophanes, in *The Frogs*, has Aeschylus say, "what I'd like to do is take him to *the scales* (*stathmos*); That's the only real test of our poetry; the weight of our utterances will be the decisive proof."[22] So *astathmēta* means 'non-standing-place; no *stathmos* (a balance-beam, scale)', thus, 'unstable, unbalanced'.[23] Since *pragmata* are unbalanced and unstable, they pull this way and that, and are unsettling. They make us feel uneasy and susceptible to passions and disturbedness.

[21] This is a fundamental epistemological problem. In Antiquity it was generalized and became known as the Problem of the Criterion. It was taken up again in the Enlightenment, most famously by Hume; see Chapter Four.

[22] Aristophanes, *The Frogs* 1365: ἐπὶ τὸν σταθμὸν γὰρ αὐτὸν ἀγαγεῖν βούλομαι,/ ὅπερ ἐξελέγξει τὴν ποίησιν νῷν μόνον·/ τὸ γὰρ βάρος νὼ βασανιεῖ τῶν ῥημάτων. Text and translation from Henderson (2002), emphasis added. Aeschylus and Euripides then go over to the large measuring scales, and each speaks a line into his measuring pan. Dionysus, the judge, says (of the measuring scale pans), "Look, this one's going much lower!" Aeschylus wins a second attempt too, and Dionysus says, "His (side of the scale) went down farther again, because he put in Death, the heaviest blow." (Henderson 2002: 210–215). Henderson (2002: 209n130) comments, "This weighing scene is probably modeled on the scene in Aeschylus' *Weighing of Souls* where Zeus weighs the souls of Achilles and Memnon as they fight." See Griffith (2013) for an extremely illuminating and important discussion of this passage and of judging in general in ancient Greek culture.

[23] *LSJ* online, s.v. *stathmos*. Cf. Bett (2000: 19) "*astathmēta*—derived from *stathmos*, 'balance'—could mean 'unstable' or 'unbalanced' . . . [or] 'not subject to being placed on a balance', and hence 'unmeasurable'." The interpretation 'not measurable' would follow if *pragmata* are 'not balanced' or 'unbalanced'.

3. Anepikrita *'Unjudged, Undecided, Unfixed'*

The third term, *anepikrita*, is a negative made from *epikrisis* 'determination, judgement',[24] from the well-attested derived verb *epikrinō* 'to decide, determine; judge; select, pick out, choose'—as in Aristotle's usage "with what part of itself (the soul) judges that which distinguishes sweet from warm"[25]—which is based in turn on the verb *krinō* 'to separate, distinguish; choose; decide disputes or contests; judge; prefer'; *krinō* is the source also of the important word *kriterion* 'criterion, means for judging or trying, standard'.[26] *Anepikrita* thus means 'unjudged, undecided, unchosen, unfixed',[27] so *pragmata* are not permanently decided or fixed.

The Three Characteristics— The Buddha

Pyrrho's tripartite statement is completely unprecedented and unparalleled in Greek thought. Yet it is not merely similar to Buddhism, it corresponds closely to a famous statement of the Buddha preserved in canonical texts.[28] The statement is known as the *Trilakṣaṇa*, the 'Three

[24] Cf. Bett (2000: 19). One of its few occurrences is in D.L. ix, 92, where it means 'judgement' or 'decision'. However, its positive verbal form is very well attested in Classical period Greek. See the following note.

[25] Aristotle, *De Anima* 431a20 (text from *TLG*): τίνι δ' ἐπικρίνει τί διαφέρει γλυκὺ καὶ θερμόν. Cf. *LSJ* online, s.v. *epikrinō*.

[26] *LSJ* online, s.v. *krinō*. Cf. Griffith's (2013) illuminating discussion of judging between contestants in ancient Greek culture.

[27] Cf. Bett (2000), who regularly refers to this characteristic as a lack of "fixity", though he interprets it metaphysically.

[28] The canonical Nikāya texts of the Pali Canon are traditionally thought to reflect Early Buddhism—meaning, in theory, the state of the teachings close to the time of the Buddha. However, the actual dates of the Nikāya texts are unstated, and in general traditional studies do not reveal when they were composed, pace Wynne (2005) and many others. Their acknowledged doctrinal similarity both to early translations of Buddhist texts into Chinese and to the recently discovered Gāndhārī texts does not affirm the picture of Buddhism presented in them as being close to the time of the Buddha because these Chinese and Gāndhārī texts both date to the late Kushan period. Their similarity to the "early" Pali canonical texts tells us only that all three sets of texts date to the same period, thus confirming that traditional "early" Buddhist canonical literature reflects Normative Buddhism (q.v. below), a product of the same Saka-Kushan period. Because the Nikāya texts are also far from homogeneous in their representations of the teachings

Characteristics' of all *dharmas* 'ethical distinctions, factors, constituents, etc.' Greek *pragmata* '(ethical) things' corresponds closely to Indic *dharma* ~ *dhamma* '(ethical) things' and seems to be Pyrrho's equivalent of it.[29]

The Buddha says, "All *dharmas* are *anitya* 'impermanent'. . . . All *dharmas* are *duḥkha* 'unsatisfactory, imperfect, unstable'. . . . All *dharmas* are *anātman* 'without an innate self-identity'."[30]

1. Anitya *'Impermanent, Variable, Unfixed'*

The first term, *anitya* (Pali *anicca*) is the negative form of *nitya* 'eternal, invariant, fixed (etc.)' and means 'impermanent, variable, unfixed'.[31]

2. Duḥkha *'Uneasy; Unsatisfactory; Unsteady'*

The meaning of the second term, *duḥkha* (Pali *dukkha*), is contested by scholars and actually has no universally accepted basic meaning or etymology. The standard Sanskrit dictionary and recent scholars' interpretations of *duḥkha* include 'unsatisfactory, imperfect', and 'uneasy, uncomfortable, unpleasant',[32] and so on, but the term is perhaps the most misunderstood—and definitely the most mistranslated—in Buddhism.[33] However, at the very beginning of his definition, Monier-Williams says, "(according to grammarians properly written *dush-kha*

---

of the Buddha, scholars have determined that some elements are earlier or later, while study of the inner logic of the Buddha's own teachings (to the extent that it is agreed what they were) also allows inclusion or exclusion of various elements.

[29] I am indebted to Georgios Halkias (p.c., 2012) for this observation; I am of course responsible for any misunderstanding. Cf. the discussion of *dharma* in Appendix C.

[30] *Anguttara-nikāya* III, 134. Mitchell (2008: 34) translates it: "all [the world's] constituents are [1] transitory [S. *anitya*, P. *anicca* 'impermanent'] . . . all its constituents are [2] unsatisfactory [S. *duḥkha*, P. *dukkha*] . . . all its constituents are [3] lacking a permanent self [S. *anātman*, P. *anattā* 'containing no permanent inner substance or self']." His "constituents" translates Sanskrit *dharmā*, Pali *dhammā*.

[31] Monier-Williams (1988: 547), online edition, s.v. *anitya* and *nitya*.

[32] Monier-Williams (1988), online edition, s.v. *duḥkha*.

[33] Hamilton (2000: 12) says, "Until recent years, *dukkha* was usually translated as 'suffering', with 'pain' or 'ill' being common alternatives; now 'unsatisfactory' is more usually used." Despite Gethin's (1998: 187) reasonable definition of *duḥkha* as "unsatisfactory and imperfect", he still regularly mistranslates it as "suffering" in much of his book. Note that Hamilton (2000), which is based on the Pali Nikāya texts, rightly treats the *Trilakṣaṇa* as a key element of Early Buddhism. Nevertheless, her book presents a solidly traditional Normative Buddhism, not Pre-Normative Buddhism or actual historical Early Buddhism.

and said to be from *dus* and *kha* [cf. *su-khá*] . . .)".[34] The opposite of *duḥkha* is widely thought to be *sukha* 'running swiftly or easily (only applied to cars or chariots)'—a usage that occurs in the Rig Veda.[35] The usual meaning of *sukha* is now simply 'good', so its apparent opposite, *duḥkha,* should mean 'bad', but such an idea is explicitly refuted by the third characteristic, *anātman,* as well as by complete agreement in attested Early Buddhism that antilogies such as "good" versus "bad" are misconceived. Accordingly, although the sense of *duḥkha* in Normative Buddhism is traditionally given as 'suffering', that and similar interpretations are highly unlikely for Early Buddhism. Significantly, Monier-Williams himself doubts the usual explanation of *duḥkha* and presents an alternative one immediately after it, namely: *duḥ-stha* "'standing badly,' unsteady, disquieted (lit. and fig.); uneasy," and so on.[36] This form is also attested, and makes much better sense as the opposite of the Rig Veda sense of *sukha,* which Monier-Williams gives in full as "(said to be fr. 5. *su* + 3. *kha* , and to mean originally 'having a good axle-hole'; possibly a Prakrit form of *su-stha*[37] q.v.; cf. *duḥkha*) running swiftly or easily (only applied to cars or chariots, superl[ative] *sukhá-tama*), easy". It would seem that there were two forms of each word; Prakrit and Buddhist Hybrid Sanskrit chose the *-kha* forms instead of the *-stha* forms, which survived nevertheless in a much smaller way. The most important point here is that *duḥ* + *stha* literally means 'dis-/bad- + stand-', that is, 'badly standing, unsteady' and is therefore virtually identical to the literal meaning of Greek *astathmēta,* from *a-* + *sta-* 'not- + stand',[38] both evidently meaning 'unstable'. This strongly suggests that Pyrrho's middle term is in origin a simple calque.

3. Anātman *'No (Innate) Self (-Identity)'*

The third term, *anātman* (Pali *anattā*), means 'no (innate) self (-identity)'. As with the other characteristics, it is applied to all dharmas, including

[34] Monier-Williams (1988: 483).

[35] Monier-Williams (1988), online edition, s.v. *sukha.* Cf. below. The other meanings are later.

[36] Monier-Williams (1988: 483); Böhtlingk (1928), Cologne online edition.

[37] Monier-Williams (1988: 1239) defines *sustha* as 'well situated, faring well, healthy, comfortable, prosperous, happy'.

[38] The root of the verb in both languages (as in English) is a cognate inheritance from Proto-Indo-European *stā- 'to stand; place or thing that is standing' (Watkins 2000: 84).

humans, so it of course includes the idea of the human "self-identity", and much discussion in Buddhist texts and the scholarly literature on them focuses on that idea.[39] Nevertheless, Buddha explicitly says that "*all* dharmas are *anātman*." As Hamilton rightly points out, "In a great many, one might almost say most, secondary sources on Buddhism" *anātman* "has regularly been singled out as being the heart or core of what Buddhism is all about."[40] Like all major Early Buddhist teachings, this one is presented negatively. It rejects the idea of inherent absolutes such as good and bad, true and false, and so on. The rejection is explicit also in Buddhist-influenced Early Taoist texts as well as in early Normative Buddhist texts such as the *Pratyutpanna Samādhi Sūtra*, first translated into Chinese between AD 178 and 189 by the Kushan monk Lokakṣema, and the *Sukhāvatīvyūha Sūtra* (translated in the early third century AD), both of which belong to the Pure Land school of Buddhism, traditionally classed as a branch of Mahayana.

The "three characteristics" are said to apply to "all dharmas", that is, everything, and are central in Buddhism.[41] But for Buddha, as for Pyrrho, their reference is exclusively to ethical or moral matters, including emotions and other conflicts. Like Pyrrho, the Buddha did not even mention metaphysics. He is presented in early Normative Buddhist texts as considering metaphysics to be distracting sophism, and refuses

[39] Hamilton (2000) is one of the many extreme examples of this, but her book does contain some unique insights on *anātman*.

[40] Hamilton (2000: 19); cf. Gethin (1998), who devotes thirty pages to the topic "No Self".

[41] Hamilton (2000) stresses the centrality of the concepts in the *Trilakṣaṇa*, but also emphasizes the "Four Noble Truths" and the "Eightfold Path". It is significant that neither of the latter two lists mentions *anitya* 'impermanent' and *anātman* 'lacking an inherent self-identity', and the Four Noble Truths are fixated on *duḥkha* alone. It is pointed out by Bareau (1963: 178–181; cited in Bronkhorst 1986: 101–104), from contrastive study of Vinaya accounts of the Buddha's first sermon with the accounts in the early sutras, that the Four Noble Truths are not even mentioned in the sutras. Moreover, it has since been shown definitively by Schopen (2004: 94) that the Vinaya versions we now have are actually dated or datable only to the fifth century AD. Because the *Trilakṣaṇa* seems to be attested in Pyrrho's Greek version, it is datable to 330–325 BC, and is therefore three centuries earlier than the otherwise earliest known Buddhist texts—the Gāndhārī manuscripts—and nearly a millennium earlier than the attested Vinaya. In any case, the Four Noble Truths and the Eightfold Path are clearly developments of late, standardized Normative Buddhism, which spread far and wide and absorbed or replaced earlier forms of Buddhism in the Saka-Kushan period.

to teach it,[42] but that story has patently been concocted to explain why a topic of concern in later times was not discussed by the Buddha.

Pyrrho's version of the *Trilakṣaṇa* is so close to the Indian Buddhist one that it is virtually a translation of it: both the Buddha and Pyrrho make a declaration in which they list three logical characteristics of all discrete "(ethical) things, affairs, questions", but they give them exclusively negatively, that is, "All matters are *non*-x, *non*-y, and *non*-z." The peculiar way in which the characteristics are presented is thus the same, the main difference being the order of the first and third characteristics.[43] This passage about the three characteristics is thus the absolutely earliest known bit of Buddhist doctrinal *text*. It is firmly dated three centuries earlier than the Gāndhārī texts.[44]

Now, the *Trilakṣaṇa* is not just any piece of Buddhist teaching. It is at the center of Buddhist *practice*, which is agreed to be the heart and soul of living Buddhism of any kind. Speaking of "insight meditation", evidently the oldest, but certainly the single most important of the different kinds and stages of Buddhist meditation, Gethin (1998) says,

> With the essential work of calming the mind completed, with the attainment of the fourth *dhyāna*, the meditator can focus fully on the development of insight. . . . [45] Insight meditation aims at understanding [that

[42] *Majjhima-nikāya* I, 428. Discussed by Gethin (1998: 66–67).

[43] In view of the three centuries separating Pyrrho's version of the *Trilakṣana* from the Gāndhārī texts (and probably still more centuries for the Pali texts), the probability must be considered that the meaning of the word *duḥkha* (Pali *dukkha*) had changed so much in that long interval that its Early Buddhist meaning has been lost in Indic. In that case, Pyrrho's version may preserve something closer to the Buddha's own intentions. As for the reversal of the first and third characteristics in Pyrrho's version, it could similarly represent the earlier tradition, or it could perhaps have been deliberate, due to Pyrrho's own stress on *adiaphora*, as discussed below.

[44] The statement of the *Trilakṣaṇa* is attested in the earliest known Buddhist manuscripts, the Gāndhārī texts that are currently under intensive study, including one dated to the first century AD, or possibly even the previous century. See Baums (2009: 251, 302, 406): "*aṇica* · *dukha* · *aṇatva*", which he translates traditionally as "impermanent, painful and without self". It is currently thought that the Gāndhārī texts date to approximately the same time as the traditional date of the compilation of the Pali Canon, but that the latter has been much altered in the following centuries.

[45] Here Gethin (1998: 187) adds "and the wisdom that understands the four truths." This is no doubt relevant for practitioners of later, Normative Buddhism, but as noted above it has been demonstrated that the Four (Noble) Truths cannot be reconstructed to Pre-Normative Buddhism.

> "things"] . . . are impermanent and unstable (*anitya/anicca*), that they are unsatisfactory and imperfect (*duḥkha/dukkha*), and that they are not self (*anātman/anattā*). The philosophical nuances of these three terms may be expressed differently in the theoretical writings of various Buddhist schools, but in one way or another the higher stages of the Buddhist path focus on the direct understanding and seeing of these aspects of the world.[46]

This characterization is supported by the *Mahāsaccaka Sutta*, in which the Buddha describes his final enlightenment, ending with his achievement of the four *dhyānas*.[47] In the last and highest of these, the fourth, he says, "As a result of abandoning bliss, and abandoning pain, as a result of the earlier disappearance of cheerfulness and dejection, I reached the Fourth Dhyāna, which is free from pain and bliss, the complete purity of equanimity and attentiveness, and resided [there]."[48] What the Buddha is abandoning here is the *distinction between the opposite qualities* or antilogies that are mentioned. This is Pyrrho's *adiaphora* state of being 'undifferentiated, without (an intrinsic) self-identity', which is identical to the Buddha's state of being *anātman* 'without (an intrinsic) self-identity'. It is equated with nirvana (*nirvāṇa* or *nirodha*) 'extinguishing (of the burning of the passions)', and the peace that results from it. In the terms of the *Mahāsaccaka Sutta*, 'being free from both pain and bliss'[49] means the state of *apatheia* 'passionlessness', while "complete equanimity" is exactly the same thing as *ataraxia*. As Timon says, the result of following Pyrrho's program is first *apatheia* 'passionlessness',[50] and then *ataraxia* 'undisturbedness, equanimity'—nirvana.

[46] Gethin (1998: 187). However, it must be emphasized that the Buddha did *not* teach about metaphysics (or for that matter physics, etc.), as noted above.

[47] Sanskrit *dhyāna*, Pali *jhāna*, has been borrowed into Chinese as *Ch'an* 禪, and into Japanese via Chinese, as *Zen* 禪.

[48] *Mahāsaccaka Sutta*, MN I, 247, translated by Bronkhorst (1986: 17), who adds that the text's "description of the Buddhist Four Dhyānas . . . is standard, and recurs numerous times in the Buddhist canon."

[49] Bronkhorst's "bliss" is his translation of Skt. *sukha*, and "pain" is his translation of Skt. *duḥkha*. These are common late Normative Buddhist interpretations of the meanings of the words, as discussed above.

[50] See the passage quoted below in this chapter; *apatheia* is my textual emendation for *aphasia*, as shown in detail in Appendix A, q.v.

We Know Neither the Absolute Truth nor the Lie

Pyrrho next points out that the logical problem he has noted has specific implications for truth values of anything, and accordingly, for our epistemology: "Therefore, neither our sense perceptions nor our *doxai* 'views, theories' tell us the (ultimate) truth or lie to us (about *pragmata* 'matters'). So we certainly should not rely on them (to do it)." Because differentiae and other criteria are provided by human minds,[51] and ethical "matters, affairs, topics" are by nature unstable and unfixed, both our inductive knowledge (based on perceptions) and our deductive knowledge (views, theories, or arguments, even if based on purely internal logical calculation) must be circular, and therefore logically invalid and fatally defective in general.[52] They are thus useless for determining any ultimate, absolute truth, or its converse, untruth—the lie—about *pragmata* 'matters'; so we certainly should not expect our intrinsically flawed and imperfect sense perceptions and mental abilities to do that.[53]

Pyrrho's rejection of the antilogy of *the Truth* versus *the Lie* hearkens back to the fundamental antilogy, repeated over and over in the early Avesta and the early Old Persian inscriptions, between *Asha* or *Arta* 'the Truth', supported by Heavenly God, Ahura Mazda 'Lord Wisdom', versus *Druj* 'the Lie'.[54]

Pyrrho's point here is that humans want to know the ultimate, absolute Truth, but *the ultimate* or *the absolute* is a perfectionist metaphysical or ontological category created by humans and superimposed on everything. The same people declare our task to be to learn the

[51] Of course other animals—even the simplest ones—do the same thing.

[52] See the discussion of the Problem of Induction in Chapter Four.

[53] Pyrrho's explicit mention of the converse of telling the truth indicates not only that he was well aware of the Law of Non-Contradiction, but that he was aware of the deeper implications of his negative "declaration" about things, q.v. Chapter Four.

[54] In the Gāthās, although Zoroaster vehemently rejects the *daevas* or *daivas*, the old polytheistic gods, they are equated with *druj* only indirectly, via condemnation of the priests who worship the *daevas*. Their worship was evidently too prevalent to be stamped out, and the most important of the old gods were reintroduced under the later Achaemenids.

absolute, perfect truth, and to understand it, as if it really existed.[55] Yet such categories cannot exist without humans, as pointed out in the Buddha's teaching of *anātman*—dharmas do not have inherent self-identities—and in Pyrrho's version of it, *adiaphora*.

In several famous Normative Buddhist sutra narratives the Buddha is presented as steadfastly refusing to discuss metaphysics and other forms of speculative philosophy, declaring that they are nonsense, and harmful, because they lead one astray from one's path to passionlessness and nirvana.[56]

The attitude of the Buddha in these texts is very clear:

> Buddhism regards itself as presenting a system of training in conduct, meditation, and understanding that constitutes a path leading to the cessation of suffering.[57] Everything is to be subordinated to this goal. And in this connection Buddha's teachings suggest that preoccupation with certain beliefs and ideas about the ultimate nature of the world [i.e., metaphysics] and our destiny in fact hinders our progress along this path rather than helping it. If we insist on working out exactly what to believe about the world and human destiny before beginning to follow the path of practice we will never even set out.[58]

There has been much empty scholastic debate on why the Buddha did not answer the metaphysical and other questions posed by the novice monk Māluṅkyāputta in the sutra about him, including even whether or not Buddha knew the answers.[59] It must first be stressed that this entire problem is purely a Normative Buddhist one, and cannot be projected back to the time of the Buddha. However, from the perspective of that late form of Buddhism, the reason he did not answer is remarkably clear in the sutra itself: from the Buddhist point of view, the questions are irrelevant, but also, as the *Trilakṣaṇa* makes abundantly clear, they are "unanswerable because they assume. . . *absolute categories* and concepts—the world, the soul, the self, the Tathāgatha—that the Buddha and the Buddhist tradition does not accept or at least criticizes and

[55] This is the goal of most of the major ancient Greek philosophical schools.

[56] The most famous example is in the *Cūḷa-Māluṅkya Sutta*; see Gethin (1998: 66).

[57] Gethin's usual translation of *duḥkha*.

[58] Gethin (1998: 65–66).

[59] See Gethin (1998: 67–68) for a summary.

understands in particular ways. That is, from the Buddhist perspective these questions are ill-formed and misconceived. To answer 'yes' or 'no' to any one of them is to be drawn into accepting the validity of the question and the terms in which it is couched."[60] The Buddha's great insight, as stated in the *Trilakṣaṇa*, is that absolute, perfect categories and concepts[61] conceived by humans are among the obstacles to achieving passionlessness and nirvana; it is necessary to get rid of them in order to progress.[62] The questions of Māluṅkyāputta reveal that some Buddhists did not understand the Buddha's main overt teachings, let alone the covert ones.

What We Should Be Without

Based on the above considerations, Pyrrho advises, "So we should be *adoxastous* 'without views, theories' [about *pragmata* 'matters'], and *aklineis* 'uninclined' [toward or against *pragmata*], and *akradantous* 'unwavering' [in our attitude about *pragmata*], saying about every single one[63] that it no more is than it is not, or it both is and is not, or it neither is nor is not."

1. We Should Have *No Views*

Pyrrho says that we should have "no views, theories" because they force us to be inclined in one direction or another with respect to *pragmata*. They thus constitute an obstacle to our attainment of passionlessness or unperturbedness—though Pyrrho does not say this himself, no doubt because stating an explicit goal would violate the principles he has just outlined. Instead, he must have taught his students to understand that the goal can be attained only indirectly, because Timon does supply this information at the end of his account, as quoted by Aristocles.

[60] Gethin (1998: 68), emphasis added.

[61] See Chapter Four.

[62] As Gethin (1998: 68) puts it, "such views (*dṛṣṭi/diṭṭhi*) about the ultimate nature of the world are, from the Buddhist perspective, the expression of a mental grasping which is but one manifestation of that insatiable 'thirst' or 'craving' which Buddhist thought regards as the condition for the arising of suffering".

[63] The phrase "every single one (of them)" here refers again to *pragmata*, explicitly echoing the beginning statement that *pragmata* are "equally"—i.e., "all"—undifferentiated, etc.

Pyrrho's explicit enjoinment that we should have "no views" corresponds exactly to the Buddhist attitude attested in some of the earliest texts in the Pali Canon. In the *Aṭṭhakavagga,*[64] several texts say unambiguously that we should have "no views". The teaching of "right views" and "the highest knowledge" are rejected as "the false science of those who are still attached to views. Moreover their attachment is not deemed to be merely the attachment to wrong views, but to views in general. Also, there is no question here of teaching the superior *dharma*, rather the point is that the true follower of the path would not prefer any dharma; he would make no claims to the possession of a higher dharma."[65] Wise men are those who "fancy not, they prefer not, and not a single dharma do they adopt."[66] Gómez points out further, "This idea is in fact well known to us through the traditional doctrine of the Middle Path—avoiding the two extremes. Thus, not to rely on views is in a certain way a form of nondualism."[67] This connection is explicit in Pyrrho's next point.

2. We Should Be *Uninclined to Either Side*

Second, Pyrrho says we should be "uninclined". One of the parallel testimonies, a poem by Timon in praise of Pyrrho, says he was "not weighed down *on this side and that* by passions (*patheōn*), theories

[64] The fifth book of the Sutta Nipāta subsection of the Khuddaka Nikāya section of the Pali Canon.

[65] Gómez (1976: 139–140). I have silently changed his past tense verbs to present tense and spelled out *Aṭṭhakavagga* here and below. Gómez (1976: 156) also notes, "Some key passages from the *Aṭṭhakavagga* could be called 'proto-Mādhyamika' passages in the sense that they anticipate some of the axial concepts of the Mādhyamika. . . . [However], the theoretical framework of the Mādhyamika is totally absent from the *Aṭṭhakavagga*. The twofold truth, emptiness, causation, and dependent origination, the indeterminables, the tetralemma, the equivalence of *saṃsāra* and *nirvāṇa*, are conspicuous by their absence." Note that by "the tetralemma" Gómez means the developed form of it used conspicuously and even profligately in Madhyamika works. However, it is very definitely odd that Madhyamika should have *revived* a dialectical fashion of the fourth to third centuries BC (see Appendix A). Something thus seems to be wrong with the periodization here. D'Amato (2009) compares the early texts discussed by Gómez to the fully developed Madhyamika system.

[66] *Aṭṭhakavagga* 803 (Gómez 1976: 140). His comment on this being "a form of nondualism" is precisely correct. It is one aspect of the Buddha's rejection of Early Zoroastrianism, which is permeated with an early kind of dualism focused on antilogies, opposed ethical categorizations.

[67] Gómez (1976: 141).

(*doxēs*), and pointless legislation". This clarifies that we should maintain our balance in the middle, *neither for nor against* passions, *doxai* 'views, theories', and vain attempts to "fix" things (i.e., to make them established, permanent).[68] With the exception that they are not in the same order, these three points correspond to the three injunctions of Pyrrho presently under consideration, which also apparently correspond to the "three characteristics" of all *pragmata* in the first line of Pyrrho's declaration, namely *adiaphora* (there are no logically differentiated *pragmata*) : *adoxastous* (be without views or theories—which require differentiae—about *pragmata*); *astathmēta* (there are no balanced *pragmata*) : *aklineis* (do not be unbalanced by inclining toward this one or that one) ; *anepikrita* (there are no fixed *pragmata*) : *akradantous* (unwaveringly avoid trying to fix or "choose" them by fiat). The ancient testimonies say that Pyrrho did not "choose." He maintained a balance between extremes, without views, and thus achieved *ataraxia* 'undisturbedness, calm'.

One of the insights of Buddhism that appears to go back to the Buddha himself is that we should not have attachments (*upādāna*) or cravings (*ṭṛṣṇā, taṇhā*) with regard to material things, human relations, views, and so on, in order to avoid disturbance. In normal daily life "we become attached to things that are unreliable, unstable, changing, and impermanent." Though we try to find something "that is permanent and stable, which we can hold on to and thereby find lasting happiness, we must always fail." The Buddha's solution is, "Let go of everything." The goal of the Buddhist path is thus the cessation of craving, equated with the cessation of *duḥkha*.[69]

One who "does not grasp at anything in the world . . . craves no longer, and through not craving he effects complete *nirvāṇa*".[70] Although this is expressed in Normative Buddhist language understood by modern Normative Buddhist exegesis, the point is the same as in Pyrrhonism: maintaining one's balance by not clinging or being weighed down by passions, which pull us, in one direction or another, away from the balanced condition of having no views, no passions, no choices, and so on. Buddhist mendicants are explicitly enjoined not to refuse whatever

[68] See Appendix A for references and discussion of Timon's poem.

[69] Gethin (1998: 74); here as elsewhere, he translates *duḥkha* as "suffering".

[70] *Dīgha Nikāya* II, 68, translation by Gethin (1998: 146).

food is given them when begging, nor to refuse a robe given to them, but to eat and wear whatever they may have without complaint—that is, they should not be choosy or picky. It is precisely the attitude and behavior of Pyrrho described in several narratives about him,[71] and it is precisely the attitude of the Buddha: according to the traditional account in the *Mahāparinirvāṇa Sūtra*, he died after eating spoiled food given him by a pious donor.

This "not choosing" is thus one of the core teachings of Early Buddhism and Early Pyrrhonism both. It is expressed in exactly the same words. The *Paramattaka Sutta* in the Suttanipāta, in stressing that holding particular views is a form of clinging, says, "One who *isn't inclined toward either side*—becoming or not-[becoming], here or beyond—who has no entrenchment when considering what's grasped among doctrines, hasn't the least preconceived perception with regard to what's seen, heard, or sensed."[72] These points thus occur in exactly the same *systemic* relationship in both Buddhism and Pyrrhonism.

3. We Should Be *Unwavering*

Pyrrho finally enjoins us to be "unwavering" in our disposition about *pragmata* '(ethical) things, matters, affairs', reciting the tetralemma formula in response to "every single one" of them so as to deny that they have any validity whatsoever. "For Pyrrho declared no matter to be good or bad or just or unjust, and likewise with regard to all matters, that not one of them is (good or bad or just or unjust) in truth, but that people manage all matters (*prattein*)[73] by law and custom, because each one is no more this than it is that."[74]

[71] See below in this chapter.

[72] *Paramattaka Sutta*, Suttanipāta 4.5, trans. Thanissaro Bhikku (1994–2012) http://www.accesstoinsight.org/tipitaka/kn/snp/snp.4.05.than.html, emphasis and clarification added. The sutra also emphasizes the importance of having no views: "Abandoning what he had embraced, abandoning self, not clinging, he doesn't make himself dependent even in connection with knowledge; doesn't follow a faction among those who are split; doesn't fall back on any view whatsoever."

[73] The construction in Greek uses not the noun *pragmata* but its corresponding verb *prattein* 'to achieve, bring something to an end', from *prak-*; it is a verbal form of *pragma* and *praxis* that means something like 'to "do" *pragmata*', i.e., 'to manage matters'.

[74] D.L. IX, 61: οὐδὲν γὰρ ἔφασκεν οὔτε καλὸν οὔτ' αἰσχρὸν οὔτε δίκαιον οὔτ' ἄδικον: καὶ ὁμοίως ἐπὶ πάντων μηδὲν εἶναι τῇ ἀληθείᾳ. Text by Hicks (1925: 474), but correcting the erroneous printed form ἀληθείᾳ in his text from the text of Decleva Caizzi (1981: 29).

The denial that *dharmas*, or "(ethical) things", exist "in Truth" is yet another pervasive teaching of Buddhism.[75] What both Pyrrho and the Buddha deny is the idea of anything existing in some ultimate, absolute sense *beyond* that of our perceptions and thoughts, as opposed to phenomenal appearance.[76]

Both Pyrrho and Buddha stress that the Way is not easy; one must struggle against our natural human inclinations to waver back and forth between this passion and that. We are not perfect beings living in a perfect world, so we sometimes err. We must stick to the path, despite occasional setbacks and other difficulties, as pointed out by Pyrrho in his response to criticism related below in Narrative 5.

Pyrrho tells us that when we are confronted by a conflict, we should recite the tetralemma, a four-part formula that negates all possible determinations. Doing this "unwaveringly" in every instance eliminates the obstructions of *pragmata* one by one.

Although it has been argued that Pyrrho's use of the tetralemma reveals that his thought derives from Buddhism, this has been shown to be an untenable view because the tetralemma already occurs in earlier Greek philosophical texts. Plato (428–347 BC) quotes a tetralemma in the *Republic* spoken by Glaucon and responded to by "Socrates", and Aristotle too quotes a tetralemma in his discussion of those who deny the Law of Non-Contradiction.[77] It also occurs in the *Chuangtzu* (composed mostly of material put together in the fourth to third centuries BC). In Normative Buddhist texts, the tetralemma is earliest attested in works ascribed to the Madhyamika philosopher Nāgārjuna (traditionally dated to the second century AD), but the tetralemma also occurs in sutras from the Pali Canon traditionally thought to reflect Early Buddhism. Moreover, as noted above, basic Madhyamika philosophy itself is found in some of the early Pali sutras.

[75] The apparent partial exception to this teaching taken by the Sarvāstivāda school ('those who say all [dharmas] exist'), an important subsect of Normative Buddhism in Late Antiquity (q.v. Willemen, Dessein, and Cox 1998), was the cause of much creative disputation, q.v. Beckwith (2012c).

[76] See Chapter Four.

[77] See Bett's (2000: 123–131, 135–137) excellent discussion of their usage of the tetralemma, bearing in mind his view of Pyrrho as a dogmatic metaphysician; see Appendix A for discussion and citations.

Passionlessness, and Then Undisturbedness—Pyrrho and Buddha

The Aristocles account ends with the quotation of Timon's conclusion: "Timon says that, for those who maintain this attitude, what is left is first *apatheia* 'passionlessness, absence of suffering', and then *ataraxia* 'undisturbedness, calm, peace'". This translation is based on a hitherto overlooked passage, later in Aristocles' chapter on Pyrrhonism, which *explicitly* paraphrases the long problematic—in fact, bewildering—received text's conclusion. In the received text the first of the two results is given as *aphasia* 'unspeakingness', rather than *apatheia*, which is what the other ancient testimonies lead us to expect. In short, the resulting textual correction totally vacates the extensive scholarly literature about what Pyrrho meant by *aphasia* because the word was never in Aristocles' text, which had *apatheia*.[78]

The passage as a whole is remarkable because once again it corresponds exactly to the Buddhist tradition. The last two of the Classical stages of realization in Buddhist "mindfulness" yoga (breath meditation)[79] are *apraṇahita* (Pali *appaṇihita*) 'passionless' and *nirodha* 'extinguishing; nirvana',[80] which correspond precisely to what, according to Timon, are the two things "one is left with" after following Pyrrho's "attitude" or path: "first *apatheia* 'passionlessness' and then *ataraxia* 'undisturbedness, peace'."[81] The earliest form of Buddhist meditation,[82] which ends with the Fourth Dhyāna and nirvana, as discussed above, explicitly states that having abandoned antilogies such as good and bad, one is free from them, that is, passionless, and

[78] For detailed discussion of the textual error in the received text of Aristocles in Eusebius, and its emendation, see Beckwith (2011b)—now Appendix A.

[79] In the Central Asian Buddhist yoga textbook (Schlingloff 2006), they are stages or steps 15 and 16 of the first phase, Development for the Present, in chapter 2, Mindfulness of Breathing. See the next note.

[80] See Schlingloff (2006) on the Central Asian manuscript in Sanskrit; he compares it to the standard lists in Sanskrit and Pali; see also Bretfeld (2003). The literal meaning of both *nirodha* and *nirvana* is 'the extinguishing (of the burning of passion)'.

[81] See Note 78 and attendant text.

[82] It seems to go back to Buddha himself. Bronkhorst (1986) shows that it is the earliest identifiable form of meditation in Buddhist literature.

one dwells in "indifference" and "mindfulness".[83] The first of these is of course *apatheia* "passionlessness", and the second is *ataraxia* "undisturbedness, calm". In Buddhism, nirvana is regularly stated to be inexpressible. Like all the rest of the basic teachings of Buddhism and Pyrrhonism, it is expressed only negatively in both.[84]

In sum, Pyrrho points out that because *pragmata* '(ethical) things, matters, questions' are inherently undifferentiated by logically valid criteria, there is no valid difference between good and bad, just and unjust, and so on. Therefore, neither sense perceptions nor *doxai* 'views, theories' can either tell the truth or lie, as a consequence of which neither the absolute Truth nor an absolute Lie can "really" exist, nor is it possible to determine "in truth" whether any *pragmata* exist. Therefore, we should not expect our senses or our *doxai* 'views, theories' to be able to tell the "real truth" or a "real lie" about anything. Instead, we should have "no views" about *pragmata*, we should be uninclined toward any extreme with respect to *pragmata*, and we should be unwavering in our attitude about them, reciting about every single *pragma* the tetralemma formula, "It no more is than it is not, or it both is and is not, or it neither is nor is not". This formula invalidates all dogmatic arguments.[85] What is left after maintaining this "attitude" or path, says Timon, is first *apatheia*[86] 'passionlessness', and then *ataraxia* 'undisturbedness, peace'. According to Diogenes Laertius, Timon says suspending judgement "brings with it *ataraxia* 'undisturbedness, calm', like its shadow".[87] Although suspending judgement is a feature specifically of Late Pyrrhonism, essentially the same thing is already advocated by Pyrrho himself in the Aristocles passage, and by Timon in his *Pythō*, where he puts it as "determining nothing and withholding assent".[88]

Pyrrho's *ataraxia* "undisturbedness" is perfectly paralleled by the early sutras' accounts of Buddha's enlightenment when he reached the Fourth Dhyāna. His enlightenment was equated with nirvana. It has been shown conclusively that in the earliest sutras Buddha is shown

[83] Bronkhorst (1986: 16–17, 82–83).

[84] See also the discussion of Narrative 4, below.

[85] Bett (2000: 30); he discusses this and other interpretations at length (29ff.).

[86] See Appendix A for the long overlooked textual problem and its solution.

[87] Diogenes Laertius IX, 107.

[88] Diogenes Laertius IX, 76. See the discussion in Appendix A.

as having attained nirvana in this lifetime, and did not lose it during the decades before his death.[89] Hundreds of years later, in Normative Buddhism, the early picture of Buddha's enlightenment as nirvana had become increasingly modified, to the point that many came to consider it impossible to attain nirvana in one lifetime. Nevertheless, this must not mislead us into thinking that such was the view of the Buddha's followers in his lifetime, or soon after his death.[90] It is logically necessary for the Buddha to have achieved nirvana and for his followers to have believed that they could do the same thing if they imitated him, in order for such later ideas to have developed in reaction to it. If the Buddha had not achieved his remarkable, heroic breakthrough, there would have been no Buddhism.[91]

The teachings in the Aristocles passage are paralleled and amplified by other ancient testimonies. Together, the corpus of material on Pyrrho's thought, though certainly quite limited, presents a very clear, consistent, unambiguous picture of it. Moreover, the main teachings of both Early (Pre-Normative) Buddhism and Early Pyrrhonism are the same. Both have the same *telos* or 'goal', which is expressed negatively and is explicitly said to be attained as an indirect result of following the path, and both express specific details of the teachings in precisely the same way, in several cases in the same words.

Pyrrho's Declaration and Early Buddhism

Pyrrho's negative statement that all *pragmata* 'discrete matters, objects of cogitation', are Not-*x* and Not-*y* and Not-*z* corresponds to the Buddha's negative statement about all *dharmā* 'discrete matters, objects

[89] This is shown already by Bareau (1963: 72–77; cited in Bronkhorst 1986: 93).

[90] Bronkhorst (1986: 93–95 et seq.), q.v. for analysis and citations.

[91] Cf. Bronkhorst (2011: 10–11): "[T]he buddhist texts state repeatedly that the Buddha taught something new, something that had not theretofore been known in the world. . . . [The texts indicate that] the original teaching of the Buddha was in various respects radically different from other teachings that were current in its time and region. The buddhist texts themselves insist that the Buddha had discovered something new, and that he therefore taught something new. Scholars have not always believed this, but their scepticism was not justified."

of cogitation, dharmas'. Both of them include the statement that individual *pragmata* ~ dharmas have no inherent self-identity. Logically, then, we cannot say for certain if anything is "true" or "false", and so forth, so we should have "no views" (such as that a given *pragma* is true or false), and we should "not incline" toward any choice. If we are "unwavering" in this "attitude", we will be passionless, and then calm.

No other Greek system proposes such a program as a coherent system, and no one has ever suggested that there is one. It is equally the core of the Early Buddhist system. Pyrrhonism and Buddhism alone propose it, and they match down to details.

Pyrrho's Practice

Some of the most striking bits of information about Pyrrho make almost no sense in the Greek tradition, and have been treated with some puzzlement by scholars, but they make very good sense as attestations of Buddhist practice, and are completely consistent with Pyrrho's—and the Buddha's—teachings.

The most literally solid statement of all is the remark by Pausanias (fl. ca. AD 150–175) in his *Description of Greece* that the city of Elis erected a statue in Pyrrho's honor. "On the side of the roofed colonnade facing the marketplace stands a statue of Pyrrho, son of Pistocrates, a sage[92] who would not give firm assent to any proposition."[93] Pausanias's book is a travelogue or guidebook rather than a history, but he has been shown to be a faithful and extremely accurate observer. He saw the statue himself, as well as Pyrrho's tomb nearby in his home village, Petra.[94]

[92] The text has σοφιστοῦ. Greek σοφιστής is usually rendered into English as 'sophist', even though it often does not have the negative meaning of the *English* word *sophist.* Considering what Pausanias says here about Pyrrho it is impossible to imagine that he could have intended the meaning 'sophist'. I have translated it as 'sage', one of the alternative translations frequently used for instances when the Greek word is applied to people we might properly call 'philosophers'.

[93] Pausanias VI, 24.5: κατὰ δὲ τῆς στοᾶς τὸ ἐς τὴν ἀγορὰν ἕστηκε Πύρρωνος τοῦ Πιστοκράτους εἰκών, σοφιστοῦ τε ἀνδρὸς καὶ ἐς βέβαιον ὁμολογίαν ἐπὶ οὐδενὶ λόγῳ καταστάντος. Text from Perseus online version of Spiro (1903); cf. Jones (1917: 3:148–151).

[94] Pausanias VI, 24.5: ἔστι δὲ καὶ μνῆμα τῷ Πύρρωνι οὐ πόρρω τοῦ Ἠλείων ἄστεως: Πέτρα μὲν τῷ χωρίῳ τὸ ὄνομα. "Not far from the town of the Eleans, at a place called Petra, there is also a tomb of Pyrrho."

This accords very well with a report, on the authority of Nausiphanes, who had personally studied with Pyrrho: "So revered was he by his home town that they appointed him high priest, and because of him they voted to make all philosophers exempt from taxation."[95] The veracity of this testimony has been doubted, and perhaps for a typical Greek philosopher such consideration is difficult to imagine. But for Pyrrho, who in his own lifetime was viewed by nearly everyone—even those who did not agree with him—as a kind of holy man,[96] much like the Buddha, it is easy to understand. The agreement of this strand of thought in the testimonies adds further support to the report of Nausiphanes. It should not be surprising then to learn that it also accords very well with the historical treatment of Buddhist teachers.

It is well established from the earliest accounts of Normative Buddhism that monks, nuns, and their monasteries were not taxed in ancient India.[97] The ancient Greek accounts of Early Buddhism do not mention whether or not the Śramaṇas were taxed, but since they are explicitly described as living extremely frugally, it is difficult to imagine how they could have been taxed. The Forest-dwelling Śramaṇas, in particular, essentially owned nothing and had no property—in fact, they did not participate in economic activity of any kind, as noted in Chapter Two—while the Town-dwelling Śramaṇas, the Physicians, begged for their food and stayed with people who would put them up in their houses, so it would have been next to impossible to collect any taxes from them.[98] Not only does Megasthenes present this as the normal state

[95] D.L. IX, 64: οὕτω δ' αὐτὸν ὑπὸ τῆς πατρίδος τιμηθῆναι ὥστε καὶ ἀρχιερέα καταστῆσαι αὐτὸν καὶ δι' ἐκεῖνον πᾶσι τοῖς φιλοσόφοις ἀτέλειαν ψηφίσασθαι.

[96] The testimonies contain repeated reference to such opinions by many well-known contemporaries of Pyrrho who knew him personally, including some who are said to have remarked that they did not agree with Pyrrho's philosophy.

[97] The tax-free status of religious foundations was one of the main reasons for their proliferation. On the tax-free status of Buddhist *vihāras*, see Beckwith (2012c: 41–42) and references. On the de facto continued ownership of *vihāras* by donors in India, see Schopen (2004: 219–259); cf. the continued ownership by the Barmakids of the famous Nawbahār (Nava Vihāra) of Balkh and the lands that were donated to support it, surviving Islamization and several wars (Van Bladel 2010).

[98] The Brāḥmaṇas, by contrast, had extensive possessions, including land, so one would imagine that they were taxed even during their ascetic stage, which according to Megasthenes was thirty-seven years long. The period is given as forty years in the accounts of Calanus, but he was not a Brahmanist at all, based on Megasthenes' description of the beliefs and practices of his sect; cf. the Epilogue. The insistence of modern scholars

of affairs, the *gymnosophistai* 'naked wise-men' (or "Gymnosophists") of ancient Greek tradition—who were *neither* Śramaṇas *nor* Brāḥmaṇas—are described in all accounts as having lived extremely frugally, and they openly encouraged the Greeks to join them and live the same way so as to learn their philosophy and practices. Did Pyrrho actually live as a Śramaṇa for a while when he was in India? We do not know. But the account of Megasthenes tells us that the "philosophers" or "holy men" of ancient Gandhāra were undoubtedly not taxed; they were left alone to practice and teach.[99]

In view of the high esteem, and even veneration, accorded him by his contemporaries, it is not difficult to imagine the elderly Pyrrho—a companion of Alexander, as well as an esteemed teacher—being honored by his fellow citizens in the way described, perhaps after suggestions and encouragement from Timon and others who had heard Pyrrho's stories about his experiences in India.

From Eratosthenes, reported by Diogenes Laertius, it is well established that Pyrrho also remained celibate.[100] Diogenes Laertius, quoting from Antigonus of Carystus's book about Pyrrho, says, "He would withdraw from society and live as a hermit,[101] rarely making an appearance before his family."[102] Later in the same section of quotations Diogenes says, "Often . . . he would leave his home and, telling no one, would go roaming about with whomsoever he chanced to meet."[103] That is,

that Megasthenes' description does not accord with what "we know" about ancient Brahmanism is based not on ancient Brahmanism (of which we have absolutely no record for at least half a millennium after Megasthenes' time, and typically much longer), but on the imaginations of medieval to modern writers.

[99] Plutarch makes this explicit, insofar as he quotes Alexander himself as having said that the naked wise men of India did not even have a wallet, unlike Diogenes the Cynic, whom Alexander had met in Corinth and had been impressed by. Plutarch's account, however, seems to have been influenced by Megasthenes' account of the Forest-dwellers. The actual "philosophers" met by the Greeks when Alexander was there depended on other people for many things, as the accounts make clear. See further in Chapter Three.

[100] D.L. IX, 66: "He lived in fraternal piety with his sister, a midwife" (translation by Jones 1933: 3:479).

[101] Greek ἐρημάζειν; derived from ἐρῆμος 'desolate, desert, solitary, lonely', the source of the English loanwords "eremitic", "hermit", etc.

[102] D.L. IX, 63: ἐκπατεῖν τ' αὐτὸν καὶ ἐρημάζειν, σπανίως ποτ' ἐπιφαινόμενον τοῖς οἴκοι. Text and translation by Jones (1933: 3:477); cf. Narrative 1 below.

[103] Translation by Jones (1933: 3:477). The quotations are of course in *oratio obliqua*.

he *wandered.* Both of these reports accord perfectly with the itinerant wandering, hermetic life of the Buddha, according to the traditional accounts, as well as with that of a Buddhist *śramaṇa,* particularly the Forest Śramaṇa type attested in the *Indica* of Pyrrho's contemporary Megasthenes.[104]

The Narratives about Pyrrho

The Greek version of the Trilakṣaṇa text and its parallels,[105] some statements directly connected to them, and a number of verbatim quotes of Timon's poems praising Pyrrho are the most important testimonies about Pyrrho's *teachings.* By contrast, the most important testimonies on his *practices* are narrative vignettes about his life. These "anecdotes" typically describe him in the context of events involving other actors and spectators, and conclude with a moral, or judgemental comment.

No previous attempt seems to have been made to organize these narratives[106] and analyze their purpose.[107] They are moralistic or didactic stories. Regardless of their subject matter, the narratives are concerned to show whether Pyrrho behaved in accordance with his teachings or in violation of them. This is significant in the Greek context because "philosophers" were expected to follow their teachings in daily life.[108] Most strikingly, all of them show Pyrrho as an imperfect being living in an imperfect world. In this respect they contrast sharply with the panegyrical verses of Timon that praise Pyrrho as a perfected being beyond ordinary men. Accordingly, the narratives cannot be attributed to Timon.

[104] See Chapter Two.

[105] Discussed above; for a detailed study of this material, see Appendix A.

[106] This is a rather Aristotelian enterprise, fully un-Pyrrhonian, so I doubt Pyrrho would approve of it as such, but I hope that the clarification of his teachings that results from it would have met with his approval.

[107] When they are discussed by scholars, they have usually been given ad hoc explanations, rather than ones that fit the points of the vignettes into the picture of Pyrrho's thought and practice known from other sources. Clayman (2009: 44–46) argues that the "essentially Skeptical portrait" of Pyrrho in the narratives "was a deliberate creation of Timon who embodies the principles of Skeptic practice in Pyrrho." However, there is no evidence for this claim. Bett (2000) notes the practical impossibility of distinguishing Pyrrho from Timon in the sources; cf. Appendix A.

[108] Cf. Clayman (2009: 35) on this Greek tradition.

As reports apparently written in most cases by non-Pyrrhonists who were contemporaries of Pyrrho, the narratives are important for understanding what Greeks in general thought of Pyrrho's teachings and practice, and how Early Pyrrhonism contrasted with what might be called "normal traditional Greek thought and behavior".

The narratives begin with Pyrrho's experiences as a member of Alexander's court for over ten years, five years of which were spent in Central Asia and India. According to all accounts, Pyrrho had an experience there that permanently changed him.

1. *Pyrrho in India*

The first narrative about Pyrrho survives in two pieces found as quotations or paraphrases in different works, though each piece assumes or refers to the other. The main versions are in Diogenes Laertius, Sextus Empiricus, and Plutarch.[109] The story relates that while in India, "Pyrrho heard an Indian reproach [his teacher] Anaxarchus, telling him that he would never be able to teach others what is good while he himself danced attendance on kings in their courts. Since Pyrrho himself had written a poem in praise of Alexander, for which he had been rewarded with ten thousand gold pieces,[110] he withdrew from the world and lived in solitude, rarely showing himself to his relatives."[111] This narrative seems to go back ultimately to a personal account by Pyrrho himself or someone very close to him. Its moral is simple and clear, but the effects of the Indian's remark on Pyrrho are stunning. As

[109] Bett (2000: 1n4).

[110] Sextus Empiricus, *Adversus Mathematicos* ("Against the Learned" = *M*), I, 282, ed. and trans. Bury (1933: 4:162–163): λέγεται γὰρ αὐτὸν καὶ ποίησιν εἰς τὸν Μακεδόνα Ἀλέξανδρον γράψαντα μυρίοις χρυσοῖς τετιμῆσθαι "for Pyrrho himself, it is said, wrote a poem for Alexander of Macedon and was rewarded with thousands of [or 'ten thousand'] gold pieces." Plutarch has: Πύρρωνι δὲ τῷ Ἠλείῳ πρῶτον ἐντυχόντι μυρίους χρυσοῦς ἔδωκε "To Pyrrho of Elis he (Alexander) gave ten thousand gold pieces when he first met him". Plutarch, *Moralia* 331 E ("On the Fortune of Alexander"), ed. and trans. Babbitt (1927: 4:411). The significant difference in Plutarch's version is his omission of the reason for Alexander's gift, as noted by Bett (2000: 1n4).

[111] The first and third sentences are in chronologically reversed order in D.L. IX, 63, the first being intended to explain the third, which reads in Hicks's (1925: 2:477) translation, "He would withdraw from the world and live in solitude, rarely showing himself to his relatives."

a result, Pyrrho not only ceased writing poetry, he adopted a "philosophy" that was unprecedented and bewildering (for a Greek). In particular, though, he "withdrew from the world", and "lived in solitude", and "rarely showed himself to his relatives".

These three things are stereotyped expressions for what a person beginning Early Buddhist practice did, especially one following the way of the Forest-dwelling *śramaṇas*. Buddhist texts regularly refer explicitly to *śramaṇas* as those who have "left their families (or homes)" and have "withdrawn from the world".[112] The early *śramaṇas* who are thought to have best preserved the original practices of the Buddha before he achieved enlightenment are those who "lived in solitude" in the forest and practiced greater austerities than the other *śramaṇas*. Megasthenes, a contemporary of Pyrrho who gives an eyewitness account of the Indian "philosophers", tells us explicitly about these Forest-dwelling *śramaṇas* and their austerities, thereby confirming the antiquity of the Indian tradition in this case. Pyrrho himself is said to have behaved as a hermetic ascetic.

2. Pyrrho's Continuing Issue with Wealth

The first narrative tells us that Pyrrho took the Indian's admonishment to heart specifically because of his own acceptance of a fortune in gold from Alexander. In the next story, from Athenaeus, Pyrrho says to a host who has just lavishly entertained him, "I'm not going to visit you in the future, if you entertain me that way, so that I don't feel bad when I see you wasting your money unnecessarily, and so that you don't run short of funds and suffer. Because it's better to favor one another with our company than with a large number of dishes, most of which the servants consume."[113] The other quotations in that section of Athenaeus are mostly dated to Pyrrho's time, or slightly earlier or later, so it is quite possible that Pyrrho actually said something like this, but even if he did not, his statement is specifically Pyrrhonian and is certainly the kind of thing he would have said to a friend. Pyrrho does not want either of

[112] In Normative Buddhism, these expressions are specifically equivalent to saying "became a monk". Cf. Gethin (1998: 85, 87) on "becoming a Buddhist monk . . . : 'going forth' (Sanskrit *pravrajyā* ~ Pali *pabbajjā*) . . . from the household life into homelessness".

[113] Athenaeus X, 419, d-e, translation by Olson (2008: 4:469).

them to feel distressed because of the banquet or, to put it in more Pyrrhonian terms, to become "disturbed" or "unbalanced" by excesses.

The narrative about the Indian's reproach and the narrative about the banquet could simply be written off as traditional morality—either generic or, as Bett suggests, that of a specific Greek school, the Cynics.[114] But the point of the first text is that Pyrrho reacted to the Indian's remarks because he felt bad about having accepted a lavish reward from Alexander. The second says explicitly that he wanted to avoid being distressed by receiving the "gift" of a luxurious banquet. In both cases his remarks are strictly about the effects of excess on the *individual*. He says nothing at all about waste or unfairness themselves, both of which have to do with *social* morality.

This focus on the individual is a specific characteristic of Early Buddhism, which encourages people to "leave the family" to pursue individual enlightenment, just as Pyrrho himself did. Both narratives are in full accord with the Early Buddhist reason for not accepting wealth, or anything luxurious: to avoid extremes and attachments to things, with their attendant emotional disturbances.

3. Pyrrho's Humility

A narrative in Diogenes Laertius, taken from Eratosthenes, presents Pyrrho performing humble, everyday tasks without either complaint or excessive enjoyment: "He lived in fraternal piety with his sister, a midwife, . . . now and then even taking things for sale to market, poultry perchance or pigs, and he would dust the things in the house, quite indifferent as to what he did. They say he showed his indifference by

[114] Bett (2000: 64); he summarizes the account, saying, "Pyrrho goes to a sumptuous dinner with a friend, and says that he will not see him again if he is received in this fashion, because what is important is good company rather than a display of unnecessary luxury." He then remarks, "Here, as in some of the other anecdotes, Pyrrho's behaviour is reminiscent of that of the Cynics . . .". This misses the point or moral of the story (see the discussion above), which is given explicitly in Athenaeus, who has taken the passage from the second century BC writer Hegesander (Bett 2000: 64). Certainly Pyrrho's thought is sometimes reminiscent of Antisthenes (ca. 445–ca. 365 BC), a student of Socrates who focused on ethics and is considered to be a forerunner of the Cynics, but Antisthenes also promoted monotheism, among other interesting and non-Pyrrhonian things. It is even more difficult to find much in common between Pyrrho and Diogenes the Cynic (ca. 404–323 BC), the practical founder and model of the school.

washing a porker."[115] This account twice uses the term *adiaphora* or a derivative; Hicks translates them as "indifferent" and "indifference", and the text itself apparently suggests that meaning—in other words, that Pyrrho did not care one way or the other what he did. However, this is certainly an error, perhaps going back as far as Pyrrho's own day, when the original anecdotes may have been recorded, because in the Aristocles passage, quoted and discussed at length above, Pyrrho uses the word *adiaphora* as it was used by Aristotle, meaning "undifferentiated by a logical differentia". Pyrrho does not refer to himself, Timon, or any other person, as *adiaphora* or the like. He uses the term explicitly in reference to *pragmata* "matters, affairs"—which almost exclusively meant for Pyrrho, as for Buddha, conflicting ethical or emotional matters, with attendant antilogies such as good versus bad, true versus false, and so on. Moreover, neither Pyrrho nor the Buddha ever hints at a metaphysics, or even an epistemology. To the contrary, Pyrrho says explicitly that we should have "no views" or theories, and the Early Buddhist tradition says precisely the same thing.[116] The concept embodied in *adiaphora*, in the sense used by Pyrrho, is one of the characteristic and most important elements of his teachings. The comments *about* Pyrrho's behavior in this narrative are therefore technically inaccurate, and the narrative as we have it is perhaps not datable to Pyrrho's own time (though misunderstanding knows no chronological bounds). Nevertheless, the points made by the story are close to those of Early Pyrrhonism. In the story Pyrrho shows graphically, in a way anyone can understand, that conventional theories about what is *truly* or *ultimately* or *absolutely* good or bad are logically unfounded and therefore invalid. He also teaches those around him about humility, simplicity, and morality, virtues that seem to have been expressed by the Buddha, and by Buddhist teachers ever since.

[115] Diogenes Laertius IX, 66. This narrative is strongly reminiscent of the story about the Early Taoist master Liehtzu in *Chuangtzu* 7.5: "He went back home, and for three years did not leave his house. He did the cooking for his wife; he fed the pigs as though he were feeding people. *He did not prefer one thing over another*, from fine carving he reverted to the plain material. He took his place like a clod of earth. Amidst confusion, he was secure." Translation by Brooks and Brooks (2015: 195–196), emphasis added. See Chapter Three on the influence of Early Buddhism on Warring States Chinese thought.

[116] See the discussion above in this chapter.

4. The Seaworthy Pig

The association of Pyrrho with animals recurs in the fourth narrative. This version of it is from Plutarch:[117] "[When Pyrrho] was on a voyage, and in peril during a storm, he pointed to a little pig contentedly feeding upon some barley which had been spilled near by, and said to his companions[118] that such passionlessness (*apatheia*) must be cultivated through reason and philosophy by anyone wishing not to be thoroughly disturbed by the things that happen to him."[119] Once again, Pyrrho is shown in humble circumstances and uses them to teach the cultivation of passionlessness "through reason and philosophy" in order to attain, indirectly, *ataraxia* 'undisturbedness'—which he explicitly refers to in the text via a negative plus the word *tarattesthai* 'to be disturbed', a positive verbal form of the same word, that is, *ataraxia*.

5. Pyrrho and the Dog

The next narrative is also set in everyday conditions that any audience could understand. It relates how Pyrrho responded upon being attacked. "When a dog rushed at him and terrified him, he answered his critic that it was not easy entirely to strip oneself of one's human nature, but one should strive with all one's might against *pragmata* '(conflicting ethical) matters, events', by deeds if possible, and if not, then through reason."[120] The quotation of Pyrrho's statement in this

[117] Plutarch, *Moralia* 82 F ("Progress in Virtue"), ed. and trans. Babbitt (1927: 1:441), online version from Perseus, http://www.perseus.tufts.edu/hopper/text?doc=Perseus:text:2008.01.0153:section=11&highlight=pyrrho. The other version is in D.L. IX, 68, taken from Posidonius.

[118] Babbitt's (1927: 441) translation from this point on reads, "a similar indifference must be acquired from reason and philosophy by the man who does not wish to be disturbed by anything that may befall him."

[119] This is my translation of καὶ πρὸς τοὺς ἑταίρους εἰπεῖν ὅτι τοιαύτην ἀπάθειαν παρασκευαστέον ἐκ λόγου καὶ φιλοσοφίας τὸν ὑπὸ τῶν προστυγχανόντων ταράττεσθαι μὴ βουλόμενον, text from Babbitt (1927: 1:440).

[120] D.L. IX, 66. I have revised the translation of Hicks, which reads, "When a cur rushed at him and terrified him, he answered his critic that it was not easy entirely to strip oneself of human weakness; but one should strive with all one's might against facts, by deeds if possible, and if not, in word." The phrase "through reason" (or perhaps "through logic") here translates the last word in the Greek passage, λόγῳ, in the translation of Hicks, "in word". Cf. Bett (2000: 66).

narrative agrees very closely with the content of his statement quoted in the Aristocles account.[121] The dog narrative is vivid, and Pyrrho's words are characteristically idiosyncratic. The story thus seems to go back ultimately to an actual event involving Pyrrho himself. It is particularly helpful for understanding the Aristocles account of his teaching about the three characteristics of *pragmata*—which word means for Pyrrho conflicting ethical or emotional things.

Significantly, this narrative shows that Pyrrho behaved completely according to normal human reactions. Aristocles' version even has him climb a tree to get away from the dog.[122]

Pyrrho also says one should struggle to free oneself of one's human nature. It is impossible to achieve undisturbedness if one is continually disturbed, but it is not *easy* to achieve undisturbedness, nirvana. One must struggle against one's own *human nature*, using deeds (that is, the physical body), and if that does not work, reason (that is, the mind). This corresponds exactly to the Buddhist use of yoga (or "meditation"), a method of physical training of the body as well as the mind to overcome human nature. Timon and other ancient Pyrrhonists say that it worked for Pyrrho and those who followed his path, and it apparently did for the Buddha before him. Pyrrho's teaching in this narrative is identical in all essentials to the Buddha's teaching, the way of the *śramaṇas*. Pyrrho tells us straight out that to be disturbed is ordinary human nature. It is thus in effect heroic—superhuman—to achieve undisturbedness. And that is exactly how Timon praises Pyrrho in his poems, as many Buddhist writers too have praised the Buddha down through the ages.

Some Thoughts on the Narratives

It should by now be clear that none of the narratives about Pyrrho are versions of the well-known, traditional, and *late* Normative Buddhist narratives about the Buddha.[123] All of Pyrrho's take place in his

[121] See Appendix A and above in this chapter.

[122] Bett (2000: 68n16).

[123] As Bareau, Schopen, and other scholars have begun showing, the traditional stories, including even much of the canon, cannot be dated to anywhere near the time of the Buddha himself. Even the epithet "Buddha" does not appear in the Greek sources

lifetime; they are about Pyrrho himself, who was a Greek "philosopher" by training, and despite his Indian experience, still a Greek; and all but one of them take place in Greece and are clearly Greek in color and detail.[124iii] The narratives present Pyrrho as an ordinary man, somewhat ascetic and hermetic, who understood much about the human condition and what one needed to do to overcome it. He does not attempt to hide his lapses, but instead uses them as a way to explain about imperfection and to teach others a practical way to *ataraxia* 'undisturbedness, peace'.

Although the narratives are not versions of the later Indian stories of Normative Buddhism, the didactic elements of the narratives provide important clarification of Pyrrho's teachings and practices, which are in their intention thoroughly Early Buddhist in nature. Together with the contemporary account of 'India' by Megasthenes, the texts relating to Pyrrho provide us with valuable information about late fourth century BC Buddhism, and show that it corresponds well to traditional accounts of what it was like in the Buddha's lifetime. One thing clear from Pyrrho's teachings, from the account of Megasthenes, and from the portrayal of Gautama in Early Taoism is that Buddhism had not yet become fixated on the person of the Buddha as a kind of divinity. As recent research by Gregory Schopen has shown, Buddhism had also not yet developed other devotional and organizational elements that did eventually appear.[125]

The conclusion to be drawn from the evidence about Pyrrho's thought and practice is that he adopted a form of Early Buddhism during his years in Bactria and Gandhāra, including its philosophical-religious and pragmatic elements, but he stripped it of its alien garb and

---

until Clement of Alexandria (mid-second to early third century AD), though it does appear on a Kushan coin of Kanishka I (r. first half of the second century AD), where it is written in Bactrian spelling BoΔΔo 'Buddha' http://www.bpmurphy.com/cotw/week2.htm, and *bodhi* 'awakening' is attested in the early third-century AD Major Inscriptions of king Devānāṃpriya Priyadarśi, q.v. Chapter Two and Appendix C. Megasthenes, Pyrrho's contemporary, refers to Buddhists as Sarmanes, the *Sramanas* of the Mauryan inscription fragments in Greek. The word *Śramaṇa* was the unambiguous term for 'Buddhists', and was still used exclusively in that sense in the Middle Ages, as shown in Chapter Two.

[124] The poetic fragments of his disciple, Timon, praise Pyrrho, but they are not narratives; they are basically panegyrics. The most outstanding example of them is a poem in which Timon compares Pyrrho to the Sun God. See Endnote iii.

[125] In particular, the works collected in Schopen (1997, 2004, 2005).

reconstituted it as a new 'Greek Buddhism' for the Hellenistic world, which he presented in his own words to Timon and his other students.

The Problematic Narratives

Perhaps not surprisingly, the most popular and widely quoted narrative about Pyrrho is utterly spurious—it occurs already in Aristotle and has been shown to have been wrongly applied to Pyrrho.[126] It is placed prominently by Diogenes Laertius at the very beginning of his long, detailed account of Pyrrhonism, and perhaps for this reason it has given far too many scholars the wrong impression about Pyrrho and his thought. So as not to perpetuate the tradition, it and a textually corrupt narrative have been deliberately placed at the end of this chapter rather than at the beginning.

1. The Topos of the Madcap Fool Philosopher Applied to Pyrrho

Diogenes Laertius gives a succinct summary of Pyrrho's teachings at the beginning of his chapter on him.[127] Referring to Pyrrho's experiences in India, he says, "he even forgathered with the Indian Gymnosophists and with the Magi," and he says, "This led him to adopt a most noble philosophy, to quote Ascanius of Abdera. . . . He denied that anything was honourable or dishonourable, just or unjust. And so, universally, he held that . . . custom and convention govern human actions; for no single thing is in itself any more this than that."[128]

Immediately following this summary of his teachings, Diogenes gives his first narrative about Pyrrho: "He led a life consistent with this doctrine, going out of his way for nothing, taking no precautions, but

[126] See Bett (2000: 67–69). The story was used as a criticism of Pyrrho already in Antiquity.

[127] His account of Pyrrho's thought is unfortunately contaminated in part with features of Late Pyrrhonism and simple errors (some of which are discussed below), though on the whole it is rather accurate. However, some scholars have unwittingly thought that the entire long chapter is supposed to be about Pyrrho himself and his thought, whereas the bulk of it is about the Late Pyrrhonism of Diogenes' own times and shortly before him.

[128] D.L. IX, 61, translation of Hicks, from Perseus online.

facing all risks as they came, whether carts, precipices, dogs or what not, and, generally, leaving nothing to the arbitrament of the senses; but he was kept out of harm's way by his friends who, as Antigonus of Caristus tells us, used to follow close after him."[129] Diogenes himself then remarks that this passage is contradicted by a sober comment of Aenesidemus, a later Sceptic who adopted much of Pyrrho's thought, saying that Pyrrho "did not lack foresight in his everyday acts." Diogenes concludes—significantly, in view of the life-threatening nature of the philosopher's supposed behavior in the anecdote of Antigonus—that Pyrrho "lived to be nearly ninety."[130] Yet despite Diogenes' correctives, the image of a batty eccentric has been painted from the outset upon the unwary reader's mind.

While other testimonies—including those in Diogenes Laertius—do portray an unusual person, they do not show us a foolish or crazy one. His actions all make a philosophical point. Moreover, this particular narrative reveals its source. The main point, along with the example of walking over a cliff, is found in Aristotle's *Metaphysics*, in the discussion of what would happen to someone who denied the Law of Non-Contradiction.[131] It has thus been applied to Pyrrho despite the fact that he is not known to have denied the Law of Non-Contradiction, and hardly could have done so, since that would have meant he held a *doxa* 'view, theory, dogmatic belief', among other violations of his teachings. The statement of Diogenes Laertius in his introduction has often been interpreted to mean that Pyrrho denied anything exists, suggesting that the behavior ascribed to him by Antigonus followed his beliefs, but Pyrrho

[129] D.L. IX, 62, translation of Hicks, from Perseus online.

[130] D.L. IX, 11.62.

[131] Many scholars report this story as if it had some basis in fact. Clayman (2009: 35) says that in it "Pyrrho is making himself a living example of the Skeptic view that appearances are not to be trusted", but later in the same work she rightly notes and discusses the Aristotelian parallel, as pointed out and briefly discussed by Bett (2000: 68, 88). There are also points of textual similarity, most notably the expression ἐάν τύχῃ 'if he comes to it' in Aristotle (*Metaphysics* IV, iv, 40 [1008b], ed. and trans. Tredennick 1933: 1:178) and εἰ τύχοι 'as [= if] they came' in Antigonus as quoted in D.L. IX, 11.62; they are used the same way in both texts. Clayman (2009: 43–44) says, "This story comes not from Pyrrho's own life, but was invented by someone familiar with Aristotle's *Metaphysics*. . . . He is obviously not describing Pyrrho himself, who was a much younger contemporary". Unfortunately, she then suggests, "but it may also have been Timon who meant to capture the charming simplicity of Pyrrho's disposition."

does not and could not deny that anything exists—it makes absolutely no sense on the basis of what we know about his philosophy and religious practices—and Diogenes does not actually make such a claim.[132] Pyrrho is quoted by Timon as saying not to have any *doxai* "views, theories", and Timon and others praise him repeatedly for his success in not having any. More could be said, but all of the evidence tells us that this particular narrative is spurious and must be eliminated from the corpus of authentic information about Pyrrho and his teachings.

Having done that, one might then ask if we can determine to which philosophical or religious tradition the topos of the devil-may-care philosopher who denies the Law of Non-Contradiction could belong.[133] Although we do not of course have any information about the people who proposed such a view (assuming that Aristotle got it right),[134] it would seem at least arguable that they correspond to the school of Indian philosophy most familiar to the Greeks, namely the sect of men exemplified by Calanus, an Indian philosopher from Taxila who joined Alexander's court there, left India with him, and after spending a year in the West committed suicide at Pasargadae by burning himself to

[132] See above and Appendix A for a correct translation of Diogenes' parallel to the Aristocles passage. Bett's (2000: 51) argument that in a sense Pyrrho "does away with all existing things" depends on accepting Bett's thesis that Pyrrho's thought is founded on dogmatic metaphysical ideas; see Appendix A.

[133] Bett discusses at length the identity of the unnamed opponents of Aristotle who denied the Law of Non-Contradiction (Bett 2000: 123–131). He rightly concludes that their position "is not, in fact, particularly close" to Pyrrho's, and "whoever are the people who Aristotle is attacking [in *Metaphysics* IV], there is no serious basis for the belief that they were associates of Pyrrho, or that they and Pyrrho were of like mind" (Bett 2000: 131).

[134] An anonymous reviewer of the manuscript of this book states, "The idea that Aristotle is addressing Indian ideas in his discussion of the Law of Non-Contradiction in *Metaphysics* gamma is completely unsupported, and very unlikely. Aristotle names a great many Greek thinkers as his opponents in these chapters; and, while we can hardly doubt that he also has in mind other thinkers whom we can no longer identify, there is no reason to think that they are not Greek. Pyrrho and others may have been open to influence from other cultures, but Aristotle was a determinedly chauvinist Greek." However, as he rightly notes, Aristotle does not give the slightest hint who these people were, and there is no reason to think he could not have heard the idea from one of the many Greeks who knew, or knew about, Calanus. Without insisting that the idea must have an Indian source, I think it is better to present the data and an argument for the identification than to ignore this particular motif.

death on a funeral pyre in 323 BC.[135] The Indians made interesting comments to the Greeks about why his sect did this:[136] "Megasthenes says that suicide is not a dogma among the philosophers, and that those who commit suicide are judged guilty of the impetuosity of youth; that those who are tough by nature throw themselves against a blow or over a cliff;[137] whereas others, who shrink from suffering, plunge into deep waters;[138] and others, who are much suffering, hang themselves; and others, who have a fiery temperament, fling themselves into fire; and that such was Calanus, a man who was without self-control and a slave to the table of Alexander; and that therefore Calanus is censured."[139] The accounts of this particular sect of Indians do not say much more than this, but there is an exception, also in Megasthenes. As discussed in Chapter Two, some Indians denied that there was any difference between good and bad—according to Aristotle's misinterpretation, they therefore denied the Law of Non-Contradiction. They also believed that death was "birth"—that is, necessarily, *rebirth*—into the "true life", which is the "happy life", so they devoted themselves to preparing for death. This is what the sect of Calanus is said to have believed.[140] The identity of his sect within the Indian philosophical tradition is not certain, probably because all written evidence of such traditions in Indic languages is very late, and scanty until even later, while not surprisingly, the sect seems to have died out very early. However, its teachings are similar *in part* to those of the early Pure Land sect of Buddhism which is first attested when texts introduced from the Kushan Empire to China in the mid-second century AD were translated into Chinese.[141]

[135] Calanus reached Persia with Alexander the year before his suicide, so Aristotle outlived him by about a year. Since we know from Arrian that Calanus had a good number of disciples among the Greeks, it is reasonable to assume that they learned something on Indian beliefs and practices from him.

[136] Strabo XV, 1, 68 (text from Radt 2005: 4:220).

[137] The Greek here reads: τοὺς μὲν σκληροὺς τῇ φύσει φερομένους ἐπὶ πληγὴν ἢ κρημνόν, translated by Jones (1930: 7:118–119), "some who are by nature hardy rush to meet a blow or over precipices".

[138] I.e., they drown themselves.

[139] The text continues, contrasting Calanus with another Indian, Mandanis, who criticizes Calanus severely. However, Mandanis does not seem to have belonged to the same sect, though the sources suggest they shared some values, at least.

[140] Strabo XV, 1, 59, 64, 68.

[141] It has been much noted that some Pure Land followers committed suicide by self-immolation (Keown 1996: 9n2; Kleine 2006: 167n1). Most examples that have been

This is the same sect that worshipped the Buddha Amitābha essentially as a sun god, a belief that might be responsible for Timon's similar treatment of Pyrrho in some of his poems, as noted above. Moreover, one of their key teachings mentioned by Megasthenes is that there is no real difference between good and bad, a key teaching of Early Buddhism in general that is also attested in Early Taoism,[142] as well as in Pyrrhonism.

Nevertheless, with respect to the opponents of Aristotle who denied the Law of Non-Contradiction, and the madcap behavior described in the *Metaphysics* (and based on it, in Antigonus's putative account of Pyrrho), there is again no reason to connect such people to the Pre–Pure Land practitioners in the early Greek accounts. The key point is that in Aristotle and Antigonus, the individuals in question—because of their philosophical position—*do not care* what happens to them. However, that is simply not true of the Pre–Pure Land practitioners[143] in Megasthenes, nor even of Calanus. Both cared very much, and spent their entire lives preparing for death, which they considered rebirth into a true, happy life. Pyrrho's teachings and practices are all directed specifically toward freedom from passion, and eventually undisturbedness, but that is hardly "uncaring". Moreover, there is not a single suggestion in any authentic testimony that shows Pyrrho being "uncaring" in this sense. His practice of being "uninclined" about "matters, affairs" in order to be calm and undisturbed is ample proof that he cared, and is further supported by the fact that, like Buddha, he went to the trouble to teach others the secret of how to achieve the same passionlessness and internal peace.

2. The Corrupt Account of Pyrrho and His Sister's Offering

Another problematic narrative is the story, also deriving from Antigonus, about Pyrrho losing his temper at someone who broke a promise to help Philista, his sister, in connection with a temple sacrifice. As

cited, however, are medieval, so it is not at all certain that this was a feature of early Pure Land Buddhism; a chronologically sensitive study would seem to be needed; cf. Chapter Two.

[142] See Chapter Three.

[143] For discussion of theories about the possible non-Indic origins of Pure Land, see Halkias (2012).

in the narrative about the dog, he is said to violate his own advice or principles, though the main point seems to be, again, that he was not perfect, he had to work to control his human nature, and he cared—in this case, about his sister. As with the authentic and textually unproblematic narratives in general, this one also has a concluding statement by Pyrrho explaining the event in the context of his philosophy.

However, although the narrative does seem to have been originally as authentic as the others,[144] something happened to the text very early in Antiquity, so that the two surviving versions give significantly different concluding statements, one of which (the longer version in Aristocles) seems to support Pyrrho and the other (the shorter version in Diogenes Laertius) to criticize him. Although Brunschwig has argued cogently in favor of the former,[145] in fact the texts of both accounts are problematic and unclear, as concluded by Bett.[146] They must therefore be set aside until or unless someone is able to solve this problem.

[144] I.e., excluding the fake "careless Pyrrho" story in Antigonus, which evidently derives from the same source drawn on by Aristotle (or more likely by an Aristotelian of his school) for the argument in his *Metaphysics* discussed above in this chapter.

[145] Brunschwig (1992).

[146] See Bett (2000: 66n9).

CHAPTER 2

No Differentiations

THE EARLIEST ATTESTED FORMS OF BUDDHISM

The earliest attested philosophical-religious system that is both historically datable and clearly recognizable as a form of Buddhism is Early Pyrrhonism, the teachings and practices of Pyrrho of Elis and Timon of Phlius, as shown in Chapter One. Its central features correspond exactly to some of the central features of the traditional putatively "early" form of Buddhism presented in Pali canonical texts. However, the latter tradition of Buddhism also contains many elements—beliefs, institutions, devotional practices, and so on—which developed at the earliest in the Saka-Kushan period, three centuries after Pyrrho. They spread throughout the ancestors of the attested forms of Buddhism,[1] creating Normative Buddhism.

The elements that are attested only from approximately the Saka-Kushan period on—the exact time remains to be established—are far from trivial. They include the Saṃgha, the community of monks; the idea of the *bhikṣu* 'monk' per se, as well as of the *bhikṣunī* 'nun'; the *vihāra* or monastery;[2] the Vinaya, or Buddhist monastic code;[3] worship of the

[1] It appears that they had less influence on the highly divergent sect of Devadatta, traces of which still existed in Hsüan Tsang's day (Lamotte 1988: 517). Perhaps other forms of Pre-Normative Buddhism also survived long enough to be recorded in the Kushan period or afterward.

[2] Beckwith (2014).

[3] All extant versions of the Vinaya date to the fifth century AD (Schopen 2004: 94).

Buddha;[4] development of the idea of reincarnations of the Buddha, both human and godlike; *abhidharma* or "Buddhist scholasticism"; and many others. They are now considered to be essential elements of traditional Buddhism, yet there is no historically sound evidence that they existed at all[5] (and some evidence that they did not yet exist) until long after the visit of Pyrrho in 330–325 BC and that of Megasthenes in 305–304 BC. The lateness of the development of devotion for the Buddha and Buddha incarnations, as well as reverence for the Buddha's teachings (the *Dharma*) and the community of monks (the *Saṃgha*), means that the invention of the *Triratna* ('Three Jewels') formula is even later (perhaps as a "popular" substitute for the difficult *Trilakṣana* 'Three Characteristics' formula, which is phonetically similar.

While "genuinely Early" Buddhism (or *Pre*-Normative Buddhism) is attested earliest and best in Early Pyrrhonism, it is also attested in the travel account of the Greek ambassador Megasthenes, a Seleucid envoy sent from Alexandria in Arachosia (today's Kandahar) to the court of Candragupta Maurya to negotiate a treaty that was agreed on in 305–304 BC, only twenty years after Pyrrho's departure from India. The fragments of Megasthenes' lost book *Indica*, which are preserved as quotations in other works (most importantly Strabo's *Geography*), include his report on the "Indian" *philosophoi* 'religious-philosophical teachers and practitioners', which include not just the distinction between Brahmanists and Buddhists but a half dozen other religious-philosophical groups or "sects". Megasthenes emphasizes some aspects typical of a travel account, so he provides information that confirms and supplements the picture of Pre-Normative Buddhism presented by Early Pyrrhonism. Unfortunately, the explicit categorizations and many of the details in his remarkable account have been treated extremely cavalierly, at best, in the scholarly literature.

[4] It is now believed that he was first venerated as *Bodhisattva* "the one with a mind set on enlightenment", the Buddha before he achieved enlightenment (Schopen 2005). *Amitābha*, the Buddha "Measureless Light", is said to have originally been a monk, Dharmakāra, who took the Bodhisattva vow (Halkias 2012: 16). He and related figures venerated as "Buddhas" dwelling in their respective Heavens might also be dated to this period, but see below.

[5] See Chapter Three for detailed discussion of the Mauryan inscriptions.

The Attested Early Indian Sects

Because of the existence of fragmentary reports by members of Alexander's retinue, the fragments of Megasthenes, and still other sources (including some in Chinese), Pyrrho's teachings and practices are thus not the only datable attestations of Early Buddhism that are known. It seems to have been quite overlooked that the sources describe *a number* of philosophical-religious systems, some of which are clearly related to the type of Buddhism reflected in Early Pyrrhonism. Others may be characterized as Buddhist, but different from Pyrrhonism, and several are non-Buddhist. The five Buddhist varieties are as follows:

1. Early Pyrrhonism (Greek testimonies): things have no inherent self-identity (no differentiations), they are unstable, and they are unfixed (*Trilakṣaṇa*); both perceptions (induction) and views (deduction) are unreliable; rejection of difference between absolute Truth and absolute Lying; "no views"; passionlessness; undisturbedness, calm; yoga; celibacy; wandering; piety (*eusebeia*).
2. The Śramaṇas (Megasthenes' account in Strabo): yoga; celibacy; piety and holiness; special knowledge about the *causes* of things; women study with them too, but without sex; there are two distinct lifestyles: Forest-dwellers and Town-dwelling "Physicians"; they are called *Śramaṇas* 'Buddhist practitioners'.[6] Megasthenes further describes a third group of Śramaṇas, "others, diviners and charmers experienced with the rites and customs for the dead, who beg as mendicants in the villages and towns" and teach about karma and rebirth.[7]

[6] See the discussion below in this chapter.

[7] Megasthenes says (Strabo XV, 1, 60) they repeat "common sayings about the afterworld . . . to promote piety (*eusebeia*) and holiness" among the people. Note that *eusebeia* 'piety, holiness, reverence' is regularly used to translate *Dharma* in the fragments of the Greek version of the Major Inscriptions attributed to Aśoka, and Megasthenes was from Alexandria in Arachosia (now Kandahar), where the fragments of the Greek translations were found, so it is quite possible that it corresponds to *Dharma* here, too. See Halkias (2013: 85–89). Megasthenes explicitly says "Hades", which in itself would be unclear because it refers to the shady world of the afterlife, neither Heaven nor Hell. However, this remark in the Greek sources corresponds perfectly to the comments about Heaven in the Mauryan inscriptions; its intention is clearly identical, and the conclusion must be the same: some Buddhists by this time believed in karma and karmically determined rebirth in Heaven or Hell.

3. Early Taoism: no differentiations; perceptions are like dreams; karma; philosophers attain tranquility; the *Tao* "way" corresponds exactly to the *Dharma*, the "way" of early Normative Buddhist texts; founding teacher, "Laotzu", named *Gautama.[8]
4. The *Dharma* (Greek *eusebeia* 'piety, holiness') of the Mauryan king Devānāṃpriya Priyadarśi (fl. 272–261 BC, traditionally referred to as "Aśoka");[9] accumulate good karma in order to win next life in Heaven, bad karma suggested to lead to the opposite; gods mentioned but no God; best to renounce possessions; obey parents and elders; honor Śramaṇas, Brāḥmaṇas, and practitioners of other (unnamed) sects; no killing of animals (an anti-Brahmanist measure); ruler's Dharma inspired by visit to Saṃbodhi (Bodhgayā), where the Buddha was enlightened.
5. Pre–Pure Land (accounts in Strabo from Megasthenes): no differentiations; perceptions are like dreams; karma; philosophers discipline themselves to prepare for death; they are reborn to the true, happy life (probably in Heaven, but where exactly is unstated).

The sect of Calanus, the Indian "Gymnosophist" or "naked wise man" best known to the Greeks and most described in Greek sources, is a non-Buddhist sect. Strabo refers to them as the Γυμνῆται *Gymnetae* "the naked ones".[10] The sect is similar in some ways to the Pre–Pure Land sect described in Megasthenes:[11]

[8] See Chapter Three. "Tao" and "Taoism" are also spelled "Dao" and "Daoism".

[9] See the detailed discussion in Chapter Three.

[10] Strabo XV, 1, 70.

[11] Most of this capsule description is supported by accounts in the Alexander histories, but Strabo, who calls them the *Gymnetae*, has a specific item on them: "The Gymnetæ, as their name imports, are naked and live chiefly in the open air, practising fortitude for the space of thirty-seven years; this I have before mentioned; women live in their society, but without cohabitation. The Gymnetæ are held in singular estimation." (Strabo XV, 1, 70, translation by Hamilton and Falconer, from Perseus online). Strabo also notes, on the authority of Nearchus, that "[t]he Brachmanes engage in public affairs, and attend the kings as counsellors; the rest are occupied in the study of nature. Calanus belonged to the latter class. Women study philosophy with them, and all lead an austere life." (Strabo XV, 1, 66). Some remarks about them stem from Onesicritus, whom Alexander supposedly sent to talk to the *gymnosophistai* 'naked wise men'. Although much of what is attributed to Onesicritus is suspect (see Appendix B), and a careful examination of the sources is needed, one part of his account reported by Strabo (XV, 1, 65) agrees with other accounts and with the actual history of Calanus: "Disease of the body they regard as most disgraceful, and he who apprehends it, after preparing a pyre, destroys himself by fire; he (previously) anoints himself, and sitting down upon it orders it to be lighted, remaining motionless while he is burning."

6. Gymnetae: go naked; believe disease in the body is bad; practice physical yoga; beg for food; women study with them; believe in karma; study nature; practitioners expect to be reborn to a better and purer life; believers commit suicide by funeral pyre.[12]

This sect is clearly distinguishable from Buddhism in several specific ways: the Gymnetae go completely naked; they commit suicide by burning themselves to death;[13] and they are not called *Śramaṇas* in any ancient account.[14iv] According to Arrian, Calanus had "philosophy students" among the companions of Alexander, including even Lysimachus, who is explicitly named as having been one of these students.[15]

The Brāḥmaṇas or "Brahmanists" constitute a well-known non-Buddhist sect. Described at some length by Megasthenes, and also mentioned (and regulated) in the Mauryan inscriptions, it contrasts sharply with the other sects:

7. Brāḥmaṇas: followers are born householders (wealthy landlords), who receive an aristocratic upbringing; for thirty-seven years[16] they remain unmarried, frugal, vegetarian,[17] and celibate; after the thirty-seven years they retire to their estates, have many wives and children, eat meat, wear jewelry, and so on; they try to prevent their wives from learning philosophy; they believe God created the universe and

[12] Although other methods are mentioned (see above in this chapter), all actual instances reported by the Greeks are of self-immolation.

[13] On Chinese monks, including early Pure Land monks, committing suicide by self-immolation, see Keown (1996: 9n2) and Kleine (2006: 167n1). However, Georgios Halkias (p.c., 2013) astutely remarks, "A few instances of the Chinese interpreting the *Lotus Sūtra*, who were also Pure Land practitioners, does not make self-immolation a feature of Pure Land Buddhism." This issue thus needs to be reexamined carefully. In any case, it is quite clear that the sect of Calanus was not Buddhist, nor was the similar sect described by Megasthenes.

[14] Modern scholars have often referred to them as Śramaṇas (in one or another spelling), but no ancient writer does. See Endnote iv.

[15] Arrian, *Anabasis* VII, 3:3–4.

[16] Strabo reports on the authority of Megasthenes that Calanus said "he had completed the forty years of discipline which he had promised to observe" when he joined Alexander's court (Strabo XV, 1, 61), translation by Hamilton and Falconer (Perseus online). However, Calanus belonged to the Gymnetae sect, and despite remarks in the Greek sources he was hardly a normal Brahmanist. Strabo adds that "Alexander made presents to his children" (Strabo XV, 1, 61).

[17] But they recline on straw mattresses and *skins* (Strabo XV, 1, 59).

> regulates it and pervades the whole of it; they believe the soul is immortal and judged in Hades.[18]

This Brahmanism also contrasts sharply with the very late form of it that is known from very late sources, nearly all of them medieval or later. Scholars who specialize in ancient Indian philosophies or religions have founded their beliefs exclusively on these late sources. Because of them they claim that the Greek sources, which are at least a half millennium older than the earliest Indian sources (the Major Inscriptions of the Mauryas scarcely tell us anything about Early Brahmanism except for the practice of ritual sacrifice of animals), describe someone else, not Brahmanists. Since the fallacy behind their assumptions is evidently not obvious, it must be stated in plain words here: Megasthenes describes what may be called "*Early* Brahmanism". By contrast, late sources describe "*Late* Brahmanism". Some of the key features of the Early Brahmanist system are belief in one universal creator God, belief that the soul is immortal and judged in the world of the afterlife, and therefore belief in karma and rebirth.

Although Vedic religion is generally thought to be the ancestor of Brahmanism, these Early Brahmanist beliefs are unknown in the Rig Veda. But they are core beliefs of Early Zoroastrianism, which we know was introduced to Central Asia and northwest India by the Achaemenid Persians. Unlike the Buddha, the Brahmanists did not reject the Zoroastrian ideas, they accepted them.

The long Achaemenid rule over Gandhāra ensured that there were Zoroastrians in the region at least during the early and middle period:

8. Early Zoroastrianism. Overtly attested practice: the custom of exposing dead human corpses to wild animals; covertly attested beliefs (as rejected in Early Buddhism or accepted in Early Brahmanism): a Heavenly God who created the world; the Truth versus the Lie; humans have an immortal soul; good or bad karma determines rebirth in Heaven or Hell.

The non-Buddhist sects are better known than any of the Buddhist sects. The simple reason seems to be that the Greeks were fascinated

[18] In this case, *Hades* means simply "the afterworld" or "the afterlife", neither positive nor negative, but the element of judgement indicates that it leads to a positive or negative outcome, ergo Heaven or Hell.

by the naked ascetics of the Gymnetae sect, and somewhat interested in the Brāḥmaṇas, whose thought they considered to be somewhat like their own tradition. Leaving aside the Zoroastrians, the Greeks also had much more personal contact with the Brāḥmaṇas than with any of the others, with the sole, outstanding exception of the Gymnetae, the sect of Calanus; though of course Pyrrho's contact with his Buddhist teacher must have been quite intensive for him to have learned Early Buddhism so well. While Megasthenes' description of the early beliefs and way of life of the Brāḥmaṇas is our best source of information on Early Brahmanism of any kind,[19] the Gymnetae are better described because the Greeks were interested in them, sought them out, and had the closest interaction with them both in India and back home. Unfortunately, they are nevertheless one of the most poorly known sects doctrinally. They are discussed further below.

Attested Early Buddhism according to Megasthenes

The best known of the Buddhist systems is that of the *Śramaṇas*,[20] whose practices and beliefs, like those of Early Pyrrhonism, belong solidly to Pre-Normative Buddhism. They are described most extensively in the Greek account by Megasthenes in his book, *Indica*. Though it is lost, the geographer Strabo preserves passages culled from it in his *Geography*. Unfortunately, the version of *Indica* that Strabo used seems already to have been interpolated and expanded by others, so that the text does not always distinguish clearly between passages owing to Megasthenes or to other authors Strabo cites. In addition, the typical Hellenistic-period preference for light, chatty, titillating stories adversely affected Strabo's selection from and treatment of Megasthenes' work. To make

[19] For the scholarly literature on the Greek accounts of India, see the volumes by Karttunen (1989; 1997), which, however, contain many doubtful identifications. He says, for example, that the Sarmanes of Strabo were generic ascetics: "There used to be a lively discussion about the exact nature of the Sarmanes, whether they were Buddhist or Brahmanist, but now it seems clear that the word referred to wandering monks in general, including different groups" (Karttunen 1997: 58). This conclusion should raise questions about the recent scholarship upon which Karttunen's remark is based. See the detailed discussion of this issue below in this chapter. The bibliographical value of Karttunen's two volumes is undoubted, but very scant attention is paid in them to Megasthenes' account of the Indian thinkers.

[20] See below in this chapter for detailed analysis of the meaning of *Śramaṇa* in the Pre-Normative Buddhist period.

matters worse, in the medieval process of scribal copying and transmission of ancient Greek texts, material on foreign nations—especially proper names—typically suffered the most corruption.[21] Nevertheless, although the received version of Strabo is not perfect,[22] it preserves part of the earliest *dated* eyewitness account of Indian philosophical-religious practices and ideas by far. It is therefore incalculably more important than any of the other texts traditionally considered to represent or reflect Early Buddhism.[23]

Most importantly, Pyrrho learned a form of Early Buddhism in 330–325 BC, when he was in Bactria and Gandhāra with the court of Alexander the Great. Because some knowledge of Early Buddhism reached China via Bactria no later than the beginning of the third century BC,[24] the Buddha's teachings and practice must have been known in Bactria, through which country Buddhists had to travel to reach China, and therefore they must already have spread throughout Gandhāra, the country located southeast of Bactria in what is now eastern Afghanistan and northwestern Pakistan.

Megasthenes stresses that the Śramaṇas were divided into two basic forms of practice: the "rural" Śramaṇas, who lived out in the open, and whom he calls the *Hylobioi* 'Forest-dwellers', and the "urban" Śramaṇas, whom he calls the *Iatrikoi* 'physicians, healers'. Little attention has been paid to this bifurcation, which could have originated only when Buddhism spread outside the South Asian monsoon zone, allowing the more ascetically inclined Śramaṇas to live in the open

[21] For example, the word *Sarman(es)* is always misspelled "*Garman(es)*" in Strabo. The mistake was made in or before the earliest extant Strabo manuscript, but is not an ancient error because the correct spelling is found in all other sources, most importantly in Clement of Alexandria, whose account depends ultimately on Megasthenes. Clement (*Stromateis* I, XV, 71, 3–5) gives the form correctly with *S*-. See Stählin (1906: 2:45–46). The textual error, remarked already in the nineteenth century by McCrindle (1877: 98, note), perhaps goes back to a medieval manuscript in which the initial *S*—written *C* in ancient Greek—was misread as the similar Greek *Γ G*, due to ligature with the following α.

[22] For perfection, see Chapter Four.

[23] It must be noted that Indologists in particular are wont to discount Greek sources on early India, referring to all the above-noted problems. However, the same problems, and much worse ones, affect Indian sources, which are mostly a *millennium* or more younger, have never been properly edited, and consist largely of fantasy.

[24] See Chapter Three.

all year round. This division, originally, is specifically and exclusively characteristic of Buddhism.[25]

In the Pali Canon, in Buddhist sutras thought to have been composed before the appearance of what is traditionally known as the Mahayana, there is a standard background story against which the Buddha's lifetime and teachings are portrayed. We see mostly a quiet world of agriculture, towns, and estates of the wealthy who offered Buddha and his followers shelter and food during the monsoon season, when it is necessary to take shelter in India.

Such a temporary shelter is called an *ārāma*.[26] Individuals who practiced Buddhism, including Buddha and his followers, were called *Śramaṇas*, a term that specifically and exclusively meant 'Buddhist practitioners'.[27]

Similarly, although the specifically Buddhist word *bodhi* 'awakening, enlightenment' occurs in the Major Inscriptions of the Mauryas (early third century BC),[28] and the Buddha's personal name Gautama is attested in Chinese sources, no references to the epithet *Buddha* are attested in dated or datable sources before the Saka-Kushan period, when many other names, terms, and features of Normative Buddhism also appear, including the term *saṃgha* 'the community of Buddhist monks', *bhikṣu* 'monk' and *bhikṣunī* 'nun', and the fully developed *vihāra* 'monastery'.[29] After careful consideration of the archaeological and literary evidence Schopen says,

[25] Beckwith (forthcoming-a). Examples of non-Buddhist practitioners following similar practices, such as in the *Taittiriya Āraṇyaka*, are patently late and have nothing to do with traditional Brahmanism; they are modeled on Buddhism. See Bronkhorst (1986), who demonstrates conclusively that the *Bṛhadāraṇyaka Upaniṣad* (the only supposed "Vedic" text in which the term *śramaṇa* is not used specifically to mean 'Buddhist practitioner') imitates Buddhism and dates to well after the time of the Buddha.

[26] One dedicated to Buddhist use eventually came to be called a *saṃghārāma*, but this happened only after the development of the *saṃgha*, which means after the Major Inscriptions of the Mauryas (q.v. Chapter Three and Appendix C).

[27] See the detailed discussion below in this chapter.

[28] See Chapter Three and Appendix C.

[29] Schopen (2004: 74–79); see Dutt (1962) for the respective archaeological plans, and cf. Beckwith (2012c and 2014) for the Central Asian origin of the *vihāra* plan. The Kushans' own word for the monastery-college must have been Aramaic *dērā* (not Sanskrit *vihāra* or a Prakrit form of it), which term is attested for certain in China in the mid-second century AD but could well have been there already from the first century (Beckwith 2014).

> Marshall, again, noted some time ago that the *vihāra* that Lamotte seems to have had in mind, the ordered "quadrangular, high-walled monastery or *vihāra* . . . seems to have made its appearance in the *saṃghārāmas* of the northwest during the first century A.D., and thence to have found its way southward and eastward to the rest of India." . . . The standardized, ordered *vihāra*, then, began to appear almost everywhere in the archaeological record just before and just after the beginning of the Common Era. . . . Marshall explained the observable change in type and construction of the *vihāra* by saying, in part, that the wide acceptance of the standard form "was probably due in large measure to the changing character of the [Buddhist] church, which was everywhere tending to substitute regular, settled monasticism for the wandering life."[30]

As ascetics,[31] the Śramaṇas owned little more than a simple robe and a few other necessities. Thus did Gautama Śākamuni,[32] 'sage of the Scythians', wander, meditating and searching for answers, before his "awakening". He may well have met others doing the same thing, and studied with some of them, but we have *no remotely credible evidence* that he knew anything about Jains, Ājīvikas, or other non-Brahmanist sects. The traditional view, which actually accepts this problematic notion as dogma, has not been seriously questioned for a long time. Yet these sects are unattested in any dated or datable Pre-Normative Buddhist sources. It is because their teachings needed to be refuted and rejected by *much later* Buddhists that they eventually appeared in the written Buddhist tradition, but in works that are patently late doctrinally, full of magic and other forms of fantasy, and unreliable in every other way. Chronological incongruities reveal that the putatively "early" forms of

[30] Schopen (2004: 79), quoting Marshall (1951: 1:233, 320, 324). Schopen (2004: 77) also notes, "Even considerably after Aśoka, however, there are no references to *vihāras*. In none of the hundreds of donative records from Bhārhut, Sāñcī, and Pauni does the term occur." See now Beckwith (2014).

[31] The Major Inscriptions of the Mauryas regularly refer to "ascetics, religious mendicants", but the term used is *pravrajita-* (variously spelled; literally "one who has gone forth"); they never use for that purpose the word *śramaṇa-*, which the inscriptions repeatedly, explicitly, tell us is a term for members of a particular sect, in contradistinction to the one other named sect, the *Brāḥmaṇas* "Brahmins". See further in Chapter Three and Appendix C.

[32] This epithet (better known in later Sanskrit guise as *Śākyamuni*) is attested only from the Saka-Kushan period on, the earliest examples to date having been found in the Gāndhārī documents, but it is very difficult to imagine such an epithet being applied to a native Indian. See also Appendix C.

what eventually became identifiably Jain, Ājīvika, and so on, did not yet exist as such anywhere near the time of the Buddha, but took on recognizable forms only much later due to heavy influence from Normative Buddhism, therefore no earlier than the Saka-Kushan period.

After Gautama became *Buddha* 'the Awakened One', he wandered the same region for many years during the dry season, teaching and gradually acquiring a substantial following and a number of permanently donated *ārāmas* for use in the monsoon season, according to the Normative Buddhist accounts. After his death, Buddhist practitioners continued to do the same thing, wandering and acquiring new *ārāmas* further and further afield. Archaeological finds show that these were quite primitive, temporary affairs.[33] Moreover, since the monsoons seem to have been a determining factor in the eventual development of the traditional bifurcation in Buddhism between the "rustic" and the "urban" Śramaṇas, the division could not have occurred before Buddhism spread over the Hindu Kush into western (Central Asian) Gandhāra, where there were and are no monsoons. In any case, the development of the bifurcation must have happened before the visit of Megasthenes in the late fourth century BC. The fact that some Buddhist thought made its way to China from Bactria by the late fourth to early third centuries BC confirms this. One assumes that this bifurcation did not spread southeastward into India itself before the appearance of the *vihāra* in the Kushan period. Since Megasthenes describes premonastic Śramaṇas who were already divided into the two types, his description undoubtedly applies to Gandhāra, the northeastern neighbor of his political home, Arachosia (now southern Afghanistan).

The Account of Megasthenes

The earliest and richest eyewitness report on the ancient religious-philosophical beliefs of Gandhāra, and perhaps as far east as Magadha,[34] is that of Megasthenes, dated to 305–304 BC. Megasthenes is most

[33] Schopen (2004: 74–80).

[34] Except (partly) for Megasthenes, the Greeks were familiar only with the northwestern Indian region, eastern Gandhāra, but they referred to the entire subcontinent as "India". Unfortunately, the fragments of Megasthenes in Strabo do not tell us which city is meant when the text simply says "the city". Radt (2009: 195) quotes Jacoby's question about its location: "Palibothra?" A better-supported question would have been "Taxila?"

familiar with the northwest, so he must have spent much of his time in Gandhāra. He does describe ancient Pāṭaliputra (Greek *Palimbothra* ~ *Palibothra*, modern Patna, in ancient Magadha, now the province of Bihār) accurately and in some detail, so it is accepted that he did travel across northern India as far as Magadha, but it is also clear from his description and from archaeology that the city seems to have been newly and rapidly built by Candragupta. At the time of Megasthenes' visit it had wooden stockades and seems to have been primarily a military camp, since most of his comments about it refer to the military and related political topics. He says nothing about *philosophoi* "philosophers" there. His account of the latter transparently describes exactly the same people noted by the companions of Alexander, revealing that he undoubtedly got his information in the same place—Taxila. Like other ancient Greek writers, Strabo quotes only indirectly (*oratio obliqua*), no doubt also modernizing the language of his source, though he usually does tell us the name of the author he is quoting. However, as noted above, the grammar of *oratio obliqua* in Greek clearly and explicitly marks a passage *as* a quotation, even if it is technically an "indirect" quotation.[35] In this particular case, textual analysis shows that Strabo collected his information about the "Indian" *philosophoi* 'religious-philosophical practitioners' from different parts of Megasthenes and then strung the bits together mechanically one after the other, usually (but not always) in sections explicitly marked by Strabo's own introductory or concluding words. It is clear that in at least one instance—a short passage containing two quoted sentences—some material has been wrongly placed by him in the *Brāḥmaṇas*' section. This is clear from the contents of the statements and the peculiar division of the text following them. As a result, the correct attribution or attributions of that short section must be established on the basis of its content.

Megasthenes' account of the *philosophoi* 'philosophical-religious practitioners' of India divides them, explicitly, into two sects:[36] the

[35] The variation in prose quotations among different ancient authors is due primarily to the fact that they did not have the modern idea of quoting *identically*, except when they quoted poetry.

[36] Strabo XV, 1 (Jones 1930: 7:104–105; Radt 2005, 2009). The material Strabo presents from Megasthenes also describes several other kinds of practitioners. It deserves much more careful and insightful attention. The most recent studies are Karttunen (1989; 1997) and Parker (2008).

Βραχμᾶνες *Brachmanes*, corresponding to Sanskrit (plural) *Brāḥmaṇā* 'Brahmanists';[37v] and the Σαρμᾶνες *Sarmanes*, corresponding to Northwestern Prakrit and Sanskrit *Śramaṇā* ~ Pali *Samaṇā* 'Buddhists'.[38vi] Strabo quotes Megasthenes:

> He says that the most honored of the Sarmanes are called the Forest-dwellers (ὑλοβίοι), who live in the woods on leaves and tree-fruits, wearing clothes of tree-bark, abstaining from sex and wine. (He says) that they confer[39] with the kings, who through messengers inquire (from the Forest-dwellers) about the causes of things, and through them they [the kings] honor and pray to the divine one (τὸ θεῖον). (He says) that next in honor after the Forest-dwellers are the Physicians (ἰατρικόι), philosophers concerned about Man, (who are) frugal, but do not live in the wild, and eat rice and barley that is offered to them by all from whom they beg and who invite them into their homes. (He says) that they are able to cause people to beget many children, both male and female, by use of drugs; but (that) their medical treatment is accomplished mostly through food, not through medicines; and (that), of their medicines, the most esteemed are their ointments and plasters, while the others contain much that is evil. (He says) that both these and the others practice endurance, both of pain and of immobility, such that they remain in a single position, unmoved, all day long. (He says) that there are also others, diviners and charmers experienced with the rites and customs for the dead, who beg as mendicants in the villages and towns; but though some of them are more elegant and refined than these, they do not abstain from (using) as many of the common sayings about Hades as seem best for promoting piety (εὐσέβειαν)[40] and holiness. (He says) that women also study philosophy with some of them, but they abstain from sex.[41]

[37] Megasthenes' description makes it certain that his *Brachmanes* are the ancient Brāḥmaṇas, although it is important to examine the way quotations from his lost *Indica* have been assembled by Strabo, who did not always get it right. On the Pramnae, see Endnote v.

[38] As previously noted, in manuscripts of Strabo the name Σαρμᾶνες *Sarmanes* is written Γαρμᾶνες *Garmanes*, long ago recognized as a copying mistake due to the similarity of ancient Cα- (modern Σα-) to Γα- because Clement of Alexandria and all other ancient texts have Σαρμαν- or Σαμαν- for this word. See Endnote vi.

[39] Radt (2009: 8:198).

[40] In the Greek fragments of the Thirteenth Rock Edict from Kandahar, the Greek word εὐσέβεια "piety" translates the Indic word *Dharma* (Pali *Dhamma*).

[41] Strabo XV, 1, 60: τοὺς δὲ Σαρμᾶνας τοὺς μὲν ἐντιμοτάτους ὑλοβίους φησὶν ὀνομάζεσθαι, ζῶντας ἐν ταῖς ὕλαις ἀπὸ φύλλων καὶ καρπῶν ἀγρίων, *ἐσθῆτος* δὲ φλοιῶν δενδρείων, ἀφροδισίων χωρὶς καὶ οἴνου· τοῖς δὲ βασιλεῦσι συνεῖναι δι' ἀγγέλων πυνθανομένοις

Megasthenes thus clearly divides all *Śramaṇas* into two distinct types. The division begins by contrasting the places where the Forest-dwellers live—outdoors, in the woods—with the places where the Physicians (or "Healers") do *not* live. The Physicians do not live outdoors, in the woods, and it is further indicated that they sleep indoors as guests of donors. Therefore they live in villages or towns. This seems to be the fundamental distinction, as no mention is made of any seasonal differences. The Forest-dwellers are also said to live on wild food ("leaves and wild fruit") and to wear clothes made of bark. The wearing of bark is mentioned as a practice of Forest-dwelling Buddhist ascetics in early Normative Buddhism.[42] The comment further establishes that they are not *Brahmanist* ascetics, who are said by Megasthenes (correctly, according to Indian tradition) to wear clothing made of deer skin. Nothing is said about precisely how the Forest-dwellers obtain their food and clothing, but it comes from the wilderness itself, not from other people; no economy is involved. By contrast, the Physicians obtain from others cultivated food: "rice and barley". The same is no doubt true of their clothing, which is not mentioned.[43] Significantly, the Śramaṇas are *not*

περὶ τῶν αἰτίων καὶ δι' ἐκείνων θεραπεύουσι καὶ λιτανεύουσι τὸ θεῖον. μετὰ δὲ τοὺς ὑλοβίους δευτερεύειν κατὰ τιμὴν τοὺς ἰατρικοὺς καὶ ὡς περὶ τὸν ἄνθρωπον φιλοσόφους, λιτοὺς μὲν, μὴ ἀγραύλους δέ, ὀρύζῃ καὶ ἀλφίτοις τρεφομένους, ἃ παρέχειν αὐτοῖς πάντα τὸν αἰτηθέντα καὶ ὑποδεξάμενον ξενίᾳ. δύνασθαι δὲ καὶ πολυγόνους ποιεῖν καὶ ἀρρενογόνους καὶ θηλυγόνους διὰ φαρμακευτικῆς. τὴν δὲ ἰατρείαν διὰ σιτίων τὸ πλέον, οὐ διὰ φαρμάκων ἐπιτελεῖσθαι· τῶν φαρμάκων δὲ μάλιστα εὐδοκιμεῖν τὰ ἐπίχριστα καὶ τὰ καταπλάσματα, τἆλλα δὲ κακουργίας πολὺ μετέχειν. ἀσκεῖν δὲ καὶ τούτους κἀκείνους καρτερίαν τήν τε ἐν πόνοις καὶ τὴν ἐν ταῖς ἐπιμοναῖς, ὥστ' ἐφ' ἑνὸς σχήματος ἀκίνητον διατελέσαι τὴν ἡμέραν ὅλην. ἄλλους δ' εἶναι τοὺς μὲν μαντικοὺς καὶ ἐπῳδοὺς καὶ τῶν περὶ τοὺς κατοιχομένους λόγων καὶ νομίμων ἐμπείρους—ἐπαιτοῦντας κατὰ κώμας καὶ πόλεις—, τοὺς δὲ χαριεστέρους μὲν τούτων καὶ ἀστειοτέρους, οὐδ' αὐτοὺς δὲ ἀπεχομένους τῶν καθ' ᾄδην θρυλουμένων ὅσα δοκεῖ πρὸς εὐσέβειαν καὶ ὁσιότητα· συμφιλοσοφεῖν δ' ἐνίοις καὶ γυναῖκας ἀπεχομένας καὶ αὐτὰς ἀφροδισίων. Text from Radt (2005: 4:210–212), deleting his two editorial additions and his suggestion of an omission. Cf. the passage on the Forest-dwellers in Clement of Alexandria, discussed below in this chapter.

[42] Schopen (1997: 92).

[43] It is significant that unlike the nakedness—much noticed by the Greeks—of the sect of Calanus, the Śramaṇas wore clothing. In fact, not only are the practitioners of Buddhism throughout its long history *never* said to go naked—for the explicitly "non-Buddhist" character of nakedness see Freiberger (2006: 237)—a robe of some sort is part of the minimum equipment of a Buddhist practitioner in the earliest traditional Buddhist texts. The accounts of Devadatta and other radically ascetic practitioners mention

said to abstain from eating meat (unlike the Brāḥmaṇas, who Megasthenes says abstain from it during their ascetic period). Because the Physician Śramaṇas beg for their food, or are freely offered it, along with shelter, by charitable people who are not Śramaṇas, the Physicians are part of a much larger economy involving several socioeconomic categories besides the Physicians themselves. Megasthenes does not say that the Physicians receive payment for treating patients, but obviously they do, even if indirectly, in the form of food and housing. His account also reveals that there already were pious Buddhist laymen who supported the full-time practitioners, the Śramaṇas.

Megasthenes not only explicitly remarks that the Forest-dwellers were more highly esteemed than the Physicians, his description contains material indicating some specific ways in which the rustic Śramaṇas were considered to be better, ethically, than the urban ones. The Forest-dwellers, who "abstain from sex and wine", contrast with the Physicians who by implication do not so abstain, though Megasthenes does not tell us. Moreover, the Physicians not only "do not live outdoors",[44] they eat cultivated food. While the Physicians are explicitly said to be frugal and to beg for their food, they nevertheless live better and more easily than the Forest-dwellers. On the other hand, from a wider perspective, Megasthenes says that the Forest-dwellers were in contact with the king, though indirectly via his "messengers", who were perhaps similar to the *mahāmātras* mentioned in the Major Inscriptions of the Mauryas half a century later. Significantly, these Śramaṇas "honor and entreat the divine one"—the word used here, *to theion*, is neuter and does not mean

---

disagreement about various things, including the robe, but no matter how extreme Devadatta and his followers might have been, they did not go naked. The Vinaya (which of course in its attested forms is centuries later) contains rules regulating exactly what can and cannot be worn.

[44] Clement of Alexandria, *Stromateis* I, XV, 71, 3–5 (Stählin, *Clemens*, 2:45–46) says specifically, "Those among the Sarmanas called Forest-dwellers inhabit neither cities nor houses." Clement's account of the Śramaṇas is ultimately derived from Megasthenes, either from the original work or, more likely, via an epitome of it or of Strabo, but Clement does not cite his sources. His comments on the *Sarmanai* "Śramaṇas" are *textually* quite different from those in Megasthenes. Thus, although his comment is perfectly supported by the Indian tradition (which specifies that the Forest-dwellers do not live under a roof, not to speak of in cities), it is probable, but not entirely certain, that Megasthenes himself mentioned this in his *Indica*.

'God' per se, but rather 'the divine one' or the like.[45] The Physicians, by contrast, were "philosophers of Man", and performed the good work of healing the sick and helping people conceive children, though Megasthenes adds the comment that many of the Physicians' medicaments "contain much that is evil". As a whole, then, the text presents the picture of a more ascetic, noble, virtuous, and idealistic rustic group, the Forest-dwellers, and a less ascetic and less noble, but more practical and helpful, urban group, the Physicians.

The distinctions Megasthenes notes between the two different types of early Śramaṇas coincide with their presentation in traditional Buddhist literary accounts, in which precisely the same two types are contrasted in the same way.[46] Most especially, he calls the "rustic" variety the *Hylobioi* 'Forest-dwellers', an exact calque translation of the Indic equivalent, *Araṇyavāsin* 'Forest-dweller'.[47] The higher ethical valuation of this variety, a consistent theme throughout the text, replicates the same valuation in Early Buddhist texts. Tambiah stresses the pervasiveness and importance in southern Buddhism of the "celebrated differentiation between the village dwellers ([Pali] *gāmavāsin*) and the forest dwellers ([Pali] *āraññavāsin*). Forest dwelling emphasizes living apart from society and having minimal transactions with laity, while village/town dwelling implies regular interaction, as for instance ensues from teaching laymen the doctrine, performing rites for them",[48] and so forth. "Throughout the history of the Buddhist polities of Sri Lanka, Burma, and Thailand, one grand division of the *saṃgha*—that between monastic fraternities and/or communities labeled as forest dwellers on the one hand and as town/village dwellers on the other hand—has persisted . . .".[49] In Sri Lanka there was a formal "constitutional" division of the *saṃgha* into two moieties, the Āraññikas or *āraññavāsins* 'Forest-dwellers' and the *gāmavāsins* 'Town-dwellers'. However, the Sinhalese

[45] As noted above, it is quite possible that this refers to reverence for the Buddha, which becomes fully attested with the mention of Saṃbodhi (Bodhgayā) in the Major Inscriptions of the Mauryas, q.v. Chapter Three and Appendix C.

[46] On *Araṇyavāsin* 'Forest-dweller' and *Grāmavāsin* 'Town-dweller' in early Buddhist texts, and especially attitudes toward the former in the Vinaya and early Mahayana works, see Schopen (2004; 2005).

[47] That is, the Greek is a literal translation corresponding part by part to the Indic equivalent.

[48] Tambiah (1984: 16).

[49] Tambiah (1984: 2).

chronicles "do not mention the Āraññikas before the tenth century, and references to them in other sources are rare."[50] Why does this bifurcation appear so late in Sri Lanka, and by extension, in Southeast Asia, to which Ceylonese Buddhism spread in the Middle Ages? Surely the reason is that Sri Lanka is in the monsoon zone, and year-round living in the forest would require the Forest-dwellers to live in sheltered dwellings of some kind for at least part of the year, which would have made them identical to the Town-dwellers—and in fact, that is precisely what happened; both types lived in *vihāras*. The logical explanation is that the bifurcation arose in a non-monsoon zone, and only later spread southward into the monsoon zone, where the ecological distinction could not be maintained.[51]

According to the putatively early accounts in the Pali Canon, Buddha himself was a wandering rustic ascetic, and he definitely won the high ground as far as virtue and enlightenment are concerned. Nevertheless, despite the difference in lifestyle (and perhaps partly in religious practice), which eventually developed after his time, the *teachings* of the two types of Śramaṇas, both in Megasthenes and in the later Pali accounts, are not known to have differed in any substantial way.

Attested Early Brahmanism according to Megasthenes

Megasthenes clearly distinguishes the Śramaṇas from the Brāḥmaṇas, though he does not compare the two sects explicitly item by item.[52] Instead, he does it implicitly. At the very beginning of his discussion of Indian religious-philosophical practitioners, Strabo says, "Megasthenes makes another division in his discussion of the philosophers, asserting that there are two kinds of them, one kind called Brachmanes and the other Sarmanes; [and] that the Brachmanes, however, enjoy fairer repute, for they are more in agreement in their dogmas."[53] It is notable

[50] Tambiah (1984: 56–57).

[51] Further study of this subject is needed by specialists in early Sri Lankan Buddhism.

[52] The Brāḥmaṇas are in general not relevant to the present investigation, but they are presented by Megasthenes partly in contrast to the Śramaṇas, and their sect, like Buddhism, formed partly in reaction to Zoroastrianism, so they are discussed briefly here. The scholarship on this material has hitherto been devoted to finding ways to ignore it and its significance for understanding *actual* Early Brahmanism. The scholarly fantasy preferred by most modern scholars is based on the same kind of very late works that have made a mess out of the history of Early Buddhism.

[53] Strabo xv, 1, 59.

that the section in Strabo on the Śramaṇas does not have a subsection specifically devoted to their ideas—a major omission in an account of a sect of "philosophers" who, Megasthenes explicitly remarks, were disunited in their views, and thus less esteemed than the more "united" Brāḥmaṇas. In addition, again unlike the section on the Brāḥmaṇas, the section on the Śramaṇas does not end with an explicit concluding statement by Strabo saying something like, "This is what Megasthenes says about the Sarmanes." These and other problems suggest that Strabo's collection of quotations from Megasthenes, at least in part, does not represent their original arrangement in the *Indica*.

After telling us that the Brāḥmaṇas, unlike the Śramaṇas, are more or less in agreement on their teachings, he says that the Brāḥmaṇas practice a kind of "temporary" asceticism for thirty-seven years.[54] Though he says nothing about them doing physical yoga or any other demanding practices, he describes these "philosophers" as "leading a frugal life, lying on straw mattresses and skins, abstaining from animal food[55] and from sex", and talking "earnestly" about philosophical matters. Although during this period the Brāḥmaṇas do not eat meat or

[54] Strabo XV, 1, 59. The number 37 is repeated later in Strabo, in the account of Indian *philosophoi* taken from "other writers", where he says "37 years, as I mentioned before" (Strabo XV, 1, 70). As noted above, Megasthenes (in Strabo) quotes Calanus as saying he had practiced asceticism for the required period of 40 years, but he clearly belonged to a different sect than the Brāḥmaṇas, the mainstream Brahmanists. There is no explanation for the discrepancy. The Greeks had plenty of contact with them, and there is no reason to doubt the basic veracity of their reports. Of course, Megasthenes and the companions of Alexander who mention the Indian *philosophoi* do not describe *all* such groups wherever they existed in India, at *all* periods, including *all* Brāḥmaṇas. If a scientific approach to early Indian history were conceivable here, the matter would be treated in exactly the reverse order: Megasthenes gives us a sober, fantasy-free first-person narrative account of *some* Brāḥmaṇas that is at least half a millennium earlier than any account in any Indian source.

[55] The fact that they lie on "skins" indicates that they were not strict vegetarians, or that their vegetarianism did not have anything to do with *ahiṃsā* 'not hurting (living beings)', or that they were hypocrites about it, or possibly all three. The account of the *Pramnae* in Strabo says the mountain-dwellers wear clothes made of deer skin, a classic Brahmanist trait and an indication that they were, in fact, Brahmanists, not Buddhists. Moreover, the Major Inscriptions of the Mauryan period specifically prohibit the killing of most animals—despite the fact that animal sacrifice was a religious necessity for Brahmins in Antiquity—and stress at some length that the law was an innovation of the ruler himself.

have sexual relations with women, they retain their possessions (which are by implication considerable), and after their thirty-seven years they abandon the restrictions: "They retire, each man to his own possessions, where they live more freely and under less restraint," they eat meat, and they marry as many wives as possible, with the aim of having many children. They also wear adornments of gold. Megasthenes briefly describes some of the beliefs of the Brāḥmaṇas about the natural world, metaphysics, and ontology, among which the most significant are their beliefs about the immortality of the soul, the judgement in the afterworld ("Hades"), and so on.[56] Finally, the Brāḥmaṇas are a strictly male group, both during their ascetic training and afterward: "The Brachmanes do not communicate their philosophy to their wives, for fear they should divulge to the profane, if they became depraved, anything which ought to be concealed or lest they should abandon their husbands in case they [the wives] became good (philosophers) themselves."[57]

The Śramaṇas, unlike the Brāḥmaṇas, are described as permanent ascetics. Much more importantly, again unlike the Brāḥmaṇas, there are two different kinds of Śramaṇas.[58] As discussed above, this dichotomy is solidly attested throughout the history of Buddhism. It is undoubtedly to this division—as well as the one between these Śramaṇas and the "other" kind of Śramaṇas expert in funeral rites—that Megasthenes refers in his remark that the Śramaṇas are less united in their beliefs than the Brāḥmaṇas. Although according to Megasthenes both Brāḥmaṇas and Śramaṇas live frugally, the Brāḥmaṇas do not wander, beg, or live in the wilderness. Their inherited land and other wealth is more than sufficient to pay for their upper-class upbringing, their many wives and children, and their gold jewelry, and to support them

[56] Strabo XV, 1, 59, translations from Jones (1930: 7:103).

[57] Strabo XV, 1, 59, translation by Hamilton and Falconer (Perseus online). It is interesting that Megasthenes should mention this. The ancient Greeks were at least as androcentric as most human societies, and seem to have thought highly of the Brāḥmaṇas (in any case, they thought better of them than they did of the Śramaṇas), so this practice should presumably have been heartily approved by him. Instead, he goes out of his way to give a lengthy explanation of why the Brāḥmaṇas do not share their philosophy with their wives. Accordingly, Megasthenes' account is rather critical of the Brāḥmaṇas in this respect.

[58] Cf. Beckwith (forthcoming-a).

in a life of ease before, during, and after their thirty-seven years. This contrasts very sharply with the Śramaṇas, who all live frugally, deriving their livelihood from nature (for those who live outside, in the forests) or from other people (for those who live inside, in towns). His remark that even the more elegant and refined among the "other" kind of Śramaṇas "do not refrain from using as many of the common sayings about Hades as seem best for promoting piety and holiness" suggests that unlike many Buddhist lay believers and also unlike the Brāḥmaṇas, at least some Śramaṇas did not *themselves* believe in "Hades",[59] and therefore did not believe in karma and rebirth. Finally, he explicitly says that the Brāḥmaṇas exclude their married women from their "philosophical" studies, unlike the Śramaṇas: "Women, as well as men, study philosophy with some of them [the Śramaṇas], and the women also [like the men] abstain from sex." Although he says nothing about the Brāḥmaṇas' relationships with women other than their wives, it would appear that for the Brāḥmaṇas, women *are* wives, and they attempt to acquire as many of them as possible. By contrast, the Śramaṇas are unmarried and celibate lifelong, and include both men and women aspirants.

The Pre–Pure Land Sect according to Megasthenes

Strabo does not include a separate section about the Śramaṇas' views, and says very little about their ideas in the section he explicitly marks as devoted to the Śramaṇas. This contrasts with the preceding section on the Brāḥmaṇas, which contains two subsections, the first on the lives of the Brāḥmaṇas and the second on their views. He does have two subsections on the Śramaṇas, but they are about the two subtypes' practices, not about their ideas.

However, as noted above, his Brāḥmaṇas section is problematic because one subsection of it contains views that are diametrically opposed to well-known basic Brahmanist views, *including those given by Megasthenes himself* in his section on the Brāḥmaṇas. The subsection is therefore intrusive in that section, and must have been wrongly placed there, by whom is unknown, though surely not by Megasthenes. The misplacement probably occurred because the first topic *seems* to follow

[59] The text uses the Greek word.

the topic of the immediately preceding sentence in the genuinely Brahmanical section before it, while the second intrusive sentence also *seems* to follow that section's apparent contrast of pleasure and pain, life and death.

The intrusive section shows specific textual signs of having been put there by mistake. It is immediately followed by a completely unexpected new finite verb, where Strabo tells us that he (Megasthenes) says what "they" say about nature, including well-known Brahmanical teachings, the subject matter of which perfectly follows the material *preceding* the evidently intrusive sentences, which are glaringly out of place. If the problematic sentences were not intrusive, there would have been no reason not to continue the laundry list of Brahmanical things to the very end of the section on Brahmanism, without this odd comment. It seems that Strabo (or an interpolator) introduced the problematic section and then felt the need to tell readers it was still the same list.[60] The preceding clearly Brahmanist subsection ends with the comment that the Brāḥmaṇas "despise pleasure and pain as well as life and death".

The first sentence of the intrusive section says essentially the opposite: the unmentioned practitioners consider "this life to be like that of babes still in the womb and death to be birth [therefore, *rebirth*] into the true, happy life". The second sentence says, "There is nothing absolutely good or bad that happens to people, otherwise some would not be annoyed and others pleased by the same things—which are, after all, just dreamlike impressions—and the same individuals would not sometimes be annoyed and at other times change and be pleased by the very same things."[61] Precisely this idea is also prominent in the teachings of Pyrrho, who denied there was any "absolute" difference between good and bad, just and unjust, in human life.[62] This is a logical inference from his teaching of *adiaphora*—Buddha's *anātman*—namely,

[60] Radt (2009) seems not to have noticed this particular problem, since he says nothing about it.

[61] Strabo xv, 1, 59 (text from Radt 2005: 4:208): ἀγαθὸν δὲ ἢ κακὸν μηδὲν εἶναι τῶν συμβαινόντων ἀνθρώποις· οὐ γὰρ ἂν τοῖς αὐτοῖς τοὺς μὲν ἄχθεσθαι τοὺς δὲ χαίρειν ἐνυπνιώδεις ὑπολήψεις ἔχοντας καὶ τοὺς αὐτοὺς τοῖς αὐτοῖς τοτὲ μὲν ἄχθεσθαι τοτὲ δ' αὖ χαίρειν μεταβαλλομένους.

[62] See Appendix A for the testimonies and discussion.

that "things" (including people) do not have inherent self-identities, flatly contradicting one of the central doctrines of Brahmanism, which teaches that everything *does* have its own immortal *ātman* "inherent self-identity; soul",[63] as Megasthenes tells us twice. The intrusive passage thus cannot possibly represent an Early Brahmanist view. Quite to the contrary, the idea that "things" are unstable, unfixed, dreamlike impressions is specifically, famously Buddhist.

The Buddhist idea of *anātman* ~ *adiaphora* is expressed in this peculiar way, by denial of opposites, not only in the earliest dated testimonies to Buddhist beliefs—Pyrrho, Megasthenes, and Early Taoist texts—but in what are considered to be some of the earliest texts in the Pali Canon as well.[64] Significantly, the ideas are also found in the very earliest preserved texts of the Pure Land school of Buddhism, which seems to have developed in Bactria and Gandhāra, right where both Pyrrho and Megasthenes learned about Buddhism. For example, in the *Pratyutpanna Samādhi Sūtra*, the earliest known Pure Land work, which was first translated into Chinese by Lokakṣema, a Kushan monk,[65] between AD 178 and 189,[66] the Buddha presents negating antilogies.[67] They are introduced by his rhetorical question, "On what sort of things does one do mental concentration?"[68] Among the many things listed are a number of antilogies, including "not forsaking the people of the ten quarters [of the world] : saving the lives of the people of the ten quarters"[69] and "regarding the people of the ten quarters as one's own : regarding the people of the ten quarters as not one's own".[70] An item toward the end the list is "everything being non-dual".[71] A slightly later

[63] Cf. D'Amato (2009: 42): "We might understand . . . the tendency toward emphasizing the efficacy of removing all views whatsoever, as an extension of the fundamental Buddhist doctrine of *anātman*—the absence of self."

[64] Gómez (1976).

[65] More precisely, a Śramaṇa (沙門); see Nattier (2008: 73n165). For an English translation, see Harrison (1998).

[66] Nattier (2008: 73), q.v. for discussion of his name.

[67] In his chapter 2, on "Practice".

[68] *Taishō* 418, 12.0904b26: 何等爲定意.

[69] *Taishō* 418, 12.0904c03–04: 不捨十方人 活十方人. Translation by Harrison (1998: 15).

[70] *Taishō* 418, 12.0904c04–05: 十方人計爲是我所 十方人計爲非我所. Translation by Harrison (1998: 15), substituting colons for his semicolons.

[71] *Taishō* 418, 12.0904c26–27: 一切不二. Translation by Harrison (1998: 17).

version of the text gives a long list of antilogies in the same chapter, such as "Do not think of loveliness, do not think of ugliness; do not think of evil, do not think of good".[72]

This suggests an identification also for the *first* sentence in the intrusive (non-Brahmanist) sentence of Megasthenes' account, which says, "They converse more about death than anything else, for they believe that the life here is, as it were, that of a babe still in the womb, and that death, to those who have devoted themselves to philosophy, is birth into the true life, that is, the happy life; and that they therefore discipline themselves most of all to be ready for death."[73] This again sounds like Pure Land Buddhism, a branch of Mahayana that is practically theistic in all but name and technical doctrinal details, with a monotheistic God, typically called Amitābha—he can differ in name and attributes from text to text, but is *functionally* the same nevertheless—and a Heavenly paradise, in which the faithful who devoutly recite his name (or occasionally something else) are reborn. Although in recent decades there has been much resistance to studying the origins of this system, it was formerly thought that it originated in Central Asia (or at least somewhere in Central Eurasia), and represents a mixture of Buddhist and other beliefs.[74] This remains the most likely answer.[75] Megasthenes' account attests to the existence of a "Pre–Pure Land" complex

[72] *Taishō* 417, 13.898b28–29: 勿念好, 勿念醜; 勿念惡, 勿念善. Another version of the *Pratyutpanna Samādhi Sūtra*, *Taishō* 418, is accepted to be a genuine translation by Lokakṣema (fl. AD 178–189), though it has been much revised since his time; see Nattier (2008: 81–83, 119n25) for detailed discussion and references to the scholarly literature. The verse section containing the passage translated above is from *Taishō* 417. It is missing from *Taishō* 418, and seems to be a later addition in *Taishō* 417, perhaps drawn from the *Sukhāvatīvyūha Sūtra* translated by K'ang Seng Hui (fl. 247–280), which contains a similar section, e.g., 設我得佛、國中人天、形色不同、有好醜者、不取正覺 (*Taishō* 360, 12.0267c23–24) "If I were to attain Buddhahood, but [were to perceive or think that] people and nature in the land [still] had different shapes and colors, and some were good[-looking] and some ugly, I would not have attained true enlightenment". The negation of opposites is of course similar to Madhyamika, but as Gómez (1976) has shown, most of the key elements of Madhyamika already appear in texts thought to be among the earliest of the Pali Canon.

[73] Strabo XV, 1, 59, trans. Jones (1930: 101).

[74] Helmut Hoffmann (p.c., ca. 1975).

[75] The problems are significant and need to be studied. See the interesting discussion in Halkias (2012: 20ff.); cf. Beckwith (2011a).

of ideas in 305–304 BC, half a millennium before full-blown Pure Land per se is attested in any written text. When it is finally attested in a Buddhist text—in the second century AD—it is in a "Mahayana" work translated into Chinese from Gāndhārī Prakrit by a Kushan monk.

Although it might seem odd that Megasthenes' description of this non-Brahmanist sect is preserved in the section of Strabo on the Brāḥmaṇas, the Greeks' interests might explain its location and the apparent identification with Brahmanism. As remarked above, the Greeks were somewhat more interested in Brahmanism (with which they evidently sympathized, perhaps due to some shared ancestral beliefs) and in the Gymnetae, the sect of naked Indian philosophers represented most famously by Calanus, who committed suicide by funeral pyre in front of them in 323 BC. The location of the two sentences on the non-Brahmanist sect in Strabo's subsection on Brahmanism then makes sense, from the point of view of Greek interests,[76] even though analysis of its key ideas points to a Pre–Pure Land sect of Buddhism[77] and specifically rules out identification with the Gymnetae.

To summarize the Pre–Pure Land sect, its followers believe in rebirth, karma, the illusory or dream-like nature of existence, and *anātman* 'no inherent self-identity'. They discipline themselves to prepare for death, which is for them the most important thing, because those who prepare themselves properly ("philosophers") are *reborn* to the true, happy life. Based on the very similar beliefs in inscriptions by the Mauryan king Devānāṃpriya Priyadarśi, who specifically and repeatedly mentions that those who have accumulated good merit will go to Heaven, this passage in Megasthenes refers to the practitioners' belief in rebirth in Heaven. It is supported further by Megasthenes' remark about some of the Śramaṇas using their simpler followers' belief in Heaven and Hell to "encourage" them to be pious, as discussed above. Belief in *anātman* and in rebirth at the same time (as well as in anything being "true" or "happy") is obviously problematic philosophically.

[76] However, since the intrusive passage appears to have been moved there from somewhere else in the *Indica*, it seems probable that Megasthenes did not indicate the sectarian affiliation of the people described in it.

[77] Because Strabo's text tells us so little about them, it is not possible to say more than that they were evidently *Pre*–Pure Land Buddhists.

Compared to the Brāḥmaṇas, the Śramaṇas struck the Greeks as odd, if not alien. The fact that they are given their own subsection, evidently by Megasthenes himself, suggests that the Śramaṇas were at least as numerous as the Brāḥmaṇas—as explicitly suggested by the usage in the Major Inscriptions of the Mauryas a few decades after Megasthenes.[78] It is significant that the followers of the suicide cult (Gymnetae) are *never* called Śramaṇas 'Buddhists', despite scholars' frequent, erroneous claims to that effect,[79] and the relatively full description of Śramaṇa daily life given in a late Greek source is very clearly of garden-variety Normative Buddhism, not of a Pure Land–type sect.[80]

In any event, Buddha's teaching of *anātman*, Pyrrho's *adiaphora*—expressed commonly as the idea that there is no "difference" between *x* and *y*—is recorded also in Megasthenes, as well as in the earliest texts of the Pure Land and Madhyamika traditions. It is a non-Brahmanist view, and at the same time a fundamentally Buddhist view. The fact that Aristotle (or, more likely, one of his students) argues about a similar idea in his *Metaphysics*, despite his apparent misunderstanding of it, probably indicates that it was known in Greece by the time of Pyrrho's return from Central Asia and India, or shortly beforehand. News of the spectacular self-immolation of Calanus would have reached Greece before the death of Aristotle in 322 BC, very likely via eyewitnesses to the event, no doubt bringing with it some representations of Indian ideas, while at about the same time the "philosophy" students of Calanus—who were present at his public suicide—must have brought with them some information about Indian views as well, including perhaps the very idea that Aristotle or one of his students felt compelled to argue about in the *Metaphysics*.[81]

[78] See Chapter Three.

[79] The Indian envoy "Zarmanochegas" or "Zarmarus", who committed suicide in Athens in the first century AD (Strabo XV, 1, 73), is no exception. See Endnote iv.

[80] The Indian ambassador Dandamis (whose name appears in many highly divergent spellings), who was sent to the Roman emperor Elagabalus (r. 218–222), met Bardaisan (Bardesanes) of Edessa, who is believed to have gotten his excellent description of life in a Buddhist monastery (Beckwith 2014) from him. It is preserved in Porphyry, *De abstinentia* (Patillon and Segonds 1995: 3: xxxviii–xlii, 28–30); cf. below. Note that this Dandamis is to be distinguished from the earlier Indian Mandanis (also sometimes called "Dandamis"), who lived at the time of Alexander.

[81] See the discussion in Chapter One and Appendix A.

Our earliest sources on Buddhism thus unanimously agree on some of the most basic teachings of Early Buddhism per se, and they also show us that they were found in the Bactria-Gandhāra region at the end of the fourth century BC.

The traditional analysis of the rise of the Mahayana claims that the bodhisattva ideal, or Bodhisattvayāna, arose out of 'popular' Buddhist practices and beliefs of non-monastic laymen and laywomen, in India. However, little or no evidence has ever been found to support such a connection, and the idea has lost favor. Recently, Schopen and Boucher have presented arguments, based on textual evidence, that the bodhisattva ideal actually arose among rustic Forest-dwelling Śramaṇas, who objected to the abuses of the monks living comfortably in town, often with wives and slaves, no different than any lay householder. The rustic Śramaṇas called for a return to the pure Buddhism of the Buddha himself when he was still a *bodhisattva* 'one with a mind bent on enlightenment', as they saw themselves.[82] This particular strand of the Mahayana thus seems to have developed out of the reformist movement.

It is significant that the Bodhisattvayāna, Madhyamika, and Pure Land traditions, which ended up being included among the constituent elements of "Mahayana", appeared on the Central Asian frontiers of India and China around the second century AD in connection with the expansion of the Central Asian empire of the Kushans.[83] These three pre-Mahayana traditions appear to have developed there as a result of contact with ancient, similar Central Eurasian beliefs and recently introduced Zoroastrian beliefs. The same region is also the home of the *vihāra*, the Buddhist monastery, which is earliest attested at exactly the same time as the appearance of the above-mentioned elements of the later Mahayana, the first to second centuries AD.[84] That is, the *ārāma* or *saṃghārāma* existed earlier in India, but it was in architectural form and function (and probably all other details) nothing like what we think of as a *vihāra*,[85] or fully developed Buddhist monastery,

[82] Schopen (2005: 16); Boucher (2008).

[83] Cf. Halkias (2012: 12–15 and the very pertinent endnotes).

[84] Beckwith (2014).

[85] See Beckwith (2012c) for the later development of the *vihāra* as a monastic college, and the growth of Buddhist scholasticism in Kushan Central Asia—mainly Bactria and Gandhāra—evidently due in part specifically to lingering Greek influence there.

which was introduced via the Kushans to both India[86] and China and therefore could have developed only in Central Asia.[87] Accordingly, the development of the rustic Śramaṇas' path into the Bodhisattvayāna in Central Asia was matched by the urban Śramaṇas' development of their communal dwellings into true monasteries, much as suggested long ago by Marshall.[88]

As mentioned above, it would seem that the Śramaṇas' differentiation by lifestyle was at least partly seasonal in origin. In the earliest period they practiced seasonal "rustic" dwelling, wandering in the wilderness in the dry season, and "urban" dwelling communally in *ārāmas*, which were originally, according to tradition, purely temporary shelters necessitated by the monsoons. The development of this seasonal difference into two permanently distinctive year-round lifestyles therefore could not have taken place in the monsoon zone. It must have happened after Buddhism expanded outside the Indian subcontinent into Central Asia, where there was no monsoon and Śramaṇas could live outside all year-round. The two permanent types of śramaṇa practice thus appear to have evolved in Central Asia.[89]

In any event, the two kinds of Śramaṇas were certainly in place as distinct types in Gandhāra no later than the end of the fourth century AD, when Megasthenes visited and learned about them. Therefore, from the beginning of the strictly historical, textual attestation of Buddhism—which begins with Pyrrho and Megasthenes—the two types already existed in what linguists call "complementary distribution". The more ascetically inclined, who were perhaps also less socially inclined and more dedicated to pursuing their own enlightenment, favored the solitary, eremitic "rustic" ideal, according to which they had to fend for

[86] See Dutt (1962) for discussion and plans.

[87] The Central Asians' own word for it was not Sanskrit *vihāra* or a Prakrit form of that word, but rather Aramaic *dērā*, which is the source of the word for 'monastery' in Chinese, Jurchen, Korean, and Japanese, as well as in many Middle Eastern languages. See Beckwith (2014).

[88] See above in this chapter.

[89] Perhaps careful archaeological and palaeoclimatological work could throw some light on the development of the two types of Śramaṇa practice. The theory appears to be supported by the relative lateness of Forest-dwelling monks (*Āraññikas* or *Āraññavāsins*) in Sri Lanka, where they are attested in the chronicles only from the tenth century (Tambiah 1984: 56–57).

themselves, because in the wilderness between the urban centers there was no one from whom they could beg food or clothing. The less ascetically inclined, more social Śramaṇas gravitated to a pre-monastic ideal, in which they were provided with shelter, and—being in urban areas with many other people—they could beg for their food and clothing, or were provided with it by pious donors. The rustic Śramaṇas could achieve greater success on the path to enlightenment, as *bodhisattvas* in the original sense of the Buddha himself, and they achieved a reputation for saintliness, so that they were more highly honored by Buddhists as a whole. The urban Śramaṇas, who lived together in a sizeable group in any climate, maximized their ability to learn from each other and to pass on what they learned to following generations.

Not only in Megasthenes' report, but throughout recorded history, the Forest-dweller Śramaṇas seem to have been consistently valued more highly than the Town-dweller Śramaṇas. Nevertheless, some of the greatest teachers of Buddhism actually belong to the 'urban' category. Not surprisingly, then, the later development of the full-blown Mahayana tradition was also accompanied by the adoption of a primarily urban-type monastic tradition, including the Central Asian monastery,[90] though not to the exclusion of the rustic ideal, which continued to exist.

It has recently been noted that the Forest-dweller ideal might have been just that, an ideal, which was only rarely followed in actual practice. Certainly, despite their ideal, many of its purported practitioners too eventually adopted the *vihāra*, so that there came to be a distinction between "Forest *vihāras*" and "Town *vihāras*", and in some instances—at least in the stories—the monks from the Town *vihāras* were the ascetics, while those from the Forest *vihāras* were spoiled by luxury. The Vinaya, the source of many such stories, also contains other critical, belittling remarks about Forest-practitioners or monks of any kind who were serious about meditating and achieving enlightenment.[91] If one considers that the Vinaya is, essentially, the Buddhist monastic

[90] It seems likely that the spread of the monastery from Central Asia coincided also with the introduction of the early Mahayana tradition, even though the later Central Asian *vihāras* were predominantly non-Mahayana.

[91] Schopen (2004: 15, 25–26, 91–93).

code, that is, a kind of law code, and its authors were therefore lawyers and administrators, it is hardly surprising that such people—who were by their own descriptions pragmatic, worldly centered, politically inclined individuals—disliked intellectuals, mystics, and holy men, even though the lawyers and political administrators could hardly have been unaware of the fact that the stated purpose of the *vihāra*, the institution they governed, was to house intellectuals, mystics, and holy men. Nevertheless, all this does not mean that laymen, and other monks, agreed with such views, it means only that *some* of the *authors* of the Vinaya had such views. According to standard historiographical analysis, the negative remarks in the Vinaya are classic examples of the criticisms, restrictions, and prohibitions of a legal code revealing what people are really doing. In this case, the strongly worded criticisms and sharp, sarcastic remarks of the Vinaya authors constitute irrefutable evidence not only that some monks looked down on the Forest-dwelling monks and their ideal, but also that some monks really were practicing that ideal even at the time these Vinaya texts were finalized.

The dichotomy between the two Buddhist practitioner lifestyles (and to some extent the tension between them) has continued down to the present day. Although the number of Forest-dwellers has at times dwindled to a handful, their tradition has survived. The two approaches to Buddhist practice are found in all of the major living Buddhist traditions—there are none in which only "rustic" practitioners are known, and none in which only "urban" ones are known.

Returning to pre-monastic early Buddhism, we may note again that Megasthenes' account of the Śramaṇas in Strabo does not contain a section that explicitly describes their philosophical-religious *views*. However, careful analysis of Strabo's section on the "philosophers" of "India" as a whole makes it possible to ascribe the strictly Early Buddhist views recorded by Megasthenes to two distinctive approaches: a conservative and elitist group, versus a more popularly oriented group.

The system ascribed to the "more elegant and refined" Śramaṇas appears to include *Dharma* (Greek *eusebeia* 'piety'), honoring and praying to "the divine one"[92] on behalf of the kings, the practice of strenuous

[92] Perhaps already the Buddha, but in any case not "God" (*ho theos*), belief in whom is explicitly mentioned, by contrast, in Megasthenes' account of the Brāḥmaṇas.

unmoving yoga 'meditation', and knowledge about "the causes of things". The latter point may sound odd, but not for Buddhism, with its highly distinctive central teachings about causation. The teaching, generally speaking, must go back to the Buddha himself, since without it one can hardly make much sense out of his logic.[93] Pyrrho too taught about the causes of *pathē* 'suffering, passion' and a way to be *apathēs* 'without suffering' and thus achieve *ataraxia* 'calmness, nirvana'. Megasthenes' description of the Śramaṇas also accords closely with the descriptions of Pyrrho's wandering, his physical yoga,[94] and his unmarried celibacy.[95]

The "popular" system ascribed to "other" Śramaṇas includes—presumably in addition to the above practices and beliefs—expertise in funeral rites and teaching about good and bad karma and its consequences for rebirth in Heaven or Hell.[96] The approach of this group of Śramaṇas is thus apparently identical to that of King Devānāṃpriya Priyadarśi[97] in the genuine Major Inscriptions of the Mauryas, which were erected only two or three decades after the visit of Megasthenes.

It is significant that Megasthenes does *not* say that the Śramaṇas were vegetarians This suggests a Buddhist explanation for Devānāṃpriya Priyadarśi's law prohibiting the *killing* of animals. Accounts of the Buddha's death from food poisoning say he had eaten spoiled pork, but this does not mean he was not a vegetarian from the Buddhist point of view The explicit directions concerning vegetarianism are actually that Buddhists should not intentionally *kill* any sentient being (human or animal), which is what the law of Devānāṃpriya Priyadarśi expressly prohibited.[98] It is specifically anti-Brahmanist, because the Brahmanists

[93] However, the scholarly consensus about the fully developed treatment of *pratītyasamutpāda* (dependent origination, or dependent causation; the arising of *dharmas* 'things' in dependence upon conditions, etc.) is that it developed long after the Buddha's lifetime. It seems most likely to have developed as part of Normative Buddhism.

[94] The ancient testimonies specifically mention his tolerance of extreme pain; such toleration was a characteristic of early yoga. See below.

[95] The ancient testimonies on Pyrrho are silent about whether he did or did not practice vegetarianism.

[96] This follows from the comment that these Śramaṇas teach the people about "Hades" in order to urge them toward piety and holiness.

[97] The Mauryan ruler traditionally identified with "Aśoka"; see Chapter Three.

[98] See Freiberger (2006: 241).

needed to perform ritual blood sacrifices. In his First Rock Edict the king actually uses the Brahmanist *technical* terms for "ritual slaughter (*ā-labh*) and offering (*pra-hu*) for the ritual killing of animals",[99] making it absolutely clear that the Brahmanists were the specific target of the law. The teachings of the second group of Śramaṇas thus apparently included *ahiṃsā* 'not killing' (literally, 'not injuring').

At the time of Pyrrho, Megasthenes, and Devānāṃpriya Priyadarśi, Buddhism existed, but it was not called "Buddhism", nor does it seem likely that the Buddha himself was personally worshipped, though he was venerated.[100] The *saṃgha* is not mentioned because the *saṃgha*, as an organized or regularized type of community that had a clear monastic rule, did not yet exist. Buddhist practitioners were known as Śramaṇas, as they apparently were from the Buddha's day on, and as they were called into the Middle Ages.[101] Their teachings were above all about *Dharma*, which is translated into Greek in the fragmentary texts of the Mauryan inscriptions from Afghanistan as *eusebeia* 'piety', which is mentioned also in Megasthenes' account. The 'Forest-dwelling' or rustic Śramaṇas were considered to be more moral, or pious, than the 'physician' or 'Town-dwelling' Śramaṇas. The version of the Dharma taught by the "popular" group of Śramaṇas held that pious behavior in this life would be rewarded in the next life in Heaven; that is to say, good people would be *reborn* in Heaven, not on Earth, thus indicating belief in karma, karmic retribution, and rebirth among some Buddhists.[102] This is explicitly mentioned not only in Megasthenes' account but, repeatedly, in the Major Inscriptions of Devānāṃpriya Priyadarśi.

[99] Olivelle (2012: 183n26).

[100] The *Chuangtzu* refers, at about the same time, to the highly respected—but also not yet worshipped—founder of Taoism, Laotzu ~ *Gautama (q.v. Chapter Three). Cf. above on Megasthenes' mention of the Forest-dwellers venerating "the divine one", which could perhaps refer to an already deified Gautama.

[101] At some point in late Antiquity or the Middle Ages the Jains began to copy the Buddhists and say that they too had Śramaṇas, as well as many other once uniquely Buddhist features, such as *vihāras*. In modern times this has become endemic, causing much confusion about the early history of both Buddhism and Jainism. See the discussion of this problem in the Preface.

[102] It is now generally believed that salvation for such people was to escape samsara, the cycle of rebirth. This is, however, problematic. Indians are traditionally thought by scholars to have believed in rebirth already long before the time of the Buddha, and to have perhaps contributed the idea to early Greek thinkers, particularly Pythagoras.

What else did the Dharma teach? Neither Megasthenes nor the inscriptions tell us directly. Fortunately, however, Pyrrho does. The most important single element of the Early Buddhist teachings, known as the *Trilakṣaṇa*, or 'three characteristics' (of *dharmas* 'things'), was a slap at authentic, attested Early Zoroastrianism and attested Early Brahmanism.[103] He taught that *pragmata* 'matters, affairs'—including people—do not have their own innate self-identity (Skt. *anātman*, Greek *adiaphora*). This denies the Zoroastrian and Brahmanist belief in the soul—explicitly mentioned twice in Strabo's account[104]—and suggests that the only connection between a person in this life and a person born in another life was the good done in this life, the "merit" repeatedly mentioned by Devānāṃpriya Priyadarśi, and perhaps also the causation mentioned by Megasthenes in his section on the Śramaṇas. Although as noted above he remarks that *some* Śramaṇas preach about the afterlife ("Hades") to try to influence people to be good, clearly other Śramaṇas taught the *Trilakṣaṇa* and other more challenging things, as study of Pyrrho's thought reveals, and as is partly recorded by Megasthenes as well. The approaches of the two different groups of Śramaṇas thus appear to represent *two distinct Buddhist sects* in the process of formation.

That brings us back to Pyrrho. Both he and Megasthenes visited northwestern India, mainly Gandhāra, but Alexander—and perhaps his court—apparently campaigned as far east as Magadha, though not all the way to Pāṭaliputra. Their reflections of the Buddhism—or rather, "Buddhisms"—they encountered are fully compatible, but there is much more depth to what is reflected in Pyrrhonism, including some

---

However, it seems highly doubtful that these ideas existed in India much before the time of Buddha. Even traditional Normative Buddhist accounts indicate that what motivated Buddha to set out on the difficult path leading to his enlightenment was his perception of sickness, old age, and death—or, simply, death—without any suggestion of the ideas of rebirth or samsara. Belief in karma and rebirth is now generally thought to have appeared at about the same time as Buddhism. See the Prologue for discussion of its clear Early Zoroastrian source.

[103] I.e., the forms of these belief systems attested in contemporaneous or nearly contemporaneous texts.

[104] Strabo XV, 1, 59. An additional passage that does *not* go back to Megasthenes—as Strabo explicitly tells us—might not represent actual Indian beliefs: "And writers mention similar opinions of the Brachmanes about the seed and the soul, as also several other opinions of theirs. And they also weave in myths, like Plato, about the immortality of the soul and the judgments in Hades and other things of this kind." (Jones 1930: 7:103). However, the Brahmanists' core belief in an immortal *soul* is separately and explicitly attested in Megasthenes' account.

apparently isolated practices and comments in the ancient testimonies best explained as artifacts of Pyrrho's Buddhism, which clearly belongs to the more "elegant" variety.

Pyrrho's radically new *philosophia* taught about *causes*, specifically, the causes of *pathē* 'suffering, passion' and a way to achieve *apatheia* 'passionlessness; without suffering' and *ataraxia* 'undisturbedness, peace', exactly as Buddha had taught before him. Pyrrho also taught that because nothing has its own logical self-identity, our inductive and deductive faculties cannot tell us whether conflicting ethical matters are just or unjust, good or bad, or true or false "absolutely".

Like the Buddha, Pyrrho taught that his way was not easy: one needed to struggle against *pragmata* '(conflicting) matters, affairs, events' with both the body and the mind. Accordingly, he practiced a mild form of asceticism, including early yoga-meditation. Timon and others repeatedly refer to Pyrrho as being "uniformly unmoved", and Diogenes Laertius remarks that he withstood extreme pain, such as from caustic remedies or surgery on a wound, without even frowning.[105] These descriptions accord perfectly with the account of the Śramaṇas by Megasthenes and other early Greek witnesses, as well as with what is believed to be the general thrust of early Indian yoga-meditation.[106]

Pyrrho, and also his student Philo of Athens, were both observed "babbling" to themselves.[107] Unfortunately, we do not know what exactly they were saying, or why, but when asked what he was doing, Pyrrho replied that he was "practicing to be virtuous."[108] Could they have been saying something in another language?[109]

Pyrrho was celibate. He also "would withdraw from the world and live in solitude, rarely showing himself to his relatives,"[110] and

[105] D.L. IX, 67. Cf. Clayman (2009: 40), who like Bett (2000) suggests Pyrrho may well have learned this "indifference" to pain from the Indians.

[106] Bronkhorst (1986).

[107] Pyrrho, in D.L. IX, 64, Καταληφθεὶς δέ ποτε καὶ αὑτῷ λαλῶν καὶ ἐρωτηθεὶς τὴν αἰτίαν ἔφη μελετᾶν χρηστὸς εἶναι. Philo, in D.L. IX, 69.

[108] Bett (2000: 94n67) discusses this from the point of view of a possible violation of Pyrrho's own philosophy, but as he notes, it does not have to be taken that way. Cf. the discussion of Hume's "sceptical solution" in Chapter Four.

[109] Most Greeks thought foreign languages sounded like "babbling". Pyrrho liked Homer and frequently quoted him (Bett 2000: 82), but Homer's works were practically sacred in ancient Greece, and well known; no Greek would ever have referred to someone reciting Homeric verses as λαλῶν "babbling". Possibly they were reciting something from memory, such as a Buddhist oral text Pyrrho had learned in Central Asia or India.

[110] D.L. IX, 63.

frequently went off wandering. These practices accord with the wandering, solitary life of the Early Buddhist 'Forest-dwelling' Śramaṇas, according to tradition and later practice. The mention of "withdrawing from the world" and family reflects the stereotypical Buddhist expression "to leave the family", which means in practice "to become a Buddhist ascetic practitioner" (in Pyrrho's day, a *Śramaṇa*; later, a *bhikṣu* 'monk'). It is mentioned again, with a full description of what it entailed, in the later account of Buddhist monks in Porphyry's *De abstinentia*, discussed below.

Although Pyrrho himself practiced asceticism for long periods away from people, Timon, his most important disciple, remained a layman. He went off wandering sometimes with Pyrrho, but he was married, he lived in the city, and he had children. We know that he taught his son Xanthus medicine, and Diogenes Laertius remarks, "This son was a man of high repute".[111] Although Pyrrho's ascetic "rustic" path ultimately did not survive in Greece, Timon's "urbane" path did survive, and was practiced by other physicians into Late Antiquity, as attested by Sextus Empiricus, our most important source on Late Pyrrhonism. In this way, and by his introduction of the Problem of the Criterion, Pyrrho had a lasting effect on European thought, as discussed in Chapter Four.

On the Meaning of *Śramaṇa* in Premodern Sources

Until fairly recently, the traditional meaning of *śramaṇa* was clear and uncontested, at least outside India: it meant 'Buddhist practitioner', and later 'Buddhist monk'. Unfortunately, its meaning has become unclear due to the frequent, wholly unjustified misinterpretation of the word in numerous works based on late attempts to project this or that non-Buddhist system—most frequently Jainism—back to the days of the Buddha, or even earlier. It has thus been widely claimed that there were *other* ascetics in the Buddha's day (or even before him) and in Early Buddhism who were also called *śramaṇas*. The word has

[111] D.L. IX, 109–110, citing "Sōtion in his eleventh book", referring to Sotion of Alexandria, a second century BC doxographer who is one of Diogenes Laertius's most important sources; the work is undoubtedly Sotion's lost *Diadochē*, which is on philosophical lineages.

therefore been mistranslated, by too many, as "ascetic". Although such views are based on historically unreliable Indian accounts composed and written down many centuries later, they are followed now by most modern Indologists.[112]

Nevertheless, all of the *dated* or *datable* accounts of Indian religious-philosophical beliefs (most of which are in foreign sources), from Antiquity well into the Middle Ages, use the word *śramaṇa* (also spelled *sarmana, samana, ṣaman,* etc.) to refer specifically and exclusively to Buddhist practitioners,[113] often explicitly in distinction to Brahmanists. The distinction is earliest made in the account of Megasthenes. The same distinction is made in the Major Inscriptions of the Mauryan period, both in the Brahmi script versions as well as those in Kharosthi script and in Greek. The Major Inscriptions repeatedly mention the dichotomy between Brāḥmaṇas and Śramaṇas or Śramaṇas and Brāḥmaṇas, who are mentioned together in most of the inscriptions. The two are explicitly referred to as "sects", and in several instances the existence of other unnamed "sects" is mentioned.[114] This is explicit in the Prakrit versions of the synoptic inscriptions. The fragmentary Greek version of the Thirteenth Rock Edict from Kandahar also says, "And the King further considered that those living there, as many *Brāḥmaṇas, Śramaṇas* and others debating the *dhamma,* should keep in mind what are of interest to the King."[115] The expression "others *debating*" the Dharma[116] explicitly means, in Greek, "members of other sects".[117]

[112] The idea was promoted already in the early nineteenth century by Colebrooke, who is quoted at length in a footnote by McCrindle (1877: 105n1). There continue to be many arguments in support of this view, e.g., "Like Buddhism, Jainism was born in Greater Magadha. The Jina and the Buddha are supposed to have been contemporaries, and there are indeed early buddhist text [*sic*] that mention Mahāvīra's demise. The two movements were aware of each other's existence, and there are good reasons to believe that they influenced each other. This influence was, as far as the earliest period is concerned, largely unidirectional: there is for this period much more evidence for jaina influence on Buddhism than the other way round" (Bronkhorst 2011: 130); cf. Bronkhorst (2009).

[113] See further below in this chapter.

[114] See the discussion of the Mauryan inscriptions in Chapter Three.

[115] Halkias (2013), q.v. for the Greek text.

[116] As Halkias (2013: 86) notes, the text uses Greek *eusebeia* "piety" to translate *dharma* (Pali *dhamma*).

[117] The inscription's οἱ . . . διατρίβοντες means "the debaters; the sectarians (members of sects)".

Finally, where the "Seventh Pillar Edict" on the Delhi-Topra pillar mentions the sects, it gives them in the way they are mentioned in the Major Rock Edicts—that is, "Śramaṇas and Brāḥmaṇas", occasionally adding "and other sects", with two notable exceptions. It reads, "Some (*Mahāmātras*) were ordered by me to busy themselves with the affairs of the *Saṃgha*; likewise others were ordered by me to busy themselves also with the Brāḥmaṇas (and) Ājīvikas; others were ordered by me to busy themselves with the Nirgranthas [Jains]; others were ordered by me to busy themselves also with various (other) sects; (thus) different *Mahāmātras* (are busying themselves) specially with different (congregations)."[118] It is notable that this inscription explicitly mentions the Buddhists, using the term *Saṃgha* for the expected *Śramaṇa*, showing explicitly that the inscription is the product of a much later age. By using the term *saṃgha* 'the community of Buddhist monks (*bhikṣus*) and nuns (*bhikṣunīs*)'—referring specifically to Buddhist practitioners who resided in monasteries under a monastic rule (however primitive)—the inscription shows that the term *śramaṇa* had already passed out of common usage to refer to Buddhist practitioners. It is now known that organized monasteries (*vihāras*) did not exist anywhere—at least, outside of Central Asia—before the Kushan period, and were introduced to India quite suddenly in the first century AD. The earlier *ārāmas* were very primitive affairs and do not begin to suggest an organized conception of Buddhism.[119] The new monastic ideal contrasts very sharply with the earlier ideal, going back to the time of the Buddha himself, of the solitary, wandering "forest" Śramaṇa and of the less ascetic, but still solitary, "urban" Śramaṇa, as described by Megasthenes. It must also be stressed that in none of the Major Inscriptions of the Mauryas is the term *śramaṇa* used in the generic sense "ascetic". The term used throughout the Major Inscriptions that is regularly translated by Hultzsch as 'ascetic' is *pavajita-* (Sanskrit *pravrajita-*), which actually means 'wanderer, homeless one'. The word *śramaṇa* is never used in

[118] "Seventh Pillar Edict" (Delhi-Topra), line 25, text and translation by Hultzsch (1925: 132, 136), q.v. for a clear rubbing. On the spuriousness of this text (as a Major Mauryan inscription) see Appendix C.

[119] Pointed out already by Marshall (1951). As noted above, Schopen has established that the Vinaya does not reflect Early Buddhism, as once thought, but *very late* Normative Buddhism.

ancient texts of any kind as a generic with the meaning 'ascetic' used for practitioners of any and all traditions.[120] It meant specifically and only 'Buddhist practitioner'.

However, a recent study argues that there is one exception to the rule that *śramaṇa* always means 'Buddhist practitioner' in non-Indian texts.[121] The putative example is a passage from the fragmentary Greek account of India by the Syriac writer Bardaisan (Bardesanes) of Edessa (AD 154–222) quoted by Porphyry (AD 234–ca. 300) in his *De abstinentia*, a book promoting vegetarianism.[122] Porphyry's account of the Indians begins with a very brief introductory remark in which he notes that the Indian religious thinkers are divided into two kinds, the *Brachmanes* or 'Brahmins' and the *Samanaioi* or 'Śramaṇas', followed by his discussion proper, which includes a section on the *Brachmanes*, a section on the *Samanaioi*, and a section on the ancient Indian sect that practiced suicide by fire, the Gymnetae. The article claims that the word *samanaioi*—an Aramaic-Greek hybrid plural[123] of *samana*, a Prakrit form of *śramaṇa*—refers in this account to *Jain* monks, not Buddhists. It is further contended that the third section of the account, in particular, reflects Jainism, not Buddhism. It is thus necessary to discuss the argument in some detail.

To begin with, it must be remarked that even in the third part of Porphyry's account there is nothing specifically Jain in it except the general idea of planned suicide, and that is described as being by fire,

[120] It is also not so used even in more recent ones. The word *śramaṇa* occurs once in the *Āraṇyaka Brāḥmaṇa*, a text on a Brahmanist practitioner who meditates in the forest. This is an isolated occurrence, and an obvious imitation of the Buddhists' Forest-dweller *śramaṇa*, yet it has been taken as "proof" that there were *śramaṇas* before the Buddha, and so on. The *Āraṇyaka Brāḥmaṇa* is undated and undatable to any such early period, and cannot prove anything about it. Bronkhorst (1986) has already shown that another such "early" Brahmanist text, the *Bṛhadāraṇyaka Upaniṣad*, is later than Buddhism and imitates it.

[121] Deeg and Gardner (2009).

[122] Porphyry, *De abstinentia* IV, 18.1–3. It is often noted that the text is also to be found in Stobaeus, *Eclogae* I, 3.56 (Wachsmuth and Hense 1884: 1:66–70), but the references therein to Indians have nothing to do with the section on the Śramaṇas in Porphyry's *De abstinentia*, and do not even mention any form of the word *śramaṇa*.

[123] Winter (1999: 115) remarks that the ending *-aioi* of the Greek form *Samanaioi* is basically a Greek rendering of the Aramaic plural ending *-aijâ*, seen in many names of groups in the Near East.

which all scholars, including the authors, note is very un-Jain. The other details are in general very un-Jain also, as the authors themselves remark in several instances, and there are many other un-Jain things elsewhere in the account. Moreover, the term *Samanaioi* is used *only*[124] in the *second* section of Porphyry's account, which is from Bardaisan, who regularly repeats the word *Samanaioi* throughout the section. It is an absolutely clear, unambiguous description of a day in a Normative Buddhist monastery. This ought to be conclusive on its own, but there is more, and it decisively rules out all speculation.

The third section—the part the authors contend is more similar to Jainism than to Buddhism—was taken by Porphyry essentially word for word from Josephus's book *Bellum Iudaicum* 'The Jewish War', and originally had nothing whatsoever to do with the account of the *Samanaioi* in Bardaisan.[125vii] The third section describes the ancient Indian Gymnetae sect, which has been wrongly considered by most scholars to belong to the Śramaṇa sect, despite the fact that its followers are never called Śramaṇas.

The Josephus passage describes this distinctive ancient "Indian" sect of people, men and women, who were so eager to enter the next life that they often committed suicide, typically by burning themselves alive on a funeral pyre. As noted above, Strabo describes them and calls them the Gymnetae 'the Naked ones'. The best-known Classical accounts of them focus on Calanus, who joined Alexander the Great's court when the Greeks were in Gandhāra, accompanied him back to Pasargadae in Persia, and committed suicide there in the presence of Alexander and many others. This sect is thought to be unknown in Indian sources (all of which are *many* centuries later than the Greek sources), despite attempts to find it in them. It is quite clear that they were a non-Buddhist sect—a numerically very small one according to comments in

[124] That is, leaving aside the mention of the Samanaioi in the introductory section. Porphyry describes the Brachmanes, followed by the Samanaioi, and refers to both explicitly by name in their respective sections. In the third section, on the Indian Gymnetae sect, he does not mention them by name, nor does he explicitly distinguish them from the other Indian thinkers he describes. He also does not mention that he has taken his material from more than one source. This unclarity has led to modern scholars' misinterpretations.

[125] For details, see Endnote vii.

the earliest sources—which died out before the end of Late Antiquity and the beginning of the Middle Ages, at which time the Indians began to write something very roughly approximating history.[126]

Unlike the third section, the second section—the immediately preceding paragraph in Porphyry's text—is indeed from Bardaisan, who does use the term *śramaṇa*, in the form *samanaioi* (a Greek form of the Aramaic plural of Prakrit *samana* ~ Sanskrit *śramaṇa*) to refer to the people he describes, who are certainly Buddhists.[127] In fact, Bardaisan very strikingly repeats the word *samanaioi* "Śramaṇas" *five times* in that short paragraph, which is unambiguously about life in a Buddhist monastery,[128] and he stops repeating the word *samanaioi* at the point where the content no longer describes anything recognizably Buddhist.[129] Bardaisan's text quoted by Porphyry clearly describes a monastery and its inmates, monks, both late developments typical of Normative Buddhism. In the much earlier account by Megasthenes, he describes Śramaṇas, the 'ascetic practitioners' of *Early* Buddhism, who were not "monks" and did not have monasteries,[130] so the term for 'Buddhist' in foreign sources had already become fixed as *Śramaṇa* or a variant of that word. Half a millennium later, the term *samanaioi* "Śramaṇas" in Bardaisan still unambiguously refers specifically and only to *Buddhist* practitioners.

[126] See above in this chapter on the similarities and differences between this sect and the Pre–Pure Land sect.

[127] Winter (1999: 120), though unaware that the third part of Porphyry's section on the Indians has been taken from Josephus, nevertheless correctly identifies the *Samanaioi* of Porphyry with Buddhist monks, and explains the Syriac intermediary form, which comes from Bardaisan. He also cites an interesting Zoroastrian inscription relevant to the identification of the word *Śramaṇa* as the term for the practitioners of a particular religion: "Auf Gleiches weist auch die Verwendung des Terminus in der Inschrift des Kartir, eines zoroastrischen Oberpriesters, . . . wo *ṣmny* neben der Brahmanen, Juden, Judenchristen u. a. also Opfer der Religionsverfolgungen aufgelistet werden."

[128] Deeg and Gardner (2009) admit this in their discussion of the second part of Porphyry's text (which they clearly did not realize is unconnected to the third part).

[129] In fact, just at that point the text explicitly mentions Brahmanists and the section taken from Josephus begins.

[130] The term *Śramaṇa* retained its original meaning *in the Indian context* even after the development of Normative Buddhism. This semantic conservatism may be the reason for the shift to the use of *bhikṣu* "monk" and *bhikṣunī* "nun" when Buddhist practitioners mostly became inmates of monasteries.

Another mistaken argument about *Śramaṇa* has been made on the basis of a passage in Clement of Alexandria (mid-second to early third century AD),[131] in which a long "laundry list" of examples of religious practitioners among different peoples is given, including the "Indians" and others in their vicinity. Clement mentions the *Samanaioi*, the "philosophers" of the Bactrians, meaning the Kushans (who in his day ruled Central Asia and northern India);[132] the *Brachmanai* and *Sarmanai*,[133] including an account of the Forest-dweller (*Hylobioi*) subtype of the Sarmanai, in a passage specifically dependent on Megasthenes' account;[134] and unnamed "people in India who revere *Boutta* 'Buddha' like a god because of his remarkable sanctity."[135]

The argument—already made by Colebrooke in the early nineteenth century and noted by McCrindle in his translation of the fragments of Megasthenes later in the century—is that the last-named group were Buddhists, while the Sarmanai were Jains and others.[136] In fact, the text allows no such conclusion. Clement simply *lists* all "Indian philosophers" of any kind that he has found in his reading, and clearly has no

[131] Clement of Alexandria, *Stromateis* I, XV, 71, 3–5 (Stählin 1906: 2:45–46): Φιλοσοφία τοίνυν, πολυωφελές τι χρῆμα, πάλαι μὲν ἤκμασε παρὰ βαρβάροις κατὰ τὰ ἔθνη διαλάμψασα, ὕστερον δὲ καὶ εἰς Ἕλληνας κατῆλθεν. Προέστησαν δ' αὐτῆς Αἰγυπτίων τε οἱ προφῆται καὶ Ἀσσυρίων οἱ Χαλδαῖοι καὶ Γαλατῶν οἱ Δρυΐδαι καὶ Σαμαναῖοι Βάκτρων καὶ Κελτῶν οἱ φιλοσοφήσαντες καὶ Περσῶν οἱ Μάγοι (οἳ μαγείᾳ καὶ τοῦ Σωτῆρος προεμήνυσαν τὴν γένεσιν, ἀστέρος αὐτοῖς καθηγουμένου εἰς τὴν Ἰουδαίαν ἀφικνούμενοι γῆν) Ἰνδῶν τε οἱ γυμνοσοφισταί, ἄλλοι γε φιλόσοφοι βάρβαροι. διττὸν δὲ τούτων τὸ γένος, οἳ μὲν Σαρμᾶναι αὐτῶν, οἳ δὲ Βραχμᾶναι χαλούμενοι. καὶ τῶν Σαρμανῶν οἱ Ὑλόβιοι προσαγορευόμενοι οὔτε πόλεις οἰκοῦσιν οὔτε στέγας ἔχουσιν, δένδρων δὲ ἀμφιέννυνται φλοιοῖς καὶ ἀκρόδρυα σιτοῦνται καὶ ὕδωρ ταῖς χερσὶ πίνουσιν, οὐ γάμον, οὐ παιδοποιίαν ἴσασιν, ὥσπερ οἱ νῦν Ἐγκρατηταὶ καλούμενοι. εἰσὶ δὲ τῶν Ἰνδῶν οἱ τοῖς Βούττα πειθόμενοι παραγγέλμασιν. ὃν δι' ὑπερβολὴν σεμνότητος ὡς θεὸν τετιμήκασι.

[132] Clement's spelling *Samanaioi* here derives specifically from Bardaisan's Syriac works, and so too does his identification of the Bactrians with the Kushans (whose proximal homeland was indeed Bactria).

[133] Modern editors' correction of the extant manuscripts of Strabo, which all have "Garman-", is due primarily to Clement's text. The fragmentary Greek version of "Aśoka's" Thirteenth Rock Edict from Kandahar also has the expected *S*-. See the discussion above in this chapter.

[134] The information is most probably from Megasthenes' *Indica*, though whether Clement took it directly from Megasthenes or indirectly from another source is unclear.

[135] This passage, which is unique to Clement, contains the earliest reference to the name *Buddha* in any Western source.

[136] Colebrooke, cited in (McCrindle (1889: 98n1).

idea that any of them are or are not the same as any others, because he is absolutely neutral on the point.[137] Moreover, it must be stressed that the three types (including the Kushans) in the "Indian" category belong to three different sources and at least two different periods.

An additional problem with the view that there were many other kinds of *śramaṇas* at the time of the Buddha is that it requires these putative other traditions to have *ceased* using the term not long after the Buddha's lifetime (or at any rate before the testimonies of Megasthenes, the Major Inscriptions of the Mauryas, the early Chinese translations, and the medieval Islamic sources, which contain no examples of such putative non-Buddhist uses) and then, after a hiatus of over a millennium, to have resumed using the term. That is of course absurd. They clearly began using the term for their own practitioners only after it had become well established as a term for Buddhist practitioners, and after Buddhism had become widespread and extremely influential in India.[138]

A recent discussion of the Greek sources by Wilhelm Halbfass presents the typical position to the effect that *śramaṇa* refers to all kinds of ascetics. It then asks, "does Megasthenes mention Buddhism at all?"[139] The answer, citing scholars' confusion and creative attempts to overcome the resulting problem, is again negative. Yet the author asks further,

[137] The attempt of McCrindle to interpret the last statement in Clement's account as "ambiguous", so that the last example could alternatively refer directly to the previous one, is not correct. The text is not ambiguous, but it also does not tell us one way or the other if the *Boutta* worshippers had anything to do with the Sarmanes. Unfortunately, Clement does not identify his sources.

[138] One must also take into account the fact that in several other attested instances new Buddhist-like religious systems developed—including in China, Tibet, and Japan—through the adoption of many of the trappings, practices, and beliefs of the Buddhists by people who seem to have differed from them originally. The results—"religious" Taoism, Bon, and Shinto, respectively—vary in their degree of difference from Normative Buddhism in the respective countries. Bon is unattested in any form during the Tibetan Empire (Beckwith 1987/1993; 2012a), not to speak of even earlier, despite claims to that effect in traditional Bonpo texts. From its earliest attestations in actual religious texts (ca. tenth century AD), it is what may be called a variant form of the early Rnyingma school of Tibetan Buddhism, which dates to the same period (Robert Mayer, p.c., 2011). Likewise, modern Taoism is a system very similar to Chinese Buddhism, and Shinto is a system similar to Japanese Buddhism.

[139] Halbfass (1995: 204).

> But how do we account for Megasthenes' own apparent silence concerning Buddhism, in view of the fact that he visited Pāṭaliputra and should, if we accept the traditions about this city, have noticed conspicuous Buddhist monuments and, moreover, have heard about Buddhist life and thought? Dihle says that for Megasthenes the Buddhists were still too insignificant to be mentioned separately (". . . während für Megasthenes, also vor Aśoka, die Buddhisten noch keine Rolle in Indien spielten, die ihre eigene Erwähnung gerechtfertigt hätte").[140] However, this would be rather strange—"chose étrange," as Henri de Lubac notes[141]—if indeed, Buddhism had already been alive and growing, and enjoying the patronage of various rulers in this area, for a period of two centuries. Could it really have been that inconspicuous and insignificant that Megasthenes either overlooked it or, provided that he heard about it, chose not to mention it at all?[142]

Halbfass unfortunately then disregards his perceptive observation and buries it in a mass of speculation buttressed by the citation of other similar works.

In short, few, if any, scholars have carefully read and thought about the contents of Megasthenes' account on the one hand, and on the other hand at least considered the possibility that Buddhism might have changed somewhat over the many centuries of its existence, such that what Megasthenes describes must be earlier forms of Buddhism different from the forms of Buddhism attested many centuries later.

The remarkably unanimous testimony of all *non*-Indian sources, most of which are far earlier than the actual dates of any Indian sources, is that the term *śramaṇa* meant exclusively 'Buddhist practitioner' in all early languages in which it is attested,[143] including Chinese 沙門 (Mandarin *shāmén*),[144] Sogdian *šmn-* (*šaman-*), Khotanese *ṣṣamaṇa*, and

[140] Dihle (1964: 63); that is, "because for Megasthenes, that is before Aśoka, the Buddhists did not yet play any role in India that would have justified reference to them."

[141] Lubac (1952).

[142] Halbfass (1995: 205).

[143] Mayrhofer (1976: 3:387–388) cites the use of *śramaṇa* "in den buddh. Bereich und indirekt nach dem Westen", giving the examples cited here, among others; note that the usual Tokharian A stem is *ṣamn-* (Poucha 1955: 337–338). Cf. Winter (1999: 120n486).

[144] This is perhaps the most frequently used among a number of different early Chinese transcriptions of the word.

Tokharian B *ṣamāne*, Tokharian A *ṣāmaṃ*.[145] Usages by other religious traditions in India are not datable in any scientific way to a period earlier than at least a half millennium after the Buddha's death around the middle of the first millennium BC.

Observations by foreign visitors and the usage by the ruler Devānāmpriya Priyadarśi in the authentic Major Inscriptions of the Mauryas in the early third century BC agree that there were Brāḥmaṇas, Śramaṇas, and "other sects". That unambiguously means that the followers of the "other sects" *could not* be Brāḥmaṇas or Śramaṇas. Moreover, the so-called Seventh Pillar Edict on the Delhi-Topra column refers to the Jains and Ājīvīkas as *pāsaṃḍā* '(philosophical-religious) schools, sects', *not* as *śramaṇas*. All foreign sources too are unanimous in saying the Śramaṇas were specifically Buddhist practitioners, as shown above. The only conclusion that can be drawn is that the Śramaṇas in Early Buddhism and in all dated early historical sources were Buddhists, based on the unusually consistent, clear evidence, versus the lack of any reliable, dated evidence whatsoever in support of the idea that the word *śramaṇa* ever referred to "sects" or "ascetic practitioners" in general in Antiquity. At some time in Late Antiquity or the Middle Ages—if not even later—the Jains and other non-Buddhist religious practitioners in India adopted the word to refer to their own ascetics and projected themselves back to, or beyond, the time of the historical Buddha.[146] Because in the Kushan period (at the earliest), or later, the Buddhists had to defend themselves from the criticism by the Jains and others, and because by the time all this happened Buddhism had become largely

[145] Adams (1999: 649).

[146] Modern scholars' confusion about the word *śramaṇa* appears to be due above all to the Jains' creative attempts to assert their chronological and other priority over the Buddhists. As noted above, these efforts are strikingly similar to the attempts of modern Bon adherents to do the same thing. No actual hard evidence, textual or other, has ever been produced to support such claims in either instance. See the very careful comments of Mette (1995), who, though evidently pro-Jain, essentially admits that Buddhism seems to be in all respects earlier than Jainism. The Jains cannot be demonstrated to have even existed before the date of the "Seventh Pillar Edict of Aśoka", which is traditionally treated as the last part of the Delhi-Topra pillar inscription, but is an *obvious late addition* to the existing inscriptions on that monument; as noted above, the addition dates to the Normative Buddhist period, evidently under the Kushans. See Appendix C for detailed discussion.

monastic, the Buddhists included references to the founders of the other religious-philosophical traditions as contemporaries of the Buddha so that they could show how the Buddha was superior to them in wisdom and in every other way and thus defeated them. The idea of linear chronology has long been thought to have been absent in early India, and certainly there is no evidence of any conception of history per se there until well into the Middle Ages, so the Buddhists did not realize that by placing their opponents in the traditional Normative Buddhist background of Saka-Kushan period Magadha they were in effect legitimizing claims that the other religions' followers would eventually make. Scholars have been misled by this far too long. There is absolutely no evidence for the usage of the word *śramaṇa* by any non-Buddhist traditions in sources actually attested and dated to Antiquity through the early Middle Ages. The other traditions adopted the term—and much else—from Buddhism, in the Saka-Kushan period or later times.

This is not an isolated point. There is also no evidence for the existence of the term *bhikṣu* 'Buddhist monk' (or its Prakrit analogues) before the appearance of Normative Buddhism several hundred years after the Buddha's lifetime, suggesting that there was something that distinguished those who were so named from those who were called *śramaṇas* in the earlier sources. Furthermore, there is no indication of anything like a *saṃgha* 'community of monks' in Megasthenes' account, his use of the term *śramaṇa* contains no suggestion that the Buddhist practitioners he describes were anything at all like "monks" per se, and it has already been demonstrated that there were no monasteries, and no monastic code either.

The logical conclusion to be drawn is that during the period reflected in the teachings of Pyrrho and the account of Megasthenes, the late fourth century BC, and still in the early Mauryan period, there was not yet a *saṃgha*, nor monks, nor monasteries, nor a Vinaya, nor full divinization of the Buddha. These all appeared as essential elements of Normative Buddhism, which flowered in the Saka-Kushan period,[147] when the old solitary ascetic ideal was replaced (though not

[147] Although the Vinaya texts are all dated or datable only to the fifth century AD, as pointed out by Schopen (2004: 94), they are chronologically layered texts. It seems likely that the earliest layers date back perhaps as far as the Saka-Kushan period, but not earlier, because monasteries are not attested before the ones discovered at Taxila dated to the first century AD.

completely) by the communal, organized monastic ideal, which was then projected back to the time of the Buddha. However, this was not done consistently or thoroughly, so that an older picture of Early Buddhism is sometimes preserved side by side with the newer picture of it.

THE ANCIENT INDIAN GYMNETAE SECT AND EARLY BUDDHISM

The Indian philosophical-religious teacher best known in Classical sources is Calanus, who met the Greeks when Alexander of Macedon invaded Gandhāra. He joined Alexander's court and went with him to Pasargadae in Persia, where he committed suicide in 323 BC, despite Alexander's pleas that he not do it. His chosen method was to cast himself onto a funeral pyre, as did several others noted in the West, apparently with the aim of going to Heaven in the quickest, most direct way possible.[148] This made a powerful impression on the Greeks.

The Buddha says not a word about God or about Heaven and going there, he rejects the idea of inherent personal identities (including the "soul"), and he talks about *nirvāṇa* instead, Pyrrho's *ataraxia*—calm, undisturbedness—here on earth, in this life. Buddha and Pyrrho say one should have "no views" and just rely on *custom* and the *phenomena*, which is what people actually do anyway. Timon says, "The phenomena[149] are omnipotent wherever they appear."[150] The Late Pyrrhonists and the Neo-Pyrrhonians say the same thing. But if we choose phenomena, what are we *not* choosing? The converse of phenomena is "non-phenomena". The "non-phenomenal world" would be either the one in our minds (problematically conceived of as distinct from "the world") or the world of God—which is also problematically distinct from "the world". So the Buddha,

[148] Many Chinese and Japanese Buddhist monks committed suicide by burning themselves to death, from medieval to recent times, as shown very thoroughly and clearly by Kleine (2006); but the participants' motivations, which Kleine discusses, do not appear to have anything in common with those of Calanus and the other followers of the ancient Gymnetae sect.

[149] In Greek *phainomenon* 'the apparent, that which appears'; see the following note.

[150] Timon, *Indalmoi*, quoted in D.L. IX, 105: ἀλλὰ τὸ φαινόμενον πάντη σθένει οὗπερ ἂν ἔλθῃ ; text from Hicks (1925: 2:516–517), who translates it memorably, "But the apparent is omnipotent wherever it goes". Bett (2000: 85) translates it more literally: "But the appearance is powerful everywhere, wherever it comes."

and Pyrrho following him, and two millennia later Hume once again, were actually reacting against one or another theistic system.[151][viii]

This would explain the apparent problem of the "missing God" and related elements in Normative Buddhism. If the missing element were put back in, one would have a monotheistic Central Eurasian Culture Complex belief system, with the God of Heaven, the lord and his comitatus, suicide of the latter on the death of their lord, and rebirth for them all in Heaven. This must seem rather close to the sect of Calanus, but the Gymnetae cannot be identified with any known Buddhist group. In the Greek sources the sect's followers are never called *Śramaṇas*, they go naked, and suicide makes absolutely no sense in nontheistic "elite" Early Buddhism, which is openly devoted to achieving a satisfactory life on earth. However, there are similarities between the ideas of the Gymnetae and "popular" Early Buddhism, including the system described in the Major Inscriptions of Devānāṃpriya Priyadarśi. That raises the question of theistic elements or trends in attested Early Buddhism.

The earliest historically attested theistic Buddhist sect is Pure Land. The sect first appears in the *Pratyutpanna Samādhi Sūtra*, which was translated into Chinese between AD 178 and 189. This is a text radically different not only from Early Buddhism but even from the putatively "early" Normative Buddhist texts of the Pali Canon and the Gāndhārī documents, which mostly date to approximately the same period. Pure Land obviously distinguishes its teachings from something else that it strongly rejects—namely, attested Early Buddhism—in quite the same way that attested Early Buddhism, including its Pyrrhonian offshoot, distinguishes itself sharply from theistic belief systems. It is thus no surprise that the followers of Pure Land and other related sects eventually came to call themselves, collectively, *Mahāyāna* 'the Great Vehicle', in explicit contrast to what they derisively called *Hīnayāna* 'the Little Vehicle'.

The early Pure Land Buddhism of the *Pratyutpanna Samādhi Sūtra* apparently (and effectively) has God (Amitābha), Heaven (Sukhāvatī), and rebirth in Heaven. For a Central Eurasian, all of these are comfortable old Central Eurasian Culture Complex ideas, and for a Persian,

[151] See Chapter Four for detailed analysis. On the possibility that he was reacting against *Greek* theism, see Endnote viii.

they are (not coincidentally) comfortable old Early Zoroastrian ideas too. Yet the text does explicitly reject antilogies,[152] so it openly accepts the Early Buddhist teaching of *anātman* '(things have) no (inherent) self-identity', Pyrrho's *adiaphora,* and along with it the teaching of impermanence: Amitābha is actually, explicitly, *not* an eternal being. Several of the characteristic features of early Pure Land are mentioned in Megasthenes' description of the unnamed Pre–Pure Land sect inserted into the description of Brahmanism in the received text of Strabo, as discussed above.

Perhaps first there was the religious belief system of the Central Eurasian Culture Complex, which reencountered the related system of Early Zoroastrianism when the Achaemenid Persian Empire conquered Central Asia. Zoroastrianism introduced the idea of the absolute opposition of the Truth and the Lie. Then the Buddha reacted against absolutist-perfectionist distinctions and eternalism in general. When the Pre–Pure Land sect developed, it restored God (as Amitābha or another "Buddha", depending on the text) and rebirth in Heaven, while nevertheless retaining the *Trilakṣana* teaching of *anātman* (philosophically expressed as the invalidity of antilogies) and the teaching of *anitya* 'impermanence', as well as the teaching of *duḥkha* 'uneasiness'.

Although the Pre–Pure Land sect was clearly not the same as the non-Buddhist sect of Calanus, in Megasthenes' day it was evidently not yet thought of as strictly Buddhist either. His description of Pre–Pure Land, as preserved in Strabo, is in the section explicitly devoted to Brahmanism, despite the explicit Pre–Pure Land belief in the invalidity of antilogies, and thus in *anātman.* But the Brahmanists worshipped a creator God and believed in an afterlife, so it is not totally unreasonable for the Pre–Pure Land sect to be described there. The Pre–Pure Land sect is therefore, perhaps, still to be distinguished from Buddhism in the very earliest sources.

However, most of the features of Pre–Pure Land are elements of the system called the *Dharma* in the Major Inscriptions of King Devānāṃpriya Priyadarśi, a mere half century after Megasthenes. It thus appears that Pre–Pure Land became a minimally Buddhist sect,

[152] The most famous Pure Land rejection of antilogies is in the "longer" *Sukhāvatīvyūha Sūtra* (translated into Chinese as the *Wu liang shou ching* 無量壽經), a later work.

"proto-Pure Land", by the time of that king. The features of this system are discussed further in Chapter Three.

When the Pure Land we know is first attested in the late second century AD, it includes several modified absolutist-perfectionist features, but it is nevertheless still a fully Buddhist sect, regardless of the contradictions.

All of this is remarkably similar to the religious aspects of the Central Eurasian Culture Complex and its core sociopolitical-religious element, the comitatus.[153] The main focus of the comitatus was Heaven.[154] Its young aristocrat warrior members needed to associate themselves with a Lord to make sure they got to Heaven, because a real Lord had Divine ("sacral") ancestral blood, and swearing an oath or vow to be "friends" with him in this life and the next ensured rebirth in Heaven. That the comitatus and the lords would, for whatever reason, go to Heaven, explains the persistence and strength of the comitatus system.[155] It is thus not surprising that the practice of burial at the stupas of Buddhist holy men[156] closely parallels the Central Eurasian practice at the burial mounds of political lords, most famously among the Scythians.

The earliest Pure Land sutras, including the very first one translated into Chinese, tell us that the Pure Land is the paradise of Amitābha in the West—meaning the western sky, up in Heaven, but of course also located above or *over* Central Asia, which was to the west of early China. Pure Land thus reflects, in part, earlier pre-Buddhist Central Eurasian Culture Complex teachings and practices of Central Asia. Buddhism per se continued to develop its own "reformed" Early Buddhist teachings and practices in Central Asia and in India. Eventually,

[153] Beckwith (1984; 2009: 1–28). Much written on the comitatus continues to be uninformed and problematic.

[154] Beckwith (2011a).

[155] Beckwith (2009: 12–26). Unfortunately, it is rarely said precisely *where* the "home" to which they would return upon death was. The major Early Old Tibetan historical texts—the Zhol Inscription and the *Old Tibetan Annals*—tell us that the ruler, the *btsanpo*, came from *gnamgyi lha* 'the God of Heaven (*gnam*)', but when he died, they say he *gungdu gśegs* 'went to Heaven (*gung*)'. For an early attempt to explain this terminological discrepancy, see Beckwith (2011a), which must be modified to make it clear that there was only *one* God of Heaven (cf. Beckwith 2010a).

[156] Schopen (1987).

a merger of the two in Central Asia produced developed "Buddhicized" Pure Land, which spread to both India and China under the Kushans.

Mahayana may thus have developed partly under the influence of native Central Eurasian-type beliefs accommodated to Buddhism.

The Buddha's insight on *anātman* negates the theism of the Central Eurasian Culture Complex, Zoroastrianism, Brahmanism, and some of the Pre–Pure Land beliefs attested in Megasthenes. By the time full-blown Pure Land per se is attested in Chinese translations in the second century AD, it is a kind of Normative Buddhism. Enough of Buddhism had been adopted by "Old Believers" of pre-Buddhist Pre–Pure Land such that they had become essentially indistinguishable from those followers of Early Buddhism who had adopted many of the absolutist elements rejected by the Buddha. Followers of the resulting Mahayana tradition said that they were Buddhists too, though of course a better, more evolved kind. Along with the merger some very old practices—in particular the tradition of the wandering ascetic Forest Śramaṇas—were revitalized,[157] and followers of the *Mahāyāna* 'the Great Vehicle' claimed the moral high ground as the ultimate "renouncers".

[157] Boucher (2008).

CHAPTER 3

Jade Yoga and Heavenly Dharma

BUDDHIST THOUGHT IN CLASSICAL AGE CHINA AND INDIA

In the Warring States period (ca. 450 BC–221 BC), which began shortly after the death of Confucius, Chinese thought was in a nearly constant state of flux, if not turmoil. Ideas related to the Early Buddhism attested in the fragments of Pyrrho and Megasthenes are quite clearly present in Warring States writings, especially Early Taoist texts,[1] including the *Laotzu* (i.e., the *Tao Te Ching*) and even more so the *Chuangtzu*, as well as the anonymous Jade Yoga Inscription.

Although the earliest text of the *Laotzu* does not mention Laotzu 老子 himself by name,[2] the *Chuangtzu* attributes its enlightened ideas primarily to Laotzu (Lao Tan 老聃), or to Chuangtzu 莊子 (Chuang Chou 莊周), though other sages are also mentioned. Like the received versions of many early Chinese literary texts, the *Chuangtzu* is a compilation of material representing various views and different periods

[1] Despite the recent appearance of a few suggestive studies, most of the research that needs to be done on this topic has not yet been done, and because of scholars' preconceptions, academic fashion, and other factors, it may not be done for a long time to come. Nevertheless, the material is relevant to the understanding both of Early Buddhism and of Early Taoism, and does need to be discussed. I hope that the presentation in this book will raise awareness about some of the material and encourage specialist scholars to work on it.

[2] He is also mentioned under the name Lao Tan 老聃 in *Li Chi* 7, where he is portrayed as an expert on funeral rites; cf. Henricks (2006: 135).

from Early Taoism on.[3] In the case of the *Chuangtzu*, what seems to be the earliest of the positions presented (in the text and in Taoism in general) is very close, if not identical, to the *anātman* teaching of Early Buddhism, with its concomitant features, notably the denial of antilogies, some examples of which are found in the *Laotzu* as well.

Chapter Two shows that the characteristic features of Bactrian-Gandhāran Early Buddhism, as reflected in the teachings and practices of Pyrrho and as described by Megasthenes, are also found in later Buddhist works that are usually considered to reflect "early" Buddhism, but are datable only to about the first or second century AD or later and in large part reflect developed Normative Buddhism. By contrast, some of the Early Taoist material is approximately contemporaneous with Pyrrho and Megasthenes. It seems that this material's appearance in China is connected to the fact that Central Asia, including Bactria and Gandhāra, was part of the Achaemenid Persian Empire down to Alexander's invasion and conquest of the region in 330–325 BC.[4] The Early Taoist material would thus seem to be of great interest for the history of Early Buddhism in Bactria and Gandhāra and its relationship to Chinese thought during the Warring States period.

Things Change

Perhaps the most characteristic theme in the *Laotzu* and the *Chuangtzu*, which are considered to be the two earliest Taoist classics, is their frequent treatment of opposing ideas or "antilogies", mainly ethical ideas such as beauty versus ugliness, approval versus disapproval, success versus failure, and many others.

[3] Stylistically and to a large extent conceptually, some of the text—particularly the section known as the "Inner Chapters"—is evidently by the hand of one author, though it has certainly been reworked, sometimes repeatedly, by later writers who were often opposed to the ideas presented in it. Their changes seem in some cases to have started out as glosses; in any case, they have mostly been incorporated into the text, which has thus been altered to the point that some scholars argue it developed accretionally from the beginning. In any event, as a result, it now actually represents several distinct views. For the more radical proposal that the *Chuangtzu* is "a collection of short texts presenting conflicting views", see Robins (forthcoming). My understanding of this owes much to a number of discussions with colleagues on the Warring States Workshop discussion list, who are of course not responsible for any errors.

[4] Beckwith (2013).

The *Tao Te Ching*, which is attributed to Laotzu, or Lao Tan, does present many examples of antilogies, for example the beginning of chapter 2 (Guodian manuscript A:9) on the "Theory of opposites":[5]

> When the whole world knows beauty as "beautiful", "ugly" arises.
> When all know "good", "evil" arises.
> "Existence" and "nonexistence" are born together.
> "Difficult" and "easy" are achieved together.
> "Long" and "short" are simultaneously formed.
> "High" and "low" are simultaneously completed.
> "Meaning" and "sound" agree with each other.
> "Before" and "after" follow each other.[6]

In this passage, the antilogies in the *Laotzu* seem to be presented as opposite concepts that are human creations, so it agrees with the Buddhist and Pyrrhonian approach. However, the citation of antilogies in the text usually seems intended to focus on the *relationship* between the two opposing things: the opposites exist together, or one leads to or gives birth to the other. The most common approach to antilogies in the text is thus presentation of opposing concepts mostly as different facets of one thing, or as different extremes of a continuum that is not really distinct, as in the above quotation. Often, one thing (though thought to be undesirable) leads to success, while the other thing (though thought to be desirable) leads to failure. The text thus recognizes the existence of a debate about antilogies, yet it mostly rejects not only the antilogies but the debate itself. This suggests that although the *Laotzu* is generally believed to represent an earlier stage or stages of Taoism (and

[5] Brooks (2010: 144), referring to chapter 2 in the Guodian manuscript (before 278 BC), divides it into 2A "Theory of opposites; low profile" and 2B "Low-profile ruler gains his ends". The two parts of the chapter have little if anything to do with each other.

[6] *Laotzu* 2A, or the first eight lines of Guodian chapter A:9 (text from Henricks 2000: 52): 天下皆知美之為美也惡已。皆知善則不善已。有無相生也，難易相成也，長短相形也，高下相盈也，意聲相和也，先後相隨也。 I have emended the first character of line 7 in accordance with the reading in Mawangdui-a (from Henricks 2000: 149), which makes slightly better sense, unlike the usual reading 音 "sound", translated by Henricks as "tone" (though it is possible that the Mawangdui-a redactor changed it for the same reason). My own translation agrees fairly closely with that of Henricks for the first two lines, but diverges from his and the others I have checked on the remaining lines (3 through 8), which have a difficult structure (q.v. Henricks 2000: 50); partly for that reason I have varied my translation even though the structure is exactly parallel in Chinese.

this is possibly the case in some respects), its thought does not in fact represent the *earliest* period of Taoism.[7] This is not the general view, but because of the much clearer layering of some of the examples in the *Chuangtzu*, it seems difficult to deny. On the other hand, there are still some striking passages in the *Laotzu* that immediately call to mind Pyrrho's understanding of Early Buddhism. For example,

> Eliminate knowledge, get rid of distinctions,
> And the people will benefit one hundredfold.[8]

In comparison with the *Laotzu*, the *Chuangtzu* (fourth to third centuries BC), attributed to Chuangtzu or Chuang Chou, preserves what appear to be earlier stages of Taoism in the form of layers of thought that are rejected by subsequent additions.[9] In particular, the *Chuangtzu* includes many examples of the same principle as Pyrrho's *adiaphora* and Buddha's *anātman* '(all things have) no inherent self-identity',[10] such as this one about Beauty:

> Mao Ch'iang and Li Chi were considered beautiful by men, but when fish saw them, they plunged into the depths; when birds saw them, they flew high in the sky; and when deer saw them, they ran away. Did any of these four really know the true principle of beauty in the world? As I see it, the principles of benevolence and righteousness and the paths of right and wrong are tangled and confused. How should *I* know how to distinguish them?[11]

[7] Brooks and Brooks (p.c., 2007) comment, "The text must have had at least three proprietors during the long period of its growth . . . , and two shifts in characteristic emphasis may be discerned in the text, independently implying three compilers." The Guodian manuscript is dated to before 278 BC. See Henricks (2006) for presentation of the Guodian text and translation in comparison with the traditional received text.

[8] *Laotzu* 19, corresponding to Guodian A:1 (text from Henricks 2000: 30): 絕知棄辨，民利百倍; translation by Henricks (2000: 28).

[9] This is done in quite the same way as earlier Buddhist regulations are relaxed or even completely rejected in successive layers of the very same text of the Vinaya, as shown in several studies by Schopen (2004).

[10] See Chapter One.

[11] 毛嬙。麗姬。人之所美也。魚見之深入。鳥見之高飛。麋鹿見之決驟。四者 孰知天下之正色哉。自我觀之。仁義之端。是非之塗。樊然殽亂。吾惡能知其辯。 Text from http://ctext.org/zhuangzi/adjustment-of-controversies, q.v. for Legge's translation; cf. Watson (1968: 46). The passage is from *Chuangtzu* , chap. 2, "Discourse on the Equalization of Things" (齊物論). Cf. the argument of Anacharsis the Scythian on judging art, quoted and discussed in the Prologue.

The most famous single passage from the *Chuangtzu*, the story about Chuang Chou and the butterfly, makes exactly the same point:

> Once Chuang Chou dreamt he was a butterfly, a butterfly flitting and fluttering around, happy with himself and doing as he pleased. He didn't know he was Chuang Chou. Suddenly he woke up and there he was, solid and unmistakable Chuang Chou. But he didn't know if he was Chuang Chou who had dreamt he was a butterfly, or a butterfly dreaming he was Chuang Chou.[12]

The story is strikingly Buddhist in at least two ways. It questions our knowledge about the differentiation between a man and a butterfly, and it questions whether there is a difference between a dream and the "real" world.

However, two comments have been added at the end of the story: "But between Chuang Chou and the butterfly there *must* be a distinction! This is what 'Things change' means."[13] The first comment[14] says there *must* be a difference (分) between Thing One (Chuang Chou) and Thing Two (the butterfly), because after all the story talks about the states of Things One and Two. The second comment argues that this is what we mean when we say *things* change. The main Buddhist point of the story that the first comment contests is *anātman*, which denies the validity of antilogies. The second comment appears to be a simple explanatory gloss,[15] but the author apparently agrees, maintaining that the story wrongly contends that antilogies do not exist, otherwise they could not change. On the other hand, the story also seems to assert the Buddhist principle of *anitya* "impermanence", denying that things are

[12] 昔者莊周夢為胡蝶，栩栩然胡蝶也，自喻適志與。不知周也。俄然覺，則蘧蘧然周也。不知周之夢為胡蝶與，胡蝶之夢為周與。周與胡蝶，則必有分矣。此之 謂物化。Text from http://ctext.org/zhuangzi/adjustment-of-controversies, q.v. for Legge's translation. The translation here is by Watson (1968: 49).

[13] 周與胡蝶，則必有分矣。此之謂物化。Text from http://ctext.org/zhuangzi/adjustment-of-controversies, q.v. for Legge's translation; cf. Watson's (1968: 49) translation: "Between Chuang Chou and a butterfly there must be *some* distinction! This is what is called the Transformation of Things."

[14] The final comments could well be by *two* later writers, one for the first sentence, another for the second.

[15] The existence of later glosses of this kind in the Early Taoist texts has long been known.

eternally fixed and unchanging, so the second comment could simply be a reaffirmation of it.[16]

The text itself thus clearly points to two stages of its own development.[17ix] The story proper presents Classical Buddhist ideas. The first comment (much like Aristotle protesting against violation of the Law of Non-Contradiction) seems not to understand what the *Chuangtzu* voice is saying, namely that it is *logically* impossible to differentiate validly between Chuang Chou and a butterfly.[18]

The position in the story itself is very close to that in Pyrrho's teachings and the report of Megasthenes, suggesting that the latter are approximately contemporaneous with the earlier layer of the *Chuangtzu.*

The Jade Yoga Inscription

At around the same time—the late fourth century BC,[19] the period of the earliest layer of the *Chuangtzu* and the *Laotzu*—an inscription was carved on a jade staff finial, giving directions for yogic-meditational breath control. Although yoga-meditation as a whole is generally considered to be stereotypically Indian, the earliest actual dates of *Indian* texts on breath-control yoga-meditation are, as usual, very late. It is frequently said that closely comparable passages are to be found in the Upanishads—Brahmanist texts of which the earliest are traditionally thought to be contemporary with the time of the Buddha—but there is absolutely no concrete support for such belief, and in this particular case it has been shown to be false.[20] The practice of yoga by Pyrrho (see Chapter One) and the well-known Greek description of the same kind of yoga in India (see Chapter Two) agree with each other and together solidly attest to the existence of early yoga in India. Neither

[16] As with many passages in Early Taoist works, there are other interpretations.

[17] See Endnote ix.

[18] In other examples in the Early Taoist texts, the text voice goes one step further (essentially taking the same step Nāgārjuna eventually took), by explicitly denying the Law of Non-Contradiction in order to affirm a nondual mystical Unity. This later idea seems to be the dominant position in the *Laotzu* as well. For the logical problems, see Chapter Four.

[19] Brooks and Brooks (2015: 175). The finial is not made up of ten pieces of jade, but only one (E. B. Brooks, p.c., 2015), pace Mair (1990a: 159).

[20] Bronkhorst (1986).

source explicitly mentions *breath* control, but in both cases extremely few details are given, so that it is impossible to say anything about it one way or another.

The text on the jade finial has been described and translated by Helmut Wilhelm and Gil Mattos.[21] Mattos translates it as follows:

> MOVING THE BREATH[22]
> Ingest and then let it [i.e., air] accumulate.
> When it accumulates, let it spread.
> When it spreads, let it descend.
> When it descends, let it stabilize.
> When it stabilizes, let it firm up.
> When it firms up, let it grow.
> When it grows, let it mature.
> When it matures, let it return.
> When it returns, let it ascend to Heaven.
> As for Heaven, its roots are on high.
> As for the Earth, its roots are below.
> When [this regimen] is adhered to, one lives.
> When violated, one dies.[23]

It would be good to be able to discuss the Central Asian or Indian doctrinal source (or sources) of this typically Buddhist yoga text,[24] but it seems not to have been identified more precisely.[25] The *Tao Te Ching*

[21] Wilhelm (1948), Mattos (1998); cf. Mattos (forthcoming) and Kuo Mo-jo's translation, translated into English in Mair (1990a: 156).

[22] Mattos (1998) gives the title as "Moving the Qi"—i.e., the *ch'i* 氣.

[23] Mattos (1998) gives the Chinese text, in standard characters, as 行氣 : 呑則畜, 畜則伸, 伸則下, 下則定, 定則固, 固則萌, 萌則長, 長則復, 復則天, 天其本在上, 地其本在下, 順則生, 逆則死. The text is in verse, and rhymes in Old Chinese in a somewhat unusual way (each line rhymes with at least one other line, with the apparent exception of the last line, a threat), indicating in at least one case—伸 in lines 2 and 3, actually written 神 "god"—that the writer intended the character to be understood *both* as written *and* as 伸, a homonym (both in Old Chinese and in Mandarin, now pronounced *shen*). Mattos has converted 神 to 伸 in both cases, but the rhyme scheme has this line rhyming with line 9 復則天, which means literally "(When it) returns, then Heaven", so although he is surely right to interpret it as the homonym 伸 "spread", it *also* means 神 "god", so lines 2 and 3 would read literally "(When it) accumulates, then God" and "(When) God, then descend".

[24] See Chapter Two on early yoga-meditation.

[25] See the very interesting comparisons and comments in Brooks and Brooks (2015).

includes similar passages, as does the slightly later text of the *Chuangtzu*.[26] The date of the Jade Yoga Inscription text itself has been approximately established on the basis of palaeography.

Gautama ~ Laotzu

Ancient Taoist tradition ascribes the founding of Taoism to a man generally known as Laotzu (老子 *lǎozǐ*) or Lao Tan (老聃 *lǎo dān*). The most well-known account, in the *Shih Chi* (ca. 135–90 BC),[27] says that "when the virtue of the Chou Dynasty declined", he decided to leave China, and reached the border post (關), where the border official (關令) recognized him. The official, called in the story "Border Control Director Hsi" (Kuan Ling Yin Hsi 關令尹喜), noticed he was a sage, and asked him to write down his wisdom before leaving. He did so, penning the *Tao Te Ching* 'Classic of the Way and the Virtue', and then left for parts unknown[28]—in some other versions he went specifically to "the West", which the mere mention of the 關 'border post; (mountain) pass' suggests anyway. The border official is elsewhere called simply Kuan Yin 關尹 (a typical Classical Chinese two-character abbreviation of a four-character expression) 'Border-post Director'. In several instances in the *Chuangtzu* he is paired with Lao Tan, including one passage where they are presented as historical personages: "Dwelling alone, peaceful and placid, in spiritual brightness—there were those in ancient times who believed that the 'art of the Way' lay in these things. The Border-post Director and Lao Tan heard of their views and delighted in them. They expounded them in terms of constant nonbeing and being."[29]

[26] Brooks and Brooks (2015); cf. Mair (1990a: 159).

[27] Brooks and Brooks (2007).

[28] *Shih chi* 63 (Peking 1959: 7:2139–2143):居周久之, 見周之衰, 迺遂去。至關, 關令尹喜曰 :「子將隱矣, 彊為我著書。」於是老子迺著書上下篇, 言道德之意五千餘言而去, 莫知其所終。 For a full translation of the account, see Henricks (2000: 133–134).

[29] *Chuangtzu* 33 (Chinese Text Project online): 澹然獨與神明居，古之道術有在於是者。關尹、老聃聞其風而悅之。建之以常無有。 Translation by Watson (1968: 371–372); I have substituted "Border-post Director" for his "Barrier Keeper Yin" and reformatted his text. Like many other passages in the *Laotzu* and the *Chuangtzu*, this one contains phrases strikingly typical of Buddhism, but it is embedded in the unifying viewpoint widespread in Early Taoism.

The story about Laotzu's departure from China is much later than the date of the oldest manuscripts of parts of the *Laotzu* that now constitute the received text of the *Tao Te Ching*, and the tale is undoubtedly legendary. However, it does tell us one very important, strikingly unusual thing for a Chinese philosopher: even in Antiquity, Laotzu was believed to be connected to foreign lands. Since it was virtually unthinkable that a native Chinese would want to leave China in old age, he must have been thought to have originally come to China from some other country, to which he then returned to die. There are very good reasons for thinking that this ancient Chinese belief was accurate, beginning with the Early Taoism attested mainly in the older layers of the *Chuangtzu*,[30] as discussed, and extending to Laotzu's name and apparently the word *dharma* as well.

First, other than his foreign origin the only thing relatively concrete known about Laotzu is that the full form of his name—in modern pronunciation, *Lao Tan* 老聃 *lǎo dān*—is very well attested in many instances in the *Chuangtzu*, where it is used interchangeably with the name *Laotzu*, which appears to be simply a standard "philosopher" version of his name. If so, it should be like those of many other ancient Chinese philosophers such as K'ung-tzu 孔子 'Confucius', formed by taking the first syllable of his name, K'ung 孔 *kǒng* 'a surname', and adding *tzu* 子 *zǐ* 'child; master, philosopher' to it. However, *Lao* 老 is unique in that it is not an ordinary surname or other proper name per se, but the ordinary adjective meaning 'old, aged'; partly for that reason Laotzu's names have been a fertile field for folk etymologies both Chinese and non-Chinese for a very long time, right down to the present.[31] Yet the name Lao Tan not only occurs many times in the *Chuangtzu* as the full form of his name, it is given without comment and treated in the text strictly as a *name*. That means all the many folk etymologies proposed to explain the name, typically involving age and ears, are worthless. Moreover, its inexplicability and the involvement of variant characters suggest that it may be a *foreign* name—as the ancient Chinese thought too, and showed by their story of his return to his foreign home late in life.

[30] The oldest part of the *Chuangtzu* is generally thought to be the "Inner Chapters", 1–7 (Brooks and Brooks 2015: 185), though as discussed here they also contain much later thought.

[31] E.g., Mair (1990b: 26ff.); cf. the discussion in Henricks (2000: 134–136).

The name *Lao Tan* 老聃 ~ 老耽 MSC *lǎo dān*, from MChi *law$_2$ *t^{h}am ~ *təm/*tam[32] can be reconstructed fairly clearly for Old Chinese. A Tang Dynasty Taoist commentator, Chang Chün-hsiang 張君相, is quoted in the Peking edition of the *Shih chi* as saying Laotzu is not the master's name, but an epithet, and more significantly he says, "老，考也."[33] 'Lao is K'ao.' Though not cited in the notes to this comment, it is a verbatim quotation from the *Shuo wen chieh tzu* (ca. AD 100), a famous and authoritative Han Dynasty work, which tells us that *lao* 老 MSC *lǎo* is *the same* as *k'ao* 考 MSC *kǎo*: "*Lao* 老 is *k'ao* 考," and vice versa. Similarly, the *Shih ming* (a later Han Dynasty work), says that *lao* 老 is pronounced like *hsiu* 朽 MSC *xiŭ*, the phonetic of which is *k'ao* 丂 MSC *kǎo*. The two words are thus equated in sound and in meaning in these early texts.[34] Moreover, "From a study of its occurrences in ancient oracle bone and bronze inscriptions, we know that" the character now written and pronounced *lao* 老 'old' "was originally written with another" character, *k'ao* 考 'old', "that had a similar appearance but faced in the opposite direction and is now pronounced *k'ao*" in Modern Standard Mandarin. "The change from *k'ao* to *lao* has never been satisfactorily explained."[35] Therefore, the name could equally well have ended up being written and pronounced today as K'ao Tan 老聃 MSC *kǎo dān*, from Early Middle Chinese *k^{h}awtam or *k^{h}awt^{h}am. Because the expected reconstruction of the onset of *k'ao* 考 in Old Chinese is either an aspirated *k^{h}- or a voiced *g-, the first syllable of the name can be reconstructed for Central dialect Old Chinese as either *Khaw

[32] Pulleyblank (1991: 184, 70–71).

[33] *Shih chi* 63 (Beijing 1959: 2139n1).

[34] The *Shih ming* says, 老，朽也。In the *Shih ming* the second character (here 朽) is usually the text's approximation of the pronunciation of the first character. This 朽 *xiŭ* < OChi *x(r)juʔ (Bax. 798) rhymes once in the *Shih ching* (*Shih* No. 291), with 茂 *mào* < *m(r)juʔ(s) (Bax. 776), which rhymes directly (in *Shih* No. 172) with an exact homonym of 考 *kǎo*, namely 栲 *kǎo* < *khuʔ (Bax. 771), and with many other words in the *Shih ching* belonging to the 幽 rhyme, which includes 老 *lǎo* and 考 *kǎo*. Karlgren (1957: 271) gives the phonetic of 考 *kǎo* as 丂 *kǎo*, which is also the phonetic of the character 朽 *xiŭ* "rot, decay". The characters *lao* 老 and *k'ao* 考 are directly equated twice in *Shuo wen chieh tzu*. One says: 老：考也。七十曰老。 "*lao* [老 'old, aged'] is *k'ao* [考'old, aged']. 70 (years old) is called 'old, aged' (*lao* 老)." The other says 考：老也。从老省，丂聲。 "*k'ao* [考 'old, aged'] is *lao* [老 'old, aged']. It is based on the meaning *lao* [老 'old, aged'] and the sound *k'ao* (丂) 'to sob'."

[35] Mair (1990b: 26). This sentence is actually an exact quote except for my revision of the bits not within quote marks to accord with the style of the present book.

or *Gaw. However, it is extremely unlikely that it had the aspirated onset [k^h] (which is difficult to justify reconstructing as a phoneme for Old Chinese), and much more likely that it had the plain voiced onset [g], as did countless other words before the Early Middle Chinese period, when they began to be devoiced and, often, aspirated, depending on dialect and other factors. The most likely reconstruction, therefore, is OChi *go ~ *gu ~ *gaw (or *gau) ~ for the first syllable,[36] giving Old Chinese *Gotam ~ *Gutam ~ *Gautam.[37] With the recent discovery that many Old Chinese morphemes, even in the Late Old Chinese period, were disyllabic and had a short final *a that was lost when Chinese underwent canonical monosyllabicization of its remaining disyllabic morphemes in the process of becoming Early Middle Chinese,[38] we can restore the expected final vowel *-a, giving us *Gotama ~ *Gutama ~ *Gautama or *Godama ~ *Gudama ~ *Gaudama, any one of which is a good Chinese transcription of the personal name of the Buddha, which is attested several centuries later in the early Gāndhārī texts (from about the first century AD on) as *Godama* ~ *Ghudama* (and later in Sanskrit as *Gautama*), bearing in mind that organized Buddhism was transmitted to China in the early centuries AD from Central Asia, and the texts were in Gāndhārī.

[36] The current traditionalist reconstruction of the vowel of this rhyme (Starostin 1989: 554, rhyme class III 幽 A 上) is *u, but it is somewhat problematic; for the time being, I give Middle Chinese **aw* plus *o, as well as the traditional *u, because the traditional OChi midvowels *o and *e are especially doubtful phonetically for the rhymes in which they have been reconstructed, and because it appears that *aw and *o (or *ō) were dialect forms of each other in Old Chinese. However, any one of the three (*aw, *o, *u) corresponds perfectly to the probable sources of the late Old Chinese forms; see below.

[37] The second syllable, *tan* 聃 MSC *dān* 'long pendulous ears', is from Middle Chinese *t^{h}am (Pul. 71). The word, which was and is written with two other characters, one of which is 耽 EMC *təm ~ *tam (Pul. 70), has attracted many fanciful folk etymologies because of the transcriptional character's meaning, which explains the frequent but very peculiar claim that Laotzu's personal name was *Erh* 耳 *ěr* 'ear'. The transcriptional character happens to have a doublet too: *tan* 耽 *dān* 'long pendulous ears', from Middle Chinese *təm ~ *tam (cf. Takata 1988: 352 *tam*), from traditional Old Chinese *tam (OChi *tə̄m in Starostin 1989: 590). Mandarin *tan* 聃 *dān* < EMC *t^{h}am "long pendulous ears; ancient place name" (Pulleyblank 1991: 71) should go back to an Old Chinese *dam, as argued above.

[38] Beckwith (2014).

The Chinese adjusted the peculiar semantics of the original transcription of his name by writing the same sounds—in Old Chinese—with different characters to make more sense out of it *as Chinese*, despite the still unusual semantics, 'Old Long-ears'.[39]

Does this mean that full Early Buddhism per se (i.e., approximately as identified in this book) was known by the early third century in Warring States China? Undoubtedly not. But the Chinese certainly did obtain some knowledge about it, including the name of the Buddha and his most important, distinctive, striking teaching, *anātman*, as well as the idea and name of the *Dharma*, as discussed below.

Second, the *Laotzu* and the *Chuangtzu* contain much thought of a character that had previously been unknown in China and long remained the "other" with respect to more accepted mainstream Chinese thought.[40] It is rightly suspected by many to be "Indian" in origin, but such observations have been attended by needless speculation about how it could possibly have reached China, a culture still wrongly viewed by too many scholars as having been isolated throughout most of its history. The same "Indian" way of thinking is attested, approximately contemporaneously, in Greek historical sources, both in the Early Buddhism acquired by Pyrrho between 330 and 325 BC and in the account of various "Indian" sects by the ambassador Megasthenes, who visited the same region in 305–304 BC, as shown in Chapter Two. It should thus not be so surprising to find such ideas in China at this time as well.

The above material requires that we draw some conclusions if we are to make sense out of it. Research on the early names of China and other

[39] This process is characteristic for many known loanwords and transcriptions of foreign names from the Han Dynasty and later times that have been transcribed by Chinese who spoke one or another (often unusual) frontier dialect. Before the invention of air travel, and in the absence of much water transport in ancient northwestern China and adjacent areas of Central Eurasia, the way most foreign words entered Chinese was by land, so the frontier dialects were generally the ones to transmit foreign loans and transcriptions. When a word reached the Central dialects, its phonetic form was interpreted or transformed, often in unexpected ways influenced by the semantics of the transcriptional characters.

[40] Another striking feature of the *Chuangtzu* is the pervasive use of humor—including sarcastic portrayals of non-Taoist philosophers (especially Confucius) similar to those in Timon's *Silloi* "Lampoons"—something practically absent in other early Chinese literature.

countries first recorded in the early Warring States period shows that a current of what has been called "Indian" thought made its way to China via Central Asia,[41] with the result that the early Chinese were deeply influenced by it.[42x] But the concepts in question are not "generic" Indian ideas, they are demonstrably attested, known Buddhist ones, at least in part. In order to have been able to transmit what are specifically Buddhist religious-philosophical ideas to China in the fourth century BC, Bactria must already have been heavily influenced by them.

This Early Buddhist influence in China includes the explicit denial of an intrinsic difference between antilogies, or opposites. Most strikingly, yogic breathing practices appeared, spread widely, and became an integral part of Early Taoism—which also first appears at this time. The concepts in question are characteristic of Early Buddhism, but *not* of Brahmanism and the other attested early Indian sects. The influence permeates the earliest known Taoist texts, but it also would seem to have affected early Chinese "philosophical" culture as a whole, and possibly to have inspired its very inception, because it is found for a time even in strictly "Confucian" works.[43] Could this foreign "philosophical" stimulus be responsible for the fixation of Confucius, the first Chinese philosopher, on the *Tao* 道 or 'Way' of Heaven, the *Tao* of the Former Kings, and so on? It appears so, based on the history of the word *Tao*.

Tao 道 MSC *dào*, from EMC ⋆daw_2, is from traditionally reconstructed OChi *dawʁ,[44] but in view of the apparent coda *ʁ, the word probably had a final short *a vowel that was deleted in Late Old Chinese times;[45] restoring it gives us OChi *dawʁa, which could be a metathesized form of *daʁwa. In view of the alternation of *w and *m in Old Chinese (well attested also in Middle Chinese and in Japanese loanwords from Middle Chinese), this form is undoubtedly a Chinese

[41] Beckwith (2013).

[42] On the other routes, see Endnote x.

[43] See Brooks and Brooks (2013). It must not be forgotten that Buddhist ideas were unprecedented *in India*, too.

[44] On coda *ʁ, which was heard by Japanese-Koguryoic speakers as an */r/, see Beckwith (2004/2007; 2006). On the impossible recent "traditional" reconstruction *ʔ for the same phone, see Beckwith (2008: 171ff.).

[45] Beckwith (2014). Because of mergers that took place in Late Old Chinese, it is at present not possible to say for certain which words had the short final vowel *-a and then lost it.

loan-translation from Old Indic *dharma*. That is, assuming this still "experimental" reconstruction is correct, the Chinese word *tao* 道 OChi *daʁwa ~ *daʁma, that is, /darma/, was chosen to transcribe the Indic word *dharma* because its meaning "path, way" was evidently thought to be close to the perceived meaning of the word *dharma* in its sense "the Dharma".

The new Chinese fascination with the *Tao* or Way calls to mind the contemporaneous Indian concept of *Dharma*—which early became so characteristically Buddhist that the word has come to be used synonymously to mean "Buddhism" right down to the present.

> What lies at the heart of Buddhism, according to its own understanding of the matter, is *dharma*. Dharma is not an exclusively Buddhist concept, but one which is common to Indian philosophical, religious, social, and political thought in its entirety. According to Indian thought Dharma is that which is *the basis of things, the underlying nature of things, the way things are; in short, it is the truth about things, the truth about the world. More than this, Dharma is the way we should act, for if we are to avoid bringing harm to both ourselves and others we should strive to act in a way that is true to the way things are, that accords with the underlying truth of things.* Ultimately the only true way to act is in conformity with Dharma.[46]

This passage describes both Early Taoism from the Classical period and Early Buddhism equally well. The similarity of the Buddhist Dharma to the Taoist Way is striking and obvious, as it certainly was to the early translators of Normative Buddhist texts into Chinese in the late second and early third centuries AD, because they too often used *tao* 道, probably for the same reasons: at the time many Late Old Chinese words demonstrably still retained a final short *a,[47] so that *tao* could still have been pronounced *daʁwa /darwa/, and possibly even *daʁma /darma/.

The only conceivable alternative is that at *exactly the same time* as the Indians, the Chinese "independently" and "coincidentally" developed

[46] Gethin (1998: 35), emphasis added to the passage that corresponds perfectly to the presentation of the *Tao* in Early Taoist texts. Gethin says this in a section of his book that deals specifically and only with putative Indian thought, making no reference to anything foreign, not to speak of anything Taoist. Another major meaning of *dharma* that derives from the points he makes is 'law', and significantly, the standard Chinese translation of the Buddhist term *Dharma* is *fa* 法 'law'.

[47] Beckwith (2014).

the idea of the *ātman* 'breath, self' identified with the "soul"; the denial of it, and the denial that there is any absolute difference between True and False, and so on; and yogic methods of physiologically based meditation.[48] The latter two ideas and practices are solidly attested in Early Pyrrhonism and Megasthenes' *Indica,* which are dated earlier than the earliest manuscript of the *Laotzu* (terminus ante quem 278 BC). Their appearance in Early Taoism must be connected not to the much later Upanishads, or other texts of later Brahmanism,[49] which were influenced by Early Buddhism, but to Bactrian-Gandhāran Buddhism, which is attested by the Greek sources to have existed no later than the late fourth century BC.

The Achaemenids, in their earliest expansion, came into contact with the Indians and the Greeks when parts of these cultures were conquered and incorporated into the Persian Empire. Their empire continued to be in intensive contact with these two cultures down to its violent end brought about by Alexander the Great. Many ancient Greeks believed that philosophy was first developed by the *barbaroi* 'barbarians',[50] which term mainly meant 'Persians' and Scythians in Antiquity. It seems that Jaspers's theory of an Axial Age of philosophy cannot be a fantasy after all, but it was not the result of some sort of mystical *ch'i* that spread mysteriously over Eurasia, it was the result of concrete contacts, on the ground, by known peoples.[51]

The Earliest Inscriptions of Ancient India

Sometime after Alexander and his court left India for home in 325 BC, a Mauryan Dynasty ruler called Devānāṃpriya Priyadarśi (fl. ca. 272–261

[48] Complex cultural developments, both physical and otherwise, must have real-world explanations. Miraculous "coincidences", "parallel developments", and other marvels have no place in science. See the discussion in the Preface.

[49] The putative Brahmanist influence discussed at length in Brooks and Brooks (2015: 169ff.) and ascribed to the sixth century BC is based on late texts such as the *Bṛhad-Āranyaka Upaniṣad.* The latter has been demonstrated conclusively by Bronkhorst (1986) to be later than the Early Buddhist period, and to reflect Buddhist influence, not the other way around.

[50] D.L. I, 1–11 (edition and translation by Hicks 1925: 1:2–13).

[51] Beckwith (2013).

BC)[52] erected a large number of Achaemenid-style monumental inscriptions, the first known written texts in India.[53] In the Eighth Rock Edict the ruler proclaims very clearly that after he went to Saṃbodhi (an old name for Bodhgayā, where the Buddha is believed to have attained enlightenment), he began to preach the *Dharma*, and among other measures he instituted restrictions on Brahmanist sacrificial practices, showing beyond question that his Dharma was definitely not Brahmanist in nature. It was, though, strikingly different from familiar Normative Buddhism, which developed two centuries later in the Saka-Kushan period and spread far and wide, eventually subsuming or obliterating most earlier forms of Buddhism. Although it has long been debated whether his Dharma was "Buddhism", a form of Brahmanism, or his own idiosyncratic creation, the *genuine* inscriptions he erected, as the earliest written texts in India, must first be carefully distinguished from the spurious inscriptions erected much later, and then considered along with the still earlier Greek evidence, in order to establish whether his Dharma was a form of Buddhism or something else. Here only the genuine Major Inscriptions of the Mauryan king Devānāṃpriya Priyadarśi are considered as sources for Indian religious thought and practice in the mid-third century BC. The others are discussed in Appendix C.

The Dharma of King Devānāṃpriya Priyadarśi

Hultzsch compares the king's idea of Dharma with that in the *Dhammapada*.[54] "If we turn to an examination of what he tells us about the

[52] His name is spelled variously in the different inscriptions; I follow established convention and give the name (ahistorically) in its Sanskrit equivalent form.

[53] He has been identified with the ruler known in traditional histories as Aśoka, but this identification is ruled out by the inscriptions themselves. The date established by Hultzsch (1925: xxxv) follows the Greek sources, but he correlates the ruler's dates with the *Mahāvaṃsa*, an early medieval Buddhist "history". He gives the reign of the first Mauryan ruler, Candragupta, from 320 to 296 BC, followed by Candragupta's son Bindusāra (Greek Ἀμιτροχάτης [or -δης], q.v. Hultzsch 1925: xxiv–xxv) reigning from 296 to 268, and the latter's son Aśoka reigning from 264 BC on. Because of Hultzsch's view that all the inscriptions were erected by Aśoka, he proposes many changes in this or that source or identification in order to ensure that Aśoka ruled during the dated period of the Greek kings. However, this idea too is belied by the inscriptions themselves. See below in this chapter and Appendix C.

[54] Hultzsch (1925: li–liv).

nature of his *Dharma*, it appears that the latter is in thorough agreement with the picture of Buddhist morality which is preserved in the beautiful anthology entitled *Dhammapada*, i.e. 'words of morality'."[55] Hultzsch quotes Senart, "From the definitions or descriptions which the king gives us, it follows that to him Dharma ordinarily implies what we call the sum of moral duties."[56] This is not, however, what careful analysis of the texts tells us.

In addition to proper courtesy and pious behavior in general—including obedience to mother, father, and elders; telling the truth; reverence to one's master—and not killing animals, King Devānāṃpriya Priyadarśi specifically states what *Dharma* (Pali *Dhamma*) means: "compassion, liberality, truthfulness, purity, gentleness, and goodness"; also: "few sins, many virtuous deeds, compassion, liberality, truthfulness, (and) purity."[57] The inscriptions also list the evil passions: "fierceness, cruelty, anger, pride, envy".[58] It is not surprising, then, that Hultzsch translates *Dharma* throughout as "morality", despite his conviction that the king was a Buddhist "convert". There are in fact some good reasons—including explicit data—to think that Devānāṃpriya Priyadarśi did become favorably disposed toward Buddhism, but there are no explicit references to the *Saṃgha*—that is, to developed Normative Buddhism—in the genuine Major Inscriptions. The Late Inscriptions attributed to "Devānāṃpriya" or "Devānāṃpriya Aśoka" do contain explicit references to the Saṃgha, and thus to developed Normative Buddhism, but they are clearly much later in date, as shown in Appendix C, and therefore of no direct relevance here.

After discussing "many and various vulgar and useless ceremonies", the king says, "But the following practice bears much fruit, viz. the practice of *Dharma*. Herein the following (are comprised), (viz.) proper courtesy to slaves and servants, reverence to elders, gentleness to animals, (and) liberality to Brāḥmaṇas and Śramaṇas; these

[55] Hultzsch (1925: xlix). In fact, *Dhamma* in the title is simply the Pali form of *Dharma*, so it would have been more accurate for him to translate the title as "Words of Dharma".

[56] Senart (1891: 260).

[57] Hultzsch (1925: l–li).

[58] Delhi-Topra III, 19–21; also partly in the First Separate Rock Edict, Dhauli 10–11, Jaugaḍa 5–6.

and other such (virtues) are called the practice of *Dharma*".[59] He also proclaims that all *pāsaṃḍā* '(philosophical-religious) schools, sects' should be honored, and no one should overly praise his own sect or blame other sects.[60]

In the Eighth Rock Edict, he says, "But when king Devānāṃpriya Priyadarśin had been anointed ten years, he went to Saṃbōdhi".[61] The place Saṃbodhi is identified by Hultzsch, on the basis of earlier scholarship, with "Bōdh-Gayā, south of Paṭnā",[62] where the Bodhi Tree was located. He interprets this as referring to the king's "conversion to Buddhism".[63] Most scholars who support the view that the ruler (almost universally identified with "Aśoka") was a devout Buddhist do not think that he took the vows of a full Buddhist monk, but from this passage it is manifestly clear that he became favorably disposed to Buddhism and therefore began preaching the "Dharma". This is well supported by the content of the text of the Eighth Rock Edict itself, in which the quoted sentence is explicitly contrasted with earlier rulers' practice of undertaking "tours", which included hunting (and therefore killing) of animals. In the inscriptions the king also regrets having killed many people (especially in his war with the Kaliṅgas), and repeatedly refers to his restrictions on the killing of animals, urging instead gentleness to them.[64] The king specifically contrasts earlier rulers'

[59] Girnar IX, 3–5; Hultzsch (1925: 16–17). I have throughout substituted the word "Dharma" for Hultzsch's (1925) usual translation, "morality", both here and below. The original has 𑀥𑀁𑀫 *dhaṃma* (usually so spelled).

[60] Hultzsch (1925: xlix).

[61] Written 𑀲𑀁𑀩𑁄𑀥𑀺 Saṃbodhi (Girnar VIII, 2; Hultzsch 1925: 14–15); 𑀲𑀁𑀩𑁄𑀥[𑀺] Saṃbodh[i] (Dhauli VIII, 2; Hultzsch 1925: 89, 102); 𑀲[𑀁]𑀩𑁄𑀥𑀺 Sa[ṃ]bodhi (Kalsi VIII, 22; Hultzsch 1925: 36, 44).

[62] Hultzsch (1925: 15n1); "Paṭnā" is ancient Pāṭaliputra, capital of Magadha.

[63] Hultzsch (1925: xlvii).

[64] The king's specific emphasis on not killing *animals*, often repeated and explicitly declared as a legal restriction, makes it quite clear that he was not a Brahmin. It is also quite likely the source for the Jains' belief that Candragupta was a Jain, or that Aśoka started out as a Jain, though of course Buddhists also prohibit the killing of animals. (Jains are not certainly attested historically till hundreds of years later, as noted above.) The earliest source we have on religion in India is Megasthenes, who explicitly notes that the Brāḥmaṇas eat meat after their thirty-seven years of training (and no doubt in childhood too, though this is not mentioned); he says nothing about the Buddhists in this respect, but they did not forbid consumption of meat, only killing for it. This restriction appears to be Zoroastrian in origin (Boyce and Grenet 1991: 428–429).

"pleasure tours" of hunting with his own new practice of undertaking "tours of Dharma", in which the very first item mentioned is meeting with "Śramaṇas and Brāḥmaṇas" and giving them gifts. The Eighth Rock Edict reads,

> In times past the *Devānāṃpriyas*[65] used to set out on so-called pleasure-tours. On these (tours) hunting and other pleasures were (enjoyed). When King Devānāṃpriya Priyadarśin had been anointed ten years, he went out to Saṃbōdhi. Therefore tours of *dhaṃma* (were undertaken) here. On these (tours) the following takes place, (viz.) visiting *Śramaṇas* and *Brāḥmaṇas* and making gifts (to them), visiting the aged and supporting (them) with gold, visiting the people of the country, instructing (them) in *dhaṃma*, and questioning (them) about *dhaṃma*, as suitable for this (occasion). This second period (of the reign) of king Devānāṃpriya Priyadarśin becomes a pleasure in a higher degree.[66]

One of his most important statements on religion is in the Tenth Rock Edict:

> But whatever effort King Devānāṃpriya Priyadarśin is making, all that (is) for the sake of (merit) in the other (world), (and) in order that all (men) may run little danger. But the danger is this, viz. demerit. But it is indeed difficult either for a lowly person or for a high one to accomplish this without great zeal (and without) renouncing everything.[67] But among these (two) it is indeed (more) difficult to accomplish for a high (person).[68]

The king thus expresses his belief in karma and rebirth, components of the "popular" version of Buddhism (taught by "some" Śramaṇas),

[65] Here Hultzsch (1925: 37n3) comments, "Instead of this title of Aśōka's predecessors the Girnar and Dhauli versions have the word 'kings'".

[66] Girnar VIII, 1–5 (Hultzsch 1925: 14–15), Kalsi VIII, 22–23 (Hultzsch 1925: 37); I have again substituted the original text's *dhaṃma* 'Dharma' for Hultzsch's "morality"; cf. Girnar VIII, 2 (Hultzsch 1925: 14–15).

[67] I give here the usual translation, "renouncing everything", for Hultzsch's doubtful "laying aside every (other aim)". There is no reason to assume 𑀲𑀯𑀁 *savaṃ* "every" or "everything" here (Girnar X, 4; Hultzsch 1925: 17–18) refers to aims of any kind, whereas the idea as expressed—renouncing all wealth, family connections, and other attachments to the world—is reflected in the account of Megasthenes and the earliest traditional Buddhist texts. The subsequent reference to the difficulty of a high-ranking person is surely to be compared to the remarks in early Christianity, and, no doubt, other religious cultures, on how difficult it is for a rich man to enter Paradise.

[68] Girnar X, 3–4 (Hultzsch 1925: 18); cf. Kalsi X, 28–29 (Hultzsch 1925: 39–40).

but not of Early Brahmanism, according to Megasthenes, as discussed in Chapter Two.

In the Major Inscriptions the word *Śramaṇa* is always distinguished from *Brāḥmaṇa*. The normal word for a Buddhist practitioner, *Śramaṇa*,[69] occurs many times, always paired with its non-Buddhist counterpart, *Brāḥmaṇa* "Brahmanist", either as *Śramaṇa-Brāḥmaṇa* or *Brāḥmaṇa-Śramaṇa*. This pairing of the two major systems of thought and practice in India is found also in Megasthenes, as shown in Chapter Two. Both orderings of the terms occur almost equally frequently, indicating that the compounding was purely ad hoc at the time and the terms were still meaningful. This is clear not only from Megasthenes' earlier description but from the spurious "Seventh Pillar Edict" added much later to the Delhi-Topra column. It may be that the scribes who produced the written text for each locality put their preferred sect first. This would suggest that some areas were more strongly pro-Buddhist than others.

In the Twelfth Rock Edict, the pair of terms *pavajitāni cha gharastāni*[70] 'wanderers and householders' occurs. Hultzsch translates: "King Devānāṃpriya Priyadarśin is honoring all sects:[71] both ascetics and householders; both with gifts and with honours of various kinds he is honouring them."[72] The main problem here is Hultzsch's regular mistranslation of the word *pavajita-* (the equivalent of Sanskrit *pravrajita-*) as "ascetic". It actually means 'wanderer, homeless one' and is the explicit opposite of *gharasta-* 'householder'. In the Major Inscriptions both Śramaṇa and Brāḥmaṇa are the names of specific philosophical-religious schools or sects, as spelled out in the Thirteenth Rock Edict, which refers to them both as *nikāyā* 'sectarians' and as *pāṣa(ṃ)ḍā* 'schools; sects': "There is no country where these (two) classes, (viz.) the Brāḥmaṇas

[69] This word *śramaṇa* always and only meant 'Buddhist practitioner' in Antiquity, as shown in detail in Chapter Two. It is significant that in the Major Inscriptions the word *saṃgha* does not occur at all. This is further evidence (see Chapter Two) that the institution had not yet formed.

[70] The text (Girnar XII, 1) reads 𑀧𑀯𑀚𑀺𑀢𑀸𑀦𑀺𑀘·𑀖𑀭𑀲𑁆𑀢𑀸𑀦𑀺. The letter 𑀧, which Hultzsch transcribes in brackets, "[pa]", is absolutely clear in his rubbing (Hultzsch 1925: 21–22, plate facing page 22).

[71] The text of Girnar XII, 1 reads 𑀲𑀯𑀧𑀸𑀲𑀁𑀟𑀸𑀦𑀺 *sava-pāsaṃḍāni* (Hultzsch: 1925: 20–22) 'all sects (or schools)'; cf. Girnar VII, 1 𑀲𑀯𑀧𑀸𑀲𑀁𑀟𑀸 (Hultzsch 1925: 13–14) "id."

[72] Girnar XII, 1 (cf. Kalsi XII, 31), translation of Hultzsch (1925: 20–21).

and the Śramaṇas, do not exist, except among the Greeks; and there is no (place) in any country where men are not indeed attached to some sect."[73] This passage, from the earliest and best Indian written evidence, confirms that the word *Śramaṇa* (variously spelled) means *specifically* and *exclusively* 'Buddhist practitioner' in *all* testimonies,[74] including Indian sources as well as those in Greek, Chinese, Persian, Sogdian, Tokharian, and Arabic, among others, from Antiquity on, well into the Islamic Middle Ages, as shown in Chapter Two.

Devānāṃpriya Priyadarśi has further interesting things to say about "schools, sects" in his Seventh Rock Edict: "King Devānāṃpriya Priyadarśin desires (that) all sects[75] may reside everywhere. For all these desire self-control and purity of mind. But men possess various desires (and) various passions. They will fulfil (either) the whole (or) only a portion (of their duties). But even one who (practises) great liberality, (but) does not possess self-control, purity of mind, gratitude, and firm devotion, is very mean."[76] The king distinguishes between two kinds of ceremonies or rituals. One kind, "other ceremonies", he elsewhere calls "vulgar and useless", a comment that is partly connected to his specifically anti-Brahmanist prohibition of the killing of animals as sacrifices;[77] he contrasts it with the other kind, the "practice of Dharma":

> But other ceremonies are of doubtful (effect). One may attain his object (by them), but he may not (do so). And they (bear fruit) in this world only. But that practice of *dhaṃma* is not restricted to time. Even if one does not attain (by it) his object in this (world), then endless merit is produced in the other (world). But if one attains (by it) his object in this (world), the gain of both (results) arises from it; (viz.) the (desired) object (is attained) in this (world), and endless merit is produced in the other (world) by that practice of *dhaṃma*.[78]

[73] Kalsi XIII, 38–39 (Hultzsch 1925: 44–47), translation of Hultzsch. I have changed his "Yonas" (i.e., the "Ionians") to its normal translation, "Greeks".

[74] It is exactly parallel to the word *Brāḥmaṇa*, which means 'Brahmanist practitioner'.

[75] In Prakrit, *sava-[pāsa]ṃḍa* 'all schools, sects'.

[76] Kalsi VII (Hultzsch 1925: 36).

[77] Hultzsch (1925: l).

[78] Kalsi IX (Hultzsch 1925: 38–39, 44). I have again substituted the original *dhaṃma* for Hultzsch's translation "morality" throughout.

The king thus clearly states that if people do good deeds in this life they will be rewarded in the next. In the Ninth Rock Edict he mentions Heaven explicitly: "Therefore a friend, or a well-wisher, or a relative, or a companion should indeed admonish (another) on such and such an occasion:—'This ought to be done; this is meritorious. By this (practice) it is possible to attain heaven.'"[79] In the Sixth Rock Edict he indicates that his own merit would help other living beings attain Heaven in the next world: "And whatever effort I am making, (is made) in order that I discharge the debt (which I owe) to living beings, (that) I may make them happy in this (world), and (that) they may attain heaven in the other (world)."[80] Hultzsch remarks, "Instead of 'merit in the other world' [the king] often uses the term 'heaven' (*svarga*). . . . The *Dhammapada* (verse 126), however, distinguishes *Nirvāṇa* from *Svarga* . . .".[81] In this connection he also comments, "In one important point [the king]'s inscriptions differ from, and reflect an earlier stage in the development of Buddhist theology or metaphysics than the *Dhammapada*: they do not yet know anything of the doctrine of *Nirvāṇa*."[82] This is not quite correct. The nonmention of Nirvana is of course unsurprising even in a Normative Buddhist context. But the ideas of karma and, effectively, rebirth—that being good in this world

[79] Girnar IX, 7–9 (Hultzsch 1925: 17). Cf. also the Second Separate Rock Edict at Dhauli 9 (Hultzsch 1925: 99–100) and Jaugaḍa 13 (Hultzsch 1925: 118): "And if (you) act thus, you will attain heaven, and you will discharge the debt (which you owe) to me." This corresponds exactly to the promise of the oath or vow taken by the lord of a Central Eurasian comitatus in return for their oath to him (Beckwith 1984; 2009: 12–23). Olivelle (2012: 175) claims, "Aśoka's civil religion had also an other-worldly dimension; abiding by his civil religion of Dharma assured 'heaven' after death. This heaven is a generic after-death beatitude, distinct from specific goals formulated by the religions of his day." He does not provide any support for this view, which does not agree with the contexts in which the promise of heaven for those who do good is mentioned in the Major Inscriptions. However, he does argue that "Aśoka"—i.e., Devānāṃpriya Priyadarśi—was inspired by Buddhism (Olivelle 2012: 179), and he rightly doubts Bronkhorst's theory of the "Magadhan" origin of belief in rebirth and karma (Olivelle 2012: 176).

[80] Kalsi VI, 20 (Hultzsch 1925: 35), also in the other synoptic versions.

[81] Hultzsch (1925: liv); I have substituted "[the king]" for his "Aśōka".

[82] Hultzsch (1925: liii), who adds that the inscriptions "presuppose the general Hindū belief that the rewards of the practice of *Dharma* are happiness in this world and merit in the other world". However, it is now known that what is today called "Hinduism" did not come into existence until hundreds of years after the inscriptions were erected. I have again substituted "[the king]" for his "Aśōka".

will be rewarded in the other world—are now generally considered to be innovations in Indian thought which appeared at the same time as Buddhism appeared.[83] By 330–325 BC (when Early Buddhist teachings were transmitted to Pyrrho) to 305–304 BC (when Megasthenes visited India), the ideas of karma and Heaven were apparently not yet part of the teachings followed by the main two groups of Śramaṇas he describes, but Megasthenes says that even the more "elegant" ones among his other group of Śramaṇas, who specialized in funeral rites and begged as mendicants in the villages in towns, taught about karma and Heaven.[84]

Hultzsch is right that the overriding religious lesson of the Dharma taught in the Major Inscriptions is that good deeds are rewarded in this life, but *especially*—the word is stressed—in the next life, in Heaven. That is, the king's Dharma teaches about karma and rebirth, both essential points not only in Normative Buddhism but already in the account of Megasthenes, who says that some other Śramaṇas teach such ideas to the people in order to motivate them to behave better. The "Pre–Pure Land" sect, too, which taught the same ideas, was apparently just about to become Buddhist,[85] and if it can be identified with the "popular" sect of Śramaṇas, it seems to have become Buddhist by the time of Devānāṃpriya Priyadarśi. Where did these beliefs come from?[86]

The inscriptions of the Achaemenid rulers of the Persian Empire say, "The man who has respect for that *law*, which Ahuramazda has established, and worships Ahuramazda and Arta [truth] reverent[ly], he both becomes happy while living, and becomes blessed when dead."[87]

[83] See the Prologue and Chapter One.

[84] See Chapter Two.

[85] The very earliest known actual Pure Land text (translated in the mid-second century AD) is of course Normative Buddhist in content.

[86] Bronkhorst (2007) argues—certainly correctly—that karma and rebirth did not develop within Vedic religion, and that they were unprecedented in India. However, he proposes that they developed in "Greater Magadha", an area where Vedic religion did not predominate, though we have no actual data to support this. He also proposes that both Buddhism and Jainism developed *in response to* the ideas of karma and rebirth. This may be the case for Jainism, but it is attested so late and is so full of ideas and practices clearly derived from Buddhism—especially late, Normative Buddhism—that it is most unlikely it even came into being until long after the Buddha's lifetime. Cf. the Preface.

[87] Razmjou (2005: 151), quoting an inscription of Xerxes (XPh 46–56), emphasis added. Old Persian *Arta* "the Truth" is explicitly opposed to *Druj* "the Lie".

The outcome for good people who follow the law of Ahuramazda is that they go to Paradise when they die. The Persian text sounds remarkably close to the statements in the Major Inscriptions of the Mauryas in Prakrit, and reminds us of the fact that one of the main meanings of Indic *dharma* is "law". For example, "By that practice of the *law*, the desired object is attained in this world and endless merit is produced in the other (world)."[88] Comparing the two sets of inscriptions, one is struck by the "missing God" in the Mauryan inscriptions. It is the most distinctive sign of Buddhism that can be imagined.

The people of the Avesta were originally Western Old Indic speakers[89] who had a religious system like the Eastern Old Indic people of the Rig Veda, but with Zoroaster's "reforms" the people of the Avesta ended up with a monotheistic sky god and karma,[90] among other things not found in the Rig Veda or in the attested materials on pre-Avestan Western Old Indic.[91] Since it is generally believed that the idea of karma was newly introduced to India at about the same time in both the Upanishads and the Buddha's teachings, it must have come in via Gandhāra, which was conquered by the Achaemenids in the sixth century BC and formed part of the Persian Empire down to Alexander's conquest. This would seem to explain the most striking characteristics of the inscriptions—the king's sincerity, his genuine earnestness, and his devotion to the Dharma—and their remarkable similarity to the corresponding characteristics in the Achaemenid inscriptions of Darius.

In short, Devānāṃpriya Priyadarśi's Dharma is a blend of two elements. Much of it is "Buddhist-flavored", but what kind of Buddhism does it reflect? He himself tells us in the Eighth Rock Edict that he visited Saṃbodhi—Bodhgayā, where the Buddha achieved

[88] Kalsi IX, 26–27 (Hultzsch 1925: 38–39), translating *dharma* in this instance as 'law'; Hultzsch translates the passage as "the (desired) object (is attained) in this (world), and endless merit is produced in the other (world) by that practice of morality."

[89] Old Avestan (the language of the Gāthās) is an Iranicized Old Indic language. See Beckwith (2007a; 2009: 365–369).

[90] Cf. Soudavar (2010: 135).

[91] Beckwith (2012b). There is of course very little remaining of early Western Old Indic, but there does not seem to be any reason to think that the idea of karma is earlier than Zoroaster.

enlightenment—and afterward renounced violence and began preaching "the Dharma", which equally means 'the law'; that is, *Dharma* 'the Buddha's teachings', were and are collectively called 'the Law'. This surely means that the king's Dharma was, at least in his own mind, Buddhist. The fragmentary Greek versions of the Major Inscriptions translate *dharma* as *eusebeia* 'piety, holiness, morality', which is certainly a prominent explicit component of Devānāṃpriya Priyadarśi's Dharma. Megasthenes uses the same word for the same purpose (see Chapter Two), and it is notable that Pyrrho is said to have lived *eusebōs* "piously" with his sister.[92] The Buddhist elements in the king's Dharma thus apparently include his choice of the word *Dharma* to designate it; his institution of *ahiṃsā* 'non-violence' (he specifically says that killing sentient beings, whether people or animals, is bad, and pays special attention to nonviolence toward animals); his remark that the best path is to "renounce everything (wealth in particular)"; and his emphasis on the importance of the accumulation of "endless merit [good karma] in the other (world)", Heaven. Since the latter element was already part of the "popular" Buddhist teachings of some Śramaṇas, as well as the "Proto-Pure Land" belief system (see Chapter Two), Buddhism accounts for these beliefs too.

All this suggests that the king's Buddhism in general was an early, pietistic, "popular" form perhaps akin to pre-Mahayana. The other aspects of his Dharma that are specifically mentioned in the Major Inscriptions are elements of what might be called "generic" piety and morality: compassion, liberality, truthfulness, purity, gentleness, goodness, few sins, many virtuous deeds, proper courtesy to slaves and servants, reverence to elders, gentleness to animals, and avoidance of the evil passions of fierceness, cruelty, anger, pride, and envy. It must be emphasized that all of these virtues (and the vices to be avoided) are found in Normative Buddhism, so they certainly do not argue *against* his faith being Buddhism. The king also takes pains to emphasize that practitioners of all sects should be respected. However, he does proclaim explicit restrictions on bloody sacrifices, which were at the time a necessity for Brahmanists, and in his First Rock Edict he uses "the Brahmanical technical terms for ritual slaughter (*ā-labh*) and offering

[92] D.L. IX, 66 (Hicks 1925: 2:478–479).

(*pra-hu*) for the ritual killing of animals",[93] so it is absolutely clear that the Brahmanists were the specific targets of the new law. Megasthenes tells us that the Brahmanist ascetics did *not* eat meat (though after their ascetic period they did), but he does not tell us whether the Buddhists (Śramaṇas) did or not.[94] In short, of the two belief systems that are explicitly mentioned in the Major Inscriptions, the king definitely favored a form of Early Buddhism—specifically, a "popular" form of it that was close to the Pre–Pure Land sect discussed above.

THE AUTHOR OF THE MAJOR AND MINOR INSCRIPTIONS

In addition to the Major Inscriptions, there are a good number of other inscriptions in early Brahmi script, virtually all of which have also been attributed to the ruler known as "Aśoka". Most of them are explicitly Normative Buddhist in content and very different in every other respect from the Major Inscriptions. Their authenticity and dating are discussed in detail in Appendix C, but their very existence brings into question the precise identity of the author of the Major Inscriptions, which was established on very shaky grounds to begin with. It must therefore be reopened.

One of the most doubtful points is the unlikely idea that Candragupta founded his empire the moment Alexander the Great died, if not even earlier. This idea has been proposed to make the internal dates of the inscriptions match the dates given in the traditional legendary Buddhist "histories". Candragupta is well known from Greek sources and had much to do with the Greeks, but that activity took place *two decades* after Alexander's death, at the time of Megasthenes' diplomatic mission to his court on behalf of Seleucus I Nicator, who succeeded in concluding a treaty with Candragupta in 305–304 BC. The inscriptions are datable on the basis of the names of the Hellenistic rulers mentioned in the Second and Thirteenth Rock Edicts, though the possible identifications should be reexamined very carefully. For the present, the most conservative calculations give the shared date range of

[93] Olivelle (2012: 183n26).

[94] See Chapter Two.

272–261 BC,[95] which is thus the floruit of Devānāṃpriya Priyadarśi. Chronologically he hardly could have been Candragupta himself, but he could have been his son, who is called Amitrochates (or Amitrochades) in the Greek sources, which record extensive contacts with him as well.[96] This is supported by several points about the Mauryan monumental pillars.

To begin with, the explicit internal dates tell us that the Rock Edicts were inscribed first, not the Pillar Edicts. Second, the fact that only some of the pillars were inscribed indicates that they were all erected blank,[97] meaning that the ruler who erected them did not intend to have inscriptions engraved on them. That would accord with the pillars' Persian models, which are usually not inscribed. Third, the *way* that the pillars are inscribed is quite peculiar. The texts are in "panels" on one or more "faces", an odd way to engrave inscriptions on cylindrical columns.[98] This further suggests that the pillars were already erected at their respective sites before they were inscribed, and the scribal masons pasted the written texts on the pillars in order to cut the texts. Megasthenes, who travelled across northern India as far east as Magadha and visited Candragupta in Pāṭaliputra, specifically says the Indians did not have writing. Since he must have taken the "royal road" of the Mauryas along which many of the inscriptions are still to be found today, if monumental inscriptions of any kind had been erected by the time of his visit in 305–304 BC, he would certainly have seen one or more of them and would not have made his comment on the absence of writing in India.

[95] Hultzsch (1925: xxi–xxxvi), who unfortunately bases his eventual choices of Hellenistic rulers and their known or estimated dates of rule on the traditional legendary "histories" of later Indian literature.

[96] In the late Buddhist "histories", the son of Candragupta is called Bindusāra, Aśoka's father.

[97] The spurious "Seventh Pillar Edict" mentions them. Though it is no source for the early history of the inscriptions, its recognition that some pillars were still uninscribed (as some pillars still are to this day) when the "edict" was added to the Delhi-Topra column makes it clear that they were all first erected without inscriptions.

[98] The palaeographical oddities of the "Seventh Pillar Edict" could perhaps be explained in part by the difficulty the scribal masons apparently had in *writing* directly onto the stone (i.e., before trying to inscribe the text). The argument of Norman (2012) and others that they were written while horizontal, before erection, could theoretically explain the separate faces, but the existence of blank pillars (see the previous note on the "Seventh Pillar Edict") vacates that argument.

It is significant that the Early Buddhist "histories" that recount stories about Aśoka and others are not histories in any usual sense of the word, and are not "early" at all—they were written many hundreds of years after the inscriptions were erected. The inscriptions were still there in the open for any literate person to read. The writers of the legendary Buddhist "histories" no doubt did read them, because the literary language and script were little changed until around the end of the Kushan period in the mid-third century BC.[99] They thus could very well have mixed up two or more people with the author or authors of the inscriptions. It was only in the following Gupta period, when Brahmi script underwent major changes, that knowledge of its earlier Mauryan form was lost and the texts written in it became unreadable by people of the day.[100]

In sum, it seems most likely that the pillars were erected under Candragupta, founder of the Maurya Dynasty, who is well known to have had much to do with the Greek successors of the Persian Empire, and might even have had direct knowledge of the Persians before the coming of Alexander. The Major Inscriptions apparently belong to the reign of Candragupta's son, who also had much to do with the Greeks and ruled at exactly the right time for the chronology revealed by the inscriptions themselves; he can thus be identified with Devānāṃpriya Priyadarśi. Moreover, the king who ordered the creation of the Major Inscriptions could not have been Devānāṃpriya Aśoka, the ruler mentioned in traditional histories as Candragupta's grandson, because the contents of the Buddhist Inscriptions *explicitly attributed* to Aśoka belong to Normative Buddhism. But the Normative Buddhist period began two centuries or more *after* the Major Inscriptions were erected in the early third century BC. The Buddhist Inscriptions attributed to Aśoka could possibly be later forgeries, but it is perhaps more likely that in the Saka-Kushan period (or even later) there was a "king of Magadha" named Aśoka who was a patron of Buddhism and erected the apparently genuine Buddhist Inscriptions that bear his name.[101]

[99] Deeg (2009); cf. Salomon (1998: 31).

[100] Michael Willis (p.c., 2012).

[101] Nevertheless, some of the inscriptions attributed to Aśoka are simply spurious. For a preliminary study of the authenticity and dating of the Buddhist Inscriptions, including the fakes, see Appendix C.

CHAPTER 4

Greek Enlightenment

WHAT THE BUDDHA, PYRRHO, AND HUME ARGUE AGAINST

The argument known in Antiquity as the Problem of the Criterion was introduced to Western thought by Pyrrho of Elis, who learned it in Central Asia and India from Early Buddhism, as shown in the Prologue and Chapter One. The problem revolutionized ancient European thought, such that from Pyrrho's time onward ancient Graeco-Roman philosophy was focused on the epistemological question, "Can we *really* know anything?" The problem remained unsolved throughout Antiquity, but with the ascendancy of Christianity and its Aristotelian and Neoplatonic apologetics, it was sidelined and practically forgotten during the Middle Ages.

When Pyrrhonism was reintroduced to Western Europe in the late Renaissance, the problem once again revolutionized Western thought and shifted the central focus of philosophy to epistemology. The Scottish philosopher David Hume (1711–1776) is responsible for what may be called the problem's modern incarnation, known today as the "Problem of Induction",[1] which he presents in his book, *An Enquiry*

[1] Hume himself does not use the expression "Problem of Induction", and when he does use the word *induction*, it does not have its modern meaning. I use the expression as it is now generally understood and used in a considerable—and highly problematic—literature of its own.

Concerning Human Understanding (henceforth *Enquiry*).[2xi] "Hume's Problem" has been perhaps the most important single issue in Western philosophy in the two and a half centuries since his day. All of the major Western philosophers since Hume have grappled with it. Today it is generally considered "unsolvable". However, this does not mean that it really is "unsolvable"—the idea is singularly inappropriate for it—especially in view of the fact that philosophers seem not to have appreciated the overwhelmingly important role of Pyrrhonism, which Hume actually trumpets throughout his book,[3] not to speak of the crucial covert arguments that are presented in it. This chapter is devoted to analyzing these issues, which are fundamental to understanding not only Hume but also Pyrrho, and in turn the Buddha.

As shown in Chapter One, Pyrrho and the Buddha before him taught that things do not have their own absolute, inherent self-identities, or 'differentiae'. Therefore, our minds provide them. They are often marked in speech by quality words, category words, and many others.[4]

[2] The work was first published in 1748. The title given here is that printed in vol. 2 of the "new edition" published by Hume in 1772, the last of many that he himself saw through the press. Hume also revised it in 1776, but did not live to see it published in 1777 (Norton and Taylor 2009: 534). Hume wrote many other books, including an earlier, much longer, more involved version of this work, the *Treatise of Human Nature* (1739–1740), which has attracted most of the attention given by modern scholars to Hume's philosophical work, and is now generally considered to be his greatest contribution to philosophy. I understand other scholars' wish to study Hume's early work, but I also respect Hume's plea (q.v. Endnote xi) to take the *Enquiry* as the final, mature version of his work, and base my discussion almost exclusively on it. I quote it from the 1772 edition, retaining his spelling and punctuation.

[3] For example, the article on Hume in the *Stanford Encyclopedia of Philosophy* does not even mention Pyrrho or Pyrrhonism (Morris and Brown 2014). It is now accepted that Hume acquired most of his knowledge about Pyrrhonism from the *Historical and Critical Dictionary* of Pierre Bayle (1740), not from Sextus Empiricus or other primary sources. This accounts for his mixing of Pyrrhonism with Academic Scepticism at some points. Nevertheless, despite the influence of Bayle, Hume clearly understood the significance of the basic points raised by the Pyrrhonists, and overcame his sources. He contributed much to the spread of Neo-Pyrrhonism and influenced many of the philosophers and scientists who followed him.

[4] The Problems of Induction, the Criterion, and the Differentia are very closely related to each other and to the Problem of Universals, which concerns the existence or nonexistence of superordinate categories. Each problem has its own history and literature, and I am not an expert on any of them. In this chapter I attempt only to focus on the issues relevant to their Enlightenment reflex, Hume's "Problem of Induction".

For example, a child looks out the window and sees an animal. What is it? Because things do not have their own inherent differentiae, the animal does not have a little sign or label growing in its fur that spells out its genus, species, and so on, for our benefit. Accordingly, she applies her stored knowledge about things and matches the animal up: it's a "bunny". So far, so good. But did she get this category, BUNNY, and all the things she knows about bunnies, from logic, from pure deductive thinking? No, she got it from induction—from observing bunnies, or from seeing pictures of them and being told about them. Because our knowledge *about* the world comes *from* the world, it is perfectly circular. "Since induction is a contingent method—even good inductions may lead from truths to falsehoods—there can be no deductive justification for induction. Any inductive justification of induction would, on the other hand, be circular."[5] This is the Problem of Induction.

The problem is connected to the ancient Problem of the Criterion introduced by Pyrrho. In order to have absolutely correct true knowledge about anything, it is necessary to have a criterion that distinguishes perfectly between true and false ideas. In order to know if the chosen criterion is correct, we need to use another criterion. But it too has the same problem: it demands yet another criterion. And so on, ad infinitum. It is therefore impossible to have a criterion of truth.[6] We have to differentiate the category of bunnies from the category of birds, anger from happiness, and many other things, in order to be able to think or talk about them at all. Although dogmatic philosophers may claim that they have reached a conclusion about something *logically* on the basis of *a*, *b*, and *c*, we must agree with Pyrrho: because matters *a*, *b*, and *c* are not themselves inherently differentiated—they do not have their own differentiae or other criteria—the philosophers have supplied them, thus determining everything themselves, consciously or unconsciously, before even starting, making nice, neat, circular arguments. The problem is worse than it seems, because, as the Buddha and Pyrrho say, everything is also unfixed (variable, impermanent, undecided, etc.) and unstable (unbalanced, uncomfortable, etc.).

[5] Vickers (2010), specifically discussing Hume's version of the problem.

[6] Cf. Appendix A.

The views on epistemology held by the leading Western philosophers from the early Enlightenment on are nearly all based ultimately on acceptance or rejection of the fundamental position of ancient Pyrrhonism, as understood or misunderstood by them.[7] Sceptical thought became widely known in Europe following the Latin translation and publication in Paris in 1562 of the surviving works of Sextus Empiricus, a Late Pyrrhonist who argues against the rationalists, who contend that truth is obtained by reason (deduction), and equally against the empiricists, who argue that truth is obtained by the senses (induction).[8] Sextus argues that some of our perceptions, such as hallucinations, are accepted to be creations of our minds, and thus faulty, while different people often perceive the world differently, so our knowledge of the world as a whole is uncertain. He argues that neither deduction nor induction is reliable. According to Diogenes Laertius, Pyrrhonism's founder, Pyrrho of Elis, said that one must "suspend judgement"[9] with respect to philosophical arguments about anything beyond the raw perceptions of our senses. The technical expression "to suspend judgement" is now agreed to have developed after Pyrrho, but Timon's gloss on Pyrrho's use of the expression "no more" explicitly says it means "determining nothing, and withholding assent",[10] which in practice would amount to more or less the same thing. In any case, the underlying philosophical approach is an intrinsic part of Pyrrho's known position.

The dogmatic "Academic Sceptics" took the position that all knowledge is uncertain, therefore *nothing* can really be known and *everything* must be doubted. Although they are severely criticized by the Pyrrhonists, from Pyrrho and Timon through Sextus Empiricus, their view was revived in the Renaissance along with Pyrrhonism, and perhaps because the Pyrrhonist position—or rather, nonposition—is subtle and difficult to grasp directly, Academic Scepticism has been

[7] Cf. Searle (1995: 149–150, 157–158, 168ff.). Searle presents innovative, convincing arguments against the "anti-realist" position. Although he never refers to the issue discussed here as "the Problem of Induction", he does mention that it stems from Enlightenment philosophers (Searle 1995: 154).

[8] Bury (1933: xxxiii *et seq.*).

[9] See Chapter One and Appendix A.

[10] Bett (2000: 31).

the unsceptical, absolutist position of most European scepticism ever since.[11] Nevertheless, the ancient Pyrrhonist arguments about the imperfection and uncertainty of human knowledge had a revolutionary influence on the Enlightenment philosopher-scientists, most especially on the Scottish philosopher David Hume.

Hume was strongly influenced by Late Pyrrhonism, including the ideas of Sextus Empiricus.[12] In his *Enquiry*, Hume restates Pyrrho's view, as modified by the Late Pyrrhonists,[13] and tells us repeatedly in the book that he considers himself to be a "Pyrrhonian". Hume applies his formulation of one of the Pyrrhonists' most important theoretical points—that there is no philosophically valid justification for believing in the truth of knowledge acquired by induction—expressly to the results of experimental science. He concludes that we have no *logical* justification for believing in any knowledge acquired directly by induction or in inferences drawn from inductive knowledge. In fact, we not only cannot attain absolute truth about the world, we cannot even show by proper philosophical demonstration that the "real world" exists. Therefore, science, which may be roughly defined as the systematic search for correct knowledge about the world, is basically flawed and unreliable. Hume says,

> As to those *impressions*, which arise from the *senses*, their ultimate cause is, in my opinion, perfectly inexplicable by human reason, and 'twill always be impossible to decide with certainty, whether they arise immediately from the object, or are produc'd by the creative power of the mind, or are deriv'd from the author of our being.[14]

[11] It also affected the position of Pierre Bayle (1647–1706), whose famous *Dictionnaire historique et critique* (1740) includes an article on Pyrrho and one on Pyrrhonism. Bayle's *Dictionnaire* is now believed to have provided most of Hume's knowledge of ancient Pyrrhonism (q.v. the following note). For a recent account of Bayle, see Lennon and Hickson (2013).

[12] On the sources of Hume's knowledge of Pyrrhonism, see Popkin (1951); see also the previous note and Note 3 in this chapter.

[13] And of course modified again by post-Renaissance Europeans; I will not remark further on this. Cf. the following note.

[14] Hume, *A Treatise of Human Nature* (1739–1740), quoted in Norton (2009: 10). Hume adds to this an instrumentalist "sceptical solution": "Nor is such a question any way material to our present purpose. We may draw inferences from the coherence of our perceptions, whether they be true or false; whether they represent nature justly, or be

The thought of Hume is well known, so none of this is really new to anyone familiar with it. But surely we must ask *why* Hume has made this and other difficult pronouncements, and why Pyrrho and Buddha have done the same before him. Who or what are they arguing against? If we can understand Hume's modern version, we will understand Pyrrho's better, too, and in turn Buddha's. So let us take a closer look.

Hume contends that we live in the world almost completely on the basis of instinct, emotion, and very elementary analysis of the things we experience, in particular an inherent belief in *causation*.

> We have said, that all arguments concerning existence are founded on the relation of cause and effect;[15] that our knowledge of that relation is derived entirely from experience; and that all our experimental conclusions proceed upon the supposition, that the future will be conformable to the past. To endeavour, therefore, the proof of this last supposition by probable arguments, or arguments regarding existence, must be evidently going in a circle, and taking that for granted, which is the very point in question.[16]

No amount of testing or observation or experiment can prove or disprove this innate belief or feeling, the Principle of the Conformity of Nature.[17] Hume says, "It is only experience, which teaches us the nature and bounds of cause and effect, and enables us to infer the existence of one object from that of another."[18] So we cannot believe in science, which he says depends on experiments that try to predict

---

mere illusions of the senses." Hume eventually modified his view further to eliminate the doctrinaire assertion of uncertainty.

[15] This is identical in sense to many statements of the Buddha in canonical texts.

[16] Hume, *Enquiry* (1772: 47). His analysis is strikingly close to that of the late Normative Buddhist *pratītyasamutpāda* "chain of causation; dependent origination", the basic point of which apparently goes back to the Buddha, but in any case is attested in the late fourth century BC; see the discussion of Megasthenes' reference to the Śramaṇas' expertise in "the causes of things" in Chapter Two.

[17] Or "Principle of the Uniformity of Nature". We thus have no philosophical justification (according to traditional logic) for believing in scientific predictions because they depend on inductive reasoning and are unavoidably circular from beginning to end. It should perhaps be noted that Hume probably did not think science would be in any danger of disappearing because of his arguments, which he no doubt thought would be violently opposed and soon forgotten. They were certainly opposed, but have not been forgotten.

[18] Hume, *Enquiry* (1772: 182).

the future. We do not know everything that could happen, and cannot predict the future:[19] "The falling of a pebble may, for aught we know, extinguish the sun."[20] Therefore, we do not have any truly reliable knowledge about the world.

With Hume's argument, as with many arguments, the real problem is their many assumptions and premises that are not openly stated or simply unrecognized. The full scope of Hume's argument becomes visible only if we look at the converse of his main assumptions and arguments—as Hume himself suggests we should do.[21]

First let us take one's own imperfect self, and the irregularity and imperfection of one's knowledge, and consider the converse. What do we get? A *perfect* being whose knowledge is *perfect* and does know everything about the world, including about us, and therefore does know everything that can possibly happen. So, unlike us, this being *can* predict the future. The converse of Hume's sceptical argument is belief in a perfect being who is omniscient, omnipotent, uncaused, and so on.

Paul Russell remarks, "it is surprising to find that in the *Treatise* Hume barely mentions our idea of God, much less provides any detailed account of the nature and origin of this idea.[22] It would be a mistake, however, to conclude from this that theological problems, as they concern our idea of God, are far from his mind. On the contrary, neglecting this topic, in face of the ongoing debate and its obvious

[19] This particular argument is flawed because of unstated assumptions about time and related issues. Because the future, by definition, does not exist, arguments that depend on its existence would seem to be invalid.

[20] Hume, *Enquiry* (1772: 182), q.v. for the context of this and the preceding quotation: "The existence, therefore, of any being can only be proved by arguments from its cause or its effect; and these arguments are founded entirely on experience. If we reason *a priori*, any thing may appear able to produce any thing. The falling of a pebble may, for ought we know, extinguish the sun; or the wish of a man controul the planets in their orbits. It is only experience, which teaches us the nature and bounds of cause and effect, and enables us to infer the existence of one object from that of another."

[21] Hume says, "No negation of a fact can involve a contradiction. The non-existence of any being, without exception, is as clear and distinct an idea as its existence. The proposition which affirms it not to be, however false, is no less conceivable and intelligible, than that which affirms it to be" (1772: 182). This is the Law of Non-Contradiction. It is interesting to compare Hume's version to Searle's (1995: 208ff.), where the issue is approached from a quite different direction.

[22] It is surprising because Hume is widely considered to have been a firm atheist.

relevance for Hume's philosophy in the *Treatise*, plainly conveys a (strong) sceptical message."[23] But Hume has not neglected the topic at all. From the viewpoint of the converse, which he expressly suggests we should consider, Hume's "sceptical message", his *overt* argument, is the rejection of a *covert* argument about God.[24] Accordingly, the overt Problem of Induction could well be a red herring that Hume has laid in our path to throw everyone off his covert Problem—very successfully, as it turns out.

What it seems Hume might really have wanted to argue about may be called the "Problem of Perfection". If we had perfection in the world, we would have a perfect being, who knows everything, and a perfect, eternal, and unchanging world in which all events, if there were any, would be perfect too. We would have God with his perfect attributes, including his perfect knowledge of everything, and God's world, where everything is perfect, completely regular, eternal, and therefore ultimately the same. But do we have a perfect world like that? No. We have a very imperfect world, full of imperfect beings with very imperfect knowledge, and things and events that are far from perfect too. As Hume points out in his overt argument, because of our general imperfection we cannot acquire data perfectly with our senses, we cannot understand or analyze what we have acquired perfectly, and so on. Therefore, Hume declares, we cannot trust our senses, our inductions, and even our deductions, to tell us the absolute truth about anything. As a result we cannot trust the results of science, and our knowledge in general is unreliable. He says this Pyrrhonian "sceptical conclusion" is unavoidable at the philosophical level.

That would seem to be it, then. But Hume, following the ancient critics of Pyrrho, goes on to tell us that, practically speaking, we cannot live our lives according to Pyrrhonism, so we should not try to apply it to actual daily life; we should just follow convention and habit.[25] He

[23] Russell (2012). Note that he cites the *Treatise* here.

[24] Cf. Russell (2008) and the comments of McNabb (2009). It seems to be generally unrecognized that there might be serious covert arguments (whether intended or not) in the works of Hume.

[25] This last part, Hume's "sceptical solution", is in origin simply the Late Pyrrhonist recommendation for how a Pyrrhonian should deal with daily life, but it goes back directly to Pyrrho, the founder of Pyrrhonism, as discussed in Chapter One and Appendix A.

even blandly notes that everyday life seems to disprove Pyrrhonism anyway. However, this appears to be more of Hume's cleverness.[26] Perhaps if we think about it a little more we can see through all the smoke and mirrors, and avoid the traps he has laid for anyone hunting for the solution.

Like Buddha and Pyrrho, then, Hume tells us that the world is irregular, unpredictable, and imperfect, our knowledge is imperfect, *we* are imperfect. Compare that to the converse:

Imperfect being(s) ➤ imperfect knowledge : imperfect world ➤ variation

Perfect being(s) ➤ perfect knowledge : perfect world ➤ no variation

Which one do we have? Think of our chosen Modern form of government, think of our economy, think of science, think of anything.

Induction is our imperfect human way of acquiring and analyzing imperfect knowledge about our imperfect world. It might not seem to do well in comparison with God's perfect knowledge, but our world is not perfect, and not being gods, we cannot aspire to have perfect knowledge. That is not all. Imperfect induction is actually *better* for us than perfect induction.

Our imperfect world and everything in it, including ourselves, can *only* be imperfect, so everything must be full of differences. That means everything is full of variation and gradable qualities. In order to deal with our world, therefore, we need an epistemological tool full of variation and gradable qualities, and that is what we actually have: induction. Because of induction, even philosophers can go on with their everyday lives successfully—though of course, far from perfectly, as Searle demonstrates:

[26] Hume's description of the way of life a Pyrrhonian should follow may be basically correct, but its philosophical motivation or justification appears to have been either misunderstood or deliberately misrepresented by him. The problem might go back to Sextus Empiricus, who is overly defensive on this point, perhaps in reaction to the fact that the Pyrrhonists were severely criticized in Antiquity because philosophers were supposed to *live* their philosophy, and it was argued that Pyrrhonists could not. The existence of the covert argument seems therefore not to have been realized by the Late Pyrrhonists, or at least not by Sextus. It does not appear that Pyrrho himself had a problem with it, if he recognized the issue at all; he seems to have been uninterested in such philosophical niceties. It would seem that the Buddha did understand the issue, at least intuitively, and did not see a problem with it.

> First there is the assumption that unless a distinction can be made rigorous and precise it is not really a distinction at all. Many literary theorists fail to see, for example, that it is not an objection to a theory of fiction that it does not sharply divide fiction from nonfiction. . . . On the contrary, it is a condition of the adequacy of a precise theory of an indeterminate phenomenon that it should precisely characterize that phenomenon as indeterminate, and a distinction is no less a distinction for allowing for a family of related, marginal, diverging cases. . . . Second, and equally positivistic, is the insistence that concepts that apply to language and literature, if they are to be truly valid, must admit of some mechanical procedure of verification. Thus, for example, if one attempts to characterize the role of intention in language, many literary critics immediately demand some mechanical criterion for ascertaining the presence and content of intentions. But, of course, there are no such criteria. How do we tell what a person's intentions are? The answer is, in all sorts of ways, and we may even get it wrong in the apparently most favorable cases. But such facts as these . . . in no way undermine the concepts of intention, fiction, and metaphor. Our use of these concepts and our distinctions between the intentional and the unintentional, the literal and the metaphorical, and between fictional and nonfictional discourse [are] grounded in a complex network of linguistic and social practices. In general these practices neither require nor admit of rigorous internal boundary lines and simple mechanical methods of ascertaining the presence or absence of a phenomenon.[27]

To put it another way, *none* of our everyday thinking actually involves any genuine absolutes—whether perfect knowledge, perfect actions, perfect beings, or whatever. As Pyrrho says, all "matters, affairs, events" are inherently undifferentiated—therefore we do our best to provide them with differentiae—and because everything is also unstable and unfixed, we have to adjust our own stance on the ship of thought and change our judgements to accord with the shifting seas. We think by categorizing, and we have done it successfully enough to have survived for several million years as hominids. The things we attempt to categorize, our categories themselves, our process of categorization, ourselves as categorizers,[28] are all imperfect approximations;

[27] Searle (1983).

[28] On sublinguistic categories in language, see Beckwith (2007b).

they are not "absolutely" True or False, and they are not precise in any way. But as a consequence, there are by definition *differences* in precision, including differences of *quality* of the differences, such that some data (or samplings of things) can be more consistent than other data, and the judgements that some people make can be more consistent and conform more closely to the data than those made by others, and the totality of judgements about something made so far by one group of people can have more consistency than the totality of judgements made by another group, and so on. That means we have *gradability*.

In short, Pyrrho disproves the absolutist-perfectionist approach of Aristotle and others, but he leaves *practical* science possible, as Pyrrho's student Timon and the later Pyrrhonist physicians—including Sextus Empiricus—showed. Nevertheless, it is strictly *a science of phenomena perceived by our senses*; we cannot expect absolutes, and should not look for them.

The logically valid converse of Hume's *overt* "Problem of Induction" is thus Hume's *covert* "Problem of Perfection", which is inapplicable to us and our world because—as Hume points out so well in his overt argument, the "Problem of Induction"—we and our world are not perfect, among other things. All of this "imperfection" is simply the way that our world is, but *because* of its variety, gradability, changeability, and so on we have developed gradably imperfect minds, and imperfect, constantly changing languages, which allow us to deal with the gradable imperfection of everything in our gradable, imperfect world.

For example, it is possible for us to decide whether it is better to eat at Maximilian's Grand Gourmet Restaurant or Louie's Little Country Cafe. This is not exact, perfect knowledge. A lot depends on each of us as different, gradable individuals, too. The fact that old Louie has stayed in business for fifty years and is still going strong tells us that a lot of people like his cooking. Although Maximilian's has been in business even longer and serves a ritzier clientele, Louie's customers feel at home eating at his place, and they would not like the fancy food at Maximilian's, while the reverse is equally true. Some people think that Leonardo da Vinci was the "greatest" painter in Western art history, while others think that Rembrandt, or someone else, was "even greater". Even the same individual often makes different judgements at different times, depending on many variable factors. For example, right now a keyboardist might like to play the *Sarabande* from Bach's French Suite No. 5 on the harpsichord, but at another time she might like to play a Chopin *Nocturne* on the piano, or another piece of music composed back when there was living Art. The fact that we can make such judgements at all tells us not only that our minds are part of this imperfect, variable, gradable world, it tells us that they have developed precisely to deal with it. Could a perfect mind, attuned to its perfect self and its perfect world, even be able to comprehend our imperfect world, with significant differences between individual paintings or compositions? Structural harmony in Western music is based upon what are called "perfect" and "imperfect" intervals. Even though none of them are really "perfect" in an absolute sense, the greatness of a composition lies partly in the composer's ability to use the *imperfect* intervals to heighten appreciation of the perfect ones, and vice versa. But in a *perfect* world, as far as we can conceive of one at all, there could only be a *single* painting, a perfect one, which would probably all be a single perfect color, and there could only be a *single* piece of music, a perfect one, no doubt consisting of a single note. We would probably not be able to recognize either one as art or music. A being with perfect knowledge would actually be unable to comprehend our imperfect world, just as we would not be able to comprehend its perfect one. There is no room for perfect, Divine knowledge in our world. It would be useless. If Hume did not have imperfect (and thus gradable) knowledge of our imperfect (and thus gradable) world, it would have been impossible for him to have written a single word.

If it be no longer simply *assumed* that perfection exists, either as God and God's world or our own world (either in our perceptual reality or in the mind of God), or that scientists or other humans could have "perfect" or "certain" knowledge of anything, then the only kind of knowledge that can exist must by definition *not* be perfect or certain. Could this "imperfect" or "uncertain" human scientific knowledge be a problem? In fact, without the prior assumption of the existence of "perfect" knowledge, it is difficult or impossible to conceive of there being any fundamental problem with human scientific knowledge, though it is, to be sure, intrinsically "imperfect".

Human knowledge is by definition different from God's knowledge, or "supernatural" knowledge, which by definition is "perfect", and therefore not gradable into different degrees of "perfection" (or vice versa). Accordingly, human or "natural" knowledge is by definition not "perfect": it is *necessarily* gradable and therefore "imperfect". If it be assumed to begin with that human knowledge is by definition imperfect, the logical conclusion can only be that all "natural" knowledge can *only* be imperfect, including all knowledge about the world obtained by human scientists.

This circular argument corresponds to a less obviously circular argument: the one based on the assumption that the world is perfect and perfect knowledge of it exists in the mind of God, and therefore human knowledge, being imperfect by comparison, is worthless. The meaninglessness of such arguments ought to be apparent. Leaving aside God, if no knowledge in *our* world is or can possibly be "perfect", there could not be anything intrinsically wrong with knowledge that is not "perfect", because it is the only kind that actually exists in our world, and in any intrinsically imperfect world it is the only kind that *could* exist. As far as we are concerned, it is just knowledge, plain and simple—it is the way that it is—and, being natural, it is gradable, so some parts or aspects of it are naturally more accurate than others. In scientific work it is necessary to work toward the highest degree of precision possible, and it is the gradability of our knowledge which gives us the ability to do that.

Science, the attempt of humans to study the world we perceive, is explicitly based on *precise* thinking. It thus requires the careful use of logic, careful observation, careful experimentation, and so on. This emphasis on *precision* represents recognition of the fact that most thinking—and most language—is in actuality far from precise, the most carefully constructed logical argument can be faulty, our abilities to observe, test, record, and analyze are limited, flawed, and imprecise, and so forth. Therefore, professional working scientists actually do recognize that our knowledge is unavoidably imperfect. That is why science *as actually practiced* is overwhelmingly concerned with precision, protocols, replicability, and so forth. Science *is* method.[29] The point of science, then, is not to achieve the fantasy of perfect knowledge, or absolute truth, about anything. It is simply to understand the world *to the best of our abilities*. That is what is meant when it is said that "the goal

[29] On the origins of the medieval scientific method (the recursive argument method), which was born not in Europe but in distant Central Asia, see Beckwith (2012c).

of science is the truth." If it were not a *goal*, we would already have attained what we seek, and it would therefore be perfect, absolute Truth, we would be supernatural beings, we would already know everything, and we would not need science. Any knowledge attainable by humans is by definition imperfect, so if humans attain imperfect knowledge of anything, it must be the truth *as far as we know it*. Because absolute, perfect, true, Divine knowledge about anything must be totally perfect as a whole, it cannot contain any degree of imperfection and therefore it could not represent the world as we perceive it, which is full of imperfection, while if Divine knowledge *corresponded* to an imperfect world it could not be perfect knowledge either, and thus not Divine. Even if God suddenly decided to give us access to perfect, divine knowledge, and also conferred on us the divine ability to understand it, it would nevertheless be useless to us for understanding and dealing with our graded, "imperfect" world.[30]

The Problem of Induction is thus on the whole not really a problem at all, but simply a statement of the reality of our epistemological faculties. The one real problem is its unmentioned *background*,[31] which is not the real world, but rather the traditional belief in absolutist-perfectionist assumptions about categorization. For at least the last couple of millennia this belief has formed an unspoken frame of reference for nearly all consideration of epistemological questions, and perhaps for epistemology itself. Instead of analyzing the problems of the absolutist-perfectionist approach and its incompatibility with the known world, philosophers have been obsessed with the many supposed obstacles which, they claim, prevent anyone from accepting the ideas of Pyrrho, Sextus, and Hume as "practical" philosophy. In fact, Hume's reformulation of Pyrrhonism stands in stark, shocking contrast not to reality, but to the wholly imaginary absolutist background, a construct built on fantasies about perfect this and absolute that. What is perceived to be "problematic" about Hume's formulation is its frank assessment of the "real-world" situation of humans, human cognitive abilities, and human experience of the phenomenal world. It is not a perfect assessment—some

[30] This entire issue has long been understood intuitively by religious mystics, who essentially assert the same thing. For them, the problem can be overcome only through identification by the worshipper with God in the *unio mystica*.

[31] I use this term in its literal, common-parlance sense here, not the "real-world" sense of Searle (1995).

of its imperfections[32] are pointed out here—but in the main it conforms to the data, namely our knowledge about the phenomenal world, our epistemological abilities, and so on. In itself it is really unremarkable except insofar as anyone should have felt it necessary to state right up front what the real world is actually like—to tell people facts of life that they were, and generally still are, unwilling to accept. What makes Hume's Pyrrhonian view seem problematic is simply that most people have been unaware of their absolutist fantasy—or perhaps unwilling to give it up—right down to the present day.[33]

We should now reexamine the source of Hume's argument. Bearing in mind what we have found out about his variant of the logical argument of Pyrrho, ultimately going back to the Buddha—that is, nothing by nature has its own inherent self-identity—what can we learn about the assumptions and unstated beliefs in the Trilakṣaṇa or 'three characteristics'? Its converse might be, "The one perfect being or world *does* have an inherent self-identity; it *is* perfectly stable; and it *is* fixed." Exactly as with Hume, the *Trilakṣaṇa* negates the characteristics of God (as well as God's world, Heaven), presumably the Early Zoroastrian and Early Brahmanist God: an uncaused, perfect, eternal being, in—or the same as—a perfect world.[34] The "background" of

[32] The most important flaws (which are due directly to the absolutist-perfectionist background) are Hume's argument about the future, the dogmatic "Academic Sceptic" conclusion in his *Enquiry* to the effect that we cannot really know anything, and his apologetic presentation of his "sceptical solution" (or the idea that there was a problem in his argument that needed explaining by such a "solution"). All of this suggests that Hume was not as consciously aware of the converse of the Pyrrhonist argument (which he has adopted ultimately from Pyrrho, via Sextus Empiricus, via Bayle) as I have imagined, or that he was much sneakier. I must admit that the second possibility is the more appealing, and might well be confirmed by careful research: Hume is said to have remarked late in life that he was not confident enough to assert that atheism is correct, suggesting that he was at heart a true Pyrrhonian.

[33] It is true that many people have had great difficulty in understanding what it is that the Buddha, Pyrrho, and Hume have taught us. That is certainly their problem. But there is no "problem" with induction.

[34] Megasthenes summarizes the Brahmanists' view that "the universe was created and is destructible". He also says "that the god who made it and regulates it pervades the whole of it" (Strabo xv, 1, 59, Jones 1930: 7:103; Radt 2005: 208–209). Radt (2009: 196) says that the latter is "eine stoische Vorstellung", citing his trusty old (but unreliable) source Stein (1931: 262, 9ff.), though he also notes that this might be an insertion in the text. Yet it does agree with the view of attested later Brahmanism, or early

the Pyrrhonist position, and of Buddhism before it, is therefore also absolutism-perfectionism, just as with Hume's position.

However, if we *start* from God and his Godlike world, absolutely perfect and blissful in every respect, and then turn to the *exact* converse, we do not actually get back to us and our world. Instead, we get the *exact opposite* of a Godlike world, with *absolute* imperfection, *total* irregularity, and *complete* unpredictability from one instant to the next. As it is a world where only absolute imperfection exists—and just as in a perfect world, there is no possibility of gradation—so cognition (at least as we know it) is actually impossible. This is not only not our world, it is not even a possible world: it is an absolute chaos, an impossibility.[35] And its exact, perfect opposite, a perfect eternal world, must be impossible too. We are left with only one possibility: the *imperfect* converse of these "absolute" worlds, namely our own *non*-absolute *im*perfect world and *im*perfect knowledge.

This brings up the question of *why* the Buddha expressed his insight in the *Trilakṣaṇa*. Was he, too, expressing a veiled criticism of the dominant belief system known to him—Early Zoroastrianism or Brahmanism, or perhaps both—which like Christianity focused on an all-creating divinity and the perfection of things? Or, since the Buddha would seem really to have been by origin a Scythian (Saka), was it perhaps a Central Eurasian belief system, with its monotheistic, all-powerful Heavenly God and the belief that nobles went to Heaven after death? To the Buddha, either choice—the traditional perfectionist paradise (corresponding to the pursuit of pleasure) or its exact opposite, a hellish chaos (corresponding to extreme asceticism)—must have seemed untenable. The Buddha, Pyrrho, and Hume give the same solution for the problem they only partly present: a Middle Path between the extremes. That fits

---

Hinduism, and it is part of a quite consistent account of the Brahmanists' metaphysics. Why should this one bit be a Stoic or any other kind of insertion? The traditional Central Eurasian peoples' concept of God and the universe was quite similar to this, and the Greeks, the Indic peoples, and the Persians, being Indo-Europeans, all came from Central Eurasia (Beckwith 2009: 29–57). This sort of view is an example of the ad hoc smorgasbord approach to the history of philosophy and religion, q.v. Appendix B.

[35] The overly narrow, overly conceptualized ideas *labeled* "chaos" and discussed by mathematicians, logicians, etc. are actually highly regularized and not cases of chaos at all, but something else. I mean here simple common-parlance *chaos*, the variety defined in encyclopedias of philosophy as 'disorder', and then largely ignored.

well with us and our world, because we are neither *absolutely* perfect nor *absolutely* imperfect; we are somewhere in the middle.

Thus things are varied, though not absolutely, and events are not certainly predictable, though they follow more or less regular natural laws, which fit the nature of our somewhat regular world. People are as varied in their abilities and other characteristics as everything else. Accordingly, our minds too are not absolutely perfect or absolutely imperfect, they are also in between. Because of all the variation, things are gradable, so it is possible for us to think, and to analyze things—not perfectly, but on a gradable scale between "rather bad" and "rather good", depending on factors such as who is doing the thinking, what they are thinking about, under what conditions, with what data, how "good" and "bad" are usually defined for the matters in question, and so on. This Middle Path is exactly the one we see presented to us in the Buddha's *Trilakṣaṇa*, in Pyrrho's version of it, and in Hume's arguments for, basically, the same thing.

Pyrrho's teachings—which are manifestly based on Early Buddhism—say that because our limited, imperfect sense perceptions and knowledge cannot give us *perfect truth* or its *absolute opposite* about anything, we should not expect them to do it.[36] Instead, we should abandon belief in dogmatic views, resolutely follow the Middle Path,[37] and avoid the suffering that results from going to the extremes advocated by philosophers and religious teachers. With a fair amount of practice, we will eventually find ourselves free of the suffering of the passions—undoubtedly not *perfectly* free, but free enough. Pyrrho says we should be "unwavering", that is, steadfast, meaning we will still have to work at it. We will then experience that which follows passionlessness "like its shadow": calm, nirvana. This is also Buddha's teaching, as well as Hume's "sceptical solution", which now makes perfect sense.

[36] "Therefore (due to the problem [the *Trilakṣaṇa*] that he has just noted), neither our sense perceptions nor our views or theories (*doxai*) tell us the (ultimate) truth or lie to us (about *pragmata* 'things'). So we certainly should not rely on them (to do that)." See Chapter One; for detailed analysis of the Greek text see Appendix A.

[37] The middle way that the world itself suggests to us, the middle path between the extremes, which eventually leads to passionlessness.

Non-rectilinear Logic

Pyrrho shows that traditional logic, which may be called "rectilinear logic",[38] depends on a perfectionist-absolutist and logical impossibility: the idea that things do have their own naturally innate self-identities. Therefore, from the traditional point of view, all such supposedly valid arguments are in fact circular and invalid, and the beliefs of their proponents are unsupported. Moreover, because there are no valid rectilinear arguments, there are no valid "perfect" absolutes, and vice versa.

This however suggests that the converse should be fine: what we may call "non-rectilinear logic" should be valid if it is *not* rectilinear. Is this possible, or even conceivable? Certainly Pyrrho seems to have considered his logic to have been impeccable. So did Timon and the Late Pyrrhonists. In that case, having demonstrated the fundamental invalidity of all other "philosophy", which was based on rectilinear logic, was Pyrrho's own argument merely a "purgative", as the Late Pyrrhonists say, which expels itself along with the bad stuff? That would be necessary, perhaps, if we accepted the absolutist view of everything; if not, we must consider what it might mean.

First we must accept that Hume's analysis of induction is largely correct, and humans' *innate way of thinking* is, in fact, essentially and unavoidably—though *not perfectly*—"circular." This is because we always necessarily start from preformed notions, terms, and so on, and cannot think without them.[39] One might object, "Surely there is a way to argue which is *not* circular and invalid!" But we did *not* say, "Because our thought is 'circular' it is *invalid*." It is "circular" in its

[38] The most natural terms to use here would perhaps be "linear logic" (for traditional logic) versus "circular logic". However, "linear logic" has been adopted by Jean-Yves Girard and others as a term for a new variety of traditional logic; due to its use for computational purposes it has become widely known. The term "circular logic" would be easily confused with "circular argument", which is not always easy to distinguish from it. Whereas a "circular argument" is invalid within traditional "rectilinear" logic, it would evidently not necessarily be invalid in non-rectilinear ("circular") logic. These problems require serious study, and it is not certain that they can be easily ironed out. For this reason I have coined the terms "rectilinear logic" and "non-rectilinear logic". I would like to thank Michael Dunn (p.c., 2014) for his helpful comments, though he is of course not responsible for any errors.

[39] This is of course Pyrrho's point too.

underlying construction in our minds. That is not "bad". It gives us recursion—self-reflection. Most people think that is "good". It gives us the potential to do more than the primitive, reactive cognition done by most non-hominid animals, and not a few hominids too.

The Buddha's logic is "circular" as well.[40] According to the *Trilakṣaṇa*, things constantly change, and that change can *only* be conditioned change. Why "only"? The necessity follows upon the assumption that for anything to truly, absolutely exist as a discrete thing, it must have a permanent inherent identity, which therefore cannot change, and as a result causation—which involves change—is impossible. The Buddha rejects this absolutist-perfectionist view. And as Hume shows so well, causation is all around us and a fundamental feature of our mental processes, so we can hardly deny that causation seems to exist as much as anything else seems to exist. Moreover, if things do not have their own innate identities, then they cannot be fixed, balanced, and so on either. So they do constantly change, as the Buddha and Pyrrho both say. Things also cannot change by themselves, so they must change in connection with other things. As all things can appear to exist only in relation to other things, they affect each other. This is Buddha's "conditioned change", another point at which we can see the "circularity" in his thinking.[41]

Next we should consider what any valid logic might be like in a human mind that is inescapably "circular," or better, non-rectilinear, in its internal workings. A valid non-rectilinear argument must of course identify and define all points in the argument to the degree possible,

[40] The Buddha and Pyrrho say that the problem is in the mind. We see all of this, or our teachers tell us about it, and we worry about it and try to avoid it. But it is a mental trap, and we should undo it. In order to do that, we must use the mind, the very thing that is causing the trouble, and we must use the home of the mind, the body, to help too, via what we call in English *meditation* and *yoga*. All this may be normal human logical thought, but it is "circular."

[41] In traditional Normative Buddhism, the Buddha is thought to have seen the world as a kind of circular trap, samsara (Sanskrit *saṃsāra*). It is understood not to have been limited to this life, because of the widespread belief, perhaps based on inductive logic, that just as nature changes in the cycle of the seasons—plant lives, animal lives, etc.—so humans regularly die and are eventually reborn, their particular births having been determined by karma. However, the idea of samsara and this idea of rebirth (which is unlike the attested early form of the idea) is not mentioned or reflected in any hard data on attested Early Buddhism. Cf. the Prologue.

but in such a logic, *delimiting* the ends of the argument would make it rectilinear, and thus invalidate it. To be valid human logic, it must refer back to the beginning—it must be recursive somehow. We cannot cut the circle. Is that illogical, or unscientific? Consider a famous example of a model scientific argument. Einstein's Theory of Relativity defines mass and energy in terms of each other. It says, in effect, that mass is "ultimately" indistinguishable from energy.[42] It is a twice-"circular" argument *and* the theory conforms well to the data, so it is "circular" thrice over. The argument of the Buddha, Pyrrho, and Hume disproves its apparent covert opposite, a rigid *rectilinear* argument based on the fantasy of perfection, which is invalidated by its circularity. The Buddha, Pyrrho, and Hume also argue circularly, but their argument, like Einstein's, is *inherently* "circular" and thus conforms very well to the way we actually do think. It is this that gives it its great power. Its dissolution of rectilinear arguments allows the Buddhist, Pyrrhonist, or Pyrrhonian to be "left with" our native non-rectilinear logic, imperfection, and so on, and thus the realization that absolutism or perfectionism can lead only to unhappiness.

Conforming to the data as well as it is possible for anything to conform to anything else in our imperfect world is not only what "good" science is about, it is what we do to the best of our abilities in everyday life. That is why Hume's "sceptical solution", Pyrrho's pragmatism, and Buddha's Middle Path are actually not "instrumental" *exceptions* to their respective philosophies or religions after all. All three recommend that we accept what our imperfect minds tell us about our imperfect world, and accordingly reject absolutist-perfectionist thought of any kind.

If we reject absolutist-perfectionist thought, what do we do about Science, or Art? It is difficult to define terms such as these, but if we

[42] If the countless experiments done in nuclear particle physics show anything, they show that there is no such thing as "matter". Einstein's theory necessarily assumes—even if covertly—that there is a "real" difference between "mass" and energy. The "Big Bang" theory is predicated upon the assumption that there must be absolute beginnings and absolute endings, including the assumption that there had to be an event or a being or something *before* the event or being or something. All of this sounds remarkably like Aristotle's *Metaphysics*, with its Prime Mover, or the medieval Neoplatonic, Aristotle-influenced, Judeo-Christian-Islamic philosopher-theologians' version of God; it does *not* sound like science.

want to have those things we must do the best we can to define them anyway. And it is not just a matter of these and a few other disputed terms, such as *Beauty*, *Purity*, *Truth*, and so on: *all* of our words and concepts, our entire language faculty, our minds themselves, are equally undifferentiated, unbalanced or unstable, and unfixed, as Pyrrho and the Buddha said long ago. Why? Because we are not God, we are not perfect, we do not have perfect knowledge, and we do not have a perfect world, in which everything would necessarily be perfectly differentiated (i.e., self-identified), perfectly balanced, and perfectly fixed (i.e., eternal and unchanging). We are imperfect beings, with imperfect minds, in an imperfect world. If we did not have imperfect minds, we would not only be unable to define *Beauty* and other terms, however imperfectly, we would not even be able to conceive of them, because they necessarily exist and are defined strictly in the context of imperfection; there can be no absolute, perfect definition of them.

Critics of the idea of *Beauty* reject definitions of it *because the definitions are not perfect.*[43] But their rejection is based on absolutist-perfectionist premises. In fact, *Beauty* is actually easy for us to imagine, being as we are imperfect. It is also important (importance being a graded, imperfect concept), and we need to deal with it. The consequences of *not* dealing with it, or even openly rejecting it, as has been done for most of the past century, ought to be obvious by now, but they still are not.

No perfect ideals are attainable. That is why they are ideals, goals. That is why the great masterpieces of art are so few. Without the gradation made possible by our imperfect world, including our imperfect minds, we would not notice such differences, and it would be impossible for us to appreciate art at all, so there would be no art, not to speak of "great" art,[44] which *requires* artists to *aim* at "perfection"—and

[43] See Chapter Three for a discussion of Beauty in the *Chuangtzu*. Note that Kant considered it to be impossible to judge beauty according to any external criterion (Eichner 1970: 35–36, cited in Speight 2011). This is of course in line with the view of Pyrrho and other ancient writers, q.v. the Prologue.

[44] See Beckwith (2009: 263–302, 313–318) on Modernism's destruction of the traditional tension between the Ancient and the Modern, old and new, which operated in the "high art" tradition, and the failure of comparable new traditions to develop.

only imperfect people in an imperfect world can possibly imagine what that could mean.

Although Beauty is certainly not easy to define, we do have a definition of it, or many definitions, as we must have if we want to think about it, talk about it, and most importantly, *do* something about it. Not working seriously to come up with a better definition than the ones we have, which are mostly based on folklore, impairs our ability to deal with it. If we were to follow a human Middle Path in logic, our category "Beauty" would be varied, imperfect, and ever-changing—exactly as the Buddha and Pyrrho say everything is "by nature". That would mean we would have a "fuzzy category". But, those are the only categories we actually do have, *all* of them, as scholars who work on human categorization have long ago shown.[45] So we already have a nice fuzzy, furry idea of Beauty. Though most people today deny having such an idea, or *any* idea of Beauty, it should by now be clear that their denial simply confirms their acceptance of it. This is the Vise of Circular Logic (or more precisely, "Non-rectilinear" Logic).

Perfection, Imperfection, and Definitions

God/God's world ➤ Absolute Beauty : Beauty is out of this world
- Humans try to achieve absolute Beauty ➤ *some* Beauty

Humans/our world ➤ Imperfect Beauty : *some* Beauty
- Humans try to achieve or approximate *some* Beauty ➤ *some* Beauty

Non-God ➤ Absolute *non*-Beauty : Rejection of Beauty
- Humans try to do without Beauty, or do the opposite ➤ *non*-Beauty = Ugliness

Defining our terms means thinking about them—something not done very much these days, because admittedly thinking *is* hard to do—but it is worth the effort if we want artists, poets, and musicians to do Beauty again.

[45] See Beckwith (2007b).

EPILOGUE

Pyrrho's Teacher

THE BUDDHA AND HIS AWAKENING

It has long been a truism that history in India begins with Śākamuni 'the Scythian Sage', the Buddha.[1] According to current scholarly opinion, the Upanishads first appeared at about the time of the Buddha, somewhat after the Rig Veda had become a fixed oral text.

In the Jainist view, Mahāvīra, the founder of the Jains, was a contemporary of the Buddha, and they knew each other, as did the founders of the other great ancient Indian sects.[2xii] This a wonderful story, and there are many similar stories in Indian literature. Nevertheless, scholars have demonstrated, piece by piece, in many studies of individual contradictory problems in Early Buddhism and other ancient Indian belief systems, that the other traditions have reconfigured themselves so as to be as old as Buddhism,[3] or in some cases, as with the Jains, even older.[4] They demonstrate as clearly as anyone could have done that the story of the Buddha is the oldest of the lot. Although some may wonder why the non-Buddhists made such claims, there are

[1] Like the Prologue, this chapter is an essay intended to summarize some of the main points touched on in the central chapters of this book and draw reasoned conclusions; it is therefore mostly not annotated. For references, texts, and detailed discussion of topics mentioned in this chapter, please see the chapters above and the appendices.

[2] See the discussion in the Preface and in Endnote xii.

[3] They and other scholars do not always seem to realize the implications of such demonstrations.

[4] See Mette (1995) and the discussion in the Preface.

actually many close parallels in recorded Asian religious history,[5] and many good reasons for them to want to imitate the Buddhists' success.

That brings us back again to the Buddha, about whose biography we know extremely little for certain. Though most Buddhologists accept many, if not all, of the Normative Buddhist tradition's ideas about him and his genuine teachings, in fact we can say with confidence only that his personal name was *Gautama* (or *Gotama*); that he was familiar with Early Zoroastrianism and reacted against it; that he achieved a remarkable intellectual deed, as a result of which he became known as the *Buddha* 'the awakened (enlightened) one'; that he taught what he had discovered to others; and that he died in a remote area of Magadha. As shown by Bareau, Schopen, and others, we cannot believe most of the traditional accounts of the Buddha's life and teachings. However, as with the historical Jesus, we can probably accept the nonmiraculous and nonscripted parts of the account of his death as generally historical. After all, if Jesus had not been crucified, could the Christianity we know have developed? Similarly, if Gautama had not achieved *bodhi* "awakening" (or "enlightenment")—whatever that meant to him and others of his time—he would not have become known as the *Buddha*.

The Eighth Rock Edict of Devānāṃpriya Priyadarśi tells us that the king went to Saṃbodhi (now Bodhgayā) in Magadha, where the Buddha is believed to have achieved enlightenment under the Bodhi Tree. This firmly dates the story and the veneration of the particular place where the Buddha's enlightenment was thought to have happened, and probably veneration of the person of the Buddha himself, to which Megasthenes may refer.[6] After his visit the king began preaching the Dharma,[7] so in view of the solid evidence, we can be sure that these particular beliefs were widespread and apparently unquestioned by the mid-third century BC, two centuries or more before the development of Normative Buddhism.

During his life, the Buddha must have acquired enough followers, who revered him for his accomplishments, that they successfully

[5] Most notably, systematized Chinese Taoism, Tibetan Bon, and Japanese Shinto, as mentioned in Chapter Two, Note 140.

[6] See Chapter Two.

[7] Eighth Rock Edict: Girnar VIII, 2 (Hultzsch 1925: 14–15). See further in Chapter Three.

maintained, spread, and developed his teachings during his life and after his death.

So we are back to the fundamental question: What did the Buddha teach, why, and when?

First of all, *actual* Early Buddhism, as far as we can reconstruct it, must be based on what is attested in the hard data: Greek, Chinese, and Indic sources firmly dated to the fourth and third centuries BC. This is not very long after the lifetime of the Buddha, according to recent scholars' estimates, though still at least a century intervenes.[8] Therefore, what is attested sometimes is already quite different from what we can determine was the state of affairs during the Buddha's lifetime. In addition, because many connecting bits are missing in these fragmentary early sources, when necessary they must be filled out from what can be deduced from the earliest texts of later Normative Buddhism.

This section summarizes what this attested and explicit Early Buddhism looks like, based on the analysis and presentation of data in the rest of the book.

It seems from the extant evidence that the Buddha started out teaching not only what he himself came to understand through his practice, but also *how to come to the same understanding* by doing what he had done. And in fact, the key elements of the story telling how Gautama became the Buddha do correspond closely to reconstructable Early Buddhist practices actually attested both in the Greek sources and in the five *tapas* (ascetic practices)[9] of the Early Buddhist practitioners.[10]

Attested Early Buddhism

Gautama "went out" from his family and for many years wandered, living in the forest, begging for food, wearing found or donated clothing, and abstaining from sex. He did severe meditation-yoga under a tree

[8] See the discussion of his dates in the Prologue.

[9] The *tapas* belong to the earliest layer of the Vinaya, and are increasingly qualified and eventually rejected in the later layers. See Schopen (2004: 15, 25–26, 91–93); cf. Chapter Two.

[10] Points that are not explicitly stated in the sources, but are necessarily implied—either as required assumptions or things negated, or as necessary conclusions—are included in square brackets.

until he reached *bodhi* "awakening" and thus became the *Buddha* "the awakened one".[11]

He taught that all ethical "things, matters" have no inherent self-identity, so that there is no valid logical difference between true and false, good and bad; ethical things are unstable, so they are a source of emotional disturbance; and they are unfixed, so they change.[12] [These teachings negate the idea of an eternal perfect being, the idea of an eternal soul, the idea of an eternal afterlife in Heaven, the idea of a perfect world (here or in Heaven or both), the idea of perfect knowledge, the idea of perfect goodness or utter evil, the idea of ultimate truth or absolute falseness, and the idea that the world, including Heaven, is eternal.[13]] Because we cannot say anything absolutely true or false about anything, we should have "no views", we should be unattached or uninclined toward or against anything, and we should be unwavering in not "choosing" anything. If we maintain this mental "attitude" or "disposition" we will achieve passionlessness, after which nirvana, calm will follow by itself.

Having achieved this 'awakening', Buddha 'the awakened one' taught others how to do the same thing. The *Śramaṇas* are those who "went out" from their homes, leaving their families (including wives or husbands) and their possessions and followed the Buddha, who as a good Scythian wandered, living off the forest or by begging in towns. They strove to emulate him in thought and in deed.

Much more than is given in the above summary can be deduced by study of the logical implications and background of the Buddha's

[11] Traditionally translated freely as 'enlightenment' and 'the enlightened one' respectively.

[12] This three-part logical statement, the Trilakṣaṇa, is not only attested in full or in part in the earliest datable sources, it is still typically discussed in standard introductions to Buddhism today as part of the religion's early foundations, showing that it has been retained as a fundamental part of Buddhism even after the great changes of the Saka-Kushan period.

[13] The Buddha does not say anything overtly about metaphysics, ontology, epistemology, or other formal "philosophical" ways of trying to understand ourselves and our world. This apparent lacuna in the Buddha's teachings was noticed already in Antiquity. Some Buddhists then wrote stories about how one or another questioner demanded that the Buddha answer such questions, and how he declined to answer them. The reasons are, no doubt, very good reasons from the Buddhist point of view, but the whole point of the stories is, after all, to explain why there was nothing explicit in the tradition, as recorded at that time, to explain why such topics were missing. For the Buddha's logically implied covert teaching on such things, see Chapter Four.

teachings, as shown in the Prologue and Chapter Four. They are in most cases inescapably present in his thought, even though they are not explicitly stated in the sources.

In order to show more simply how the forms of Early Buddhism attested in chronologically early sources (late fourth century to mid-third century BC) compare with related forms reconstructed on the basis of critical study of Normative Buddhist texts, the elements found in the two categories are placed in two columns below, with the source of each element identified by an abbreviation. When terms occur in both columns that are exactly equivalent they are italicized.[14]

Elements of Early Buddhism

In Early Buddhist period texts	*In Normative period texts*
Gautama [Chu][15]	*Gautama* Śākamuni [Can]
leave family [Pyr Meg]	*leave family* [Can CanL]
wander [Pyr Meg Ins]	*wander* [Can CanL]
Śramaṇas [Meg Ins]	*Śramaṇas* [Can]
Forest-dwellers [MegF]	*Forest-dwellers* [Can CanD CanL]
stay as guests of donors [MegP]	stay as guests of donors [Can CanL]
wear *tree bark* [MegF]	*tree bark* clothes [Can]
eat wild food [MegF]	eat wild food [Can]
beg for food [MegP]	beg for food [Can CanD Vin]
abstain from sex [Pyr MegF]	*abstain from sex* [Can Vin]
abstain from wine [MegF]	abstain from wine [Can Vin]
frugal [Meg Ins]	frugal [Can Vin]
yoga [Ale Pyr Meg]	yoga [Can CanL]
good and bad karma [MegO, Ins]	good and bad karma (Can)

[14] *Left column:* The Greek accounts of Alexander's visit to India [Ale], Early Pyrrhonist teachings and practices [Pyr], Megasthenes' *Indica* fragments [Meg, distinguishing when relevant MegF (the Forest-dwellers), MegP (the Physicians), and MegO (the "other" Śramaṇas who repeated common sayings about "Hades" to scare the people into being good)], the Guodian manuscript of the *Tao Te Ching* [Tao], the *Chuangtzu* [Chu], the Major Inscriptions of Devānāṃpriya Priyadarśi [Ins]. *Right column*: The Pali and Chinese Canon in general, including the early Gāndhārī texts [Can], the five *tapas* of Devadatta from the Pali Canon [CanD], the Buddha's life story in or derivable from Pali Canonical texts [CanL], the earliest layer of regulations in the Vinayas [Vin], and meditation manuals such as the *Yogalehrbuch* from Central Asia [YogaL].

[15] Also attested in the *Li Chi* (Henricks 2000: 135).

knowledge of causes [Meg]	knowledge of causes [Can]
all things are not-x *not*-y *not*-z [Pyr]	*all things are not*-x *not*-y *not*-z [Can]
no self-identity (-x) [Pyr Meg Chu]	*no self-identity* (-z) [Can]
unstable, unbalanced (-y) [Pyr]	*unstable,* uneasy (-y) [Can]
unfixed, undecided (-z) [Pyr]	*unfixed,* impermanent (-x) [Can]
no antilogies [Pyr Meg Tao Chu]	no antilogies [Can]
no views [Pyr]	*no views* [Can]
no inclinations [Pyr Chu]	*no inclinations* [Can]
fight human nature [Pyr]	fight human nature [Can Vin]
passionlessness [Pyr]	*passionlessness* [Can, YogaL]
calm, undisturbedness [Pyr Tao Chu]	calm, nirvana [Can, YogaL]

It should be borne in mind that some of these elements belong to very different Buddhist groups. Attested Early Buddhism was *not* a monolithic system. Nevertheless, it would seem that most (but not all) of the elements listed can be traced back to the Buddha himself.

In addition to the above list, there are some other things that are attested archaeologically.

The stupa, the quintessentially Buddhist monument, is very early in Buddhism. According to Normative Buddhist (Saka-Kushan period) tradition, it goes back to the time of the Buddha himself. It is possible that the tradition is correct, because the stupa is archaeologically attested quite early, and in its form and early purpose it corresponds exactly to a Central Eurasian burial tumulus of the Scythian type.[16] The traditional epithet of the Buddha, *Śākamuni* (later Sanskritized as *Śākyamuni*) 'Sage of the Sakas (Scythians)' cannot therefore be easily dismissed, despite its absence from the very scanty early written sources. It is extremely unlikely that any Indian would have been called a "Saka"—a foreigner—as an epithet unless he really was a Saka. It seems, then, that his epithet is part of the core story of the Buddha too.

One must also take note of "the surprising rarity of canonical texts which locate the birth of the Blessed One at Lumbini",[17] as well as the archaeological discovery that virtually none of the cities well-known from canonical texts as the places frequented by the Buddha even

[16] M. L. Walter (p.c., 2011).

[17] Bareau (1995: 218).

existed as villages before about 500 BC,[18] and did not become cities for a long time afterward, if ever. Yet the background story of the Buddha's life that is portrayed in the Pali Canon takes place there, in Magadha, and the Buddha is shown frequenting its kings, palaces, rich merchants, pleasure groves, and cities. Therefore, something must be wrong. One possibility is that the Buddha lived at the time of Devānāṃpriya Priyadarśi or even later, in order to account for the urbanization of Magadha. However, the Buddha must have lived earlier than him, as the Greek attestations require and the tradition agrees. But this necessitates the Buddha having lived in a different region that was already urbanized, such as Gandhāra, which also agrees with his epithet "the Scythian (Saka) sage" and with his rejection of specifically Zoroastrian ideas, which were hardly known in Magadha before the Middle Ages. A third option, which applies to the others as well, is that the places mentioned in the Pali Canon were much simpler and more primitive than they are represented as having been.[19] However, this is evidently an example of trying to save one chosen part or aspect of dubious source material already falsified by hard data, in an attempt to hold onto a disproven theory. Bareau says,

> The numerous canonical texts showing the Blessed One in close company with powerful kings inhabiting splendid palaces situated in great cities, and with wealthy merchants . . . , does not prove in the least that the Buddha in fact lived in the midst of an urban and commercial civilization. Indeed, none of these texts had been fixed in writing, that we know of, before the beginning of the Common Era; and thus, they all reflect that which their authors saw at that time. . . . In order to glorify their venerated Master . . . they invented accounts and transformed other, older accounts . . . that had been transmitted by oral means only, by adapting these naturally and naïvely to the conditions in which they themselves lived. . . . [Thus] one must be extremely prudent if one wishes to use the Buddhist canonical texts, in Pāli, Sanskrit or in Chinese translation, as historical documents. In particular, one may not make use of these as arguments . . . to prove that the Buddha lived at a time when the middle basin of the Ganges already knew a very developed urban and

[18] Härtel (1995); cf. Bareau (1995: 219).

[19] Bareau (1995: 219).

commercial civilization—that which belonged to it during the last two or three centuries before the Common Era.[20]

The point here is that the hard data, alongside Bareau's careful demonstration that the Lumbini birth story is a late fabrication, and Schopen's demonstration that much of the "frame story" information found in the canonical sutras can be shown to have been fabricated as well, invalidate the traditional picture. We thus have no good reason to believe it. As a consequence, there is no reason to believe that the descriptions in the sutras and other Pali texts—or in the traditional, fantasy-filled attempts at chronology, including attempts to date the Buddha—took place where and when they are said in such texts to have occurred. That material therefore does not reveal the date or birthplace of the Buddha.

However, as noted above, Devānāṃpriya Priyadarśi explicitly states in his Eighth Rock Edict that he went to Saṃbodhi (now Bodhgayā), the name of which refers directly to the Buddha's enlightenment (*bodhi*). As a result, the king began preaching the Dharma. Information elsewhere in the same inscriptions tells us that the king flourished in the first half of the third century BC,[21] so the Eighth Rock Edict constitutes solid testimony from the Early Buddhist period that people in the early third century BC already believed the Buddha had attained enlightenment in Magadha—specifically, at Saṃbodhi. And as in the story of Jesus, the unusual details make it probable that there is some truth to the traditional cause of the Buddha's death—spoiled food—which according to the tradition in the *Mahāparinirvāṇa Sūtra* took place at or in the vicinity of Kuśinagara.[22]

[20] Bareau (1995: 219); he adds, "This would lead us to make the Blessed One at least a contemporary of Aśoka, which is obviously impossible, as the two inscriptions of Lumbinī and Nigālī Sāgar prove." This last point is incorrect. The two inscriptions in question prove nothing about the date of "Aśoka" and could not have been erected until long after the mid-third century BC, as shown in Appendix C (cf. Chapter Three). But the rest of Bareau's argument is correct, because Buddhism must have existed no later than the late fourth century BC—between 330–325 BC, when Pyrrho was in Bactria and Gandhāra and learned the basics of Buddhism there, and 305–304 BC, when Megasthenes was there and observed practicing Buddhists.

[21] See Chapter Three; see Appendix C for the other inscriptions.

[22] Bareau (1979). However, despite much searching and many claims to have found Kuśinagara, its location remains doubtful and highly disputed.

If the Pali Canon is not a reliable guide to the life and times of the Buddha, this question must surely then be raised: how reliable a guide is it to his thought and practice?

To Bareau's astute comments must be added the fact that "Aśoka" and the many inscriptions assumed to have been authored by him are the underpinning of nearly all proposed dates for the Buddha, including Bareau's. However, as Härtel has effectively shown—with extreme care not to make the significance of his points easily grasped—the (Normative) Buddhist Inscriptions (including the Minor Rock Edicts, the only texts to mention the name Aśoka) cited by nearly everyone as crucial data are at best much later than the Major Inscriptions, and at worst forgeries. In both cases they have been otherwise manipulated.[23] Yet even if they were genuine and unimpeachable, the fact remains that the Buddhist Inscriptions themselves inadvertently tell us they are later than the Major Inscriptions.[24] In particular, the Lumbini Inscription says it is an account, by someone else, about a supposed visit of Aśoka. This is unlike all of the genuine inscriptions, which are narrated by the king himself. To make matters worse, the language of the inscription is Prakrit, but the epithet of the Buddha is spelled *Sakyamuni*, representing Sanskrit *Śākyamuni* rather than Prakrit *Sakamuni* (i.e., *Śākamuni*). Sanskrit is not attested in datable written texts before the first century AD, and literary Sanskrit did not begin its spread throughout Indian culture at the expense of Prakrit before that time.[25] The Lumbini Inscription cannot be earlier than that, let alone three centuries earlier.

Archaeology, alongside the careful, critical study of the Pali Canon, essentially rules out the traditional picture of the world the Buddha lived in, including the place where he was supposedly born, and when, except that by the early third century BC it was believed that he had attained enlightenment in Magadha. The context of his earliest attested teaching, the *Trilakṣana,* and the description of Buddhist practitioners in the eyewitness account of Megasthenes, reveals that the

[23] Härtel (1995). To Härtel's study must be added that several known, publicly exposed antiquities forgers were involved in the discovery (or creation) of some of those very inscriptions (Phelps 2010). The men involved in the discovery of the Nigālī Sāgar and Lumbini Inscriptions are the very same men involved in the fraud.

[24] See Chapter Three and Appendix C.

[25] Norman (1993).

Buddha must have achieved enlightenment after the Persian conquest of Gandhāra and Sindh in ca. 518–517 BC, but before the conquest by Alexander and the visit of Pyrrho in 330–325 BC. If the epithet *Śākamuni* was given him because he really was a Saka, or Scythian, and his teachings were recognized as having been introduced to "India proper" by him, it raises the possibility—once widely considered—that Buddha and Buddhism are not quite "Indian" in origin. This is suggested by other points, including Buddhists' peculiar, specifically Central Eurasian practice of erecting stupas—huge burial tumuli for saintly figures modeled explicitly on the usage for kings—beginning, according to tradition, with the Buddha himself.

It has also long been noted by scholars that many beliefs and practices presented in the Pali Canon and in other Buddhist texts are doubtful purely on the basis of study of the contradictions found in the very same texts. For example, it is widely accepted that the Four Noble Truths and the Eightfold Path are later inventions. But if this is so, all of the sutra accounts of the Buddha's "First Sermon" at Vārāṇasī (Benares) are reflections of Normative Buddhism too.[26]

These and many of the other trappings of Normative Buddhism are thus much later developments unknown to the Buddha or his immediate successors. This is not bad; it is the normal path of development of all religions, and all human institutions. The idea that Buddhism has always been essentially the same, which underlies most of the dubious ideas presented in the traditional legendary historical accounts written during (or more often, long after) the formation of Normative Buddhism, no doubt satisfies many believers, but it has nothing to do with history.

What are some of these elements of Buddhism that are now thought by many scholars to be part of the earliest Buddhism, but are *not* in fact attested in the earliest sources? Some of them have already been excluded from the earliest Buddhism by scholars on the basis of inconsistencies and other problems in the early Normative Buddhist texts that reveal the lack of a given feature, or its difference from its characteristics

[26] The concepts of karma and rebirth are also not mentioned in Pyrrho's teachings. Their existence as popular Buddhist beliefs is attested by Megasthenes, but logical considerations indicate they could hardly have been part of the Buddha's original teachings, as discussed in Chapter One and Chapter Four.

in Normative Buddhism as a whole. Many features of Normative Buddhism are thus already thought to be centuries later than actual Early Buddhism (that is, attested, *Pre*-Normative Buddhism).

The earliest dated Normative Buddhist texts are the recently discovered Gāndhārī manuscripts from the Saka-Kushan era (circa mid-first century BC to mid-third century AD); the putatively "early" (though undated and mostly undatable) texts in the Pali Canon, which are traditionally dated to the first century BC, but are mostly much later;[27] and the earliest translations of Central Asian Buddhist texts into Chinese, beginning in the late second century AD.

Besides the new, strictly Normative Buddhist teachings and practices that appear in these later sources, *the teachings and practices of attested Early (Pre-Normative) Buddhism are included too*. This shows that Normative Buddhist sources do contain solid confirmation for the nature of Early Buddhism, or Pre-Normative Buddhism, but it is mixed together with later Normative Buddhism, which in some sects dominates or even replaces most of the attested Early Buddhist teachings and practices.[28] Normative Buddhist teachings and practices thus developed over a long period of time among Buddhist practitioners and devotees, partly as a result of the spread to India, under the Sakas and Kushans, of Central Asian forms of Buddhism, the distinctive elements of which were in many cases adopted by Normative Buddhism.[29]

Early Normative Buddhism

Siddhartha Gautama—known also as *Śākamuni*[30] 'Sage of the Scythians (Sakas)', the *Buddha* 'the enlightened one'[31]—was born a prince, but after witnessing the troubles of human life he left the palace and his

[27] The manuscripts are later still. The oldest manuscript of what is arguably a Pali Buddhist text is a fragment of the Vinaya preserved in Kathmandu and dated to the eighth or ninth century AD (Norman 1993). Most Pali texts are many centuries later than that.

[28] See Chapters One and Two.

[29] The extent to which they were adopted by the tradition that is preserved as the Pali Canon, why some elements were adopted but not others, and why some known elements were later rejected, are unclear, though some scholars are now asking these questions.

[30] In Sanskrit, *Śākyamuni*.

[31] Literally, "the awakened one".

family to become a *śramaṇa* and a *bodhisattva* 'one set on achieving enlightenment'. After he finally achieved his goal under the *bodhi* 'enlightenment' tree, he taught the Four Noble Truths, the Eightfold Path, and the Chain of Dependent Origination (*Pratītyasamutpāda*), among other things. His followers, members of the *Saṃgha* 'the community of Buddhist practitioners who take vows', were *bhikṣus* 'monks' and *bhikṣuṇīs* 'nuns', who mostly lived in highly distinctive structures called *vihāras* 'monasteries'. They shared the possessions of the *Saṃgha* bestowed by devotees, including by many of the monks and nuns themselves when they joined the *Saṃgha*. A minority of the *Saṃgha* took the more ascetic path of the Forest monks and followed a number of more difficult and demanding rules modeled on practices of the Buddha himself, if only for a short time—these held out the promise of possibly achieving enlightenment in this lifetime.

The goal of the monks was, as before, to achieve nirvana, though that was now generally interpreted to mean "liberation from samsara (*saṃsāra*), the endless "circle of rebirth". They mostly sought to do this by accumulating good karma through following the Buddha's path according to the monastic rules of the *Prātimokṣa*, which eventually developed into the *Vinaya*, the monastic code. The monks venerated the Buddha as a godlike being for having achieved liberation in one lifetime, a feat that they considered nearly impossible. As a sort of credo, an affirmation of faith, Buddhist devotees, including lay followers, recited the pious formula of "taking refuge" in the *Triratna* 'three jewels': "I take refuge in the *Buddha* (his venerated person), the *Dharma* (his teachings), and the *Saṃgha* (the monks and nuns, his followers on the path)."

It must be at least mentioned that the changes from the Buddha's teachings in his own lifetime to those of attested Early Buddhism one or two centuries later, and then to those of Normative Buddhism a further three or four centuries later, were not the only ones that took place. Buddhism continued to change and spread, and has continued to do so down to our own time. Many things thought to be typical of the forms of Buddhism we are now familiar with developed only in the Middle Ages, or in still more recent times. The modern period has been extremely fruitful for the development and spread of Buddhist thought and practices.

It is now necessary to try and explain *why* the Buddha taught what he did. The answer to this question is to be found partly in the historical changes that took place before and during the Buddha's lifetime, partly in the attested Early Buddhist teachings, and partly in the Pali Canon and other early texts.

The reason for the "negative presentation" of nearly everything in Buddhism is that the path to Buddha's enlightenment involved rejecting things, so his teachings tell us what things are *not*, what we should *not* do, and so on. That means if we determine what is negated, we can discover what the Buddha was reacting against, at least in some cases. This analysis is given in Chapter Four. It shows quite clearly that he rejected the "absolutist-perfectionist" approach to understanding the way ethical "matters, questions" are, including especially opposed ideas such as good and bad, true and false. Along with them he also rejected the ideas of karma, rebirth, and Heaven (vs. Hell), which are typical of Early Zoroastrianism, a religion introduced to Central Asia and northwestern India by the Achaemenid Persians. Nevertheless, they later became typical of popular Buddhism as well, and of Brahmanism.[32]

This brings up the question of the social, political, economic, and religious background of the Buddha's revolutionary thought. According to tradition, the Buddha lived in about the sixth century BC. Some scholars have recently down-dated his death to the fifth century or even the early fourth century, but within Indian sources themselves the Buddha's dates are probably impossible to determine very precisely because whatever they were, most of the rest of early Indian "history", such as it is, depends directly on the dates of the Buddha and must be moved along with them. However, there are some indications that can help us to place historical constraints on the Buddha's dates, and that also tell us something about his possible motivations. Considering the Greek attestations of Buddhism in Gandhāra in the late fourth century BC, and the necessity of the Buddha's contact with Early Zoroastrianism, which was introduced there in or shortly after ca. 518–517 BC, a fifth century date for the Buddha's death would seem most likely, as a first hypothesis.

The Buddha's Reaction to Zoroastrianism

The most spectacular political-economic events in all of Eurasia in the sixth century BC were the foundations of the Scythian Empire

[32] See the Prologue and Chapter Two.

and the Persian Empire. The Persian Empire began as the Kingdom of the Medes, which was taken over by Cyrus the Great, who was half Mede and half Persian. He conquered a vast territory, including the Assyrian Empire, most of the Near East, and part of Central Asia. He is said to have died in battle against a Scythian-Saka people, the Massagetae, in 530 BC.[33] After an unsettled succession finally disputed by Gaumata and Darius I (r. 522–486 BC),[34] the latter won. Darius then reconquered the territory acquired by Cyrus and expanded it even further, adding Egypt in the west and moving deeper into Central Asia and northwestern India in the east.[35] The Persian Empire became the world's first superpower. It was in contact with all of the great civilizations of the ancient world. The Persian Empire and the contemporaneous Scythian Empire in the steppe zone together dominated the world of the Axial Age. But why, exactly, did the Persians have such a pronounced effect on the peoples with whom they came into contact?

The rebel Gaumata the Magus was a Mede[36] (as Cyrus mostly was)[37] and was based in the area of Media.[38] When Darius defeated Gaumata, he condemned the cult of *daivas* ~ *daevas*[39] that Gaumata and many Magi had promoted, and he "rebuilt the temples that had been destroyed" by them. These *āyadana* 'temples' were probably Early Zoroastrian fire temples[40] (or in any case temples dedicated to Ahura Mazda, whom Darius credits repeatedly for his success), since it has been shown that a fair number of fire temples do date to the early

[33] However, there are other accounts of his death; see Dandamayev (1993).

[34] Shahbazi (2012).

[35] For a careful study of contemporaneous records of Achaemenid rule over the territories in Central Asia and India, see Wu (2010); cf. Briant (1996).

[36] Waters (2010: 70n19), citing the Akkadian version of the Behistun Inscription.

[37] Frye (2010).

[38] Razmjou (2005: 151).

[39] Old Persian *daiva* and Avestan *daeva* 'demon' are cognate to Sanskrit *deva* 'god'. See the close parallel in the "Daivā Inscription" of Xerxes, which exists in multiple copies (in Old Persian, Elamite, and Babylonian). It relates "how he suppressed a rebellion (in unspecified lands) after he became the king and (again, in unspecified lands) put an end to worship of a certain category of deities described as the *Daivā*, in places called the *Daivadāna*, and how he replaced the worship of the *Daivā* with the worship of Ahura Mazdā" (Abdi 2010: 280).

[40] As suggested by Frye (2010).

Achaemenid period.[41] Whatever the truthfulness of Darius's story about Gaumata being a usurper, a political-religious struggle certainly took place in the Persian Empire, and for some time Gaumata and his Median supporters—including the army—were in power.

It is clear that Gaumata's actions centered on his attempted restoration of an earlier polytheistic cult, an "unreformed" variety of Mazdaism in which the god *Mazdā* (attested already in the Amarna Letters from the fourteenth century BC) was venerated alongside many other Western Old Indic gods. This is supported by the discovery of what appears to be a Mazdaist fire altar in an archaeological site in Media identified with the Medes.[42]

Gaumata's rebellion was thus a reaction of the polytheistic "early Mazdaism" of the Medes against the "reformed" monotheistic Mazdaism—Early Zoroastrianism—supported primarily by the Persians. In Early Zoroastrianism, *Ahura Mazdā* 'Lord Mazda'[43] is a monotheistic Heavenly creator God; other gods are condemned, both in the Achaemenid royal inscriptions and in the Gāthās of Zoroaster in the Avesta.[44][xiii] More than half of all Achaemenid royal inscriptions begin with a formulaic declaration, "Ahuramazdā is the great god, who has created this earth, who has created yonder heaven, who has created happiness for mankind, who has made [*Name*] king, one king of many,

[41] Choksy (2007). This is certainly the case in the western part of the empire; the eastern parts have mostly not been excavated, but there are still extensive Achaemenid ruins in Sindh and Gandhāra (J. Choksy, p.c., 2013). The presence of Zoroastrian religious ideas and practices in Indian Gandhāra is attested by Persian records and by a Greek account from the fourth century BC (see below).

[42] J. Choksy (p.c., 2013).

[43] The full name Ahura Mazda is first attested in an Assyrian god list from the seventh century BC (Eckart Frahm, p.c., July 2011). Although the Cyrus Cylinder (dated 539 BC) does not mention Ahura Mazda, and presents Cyrus as a worshipper of Marduk, the god of Babylon (Curtis and Razmjou 2005: 59), it was normal for the early Achaemenids—like Central Eurasian rulers—to support the local gods throughout their realm (Razmjou 2005: 150, 153–154), at least publicly. In actual practice, they promoted their own monotheistic beliefs as much as possible.

[44] Soudavar (2010: 119) says, "Darius promoted a monotheistic ideology that exalted the supremacy of Ahura Mazdā, the god that Zoroaster also favoured, and a god that must have been popular among a certain group of Iranians. Moreover, Darius' initial fervour for Ahura Mazdā is accompanied by a total disdain for other deities. Similarly, . . . other divine beings about whom Zoroaster speaks in the Gāthās are qualified as *daevas* or demoniac beings." Cf. Endnote xiii.

one lord of many."[45] In addition, the inscriptions "speak about the *law* that was established by Ahuramazda, and life after death and the happiness and blessing for those who worship Ahuramazda".[46] With the backing of the Persian aristocracy, Darius defeated Gaumata and his followers and restored the new religion. The "reformed" Mazdaist sect of Zoroaster must therefore have suppressed the cult of daivas already under Cyrus in order for Gaumata to feel the need to oppose it. The tradition recorded in the Old Testament is that Cyrus was already a Zoroastrian,[47] but it is unknown if he was originally a Zoroastrian or an unreformed Mazdaist, or if he had became a devotee of Zoroastrianism at some point shortly before his contact with the Jews. At any rate, the overwhelming evidence in favor of the lateness of Zoroastrianism supports a date close to the traditional "low" date for the birth of Zoroaster, ca. 600 BC, even though that date is based on the dubious traditional reckoning.[48]

The rebellion thus definitely had more than mere religious "overtones". It seems to have been motivated *primarily* by religious reasons, since "[a]s his earliest act Gaumata started to demolish temples."[49] These may well have included the temples of other peoples, but it is hard to imagine righteous indignation over such destruction being the reason that Gaumata's deed is so strongly condemned in the Old Persian inscriptions. The reason the Persians were so angry must have been that Gaumata destroyed "temples" of the Persians themselves—specifically, those of the Zoroastrians. His rebellion against the new faith[50] was

[45] de Jong (2010: 87), changing his "that" to "yonder" and his "NN" to "[*Name*]"; cf. similarly Razmjou (2005: 151). Note that "one king of many" refers to the expression "king of kings", and means "one king over many kings", i.e., "emperor": a specific concept with very important political ramifications.

[46] Razmjou (2005: 151), emphasis added.

[47] Frye (2010) suggests that "the killing of the magi by Darius after attaining power may well reflect the defeat of the Median party of Bardiya/Gaumata and those magi at court who held on to old Aryan beliefs against the Zoroastrian convictions of Darius and many Persians, as well as some magi among the Medes. After the elimination of old beliefs the pro-Zoroastrian magi triumphed with Darius but later reconciled with those magi who favoured Mithra and Anahita."

[48] See Soudavar (2010) on the recent near-consensus regarding a low date of this kind; cf. Malandra (2009) on the tradition and the different theories and their problems.

[49] Razmjou (2005: 151), citing the inscription of Darius DB I 63–4 and adding that Darius rebuilt the "temples" the same year, after he defeated Gaumata.

[50] Compare the histories of early Islam and early Christianity.

clearly one of "Old Believer" Mazdaists against the Zoroastrians, who were no doubt viewed by the Old Believers as "heretics" or worse. The religious dimension of Gaumata's rebellion must therefore have made it even more heinous to Persian followers of Zoroastrianism. This might be thought to explain why the Persians accepted Darius's story about the rebellion and its suppression, but Gaumata had firm control of the army,[51] so Darius and his immediate supporters had to gather and keep the support of the leaders of the Persian ruling class in order to even attempt to defeat Gaumata. They would necessarily have been involved from the beginning, and whatever the truth of the story Darius tells in the Behistun Inscription, his compatriots had helped craft it, so they needed no convincing.[52]

The religious nature of the rebellion indicates that Zoroastrianism was fairly new, and not firmly established, in the South Iranic world (it was unknown among Scythians and other North Iranic peoples), while Gaumata's support for the worship of the daivas indicates that the Medes followed "unreformed" or "pre-Zoroastrian" Mazdaism, in which there were many gods.[53] In view of the general cultural similarity between the world of the Avestan Gāthās and the world of the Rig Veda, as well as the extremely close dialect relationship between the languages of the two texts, it appears that unreformed Mazdaism was the continuation of the ancient *West* Old Indic-speaking people's belief system, just as the Rig Vedic religion was the continuation of the ancient *East* Old Indic-speaking people's belief system. Both featured a number of gods, among whom the names of the most important ones—Indra, Mitra, Varuna, and the Nasatyas—are attested in both Western Old Indic and Eastern Old Indic.

[51] Soudavar (2010: 126).

[52] See Soudavar (2010: 126–128) on the Silver Plaque of Otanes, one of the key supporters of Darius (and the initator of the conspiracy, according to Herodotus), which states right out, "By the support (*vashnā*) of Ahura Mazdā and with me, Darius is the Great King." In the same inscription Darius says, "I punish the liar (who is a) rebel," making it absolutely unambiguous that the two men were followers of Early Zoroastrianism.

[53] See the discussion by Razmjou (2005: 150–151). The *neutral* Old Persian word for 'god' is *baga*. Ahura Mazda is often called in the inscriptions "the greatest god" or "the greatest of gods" (Razmjou 2005: 150–151), but his unique description as the creator of the world and the one who made the victories of Darius possible make it quite clear that he is the traditional monotheistic Heavenly God of the Central Eurasian Culture Complex (Beckwith 2009; 2012b).

In Early Zoroastrianism, by contrast, there is only *one true* God, Ahura Mazda, who created Heaven and Earth. Life is a struggle between the good who follow *Arta* 'the Truth' and the bad (especially "rebels") who follow *Druj* 'the Lie'. According to the Gāthās, when people die they are judged, and those whose good deeds are dominant go to Paradise, while those whose bad deeds are dominant go to Hell.

The texts Zoroaster produced were no doubt a version of the traditional ritual texts chanted for time out of mind, but he purged them of all but one of the gods of early Mazdaism, *Mazdā*, whom he equated with the Heavenly God of the Persians from the time when they were Central Eurasians and, like other early Central Eurasian peoples, believed in a monotheistic God of Heaven. Zoroaster calls him *Ahura Mazdā* 'Lord Mazda'.

Early Zoroastrianism spread around the vast Persian Empire, including Central Asian Bactria and Gandhāra, as well as eastern Gandhāra and Sindh—the latter two regions being linguistically Indic—no later than the reign of Darius I.[54] The intrusion of a new culture had a tremendous impact on the regions where Achaemenid armies and administrators settled, and constant contact via the Persian royal roads between the satrapies and the court,[55] as well as the movement of Magi and other Persian subjects from central regions of the empire to the periphery (attested as early as the reign of Cyrus[56]) ensured continued influence.

The impact of Zoroastrianism on northwestern India is attested in historical sources. One of the companions of Alexander, Aristobulus (ca. 375–301 BC), commenting on the burial customs of Taxila when the court was there in 326–325 BC, says "the dead are thrown to the vultures."[57] This is an absolutely clear reference to the Zoroastrian custom[58] already

[54] For evaluation of historical, inscriptional, and especially archaeological evidence for Achaemenid rule in Gandhāra, see Magee and Petrie (2010).

[55] This activity is attested in detailed records of payments made to official travellers by the government, recorded in the Fortification Tablets dated to between 509–494 BC, during the reign of Darius, which were found at Persepolis (Meadows 2005: 186, 197). See also the discussion and notes in the Prologue.

[56] Razmjou (2005: 153–154).

[57] Strabo XV, 1, 62, text from Radt (2005: 4:212–214): καὶ τὸ γυψὶ ῥίπτεσθαι τὸν τετελευτηκότα. In this section Strabo explicitly quotes Aristobulus, who remarks twice that he is talking about the Indians in Taxila (Strabo XV, 1, 61–62).

[58] Cf. Razmjou (2005: 154).

recorded by Herodotus (ca. 485–425 BC).[59] Aristobulus continues his discussion with a description of the well-known Indian custom of suttee, which he (or Strabo) says is described by others, too.[60] That means Indians at Taxila were also cremated in traditional Indian style. The Taxilan custom of throwing the dead to the vultures therefore reflects the Persian conquest of eastern Gandhāra by the Achaemenids, with the concomitant stationing there of Persian officials, including a satrap, subordinate officials, and a military garrison, and the documented presence of Magi—Zoroastrian priests—in non-Persian parts of the empire.[61]

As shown in Chapter Four, the Buddha's own teachings and practices, to the extent that they can be reconstructed on the basis of the earliest attested materials,[62] resoundingly reject absolutist, perfectionist thought of any kind, including the idea of a perfect, all-powerful, all-knowing God and an absolute difference between good and bad, true and false—core features of Zoroastrianism introduced to Central Asia and India by the early Achaemenids. The Buddha also does not teach anything explicitly about samsara, karma, or rebirth in a perfect, eternal world, but he does reject the underpinnings of such beliefs with his explicit rejection of any inherent personal self-identity (traditionally interpreted as a "soul")—a necessity for karma—and in his explicit rejection of the idea that anything is eternal. His teaching is all about this life in this imperfect world, the causes of uneasiness, and how to achieve peace.

Since the Buddha rejects the underpinnings of belief in God and the soul—core beliefs of Early Brahmanism attested by Megasthenes—it appears that he rejects Brahmanism, too.[63]

[59] Herodotus (I, 140.1–2) says that "the dead bodies of Persians are not buried before they have been mangled by birds or dogs", and adds, "That this is the way of the Magi, I know for certain; for they do not conceal the practice" (translation of Godley 1926). However, the kings and many others were buried in the ground, indicating that there were different burial rituals for the Magi (who were originally Medes) and for the Persians (Razmjou 2005: 154–156). Because of the key religious role of the Magi, this actually confirms the Zoroastrian nature of the custom.

[60] Strabo XV, 1, 62.

[61] Razmjou (2005: 153–154) cites examples from Cappadocia (Strabo XV, 3, 15), Egypt, and Babylon.

[62] See the presentation and analysis in Chapters One, Two, Three, and Four.

[63] Bronkhorst (1986) convincingly shows that Brahmanist belief in good and bad karma, and in rebirth, was adopted from early Normative Buddhism, not Early Buddhism. However, belief in an eternal soul was introduced to India by Zoroastrianism, and

The Buddha hardly "coincidentally" invented concepts exactly like those of Zoroastrianism purely in order to reject them. Because the Early Zoroastrian beliefs in God (Ahura Mazda), an eternal soul, Heaven, and karmically determined rebirth (the assignment of one's fate in the next life according to good and bad karma) first appear in Buddhism *as rejected beliefs*—either explicitly or implicitly—it seems clear that the Buddha reacted against Zoroastrianism, not Brahmanism. Nevertheless, the same sort of argument also applies to the pre-Brahmanists—they hardly invented the implicitly rejected concepts (primarily belief in God, an immortal soul, and attendant ideas) just to spite the Buddhists' implicit rejection of the underpinnings of such beliefs. Considering the difficulty scholars have had with all this for a very long time, it is doubtful that the pre-Brahmanists would have figured it all out. We know that some Early Buddhists did accept karma and rebirth anyway, and the Brahmanists could then have adopted those particular ideas from the Normative Buddhists, but the problem of God, the soul, and other ideas remains.[64]

The most logical solution is that Zoroastrianism was introduced by the Persians, and the local people in the occupied territories had to respond to it. Sooner or later, the Buddha reacted against the Zoroastrian ideas, while others adopted them and became Early Brahmanists. Nevertheless, it is also clear that Buddhism became a widespread, powerful influence on all religious thought in ancient India, so that it is undoubtedly the case that the Brahmanists did borrow very many things from Buddhism, just as Bronkhorst has shown. Although it remains unclear exactly when all this happened, the evidence of Megasthenes shows that belief in karma and the soul, at least, had been accepted by some Buddhists by the end of the fourth century BC.

---

it is attested as a Brahmanist belief already by Megasthenes, as is belief in one creator God, so it would seem likely that these and some of the other ultimately Zoroastrian beliefs in Brahmanism were adopted directly from that religion, rather than from Buddhism, where at least belief in God (per se) seems never to have been accepted. This problem requires further study.

[64] The few putatively early Upanishads (Brahmanist texts) in which these and other Buddhist-associated ideas appear have been definitively shown by Bronkhorst (1986) to be later than and modeled on Buddhism, and he is undoubtedly right about them; however, much further study of this important topic is needed. Cf. the discussion in Chapter Three.

Appendix A

THE CLASSICAL TESTIMONIES OF PYRRHO'S THOUGHT

Like Socrates a few generations earlier, Pyrrho himself left nothing in writing on his teachings.[1] However, his student or disciple, Timon of Phlius, wrote quite a lot on Pyrrho and his thought, and fragments of Timon's works are fortunately preserved. In addition, some contemporaries of Pyrrho and Timon have left their own observations and comments on one or both men. Scholars have attempted to reconstruct Pyrrho's thought on the basis of these testimonies, but a consensus has not been reached. This appendix discusses the major testimonies—above all one testimony that goes back to Timon's report of Pyrrho's own statements—and the major recent studies of them. Numerous difficult points are clarified and a new synthesis is presented.

[1] I am indebted to the editors of *Elenchos* for kindly giving me permission to present here a revised version of my article "Pyrrho's Logic" (Beckwith 2011b). The original article treats the Greek sources on Pyrrho alone, making no reference to Greek sources on Central Asia or India, nor to Indian or Chinese materials. (See Chapter One for a synthesis that includes discussion of materials not covered in the original article; see Chapter Two for additional Greek sources.) I have not changed the approach of the original article here, but I have taken advantage of hindsight to correct a few details, and I have made a few minor editorial changes. I have also added references to relevant chapters in this book, and reformatted the text to match that of the rest of the book.

1. Aristocles' Report of Timon's Account

The best strictly "philosophical" presentation of Pyrrho's views, according to current scholarly opinion, is given by his student Timon preserved in a book chapter by Aristocles of Messene copied verbatim by Eusebius.[2] Despite much contention, it is now agreed that the passage is the oldest, most genuine surviving testimony to Pyrrho's philosophy.[3] However, it is also thought that the text has major internal problems, the nature and extent of which differ depending on the interpreter.[4] In addition, most believe that the view presented in the Aristocles quotation is significantly different, at least in part, from the otherwise consistent picture of Pyrrho's thought presented by the other ancient testimonies,[5] to which much less attention has been paid. It is widely believed that either a metaphysical or an epistemological interpretation of the Aristocles text is called for, though it is not clear

[2] Eusebius, *Praep. evang.* XIV, 18:1–5; Chiesara (2001: 20–21). Bett (2000: 61) notes that Aristocles says his account is "of the key points (*kephalaia*)" of Pyrrho's thought, but this does not necessarily mean that Aristocles himself is the one who has summarized them. It is possible that he has paraphrased or indirectly quoted a summary made by someone else. The latter idea is pursued by Chiesara (2001: 126–136), who argues that Aristocles has taken his text from Aenesidemus. However, this argument rests mainly on the final comment "but Aenesidemus says *hēdonē*", which Chiesara contends is evidence that the text derives from a work by Aenesidemus. Cf. similarly Brunschwig (1999: 246–247). Yet since the text notes explicitly that *hēdonē* is what Aenesidemus says, which is different from what the preceding text (from Timon) says, Aristocles must have taken the comment about Aenesidemus either from a separate work by him or from a separate summary of his thought, not from the source—clearly Timon's own work—in which he (Aristocles) found his main account (see below, Notes 31 and 115).

[3] Long and Sedley (1987: 1:16–17, 2:6), which work is cited here exclusively by page numbers; Chiesara (2001: 108); Bett (2000: 15ff.; 2006). Two shorter, partly parallel texts exist (Chiesara 2001: 87ff.), but little attention has been paid to them. They are discussed below.

[4] E.g., Brunschwig (1994: 196): "the received text is wholly puzzling as it stands . . .".

[5] This is true even of Brunschwig, who in several works argues vigorously that part of the text reflects Timon's own views, not Pyrrho's. For texts and translations of a few of the most important testimonies, see Long and Sedley (1987); Decleva Caizzi (1981), which work is cited here exclusively by page numbers, gives most of them with Italian translations and commentary; selected major testimonies are translated and discussed by Bett (1994a; 2000).

to many scholars which, if either, is correct. Others see both metaphysics and epistemology in it. Aristocles considered it to reject philosophy as a whole.[6] An early overview of the literature on Pyrrho lists eight different interpretations: (1) "epistemologico-phenomenalistic", (2) "dialectico-Hegelian", (3) "scientistic", (4) "practico-ethical", (5) "metaphysical", (6) "antimetaphysical-nihilist", (7) "orientalist", (8) "literary".[7] The latest list gives recent scholars' positions: "sceptic or dogmatic, guru or epistemologist aware of his philosophical heritage, Timon's creation or authentic source of his student's exposition."[8]

It is thus not surprising that amid the recent flurry of publications on Early Pyrrhonism and related topics,[9] those which discuss the thought of Pyrrho himself in some detail continue to argue for different Pyrrhos. The metaphysical interpretation of Fernanda Decleva Caizzi, A. A. Long, and D. N. Sedley is most thoroughly developed by Richard Bett in his in-depth study of Early Pyrrhonism.[10] He argues that Pyrrho was more a dogmatic metaphysician than a Sceptic in the sense of the Late Pyrrhonism of Sextus Empiricus. Svavar Svavarsson notes that the Aristocles passage seems to present "an epistemological and metaphysical argument for an ethical conclusion."[11] He basically agrees with the traditional view of many older works that Pyrrho was an early Pyrrhonist,

[6] Eusebius, *Praep. evang.* XIV, 30; Chiesara (2001: 30–31).

[7] Reale (1981: 245–336), cited by Brunschwig (1999: 241n36); I have omitted other authorial comments and bibliographic references.

[8] Svavarsson (2010: 38).

[9] This study focuses on Aristocles' report of Timon's account and only discusses other testimonies about Pyrrho's thought in connection with it. Accordingly, literature cited here is largely restricted to the most recent studies that focus specifically on Pyrrho's own thought and include detailed analysis of the Aristocles passage. Citations are also not comprehensive. In particular, Bett and Brunschwig repeat their views in several different publications; I have not attempted to find and cite all the parallels. Bett's (2000) book *Pyrrho*, by far the most detailed analysis of the thought of Pyrrho himself, discusses many of the major testimonies. Despite Bett's arguments in favor of a dogmatic metaphysical view as the foundation of Pyrrho's thought, based on his interpretation of the Aristocles text—and, thus, despite some dubious conclusions in the light of this appendix—his analyses of the testimonies are generally insightful and often on the right track. For an extensive, up-to-date bibliography of works on ancient Scepticism, including the earlier literature, see Bett (2010a); cf. Thorsrud (2009).

[10] Decleva Caizzi (1981: 225–227), Long and Sedley (1987: 1:17–18, 2:6), Bett (2000; 2006); cf. Castagnoli's (2002) review of Bett (2000).

[11] Svavarsson (2010: 41).

arguing that the Aristocles text, together with what is known about Pyrrho in general, supports a "subjective" or epistemological reading which "preserves as fundamental the sceptical insight that one cannot decide how things are by nature."[12] Jacques Brunschwig contends that Pyrrho's thought is essentially ethical in nature, but somewhat weak in epistemology. According to him, Pyrrho's student Timon modified his teachings to make them epistemologically strong, as shown by the very Aristocles quotation under discussion. That is, he argues Timon, not Pyrrho, actually created what we know as "sceptical" Pyrrhonism.[13] R. J. Hankinson's position is similar to Bett's with regard to the foundations of Pyrrho's thought, but like Brunschwig he argues that it was otherwise mainly ethical, and that much of Early Pyrrhonism is the work of Timon, or "two Timons".[14] Harald Thorsrud argues that the Aristocles text is best understood from the traditional "epistemological" point of view.[15]

While all of these works contain much of interest, the fact remains that their interpretations of Pyrrho's thought are strikingly, incompatibly different, even though they are all largely based on the same short text.[16]

Because of the perceived difficulties of Aristocles' report of Timon's account, some scholars, mostly in older works, have concluded that the text per se is defective. Although strictly text-critical emendations of

[12] Svavarsson (2010: 44).

[13] Brunschwig (1994: 196–211; 1999: 247–251). Others argue, somewhat similarly, that Aenesidemus performed the same task a century or so later. Both ideas are connected to the question of the continuity of Pyrrho's thought into Late Pyrrhonism. Despite examination of that issue by a number of scholars, many serious problems remain. This appendix shows that he was in some important respects closer philosophically to Sextus Empiricus than to Aenesidemus, contra Bett (2000: 5–6, 214ff.), but the topic requires reexamination in a specialized study.

[14] Hankinson (1995: 61ff., 73).

[15] Thorsrud (2009: 23ff.).

[16] In his summary of the main points of his interpretation of Pyrrho's thought, as contrasted with later Pyrrhonism, Bett (2000: 40), says, "I have developed this interpretation of Pyrrho solely on the basis of an examination of the actual words in which Aristocles summarizes Timon's account." He does of course consider the other evidence quite carefully too, but his basic views about Pyrrho's thought apparently do derive from his reading of the Aristocles quotation—above all, his interpretation of the first words of the first statement attributed to Pyrrho himself.

it have recently been more or less universally rejected,[17] Brunschwig, as noted above, argues that the text itself reveals it represents Timon's modification of Pyrrho's views. In response, Bett has argued convincingly that it is essentially impossible to show that Timon's thought was different from Pyrrho's on the basis of either the Greek text of the passage per se or its contents.[18] Bett also notes that Timon unreservedly praises Pyrrho's life and teachings and promotes them to the best of his considerable abilities in his writings;[19] it would not make sense for Timon to have done this unless he agreed with Pyrrho's philosophy.[20] To this it may be added that Pyrrho lived a very long time and was undoubtedly still alive when many of Timon's works were written, making it unlikely that the two would have had any significant philosophical differences. If there had been any, it is difficult to believe that ancient critics would have ignored them. Some, such as Aristocles, considered differences of any kind to be fatal philosophical flaws for Pyrrhonism.[21]

In view of the above problems, a number of questions come to mind.

First, it is generally believed that Pyrrho's section in the Aristocles passage does not overtly refer to ethics, which is what all the other ancient testimonies regard as the main point of his thought; the final comments are clearly ethical, but they are explicitly attributed to Timon. Therefore most scholars think that the text presents a doctrinaire theory or belief on either metaphysics or epistemology, depending on one's interpretation of the beginning of the text. Yet it is undeniable that the very same text explicitly and emphatically enjoins us *not* to have any doctrinaire theories or views.[22] This is a serious problem with all of the interpretations of the text published to date.

Second, we can understand why Aristocles, a dogmatic Aristotelian, closely follows his school's approach in portraying Pyrrho's thought

[17] Bett (2000: 25ff.).

[18] Bett (2000: 8–12, 16–18); cf. similarly Long and Sedley (1987: 1:17). However, see Chapter One.

[19] On Timon's writings as literature in the narrower sense, see Clayman (2009).

[20] Bett (2000: 11–12).

[21] See below on Aristocles' criticisms.

[22] This is one of the core elements of Pyrrho's thought, and as noted by Bett (2000) it distinguishes Pyrrho from all other Greek thinkers. As shown in Chapter One, "no views" is also one of the key points of Early Buddhism.

as an extreme epistemological-metaphysical doctrine.[23] But if his summary from Timon actually represents an aberrant view of Pyrrho's thought, is it not odd that he discusses the text at great length without ever remarking critically, if not sarcastically, on the difference between its purported dogmatic metaphysical-epistemological views and the very different kind of Pyrrhonism—an ethical philosophy—that is portrayed in all of the other genuine ancient testimonies, some of which he himself quotes? The ethical element is an integral part of Aenesidemus' later "reformed" Pyrrhonism as well, as it certainly is in the Late Pyrrhonism of Sextus Empiricus.

Third, according to the received view it would appear that there are at least four early non–Academic Scepticisms in the surviving ancient literature itself: two ("rustic" and "urbane"[24]) versions of the thought of Pyrrho and Timon and their followers, the putative "dogmatic" position of Pyrrho in Timon's summary in Aristocles, and the non-Pyrrhonian "sceptical" position against which Aristotle argues in his *Metaphysics*.[25]

Finally, the usual contemporary reading of Timon's text typically includes the choice of one of the two sharply differing "dogmatic" interpretations of Pyrrho's initial inference. Because Aristocles' approach is

[23] It has been argued that Aristocles' responses to Pyrrho's initial statement about *pragmata* in the text are modeled, point for point, on Aristotle's response to the unnamed "sceptical" philosophers discussed in *Metaphysics* Γ 4 (1008a 30–34); see Chiesara (2001: 93–94, 112–114). However, Bett (2000: 180–182) demonstrates that Aristotle's opponents cannot be identified with Pyrrhonists. On the tetralemma, see Notes 28, 76, and 90.

[24] This putative distinction goes back to Galen (Chiesara 2001: 125, 133).

[25] One widely cited but spurious testimony, a passage in Diogenes Laertius (IX, 62) from Antigonus of Carystus, requires comment. It claims Pyrrho was heedless or even reckless and needed to be protected by his students from everyday dangers such as being run over by wagons or falling off cliffs. The same stereotyped characterizations are found in the arguments against the thinkers to whom Aristotle attributes "sceptical" positions in his *Metaphysics*, but Pyrrho is nowhere mentioned, and the main position criticized—denial of the Law of Non-Contradiction—is not one held by Pyrrho. In the original published version of this study (Beckwith 2011b), I remarked, "Diogenes Laertius's story is therefore that of a hypothetical straw man created by the Aristotelians or others to demonstrate what *would* happen to someone who followed the position ascribed to them by Aristotle. However, it is an impossible position for a Pyrrhonist (see below). See BETT, *Pyrrho* [2000], pp. 67–9, and cfr. note 22." Although the analysis per se is correct, I have since discovered that the Antigonus story and its reflection in Aristotle's *Metaphysics* both could derive from the description of a specific Indian sect by the chroniclers of Alexander the Great's adventures in Gandhāra, and also by Megasthenes in his *Indica*, about two decades later. For the people described, and their Gymnetae sect, see Chapter Three.

followed by E. H. Gifford—who published the first modern edition and English translation of the text of Eusebius over a century ago—it must be wondered if the usual modern reading is not ultimately a continuation of Aristocles' interpretation, transmitted by Gifford.

Let us therefore consider Timon's text once again in some detail.

2. The "Aristocles Passage"

(Πύρρων ὁ Ἠλεῖος . . . αὐτὸς μὲν οὐδὲν ἐν γραφῇ καταλέλοιπεν, ὁ δέ γε μαθητὴς αὐτοῦ Τίμων φησὶ) δεῖν τὸν μέλλοντα εὐδαιμονήσειν εἰς τρία ταῦτα βλέπειν· πρῶτον μέν, ὁποῖα πέφυκε τὰ πράγματα· δεύτερον δέ, τίνα χρὴ τρόπον ἡμᾶς πρὸς αὐτὰ διακεῖσθαι· τελευταῖον δέ, τί περιέσται τοῖς οὕτως ἔχουσι.

τὰ μὲν οὖν πράγματά φησιν αὐτὸν ἀποφαίνειν ἐπ' ἴσης ἀδιάφορα καὶ ἀστάθμητα καὶ ἀνεπίκριτα, διὰ τοῦτο μήτε τὰς αἰσθήσεις ἡμῶν μήτε τὰς δόξας ἀληθεύειν ἢ ψεύδεσθαι. διὰ τοῦτο οὖν μηδὲ πιστεύειν αὐταῖς δεῖν, ἀλλ' ἀδοξάστους καὶ ἀκλινεῖς καὶ ἀκραδάντους εἶναι, περὶ ἑνὸς ἑκάστου λέγοντας ὅτι οὐ μᾶλλον ἔστιν ἢ οὐκ ἔστιν ἢ καὶ ἔστι καὶ οὐκ ἔστιν ἢ οὔτε ἔστιν οὔτε οὐκ ἔστιν.

τοῖς μέντοι γε διακειμένοις οὕτω περιέσεσθαι Τίμων φησὶ πρῶτον μὲν ἀφασίαν, ἔπειτα δ' ἀταραξίαν (Αἰνησίδημος δ' ἡδονήν).[26]

This is translated by Long and Sedley as follows:[27]

(Pyrrho of Elis . . . himself has left nothing in writing, but his pupil Timon says that) whoever wants to be happy must consider these three questions: first, how are things by nature? Secondly, what attitude should we adopt towards them? Thirdly, what will be the outcome for those who have this attitude?

According to Timon, Pyrrho declared that things are equally indifferent, unmeasurable and inarbitrable. For this reason neither our sensations nor our opinions tell us the truth or falsehoods. Therefore for this reason we should not put our trust in them one bit, but we should be unopinionated, uncommitted and unwavering, saying concerning each

[26] *Praep. evang.* XIV, 18:2–4; cf. Long and Sedley (1987: 2:5), Chiesara (2001: 20), Decleva Caizzi (1981: 54–55). The latter omits the final comment on Aenesidemus given here in parentheses. My paragraphing follows Mras's edition. I have put what I have retained of Aristocles' introductory comments in parentheses. The uncorrected textual error at the end (ἀφασίαν) is disussed in detail in Section III below.

[27] Long and Sedley (1987: 1:14–15). Long and Sedley's translation is presented verbatim here, omitting only their section numbers, which do not correspond to Mras's paragraphing.

> individual thing that it no more is than is not, or it both is and is not, or it neither is nor is not.[28]
>
> The outcome for those who actually adopt this attitude, says Timon, will be first speechlessness, and then freedom from disturbance (and Aenesidemus says pleasure[29]).

Long and Sedley's translation in general follows the usual modern interpretation of the text—with the exception of their correct interpretation of ἀποφαίνειν, it differs very little in essence from E. H. Gifford's translation of Eusebius:

> Timon says that the man who means to be happy must look to these three things: first, what are the natural qualities of things; secondly, in what way we should be disposed towards them; and lastly, what advantage there will be to those who are so disposed.
>
> The things themselves then, he professes to show, are equally indifferent, and unstable, and indeterminate, and therefore neither our senses nor our opinions are either true or false. For this reason then we must not trust them, but be without opinions, and without bias, and without wavering, saying of every single thing that it no more is than is not, or both is and is not, or neither is nor is not.

[28] The more complex translations of the tetralemma that have been proposed—e.g., Brunschwig (1999: 245), Hankinson (1995: 60, 63ff.)—are not supported by the Greek or by logic. Bett (2000: 16) gives it simply: "saying about each single thing that it no more is than is not or both is and is not or neither is nor is not." Cf. Svavarsson (2010: 41), Chiesara (2001: 103ff.). However, Bett's (2000: 30–37, 173–178) contention that the tetralemma is used specifically to affirm Pyrrho's supposed dogmatic metaphysical beliefs depends on accepting Bett's premise that Pyrrho had such beliefs to begin with.

[29] Despite Long and Sedley's translation of ἡδονήν here as 'pleasure'—the usual translation, followed also by Bett (2000: 16; 1994a: 173–175)—the word *hēdonē* is explicitly given by Epicurus (who appears to have been influenced by Pyrrho's ethics) as synonymous with "passionlessness and undisturbedness" (the usual words in the ancient testimonies for the outcome of Pyrrho's program) together: "By pleasure [*hēdonē*] we mean the absence of pain in the body and disturbance (*tarachē*) in the soul" (*Ad Menoeceum*, in Diogenes Laertius x, 131–132), in the translation of Hankinson (1995: 323n14). This agrees perfectly with the use of the equivalent pair of terms in the Aristocles passage, as shown below. Since Epicurus's *tarattesthai* (the actual textual form, corresponding to Hankinson's "*tarachē*") is positive (*ataraxia* is negative, 'without disturbance'), the comment attributed to Aenesidemus evidently includes both *apatheia* and *ataraxia* within a single term, *hēdonē*, and suggests Epicurean influence on his thought (cf. Chiesara 2001: 108). Pyrrho's influence on Epicurus seems clear, but a detailed study of the issue is needed.

> To those indeed who are thus disposed the result, Timon says, will be first speechlessness, and then imperturbability, but Aenesidemus says pleasure.[30]

As discussed in Chapter One, it is highly significant that the core text section attributed to Pyrrho himself by Timon is explicitly construed in negatives from start to finish. Only the introductory and concluding sections, both attributed to Timon, contain positive or neutral statements. It is therefore likely that the sometimes unusual and early terms among the negative ones in the core text go back ultimately to Pyrrho himself, who would seem to have coined them from positive ones. It is worth emphasizing that the authorial attributions of the text given by Aristocles are given explicitly in it: Aristocles says he reports what Timon says (in the introductory section), what Timon says Pyrrho says (in the exposition or main section), and again what Timon says (in the concluding section). This and all other evidence indicate that Timon, basing himself on the oral teachings of Pyrrho, composed the original text, which is indirectly quoted, paraphrased, or summarized faithfully by Aristocles.[31]

[30] Gifford (1903: 2:816–817).

[31] Eusebius says he quotes Aristocles verbatim, but the same is not true of Aristocles on Timon (Long and Sedley 1987: 2:6); Bett (1994a: 172n82); cf. Note 2 in this appendix. Bett (1994a) remarks, "The passage as a whole is certainly not lifted verbatim from Timon, since everything Timon says is presented in *oratio obliqua* . . .". The text is probably a close paraphrase, but Aristocles, like other ancient writers, does quote poetry verbatim. He was a careful reporter of the views he discusses, as noted by Long and Sedley and by Bett. There is no reason to attempt to divide the text differently, and in fact, doing so would compromise its meaning. Brunschwig's (1994 and elsewhere) complex argument on this and other points is intended to solve the long-disputed meaning of the putative "zany" inference, q.v. Note 65; cf. Chiesara (2001: 99ff.). The idea of Brunschwig (1994: 194n9), followed by Chiesara (2001: 92ff., 99ff.), that only the first statement about *pragmata* is explicitly attributed to Pyrrho demands that every one of the very short phrases in this very short passage should have repeated "he (Pyrrho) says" or the like. As Decleva Caizzi (cited by Chiesara 2001: 99) remarks, this would be very poor style and is extremely unlikely in Greek (or any other language). Moreover, the text mentions Timon once again as the speaker when the final results are mentioned, thus confirming that the text in between the introductory and concluding remarks reports the statements of Pyrrho.

I

The introductory section, by Timon, tells us that in order to be happy one must note three points:[32] first, of what sort τὰ πράγματα *pragmata* "things" are by nature (πέφυκε)—that is, the way *pragmata* are inherently, by themselves; second, what attitude we should have toward them (*pragmata*); and finally, what the outcome is for those who have that attitude (toward *pragmata*).

The first significant term in the text is thus *pragmata*, the plural of πρᾶγμα *pragma*. The main section, the "declaration" of Pyrrho reported by Timon, also begins with *pragmata*, which is the understood topic of discussion throughout the entire passage. In view of the overriding importance of the word *pragmata* for the meaning of the passage as a whole, a loose approach will not do. In studies of the text the word *pragmata* has frequently been translated into English as "things". Theoretically, this should be unobjectionable. The problem is with the primary "default" meaning of *things* in English. The basic and usual meaning of the Greek word in the plural is "human affairs, matters, business, troubles", and the like.[33] This "human" part of the Greek word's definition has largely been overlooked by most commentators. To be sure, Pyrrho nowhere explicitly rules out physical objects from his logical analysis, which is applicable to everything, and several scholars have so taken it. For example, Bett suggests, "the tomato's being *not* red (but, say, green), or the earth's being *not* spherical (but, say, cylindrical)", and

[32] The Greek says only "these three" (without a noun such as "points" or "questions"), as noted by Halkias (2013: 76n31).

[33] *LSJ* 1457b, s.v. πρᾶγμα; "*deed, act* (the concrete of πρᾶξις, but freq. approaching to the abstract sense); *occurrence, matter, affair, thing, concrete reality*"; etc.; the plural form (πράγματα) is defined as: "1. *circumstances, affairs*"; "2. *state-affairs*"; "3. *fortunes, cause, circumstances*"; "4. *business*"; "5. *trouble, annoyance*". The plural, πράγματα (*pragmata*) thus differs significantly in its semantics from the singular, πρᾶγμα. The plural form occurs eight times in Eusebius's chapter on scepticism. The singular form πρᾶγμα occurs only once, in the sense "the topic currently in question". The Aristocles passage in question thus in effect has only *pragmata* (the plural form), and the same is true of the other ancient attestations. Nevertheless, the singular form also does *not* in fact mean a "concrete" thing. See also Note 45 in this appendix, and especially the extended discussion of *pragma* ~ *pragmata* in Chapter One, which includes numerous additional corrections and examples.

Thorsrud states, "If things are really no more one way than another, it becomes difficult to understand why the sun always seems warming and an icy lake always seems cooling, or why heavy objects always seem to fall to earth and very light ones to rise and float."[34] This interpretation of *pragmata* as "physical objects" appears to be one of the main underlying (but unnoticed) supports behind the metaphysical interpretation of Pyrrho's thought. Nevertheless, although *things* in the sense of "physical objects" is the default meaning for some scholars, "*human* things—problems, troubles, conflicts", and so on, is clearly the primary sense intended in the text, and by Pyrrho in general. We know this because Pyrrho himself tells us what he means by *pragmata*.

In one of the most vivid of the ancient testimonies, which relates an incident in which he was frightened by a dog that attacked him, he is quoted as having said "that it was difficult to strip oneself of being human;[35] but one could struggle against circumstances, by means of actions in the first instance, and if they were not successful, by means of reason."[36] Long and Sedley's "circumstances", like Hankinson's "affairs",[37] Bett's "things" (the usual translation),[38] and so on, is supposed to translate the Greek text's *pragmata*, but in this particular case the word obviously means something closer to 'troubling things, difficulties', and the like—things liable to cause *pathē* 'passions, emotions, suffering'. Certainly *pragmata* here has little or nothing to do with physical objects, metaphysics, or epistemology. According to Plutarch, Pyrrho was once on a storm-tossed ship in danger of sinking and he pointed to a pig, which was not afraid at all, but was calmly eating

[34] Bett (2000: 23), Thorsrud (2009: 21).

[35] I.e., "It is difficult to rid oneself of one's human nature". Bett (2000: 66) translates this as "it is difficult to 'strip off humanity' (*ekdunai ton anthrōpon*)." See Chapter One, Narrative 5.

[36] Long and Sedley (1987: 1:14), translating ὡς χαλεπὸν εἴη ὁλοσχερῶς ἐκδῦναι τὸν ἄνθρωπον· διαγωνίζεσθαι δ' ὡς οἷόν τε πρῶτον μὲν τοῖς ἔργοις πρὸς τὰ πράγματα, εἰ δὲ μή, τῷ γε λόγῳ. The text (Long and Sedley 1987: 2:3–4; Decleva Caizzi 1981: 34) is from Diogenes Laertius IX, 66–67; there is a shorter parallel to it, probably deriving from the same source used by Diogenes Laertius, in Aristocles (*Praep. evang.* XIV, 18:26; cf. Chiesara 2001: 28–31). As with several other striking remarks attributed to Pyrrho, this one has the ring of authenticity. See Chapter One for the full text and detailed discussion.

[37] Hankinson (1995: 66).

[38] Bett (2000: 66); cf. Note 43 in this appendix.

its food. He said to his worried shipmates, "such *apatheia* [passionlessness] must be cultivated through reasoning and philosophy by anyone wishing not to be thoroughly disturbed by the things that happen to him".[39] Pyrrho specifically gives the example of the passengers' fear aroused by the danger of their ship sinking as an example of "what happens to one", which easily arouses passions such as fear and anger. Pyrrho's reference to such happenings as a source of the arising of the passions is parallel and equivalent to his use of *pragmata* in the dog anecdote. In an anecdote about Pyrrho's sister, in which he is criticized for having expressed the emotion of anger or annoyance, the word used for the ideal he violated is *apatheia* 'passionlessness'.[40]

The point in these examples is the same; the emotions or "passions" (*pathē*) are the problem. The goal of Pyrrho's program in general, as frequently remarked in the ancient testimonies, is to achieve *apatheia*, literally 'passionlessness, lack of suffering' or *ataraxia* 'undisturbedness, peace', or 'freedom from worry'.[41] To achieve it one obviously must do something about the emotions or passions. The other ancient testimonies further clarify the meaning of *pragmata*. The two brief parallels to the Aristocles passage both explicitly state that Pyrrho denied there was any difference between honorable or dishonorable, just or unjust, good or bad,[42] and both follow with the same basic conclusions. Pyrrho's *pragmata* are, thus, not merely abstract 'matters, affairs, events', but *conflicting* ones, above all *conflicting ethical distinctions*. Like the examples of troubles, difficulties, discussed above, such conflicts

[39] For further discussion see Chapter One, Narrative 4. The quotation here is from the version in Plutarch (*Prof. virt.* 82e-f), which text (from Decleva Caizzi 1981: 36) reads: καὶ εἰπεῖν πρὸς τοὺς ἑταίρους ὅτι τοιαύτην ἀπάθειαν παρασκευαστέον ἐκ λόγου καὶ φιλοσοφίας τὸν ὑπὸ τῶν προστυγχανόντων διαταράττεσθαι μὴ βουλόμενον. Cf. Hankinson (1995: 325n36) and Bett (2000: 66). Note that the ideal is called *ataraxia* in the version of Posidonius quoted in Diogenes Laertius IX, 68 (Decleva Caizzi 1981: 35), but *apatheia* in Plutarch's version (cf. Bett 2000: 65), and that the word "things" in the English here has no explicit equivalent in the Greek. Note also that διαταράττεσθαι "to be thoroughly disturbed" is built on the same root as *ataraxia* "undisturbedness".

[40] So in Aristocles' version (*Praep. evang.* XIV, 18:26). It is given (somewhat oddly) as *adiaphoria* in Diogenes Laertius's (IX, 66) version; cf. Bett (2000: 66 and n. 9), who discusses the two versions and Brunschwig's analysis of them. This anecdote has textual problems; cf. Chapter One.

[41] Bett (2000: 37).

[42] Diogenes Laertius IX, 61. The parallels are discussed below.

are causes of the arousing of *pathē* 'passions, suffering', and therefore disturbance. Pyrrho thus specifies the basic problem he addresses, and refers to it again in the present text in his recommendation that we be "uninclined", or neutral, toward *pragmata.* It is further clarified in other testimonies, in particular Timon's statement that Pyrrho was not "weighed down on this side and that" by passions (*pathē*) and "views; doctrinal theories" (*doxai*), as discussed below.

For Pyrrho, then, the term *pragmata* is primarily ethical in intent[43] and refers to "troubling matters", such as conflicts over whether something is "just" or "unjust", "good" or "bad", and so on. For Pyrrho *pragmata* are significant mainly in the sense of *matters connected to humans* that may give rise to *pathē*, and thus derail one from the path he prescribes to achieve freedom from them. In short, there is no reason to think that here, or anywhere, Pyrrho refers to *pragmata* as neutral physical objects, natural phenomena such as mountains, stars, and so on, with no real connection to human beings, as in the "dogmatic" approach to philosophy, which he explicitly and sharply criticizes. Because the modern default meaning of the English word *thing* is in fact 'physical object' (usually with no particular connection to human emotions implied), using it without qualification in translations of this particular text invariably leads readers to think, erroneously, that it is about metaphysics or ontology. As shown below, the ancient attestations about Pyrrho—including the text under consideration—make it quite clear that Pyrrho taught more or less exclusively about ethics.[44] In the following discussion, the word *pragma* (singular) ~ *pragmata* (plural) is generally left untranslated.[45]

[43] Brunschwig (1994: 207–208) similarly argues that "the question about 'the nature of things (πράγματα)', should be construed not as a properly ontological question, let alone a physical one, but rather as a question about 'things' as related to our activity (πράττειν), i.e. as goals or ends for our acts of choice and avoidance." However, his proposed solution (199ff.) to the perceived problems of the text—"to suppose . . . that 'our sensations and beliefs' are [kinds of] πράγματα"—is, as Decleva Caizzi remarked to him, "hard to swallow" (199n15). Cf. below.

[44] The general puzzlement about Cicero's treatment of Pyrrho as an exclusively ethical teacher is thus unnecessary. Nevertheless, analysis of Pyrrho's thought based on Cicero (e.g., Brunschwig 1994: 207ff.) or other late writers would seem risky at best.

[45] The word *thing* or *things* can of course also be used indefinitely in English, as *anything*, which is why it is very often found in English translations corresponding to the many places in Greek texts where an indefinite noun is "understood"—i.e., when there is no explicit word whatever in the Greek corresponding to *thing* or some other explicit English

II

The exposition, or main text attributed directly to Pyrrho, has a clear logical structure of its own.

[1] He begins with an explicit statement of the topic, *pragmata*. He says *pragmata* are[46] "equally undifferentiated, unstable, and undecided".[47] The first of the three key terms here is ἀδιάφορα, which is usually translated as 'undifferentiated'. However, it also means more specifically 'without a logical differentia', and is used in this sense in Aristotle's *Metaphysics* along with its corresponding positive form διάφορα.[48] A differentia is a category marker that "truthfully" differentiates a species from a genus—that is, in distinguishing something from something else it categorizes it.[49] The second term is ἀστάθμητα

---

word, as happens in this very text. In addition, as pointed out in Chapter One, Pyrrho's use of *pragmata* is exactly equivalent to the Buddha's use of *dharmas*; in both thinkers the reference is primarily to ethically or emotionally conflicting "things", i.e., "matters".

[46] πέφυκε 'by (their own) nature' is usually understood here from Timon's introductory summary of what Pyrrho says, and I culpably followed the traditional approach to this in my original article. But it may be significant that Pyrrho himself does not mention it, so I have taken it out.

[47] Or "equally undifferentiated, both unstable and undecidable". Hankinson (1995: 60) translates this as "equally indifferent (*adiaphora*: perhaps 'undifferentiable'), unmeasurable (*astathmēta*), and undecidable (*anepikritos*)"; Brunschwig (1998) has "entirely undifferentiated, undetermined and undecided", but in Brunschwig (1999: 246) he has "equally without difference, without balance, without decision"; Bett (2000: 16) has "equally indifferent and unstable and indeterminate"; Chiesara (2001: 21, 102) has "equally undifferentiated, unstable, and indeterminate"; Thorsrud (2009: 19) gives the choices "equally undifferentiated and unstable and indeterminate" or "equally indifferentiable and unmeasurable and undecidable"; Svavarsson (2010: 41) has "equally indifferentiable and unmeasurable and undecidable". I have eliminated any typographical emphasis in these quotations. For the Buddhist parallel text, see Chapter One.

[48] *LSJ* 22b: "[I.] *not different*" (Aristotle), "*indistinguishable*" (Epicurus); "2. in Logic, ἀδιάφορα, τά *individual objects*, as having *no logical differentia*" (Aristotle). See examples of this usage in the *Metaphysics* Δ 6, 1016a18–28, Δ 6, 1057b7–1058b25 (cf. *LSJ* 22b, 418b). The next entries are mainly Stoic terms ("*indifferent*", "things *neither good nor bad*", etc.) that are patently due to influence from Pyrrho, who is older. Bett's (2000: 16) "indifferent" reflects Gifford's translation (q.v. Note 26).

[49] The term ἀδιάφορα is discussed briefly by Chiesara (2001: 94), who mentions Aristotle's frequent usage of it in the meaning ἀόριστος 'undefined' (which amounts to the same thing), notes Sextus Empiricus's mention of "the Pyrrhonian saying πάντα ἀόριστα ('everything is undefined')," and approves of Decleva Caizzi's interpretation "without any difference between things". However, this is not supportable by the Aristocles text or other testimonies, as shown below.

'unbalanced, unsteady, unstable, uncertain',[50] and the third term is ἀνεπίκριτα 'undecided, undetermined, unjudged, unfixed'—analysis of the parallels, including Pyrrho's program in the Aristocles passage, indicates that it refers to *pragmata* not being already determined, decided, or *fixed* in one particular way.[51] If they do not have differentiae and are thus *adiaphora* 'undifferentiated (without differentiae)', they are also *astathmēta* 'unbalanced, unstable' as well as *anepikrita* 'undecided, unjudged, unfixed'. In other words, the first of the three adjectives tells us that "by nature"—that is, intrinsically, or by themselves—*pragmata* are "without a differentia"; the second tells us that *pragmata* are intrinsically "unbalanced, unstable"; and the third tells us they are intrinsically "undecided, unfixed".

The crucial point is that Pyrrho says *pragmata* (such as "just or unjust", "good or bad") *by definition* cannot have their own differentiae. The differentia is needed by humans trying to find the "real truth" about anything, but nothing by itself reveals to us what category it

[50] *LSJ* 260a: '*unsteady, unstable; uncertain*'. Bett (2000: 16) translates *astathmēta* as 'unstable'. He mentions (19) that it also "could mean 'not subject to being placed on a balance', and hence 'unmeasurable'," as some scholars (e.g., Brunschwig 1999: 246) have indeed taken it. He says that this meaning is late, but the positive root form *stathmos* is used already in Herodotus (2.65) with the clear meaning of 'a balance' for weighing (*LSJ* online, s.v. σταθμός). Chiesara (2001: 95), citing Decleva Caizzi, says *astathmēta* "originally had the objective meaning of 'unstable' in fourth-century authors such as Plat. *Lys.* 214D." In a passage from Demosthenes (*LSJ*) the context suggests 'uncertain' rather than 'unstable', and other examples use it to refer to the uncertainty of human life. See now the discussion of *astathmēta* in Chapter One.

[51] *LSJ* 134a. It is "derived from *epikrisis*, 'arbitration' or 'determination' . . ." (Bett 2000: 19), from the verb *epikrinō*. In connection with the differentia it would seem to mean 'undecided, unjudgeable', in the sense of 'without a criterion for judging' whether something is *truly* just or unjust, good or bad, etc.; cf. Brunschwig's (1999: 246) "without decision". As noted by Bett, the negative form of the word (q.v. *LSJ* 641a) is attested late, in sceptical, medical, and legal texts. However, the positive forms are solidly attested in Classical texts. Diogenes Laertius (IX, 94–95), in a section of his account of Pyrrhonism that is at points reminiscent of the Aristocles passage (and thus presumably of Timon, whose works Diogenes explicitly quotes or cites in the chapter), uses ἄκριτος, an early, very well attested word (*LSJ* 55b–56a) and a synonym of *anepikrita*, in the sense 'not critically determined' (i.e., by a criterion), though his account at that point mainly represents Late Pyrrhonism. Most significantly, the short parallel (i.e., of Aristocles' account of Timon's text) preserved in Sextus Empiricus, given above, includes a *verbatim quote* of Timon that has the positive verbal form *kekritai* 'judge, decide', a word well attested from early to late Greek, showing that a form of that word was in Timon's original text or texts.

belongs to because nothing has such an intrinsic, inherent marker. All differentiae are, by definition, humanly supplied to whatever is under examination; using them entails full circularity and, therefore, logical invalidity—we supply the criteria and then talk about the things affected based on those criteria. Linguistically, differentiae and other criteria represent superordinate-level referents that necessarily do not occur in their literal sense in nature, otherwise it would be nonsensical to predicate them of anything—that is, *love* and *cats* may occur in nature, but not anything such as a "generic emotion" (or even a generic "positive emotion") or a "generic animal" (or even a generic "feline"); nor are there any natural differentiae to narrow such superordinates down for us.[52] Pyrrho tells us that we impose strictly human determinations on *pragmata* and then state that they "truly" have such and such characteristics, but they do not themselves have any such determinations.[53] How, then, can there be any difference "in truth" between "good" or "bad", "justice" or "injustice"?

[52] E.g., "love is love", or "cats are cats" tells us nothing about love or cats; in order to say something about them we must apply categorizing nonlove or noncat predicates to them, for example, "a cat is a small, useful animal". The predicates *small size*, *usefulness*, and *animal* are metaterms that do not exist per se in nature, but only in human minds. If they exist at all, they are at a superordinate level, unlike basic-level unanalyzed "things" such as love and cats. Languages typically treat basic-level nouns very differently from superordinate-level nouns (Beckwith 2007b: 111ff., 142ff.). Philosophically this is related to the well-known Problem of Universals.

[53] Bett (2000: 73) notes that the phrase *eikaiēs nomothēkēs* might well refer to "baseless theorizing". He remarks, "Indeed, if 'pointless laying-down of the law', in the . . . fragment of Timon [quoted by Aristocles in *Praep. evang.* XIV, 18:19] does also refer, as suggested, to theorizing about the world around us, the term is apt; from Pyrrho's standpoint, the problem with cosmology and related enterprises is that they attempt to impose a fixity upon that which is inherently lacking in fixity" (Bett 2000: 77; cf. 50–51). Although Bett's argument is intended to support his metaphysical interpretation of Pyrrho's first statement, it works even better as an explanation of a logical interpretation, and there is no objection to it from that standpoint. The translation by Gifford (1903: 2:820) of this much-discussed poem suggests a more prosaic meaning: "O what a man I knew, void of conceit / Daunted by none, who whether known to fame / Or nameless o'er the fickle nations rule, / This way and that weighed down by passion's force, / Opinion false, and legislation vain." Pyrrho is compared by Timon to great rulers, whether famous or infamous; unlike Pyrrho, they are weighed down by their passions, their false theories, and their vain attempts to achieve their goals by legislation—one of the typical things rulers do. However, in view of the other testimonies, including the Aristocles passage itself, this is clearly a reference to people "deciding" or "judging" things "according

This brings up the two attested parallels to the Aristocles text. They have been largely ignored, or at best their significance has been downplayed.[54] Yet they are of some importance for clarifying the highly compressed language of Timon's text in Aristocles.

1. The most well-known parallel occurs at the very beginning of Pyrrho's biography in Diogenes Laertius: "For Pyrrho declared no matter to be good or bad[55] or just or unjust, and likewise with regard to all matters, that not one of them is (good or bad, or just or unjust) in truth, but that people manage all matters (*prattein*)[56] by law (*nomôi*) and custom (*ethei*), because each one is no more this than it is that."[57]
2. The second parallel, from Sextus Empiricus, is a paraphrase of Timon followed by an actual quotation of a fragment of his verse. Sextus says, "Nothing is really (*physei*) good (*agathon*) or bad (*kakon*), but, according to Timon, 'among men these things are decided (*kekritai*) by convention (*no*[*m*]*ôi*)'."[58]

These are two different rewritings of the same text, which is ultimately related to the account of Timon recorded by Aristocles. All

to custom and habit"—i.e., they are not therefore "truly" or "ultimately" decided, and cannot be, because of their intrinsic lack of differentiae.

[54] Chiesara (2001: 87) quotes both parallels without discussion. Bett (1994b: 321–323) discusses them briefly, but essentially dismisses them because they contradict his "metaphysical" interpretation of the Aristocles text, which he considers (rightly) to be of primary importance. Here it is shown that the parallels do not in fact contradict the Aristocles text.

[55] Or "beautiful or ugly".

[56] The construction in Greek uses not the noun *pragmata* but its corresponding verb *prattein* 'to achieve, bring something to an end', from *prak-*; it is a verbal form of *pragma* and *praxis* that means something like 'to "do" *pragmata*', i.e., 'to manage matters'.

[57] Diogenes Laertius IX, 61; the text is from Decleva Caizzi (1981: 29): οὐδὲν γὰρ ἔφασκεν οὔτε καλὸν οὔτ' αἰσχρὸν οὔτε δίκαιον οὔτ' ἄδικον: καὶ ὁμοίως ἐπὶ πάντων μηδὲν εἶναι τῇ ἀληθείᾳ, νόμῳ δὲ καὶ ἔθει πάντα τοὺς ἀνθρώπους πράττειν· οὐ γὰρ μᾶλλον τόδε ἢ τόδε εἶναι ἕκαστον. Cf. Chiesara (2001: 87).

[58] Text of Sextus Empiricus from Decleva Caizzi (1981: 62): ὅτι οὔτε ἀγαθόν τι φύσει ἔστι οὔτε κακόν, ἀλλὰ πρὸς ἀνθρώπων ταῦτα νό[μ]ῳ κέκριται, κατὰ τὸν Τίμωνα. Cf. the translation by Bett (1997: 140 [p. 24]), and cf. Chiesara (2001: 87). For the emendation, see the following note. As Bett (1997: 158–159) says, "Sextus implies that, prior to this line [of verse], Timon also said something roughly to the effect that 'there is not anything either good or bad by nature' . . .". Certainly the parallels are far too close to assume anything else.

three texts make the same main points[59] about *pragmata*, and deciding or judging them. Why should one want to decide or judge them? Because they are not already judged or decided. In Aristocles' text Pyrrho says, "As for *pragmata*, they are undifferentiated (*adiaphora*), unstable (*astathmēta*), and unfixed, undecided (*anepikrita*)." The versions given by Diogenes Laertius and Sextus Empiricus say that there is nothing good or bad, just or unjust; such determinations do not really exist—they are made by humans following convention or custom—so it is impossible to make any *logically valid* decisions about them.[60] Several anecdotes about Pyrrho, which seem by their vividness to be true to life, show that he deliberately did such unconventional, unexalted things as washing a pig, taking chickens to market, and so on. He thus showed that typical views—such as that washing a pig is disgusting work fit only for a slave, or that it is unseemly for a philosopher to take chickens to market—are human judgements, which are made purely according to convention or custom; there is no way to justify them philosophically. Examples of just such conflicting ethical views—including many that contrast local customary or national differences—are cited in the works of Sextus Empiricus.

Pyrrho has pointed out that *pragmata* such as "just" or "unjust" do not come already provided with their own differentiae, and then says they are *astathmēta* 'unbalanced, unstable'. Why does he say this? If, like the dogmatists, one would attempt to establish whether something is "*truly* just" or "*truly* unjust", one would first have to determine what the *pragmata* "just" and "unjust" really are *in truth*. In order to do that, one would need a criterion or a judge external to or different from each one. Because *pragmata* themselves are all undifferentiated, their differentiae must be supplied by humans. But that makes any differentiation based on them strictly circular in nature, and thus logically

[59] The emphasis on "convention and custom" in the above two texts (though not explicitly in the Aristocles text) is further paralleled elsewhere in Diogenes Laertius's chapter on Pyrrho (IX.95, IX.108). Therefore, pace Decleva Caizzi (1981: 264–265), followed by Bett (1997: 159), the text of Timon (see the previous note) should, following Hirzel (1883: 3:56n1), be emended after all, from the very peculiar *nôi* 'by mind' (which would directly contradict Pyrrho's statement that 'things are *not* decided') to *nomôi* 'by custom, convention, law'.

[60] Of course, people do make decisions about them anyway. See below.

invalid, so it is impossible to validly "stabilize" *pragmata*, to make them "certain"—that is, to establish that there is, ultimately, some specific, fixed identity for "just" and for "unjust"—by supplying the differentiae for each. Since there cannot be any valid differentiae, we cannot logically distinguish anything (any *pragma*), and all is at best an unbroken continuum of uncertain phenomena. Purely logically speaking, therefore, *nothing* can be shown certainly to exist in any absolute sense. The textual parallels of the Aristocles passage in Diogenes Laertius (IX, 61) and Sextus Empiricus (*M.* [= *Adv. math.*] XI.140, partly a direct quote of Timon) both confirm the thrust of Pyrrho's statements in the Aristocles text of Timon: they all say that *pragmata* are not differentiated, and therefore do not really exist absolutely, "in truth".[61]

The same analysis applies to *anepikrita* 'undecided, unjudged, unfixed'.[62] How can anything be "decided, judged, or fixed" in one particular way if it does not have a logical differentia and is not certainly either "this" or "that"? The problem is directly related to (if not the same as) the Problem of the Criterion, the introduction of which into Greek thought has been ascribed specifically to Pyrrho.[63] The meaning of *anepikrita* here is clearly that *pragmata* are not decided, judged, fixed (or judgeable, fixable) validly because, as noted, Timon explicitly states—using the verbal form *kekritai* 'decide, judge' (a relative of *epikrinō*)—that people *do* "decide" or "judge" *pragmata*, but *on the basis of convention and custom*, not on the basis of logic or the theories of philosophers, and they do it because nothing is "by nature" already "decided, judged, fixed". The parallel in Diogenes Laertius IX, 61 fully supports this.

The inference drawn by Pyrrho from this analysis is perfectly logical and anything but "zany".

[2] Pyrrho says, "Therefore (due to the logical problem he has just noted), neither our sense perceptions nor our views, theories [*doxai*] (either) tell us the (ultimate) truth or lie to us (about *pragmata*). So we certainly should not rely on them (to do it)." This is because it is literally impossible for them to do it; something would need to be "differentiated"

[61] Cf. Bett (1997: 158–159).

[62] See Note 51 on *anepikrita* and its relatives in the parallels to Aristocles' version of Timon.

[63] See Section 4 below.

first via predication. But in the absence of uncontaminated differentiae, nothing can be logically distinguished from anything else; "true" categorization is impossible. We cannot make logically correct (or absolutely true) predications of anything, whether it is perceived by us as "noble" or "ignoble", "just" or "unjust", and so on. Pyrrho's inference is thus purely logical in origin. As Svavarsson notes, "The noun *alētheia* can mean 'truth,' or 'an account of reality,' but also just 'reality,' 'how things *really* are,' even 'how they are *by nature*,' as opposed to 'how they *appear* to be.' On this conception, if one tells the truth, one gives a true account, an account of the *nature* of things."[64] But without differentiae it is logically impossible for either sense perception or theorizing to tell the "real", logically valid truth *or* untruth about anything whatsoever. In fact, "truth-telling" and "lying" are Pyrrho's own examples of a pair of *pragmata* in the Aristocles passage. The logical conclusion that we neither can nor cannot know anything "absolutely true" about anything gives Pyrrho's observation profound epistemological implications.[65]

A key term here is τὰς δόξας. As used in this and related texts, *doxai* has been almost universally translated into English as 'opinions'.[66] The translation is a convention going back at least to Gifford's time, but it is an unusually misleading convention for Pyrrhonism in general, and for this text in particular. The term *doxai* is widely used in ancient Greek texts, with meanings that vary from author to author or even text to text, but in this and other philosophical texts connected to Pyrrho it very clearly means "theories, beliefs, views" or the like. In modern English, by contrast, the word *opinions* has almost the opposite sense; it refers to ideas or interpretations, especially those based

[64] Svavarsson (2010: 45), from his discussion of the verb *alētheuein* 'to tell the truth' in the Aristocles passage. Note that Svavarsson's discussion here is couched in metaphysical terms.

[65] This is the inference famously referred to by Stopper (1983), and many since, as "zany". See the apropos comments on Stopper's observation by Hankinson (1995: 324n29).

[66] *LSJ* 444b has for δόξα "II. after Hom., *notion, opinion, judgement*", "2. *mere opinion, conjecture*", "3. *fancy, vision*". The problematic use of modern English *opinion* is thus in part perpetuated by *LSJ*. "Opinions" is almost unanimously used for *doxai* in the most recent works. Hankinson (1995: 60ff.) translates it variously as "opinions", "judgements", or "views". By contrast, perhaps the most common translation in earlier works on scepticism is "beliefs", an accurate rendering for the present context.

on personal judgement, that differ in *unsubstantiatable* or *ultimately insignificant* ways from those held by other people (however stubbornly they might hold them), which is to say that *opinions* generally do not really matter, unlike *theories, beliefs*, or *philosophical views*. Bett remarks about a fragment of Timon on Pyrrho that "those thinkers who sought to discover 'what winds hold sway over Greece', etc., are said to be in a state of 'servitude to opinions' (*latreiēs doxōn*)", unlike Pyrrho. But what is meant by *doxōn* here cannot be anything like "opinions", which simply makes no sense in the context. Bett himself says that this passage "makes clear that theorizing is what Pyrrho avoided."[67] The sense "theorizing, theories, beliefs, philosophical views"—not "everyday opinions"[68] or "mere opinion, conjecture"—is clearly the meaning of *doxai* in the testimonies about Pyrrho and Timon. For simplicity's sake, the Greek word *doxai* is generally used below.

[3] In his third section, Pyrrho concludes by telling us what attitude we should have: "Rather, we should be ἀδοξάστους 'without *doxai*' (with respect to *pragmata*), ἀκλινεῖς 'uninclined, balanced' (toward or against *pragmata*), and ἀκραδάντους 'unwavering' (in our attitude toward *pragmata*), saying about every single one (of them) that *it no more is* than *it is not* or *it both is and is not* or *it neither is nor is not*."

There are several key points in this section. The attitude of not having *doxai* is known from other ancient testimonies about Pyrrho as well. If we accept *doxai*, we must accept the invalid determinations on which they are based, and that will inevitably give rise to the passions. Pyrrho logically says here that we should not have *doxai* because they force us to be inclined in one direction or another with respect to *pragmata*; they thus constitute an obstacle to our attainment of passionlessness or unperturbedness. Significantly, Timon says of Pyrrho that he found a way out "from servitude to the opinions (*doxōn*) and empty-mindedness of sophists".[69] Most importantly for the Aristocles

[67] Bett (2000: 70, 73); he nevertheless regularly translates *doxa* as "opinion", but remarks that in other contexts *doxa* "may also have the sense 'glory'," though he adds, "it is very possible that both senses are intended" here (Bett 2000: 75; cf. 77, 77n34, 78, 80). It is, however, extremely unlikely that the late meaning 'glory' is intended in the Aristocles passage.

[68] Bett (2000: 77n34).

[69] Diogenes Laertius IX, 64–65; Long and Sedley (1987: 1:18, 2:10); Decleva Caizzi (1981: 58). Translation by Bett (2000: 70; cf. 73–74).

passage, Timon praises Pyrrho for not being "weighed down *on this side and that* by passions (*patheōn*), views, theories (*doxēs*), and pointless legislation", that is, Pyrrho was not "inclined" toward or against them.[70] The phrase "weighed down on this side and that" in Timon's poetic text clarifies what Pyrrho says in the Aristocles passage we should be "uninclined" toward or against: *doxai*, as well as *pragmata* (the understood topic throughout the text). Timon adds "passions" and (necessarily pointless) "decision-making" (about *pragmata*). As shown above on the basis of other ancient testimonies, it is clear that Pyrrho considered *pragmata* to cause the arising of *pathē*. In this instance, the Aristocles text thus preserves an important detail of Pyrrho's thought.

The ideal "attitude" outlined in this section is well attested for Pyrrho himself in the ancient accounts. The younger Epicurean and Stoic traditions, which appear to have been influenced by some of Pyrrho's ideas (and are better attested in surviving ancient texts), support this analysis.

[70] *Praep. evang.* XIV, 18:19; Long and Sedley (1987: 2:18); Decleva Caizzi (1981: 57) gives the text as: βαρυνόμεν' ἔνθα καὶ ἔνθα / ἐκ παθέων δόξης τε καὶ εἰχαίης νομοθήκης. Long and Sedley (1987: 1:18) translate, "weighed down on this side and that with passions, opinion and futile legislation." Cf. Bett (2000: 70, 81), who translates, "weighed down on this side and that / By affections, opinion, and pointless laying-down of the law". On "the law" see Note 53 above. With regard to Long and Sedley's "passions" here, Bett (2000: 50n67) suggests "*patheōn*—perhaps 'passions', but perhaps more generally 'affections', including sensory experience". He also mentions ". . . 'affections' (*patheōn*) among the sources of disturbance" (Bett 2000: 74). The latter point is exactly right; however, the normal modern meaning of the English word "affections" is very far removed from the meaning of *patheōn* here or in other related texts, despite its widespread use as a calque in translations from Greek. Bett himself says the text under discussion "no doubt refers, at least in part, to emotions or passions, the kinds of states called *pathē* by the Stoics" but then adds, "it may also refer, more generally, to any kind of psychological 'affection', including sensory experience." He says subsequently, "if *pathē,* 'affections', in the same fragment, refers to sensory experience, there is another clear connection with the Aristocles passage; for that passage groups 'sensations and opinions' together as what one should not trust, because they are neither true nor false." But one cannot equate the *pathē* 'passions' of the fragment with *aisthēseis* 'sense perceptions'. As for "*pathē* as referring to passions", he continues, "it is highly probable that this is at least part of what is intended by the term" (Bett 2000: 77). To be sure, that is undoubtedly what it means in all of the testimonies on Pyrrho, as Bett himself (77) indicates: "Pyrrho's lack of susceptibility to various forms of emotional disturbance was one major component of the biographical material", though the idea that Pyrrho lacked "susceptibility" to them is belied by those very attestations, which show that he *was* susceptible to them. If he were not, there would have been no point to his philosophy and its practical program.

As Long and Sedley remark, "Epicurus, one of Pyrrho's admirers, also promises freedom from disturbance, and identifies the 'empty desires' which originate from 'empty opinion' as principal threats to its realization. The Stoic sage, like the Pyrrhonist, does not opine, and the passions, from which he is totally free, are false opinions or mistaken judgements, on Chrysippus' analysis."[71] Finally, we should also be ἀκραδάντους "unwavering, unshaken"—according to Timon, Pyrrho was "uniformly unmoved" (ἀκινήτως κατὰ ταὐτά)[72]—reciting in reaction to "every single (*pragma*)" a formula, known as a tetralemma, which states the invalidity of all possible theoretical assertions. Much effort has been expended in developing interpretations of this formula that would support one or another general view of Pyrrho's thought as a whole. As noted above, discussions of the formula that claim it really has a two- or three-part structure ignore the Greek, which has an explicit four-part structure, with the same word, ἤ 'or, than', occurring between each part, namely: "is ἢ is not ἢ both is and is not ἢ neither is nor is not". It literally means, "no more is *or* is not *or* both is and is not *or* neither is nor is not".[73]

The fact that in the *Metaphysics* Aristotle criticizes unnamed opponents who use a full four-part tetralemma is a reflection of its use by one or another school of dogmatic "sceptics"[74] whose views are different from Pyrrho's and also from the position of the school represented by

[71] Long and Sedley (1987: 1:22); I have deleted their coded source references. Cf. Bett (2000: 37).

[72] For the Greek text (Sextus Empiricus, *M.* [*Adv. math.*] XI.1), see Long and Sedley (1987: 2:10); for translations, see Long and Sedley (1987: 1:19) and Bett (2000: 71; 1997: XI.1). This is a typical characterization of his teacher, who is also said to have not even flinched when undergoing surgery. As Bett (2000: 169–170) suspects, "the notion that Pyrrho's attitudes and outlook were shaped to some degree by his encounter with Indian thinkers has something to recommend it", and remarks that this has been "widely accepted by scholars working on Pyrrho". The *Śramaṇas* 'Buddhist practitioners' in the contemporaneous Greek accounts (the Sarmanes in Megasthenes) are described as performing an early kind of meditation-yoga in which they would maintain the same position unmoved for many hours, or even all day long; see Chapter Two.

[73] The summaries in Diogenes Laertius and Sextus Empiricus have, more simply, that one should say it is "no more this than that" (lit. "no more this than this"). These later simplifications are perhaps a response to those who (like some modern commentators) mistakenly considered the longer early formula to be needlessly verbose or redundant. See the detailed analysis by Bett (2000: 30–37).

[74] See Notes 23 and 25.

Socrates' interlocutor Glaucon in Plato's *Republic*, who says, "For these things too equivocate, and it is impossible to conceive firmly any one of them *to be or not to be or both or neither.*"[75] Bett translates Plato's phrase with a tetralemma—"none of them can be fixedly (*pagiōs*) conceived as either being or not being or both or neither"—and comments, "The parallel with Pyrrho's recommended four-part way of speaking in the Aristocles passage could hardly be closer."[76] The point of the full tetralemma, as Bett explains, is "to exclude us from saying anything definite about anything".[77] Logically, Pyrrho's tetralemma says that "for the predicates under consideration, those predicates neither apply nor fail to apply to the things in question—in other words, that the things are purely indeterminate with respect to their possession or non-possession of those predicates".[78] The tetralemma is not, however, "a way of stating the inherent indeterminacy of things",[79] but rather a formulaic way of stating that *human* determinations are noninherent in things, with the implications noted above in the analysis of *adiaphora*.

The formula as given by Pyrrho begins with οὐ μᾶλλον 'no more'. In a fragment from his *Pythō* Timon says the expression "no more" means "determining nothing, and withholding assent".[80] Even without Timon's explanation there can hardly be any significantly different interpretation of the full formula's implications,[81] but the fragment confirms that Aristocles' report does closely follow Timon's text, which

[75] Plato, *Republic* V, 479c: 4–5, translation by Shorey (1937: 1:530–531), emphasis added.

[76] Bett (2000: 135). There seems to have been a fashion for using the tetralemma in the fourth and third centuries, if only to argue against it; see also the Chinese example in the Prologue. The chronological precedence of the passages in Plato and Aristotle rules out the possibility that the tetralemma was introduced to Greece by Pyrrho after his trip to India. The dates do *not*, however, rule out the probability that the tetralemma was introduced to Greece from the East.

[77] Bett (2000: 35–36).

[78] Bett (2000: 214–215).

[79] Bett (2000: 214).

[80] Diogenes Laertius IX, 76; translation by Bett (2000: 31); cf. Long and Sedley (1987: 1:15, 2:7), who translate this "determining nothing, and suspending judgement", which as Bett rightly notes is not the same thing. However, despite differences of detail in expression of the respective positions (q.v. Bett 2000: 31ff.), "determining nothing and withholding assent" would presumably have been quite similar in practice to "suspending judgement". Cf. below.

[81] Cf. Long and Sedley (1987: 1:17).

seems to have been *Pythō*, as has been suggested.[82] Moreover, it is at the end of Diogenes Laertius's discussion of *ou mallon*, after his quotation of Timon's explanation, that the process of rejecting all dogmatic assertions is compared metaphorically to a purgative. Although there is no explicit testimony that the process of rejection of *doxai* was compared to a purgative by Pyrrho or Timon, the process described in the Aristocles text seems to correspond to the well-known description in Late Pyrrhonism of such rejection as a cathartic that cleanses the body of the offending illness and (because the rejection is rejected too) eliminates itself along with it. Thorsrud remarks, "In a passage probably from Timon's *Pythō*, we find a metaphor that plays a central role in later Pyrrhonism: the sceptic applies his characteristically sceptical utterances to themselves, which shows how the utterances are like purgatives in driving out the offensive substance before eliminating themselves . . . Thus the expression 'no more this than that' applies to itself and discharges the appearance that the sceptic has asserted something definite. When he says that he determines nothing, he should not be taken as having determined even that he determines nothing. Pyrrho's disposition is *what is left* after the sceptical purgatives perform their function".[83] According to Diogenes Laertius, Timon "went to Pyrrho at Elis with his wife, and lived there until his children were born; the elder of these he called Xanthus, taught him medicine, and made him his heir."[84] Since Timon must have known medicine himself, perhaps (in view of the suggestion in the Aristocles passage) so too did Pyrrho.[85]

[82] Bett (2000: 31ff.) argues that in this quotation the term *ou mallon* 'no more' is used in its common parlance comparative sense, and cannot be connected to the Late Sceptical use of it, but in that case one must ask why Timon went to the trouble of explaining it, and why Sextus quoted it. Timon's usage was not *identical* to that of Sextus, who wrote many centuries later, but the fact of the term's use in the Aristocles text (which Bett agrees goes back to Timon himself), along with Timon's explicit explanation, appears to rule out Bett's interpretation in this instance. On the other hand, Bett's (2000: 132ff.) extended discussion of the use of *ou mallon* by Plato is illuminating.

[83] Diogenes Laertius IX, 76. Thorsrud (2009: 33), emphasis added. Thorsrud's last point is supported by the Aristocles text.

[84] Diogenes Laertius IX, 109–110; Long and Sedley (1987: 1:521–522). The fact that Pyrrhonism is known to have been popular among physicians—best known among them being Sextus Empiricus himself—is further suggestive.

[85] Exactly the same "purgative" comparison is made of Buddhism in the Pali Canon; see Chapter One. The earliest description of Buddhism, by Megasthenes, specifies that there were two varieties of Śramaṇas, one of whom he calls the "Physicians"; see Chapter Two.

Pyrrho thus says that *pragmata* 'matters, affairs' do not in fact by themselves have any differentiae, or criteria for categorizing or differentiating them, and being by definition without differentiae, they are uncertain and unfixed. Because differentiae and other criteria do not occur naturally together with whatever *pragmata* they are predicated of by humans, but are supplied by humans, they are invalid, and because truth telling or the opposite requires a criterion, which always invokes the same circular process, neither our sense perceptions nor our theories or views can tell us the absolute truth or falsity of any analysis of anything. The belief that Pyrrho did not address the Problem of the Criterion[86] is therefore explicitly contradicted by the Aristocles passage.[87] Diogenes Laertius says that if the criterion has not "been critically determined . . . it is definitely untrustworthy, and in its purpose of distinguishing is not more true than false."[88] This statement closely parallels Pyrrho's in Aristocles' account. In view of Pyrrho's early date, and the influence he evidently had on Epicurus, the Stoics, and some of the Academic Sceptics, it seems clear that he introduced this particular problem into Greek thought.[89]

Accordingly, we cannot trust our sense perceptions or theories to tell us "the ultimate Truth" because nothing is provided with criteria by means of which we can say anything certain or indisputable about it *beyond its basic-level appearance*. Theories about *pragmata* can therefore never be anything but a source of disputation (and thus emotional disturbance). As a result of this strictly logical entailment, Pyrrho says that we should be without *doxai* 'theories or views' (about *pragmata*); we should be uninclined (toward any *pragmata*); and we should be unwavering (in our attitude about *pragmata*), reciting the tetralemma in response to "every single one (of them)".

[86] Long and Sedley (1987: 1:16).

[87] Cf. Note 49.

[88] Diogenes Laertius IX, 94. For the alternative case see below.

[89] Landesman (2002: 46–47) says, "Among the ideas that Diogenes attributes to Pyrrho is the most powerful general argument in support of global scepticism, the argument from the criterion. . . . A criterion of truth is what helps us to distinguish between true and false beliefs or between beliefs that are justified or reasonable to assert and those that are not. . . . [I]t is unnecessary for us to examine the particular criteria that the various schools have offered because it is impossible to establish any criterion, whatever it may be". Landesman's analysis is correct, but although Diogenes Laertius does discuss the argument from the criterion in his chapter on Pyrrho, he does not explicitly say that Pyrrho himself was its originator.

Despite the criticism of "scepticism" by Aristotle and other "dogmatic" philosophers, who claim that "sceptics" would have to ignore their own senses, it is significant that Pyrrho absolutely does not say, either here or anywhere else in the ancient attestations, that we should ignore our sense perceptions. It would have been bafflingly illogical if he had urged us to ignore them, because his entire philosophy, as reflected in this text and other ancient testimonies, is based upon recognition of the existence of sense perceptions, which put us in contact with *pragmata*, conflicting and disputed "matters, affairs, questions, events" that cause disturbance and prevent us from attaining peace. Aristotle's argument makes no sense as a criticism of Pyrrhonism,[90] and there is no evidence that it was aimed at Pyrrhonism in any case.

III

Timon's conclusion tells us what those who follow Pyrrho's way can expect to achieve.

The received text says, "what remains for those who have this attitude is first unspeakingness (*aphasia*), and then undisturbedness (*ataraxia*)."

The "attitude" or "disposition" to which Timon refers is Pyrrho's prescribed path—the process of being without *doxai* 'views', neutralizing "inclinations", and being "unwavering" with respect to conflicting *pragmata*, the source of *pathē* 'passions' and other disturbances. By following it, one stabilizes one's disposition. Timon does not say that the final outcome is something *directly* achieved by following the path, but rather he says specifically that it is *periesesthai* 'what is left' or 'what remains' after doing so. Similarly, Diogenes Laertius cites Timon and Aenesidemus as saying that suspending judgement—the *telos* 'goal' of (Late) Pyrrhonism, according to Diogenes—"brings with it tranquillity [*ataraxia*] like its shadow".[91]

[90] See Chapter One. A considerable amount has been written, much of it taking an Aristotelian approach, on the topic of the (im)practicability of Pyrrhonism as a way of life; a number of recent studies are included in Bett (2010a); cf. his bibliography (2010a: 334–335) and Thorsrud (2009: 226). Aristotle's sarcastic comments in connection with the tetralemma do not point to anything specifically Pyrrhonian, since as noted the tetralemma apparently enjoyed a certain vogue at that time.

[91] Diogenes Laertius IX, 107.

Timon says that what remains or is left at the end of the process is *ataraxia* 'undisturbedness, tranquility, calm'. This term is found in other testimonies too, but another term used at least as often to refer to what the Pyrrhonist achieved is ἀπάθεια, literally 'passionlessness', the absence of πάθος 'passion, suffering'. In view of the very careful terminological usage throughout Pyrrho's section of the text, one assumes he did not use any significant term randomly.[92] So the question is, did he himself prefer the term *ataraxia* or *apatheia*, did he use both, or is *ataraxia* a later replacement for *apatheia*?

The argument that there was something about *apatheia* that caused the dogmatists to make fun of the sceptics, who then substituted *ataraxia* for the term,[93] is problematic. Pyrrho and Timon, at least, hardly seem to have cared much what the dogmatists thought, and openly scorned all of them and their beliefs. However, other questions have been raised about the final sentence of the Aristocles quotation, and there is little doubt that something is wrong with it.

To begin with, scholars have found it difficult to explain the unusual logic, or rather, the total lack of it. The result of following Pyrrho's path is given as "first *aphasia*", which is followed by the non sequitur, "but then *ataraxia*", and finally the addition by Aristocles, "but Aenesidemus says *hēdonē*". The other early testimonies unequivocally state that the result of Pyrrho's program was supposed to be *apatheia* or *ataraxia.*[94] Moreover, while all of the other elements of Aristocles' text have analogous or supporting testimonial support, nothing is mentioned about

[92] Bett (2000: 83–84) basically equates "the terms *adiaphoria*, 'indifference', *apatheia*, 'freedom from affections', and *ataraxia*, 'freedom from disturbance', all reported in the sources, as jointly describing Pyrrho's ideal". However, in the light of the discussion above it may be taken as certain that Pyrrho did not equate the term *adiaphoria*, if he ever used it, with the other terms, and as shown below, *apatheia* and *ataraxia* were not equated either.

[93] Chiesara (2001: 108, 133).

[94] Arguing that the third term was originally εὐδαιμονία "happiness", Brunschwig (1994: 204) notes, "It would be strange indeed to promise us happiness at the beginning, and not to say at the end that if we follow the recipe we shall eventually get it." Cf. Chiesara (2001: 107). In fact, there is further support for Timon's statement (which in this case may not have been the same as that of Pyrrho, who is not referred to by Timon or anyone else as "happy") in a fragment quoted by Sextus Empiricus, "He is happy who lives in calm and quietude" (Chiesara 2001: 129).

aphasia or the like in any other testimony about *Early* Pyrrhonism.[95] The term is certainly well established in *Late* Pyrrhonism, but it has the specific, positively valued sense of 'non-assertion'.

Most strikingly, although Aristocles, closely following Aristotle's sarcastic remarks in his *Metaphysics*, argues at length about the inability of "someone who denies the principle of non-contradiction" to say anything,[96] he never refers, either directly or indirectly, to *aphasia* in Timon's text. In fact, Aristocles does not discuss *aphasia* at all in his entire chapter on Pyrrhonism.[97] Yet it is hardly possible to believe that he would not have discussed it if it had been in his text of Timon.[98] In addition, the received text's statement that one experiences *aphasia* 'speechlessness' follows immediately after Pyrrho's statement that one should *state* the tetralemma "It no more is than is not," and so on, in response to every instance (of *pragmata*). Pyrrho has just *required* the follower of his path to continue to speak. The immediately following mention of *aphasia* as the result is therefore a blatant contradiction, and has been so noted by modern scholars.[99] One simply cannot imagine Aristocles passing up the opportunity to satirize Pyrrho and

[95] The Aristocles passage is the only text concerning Pyrrho himself that contains the word *aphasia*, as noted by Brunschwig (1997: 298). His observation refers of course to the *received* version of the text.

[96] Long and Sedley (1987: 2:6) note the "striking similarity between what the Pyrrhonist should say about each thing and Aristotle's characterization of the ἀφασία of someone who denies the principle of non-contradiction *Metaph.* Γ 4, 1008a30–5", though they also note that it "is probably right to object to any formal rejection of the principle of non-contradiction by Timon's Pyrrho." This might suggest that the substitution of *aphasia* for *apatheia* was done under Aristotelian influence, though clearly not by Aristocles (see below). However, the specific *word* in question here, *aphasia* (Long and Sedley's ἀφασία), actually *does not occur* in the passage of Aristotle that has been cited—highly misleadingly—by Long and Sedley.

[97] That is, the word does not occur in the chapter of his work as *originally* quoted by Eusebius in *Praep. evang.* XIV, as shown below.

[98] Cf. Brunschwig (1997: 304).

[99] E.g., Bett (2000: 37; 1994a: 164), observes, "It might be thought that, since we have just been told *what we should say* about things, *aphasia* cannot be used here in its literal sense of 'speechlessness'." He follows this with a long argument for his difficult position on the issue.

Timon about such an absurdity. The word *aphasia* is thus undoubtedly an error of one kind or another here.[100]

The possibility that the problem is strictly textual has already been raised, on other grounds,[101] but in view of the above discussion it must be remarked that the word αφασια is extremely close to απαθεια graphically, and there is an attested variant, απαθια, that is even closer.[102] The possibility of a simple scribal error, or such an error plus a miscorrection, must therefore be seriously considered.[103] One way or another, it seems that we should have *apatheia*, the state that other early testimonies tell us Pyrrho attained, rather than *aphasia* here.

In fact, it appears to have been overlooked that in the very same chapter of Eusebius, Aristocles' own text tells us that it originally had *apatheia*, not *aphasia*. In one of his diatribes against Pyrrho, Aristocles paraphrases the crucial part of the last line of his summary of Timon's account of Pyrrho's philosophy, remarking that "*they themselves* (Pyrrho and Timon) actually *say*" that "they are *apatheis* 'passionless' and *atarachoi* 'untroubled'."[104]

[100] It is worth mentioning that a notion of *aphasia* per se would not be problematic for Pyrrho's thought, even interpreted as "speechlessness" due to surprise or shock (Bett 2000: 37–39; 1994a: 164–165); "ineffability" or "the ineffable" is also the typical description of the result of achieving enlightenment in many religious systems, including Indian ones, with which Pyrrho is acknowledged to have had personal contact in India. Nevertheless, it seems to have been overlooked that the *expected* word for the outcome is, after all, *apatheia* 'passionlessness', not *aphasia*, and that the latter term is not mentioned in accounts of Early Pyrrhonism. For its use in Late Pyrrhonism, where it means "nonassertion", see Bett (2000: 37–38).

[101] Some have argued that the text is largely constructed around three-part statements, so that one should expect a three-part conclusion here. This idea has been examined critically, and rejected, by Bett (1994a: 173n84).

[102] *LSJ* 174b.

[103] In addition, both Pyrrho and Timon were from the Doric dialect region, and αφασια [ap^hasia] was αφατια [ap^hatia] in Doric. In the absence of other evidence, it would thus be conceivable that αφασια [ap^hasia] ~ αφατια [ap^hatia] could be a scribally miscorrected form (by metathesis of the feature of aspiration) of an original απαθια [$apat^hia$] ~ απαθεια "passionlessness". However, this is an unnecessary hypothesis, as shown below. On the extremely unusual dialect of Elis—so odd that the Eleans were sometimes seen as somehow "foreign"—see the magisterial study by Minon (2007).

[104] *Praep. evang.* XIV, 18:18: . . . πῶς γὰρ οἵ γε ἀπαθεῖς καὶ ἀτάραχοι, καθάπερ αὐτοί φασιν, ὄντες; The translations of Chiesara (2001: 26–27: ". . . for how could they, who are free from emotions and troubles, as they say?") and Gifford (1903: 2:820 [761d]: ". . . for how should they, seeing that, as they themselves say, they are incapable of

Aristocles' key words ἀπαθεῖς *apatheis* and ἀτάραχοι *atarachoi*, 'passionless' and 'untroubled, undisturbed', are adjective forms corresponding to the related noun forms *apatheia* and *ataraxia*, 'passionlessness' and 'untroubledness, undisturbedness'. They refer to the *two* sequential results of Pyrrho's program that must have been given at the end of the passage before the corruption occurred. Aristocles' version of the text of Timon thus never had ἀφασίαν, but rather ἀπάθειαν (or possibly the variant ἀπαθίαν). At some point in the subsequent transmission of Aristocles' text[105] a copyist introduced the erroneous ἀφασίαν for what Timon said is the outcome for those who follow Pyrrho's way—ἀπάθειαν 'passionlessness'. This textual correction resolves the problem with the final statement.

The text of Aristocles in Eusebius must therefore be emended[106] to read

> πρῶτον μὲν ἀπάθειαν, ἔπειτα δ' ἀταραξίαν. That is, "first passionlessness (*apatheia*) and then undisturbedness (*ataraxia*)."

To summarize, there is no reference to *aphasia* anywhere else in Aristocles' chapter, or in other contemporaneous testimonies; there is no evidence that Pyrrho practiced *aphasia* (whatever its meaning), and in fact his statements are frequently quoted in the testimonies; in the Aristocles passage he openly enjoins the practitioners of his way to speak; the word *aphasia* does not actually occur in Aristotle's discussion of "scepticism" in the *Metaphysics*; and examination of the received text of Aristocles in Eusebius shows that the word *aphasia* is a

---

feeling or of trouble?") fully mask the parallelism of these key concepts in Aristocles' chapter. The context is Aristocles' criticism of the Pyrrhonists' ability to be moral; they are not afraid of law or punishment, etc., so they could hardly be good citizens, and indeed, "how could they [be good citizens], since they are *apatheis* and *atarachoi*, as they themselves say?" Cf. Note 28 for the parallel in Epicurus.

105 The fact that the parallel occurs in the same chapter of Aristocles' own work reveals that he himself had, and transmitted, a correct text of Timon, as Eusebius probably did as well.

106 A textual problem is actually mentioned by Mras. According to his apparatus, the variants in Aristocles' report of Timon's account in Eusebius are from manuscripts O and N, which often derive (for this particular passage) from manuscript I^b. But for the word in question Mras's apparatus says: "ἀφασίαν (d.h. weder κατάφασις noch ἀπόφασις; s., worauf Giff[ord] hinweist, Sext. Emp. Pyrrh. hyp. I 192f.) ON, < I^b in einer Lücke von etwa 10 bis 12 Buchstaben" (*Praep. evang.* 306).

textual error. Therefore, all of the scholarly discussion of *aphasia* in Early Pyrrhonism is moot.[107]

3. The Logic of Pyrrho's Thought

The elimination of inclinations toward or against *pragmata* is the key part of Pyrrho's method, as solidly attested by the ancient reports. In Pyrrho's concluding section, he outlines a specific program in which the practitioner rejects all *doxai* and systematically and unwaveringly eliminates or neutralizes inclinations with respect to *pragmata* 'disturbing matters that happen to one, or conflicts one is faced with, which arouse the passions'. The overt reason he gives for doing this is that we cannot *logically* find out any *eternal*, *absolute* "truths" about anything—the goal of many nonsceptical philosophical systems—because there is no logically sound way of differentiating anything, including "true" and "false". All "dogmatic" theories are therefore by definition misleading at best, and desiring to discover "truths" or believing in one or another dogmatic view is a source of frustration and unhappiness. It is thus perfectly logical to say that unwaveringly, steadfastly being without theories or beliefs, and eliminating inclinations toward or against unavoidably "undifferentiated, unstable, and unfixed" *pragmata*—which are therefore disputed and cause the arising of *pathē* 'passions, suffering' and accordingly, "disturbance"—leaves us with, first, *apatheia* 'passionlessness, absence of suffering' and then, *ataraxia* 'undisturbedness, peace'. In short, the text supports Brunschwig's argument that Pyrrho was primarily "a moralist, the inventor of a new art of happiness based on impassibility and imperturbability",[108] which is to say, on *apatheia* and *ataraxia*. Bett concurs: "The idea that one is *better off*, in practical or emotional terms, adopting an attitude of mistrust or withdrawal

[107] This is not to say that the meaning of *aphasia* in Late Pyrrhonism, 'nonassertion', does not grow out of Early Pyrrhonism, but merely that we have no evidence of the word *aphasia* being used for it in Early Pyrrhonism. The Aristocles passage itself clearly indicates that the practitioner should not assent to anything dogmatically. On the sequence "first passionlessness" and "then" the final stage, "undisturbedness, calm", note the identical sequence at the end of the stages of meditation in the *Yogalehrbuch*; see Chapter One.

[108] Brunschwig (1999: 241).

than if one persists with a conventional, optimistic attitude[109] toward enquiry belongs to the Pyrrhonists and to them alone."[110]

It is Pyrrho's demonstration of the invalidity of "dogmatic" philosophical analysis in general that leads him to urge us not to have any theories or "views". This is similar, though not of course absolutely identical, to the "suspension of judgement" of later Pyrrhonism.[111] As noted above, neither Pyrrho and Timon nor the Late Sceptics advocate *abandoning* judgement with regard to our sense perceptions or ordinary commonsense "basic-level" cognition, both of which are necessary in order for us to be able to follow the Pyrrhonist path. Pyrrho's point is that we cannot say anything logically valid *about* our sense perceptions (induction) or views, theories (deduction). They do not provide us with anything we can believe absolutely because nothing comes naturally provided with its own differentia telling exactly what a potential matter of belief really is. We cannot state anything ultimately "true" or "false" (logically valid) about anything because we cannot say anything of that kind without imposing our own criteria, which depend in turn on our own sense perceptions and cognition, a fully circular process. Everyday basic-level cognition does not enter into this (and is therefore not a problem) because phenomena—whatever can be perceived

[109] Bett seems to assign negative values ("mistrust", "withdrawal", the opposite of "optimistic") to the Pyrrhonian approach, but it would seem more accurate to characterize the Pyrrhonian ideal—at least from Pyrrho and Timon's Pyrrhonian-internal perspective—as "contentedly neutral".

[110] Bett (2000: 220–221), who also says, "What is unique about the Pyrrhonists . . . is the connection they draw between these two elements" (the "goal of a trouble-free existence" and "an attitude towards our prospects for understanding that can be broadly described as sceptical"). He adds, "Others who adopt the goal of *ataraxia*, or some related form of tranquility, typically aspire to achieve this goal as a result of coming to understand the nature of things through painstaking enquiry, and being able to ascribe to them some set of definite characteristics—not through a renunciation of any attempt at such understanding. . . . And none of the others who express some form of sceptical attitude towards our prospects for understanding see *ataraxia*, or anything like it, as the result (nor trouble and torment as the result of continuing to strive for such understanding)." Bett (2000: 119–121) further points out that this same connection is to be found in the Late Scepticism of Sextus Empiricus.

[111] See also Note 80. The belief of most scholars in one or another "dogmatic" interpretation of Pyrrho's thought, which has of course obscured this similarity, is founded on belief in the validity or possibility of "ultimately" noncircular reasoning, as well as of "ultimate" truth and so on; q.v. Chapter Four.

or conceived of by our induction or deduction—are literally defined as whatever *seem* to us to be. This kind of circularity is thus built into the very definition of the phenomenal world, telling us once again that we cannot logically investigate beyond it the way "dogmatists" attempt to do, and that trying to do so can only be a source of dissatisfaction.[112]

Pyrrho concludes that because it is not possible to decide the truth of anything without differentiae or other criteria, which can be supplied only by ourselves, invoking a vicious circle, our sense perceptions and theories are simply irrelevant to fantasies such as the "real truth" about anything. We cannot make any logically valid assertions about the "real nature" of anything because it is necessary for us to use human cognitive tools to analyze or discuss anything beyond the "basic level" of phenomena. Doing so imposes our human cognitive conceptual criteria on the matter in question, contaminating the input, further contaminating the analysis, and finally producing a contaminated output or statement of results. Pyrrho has therefore identified the basic epistemological (and metaphysical) dilemma expressed by Pyrrhonist sceptics in Antiquity, and faced once again by Descartes, Berkeley, Hume, and many others down to the present.[113]

Despite the overriding interest of earlier Greek philosophers in "dogmatic" philosophy, Pyrrho taught that it is meaningless and should be avoided. We should eliminate both views and inclinations with respect to *pragmata*, and by steadfastly eliminating them, experience passionlessness and undisturbedness, which are equated with "happiness" by his disciple Timon (and by Epicurus, who is said to have been influenced by Pyrrho). Aristocles' explicit emphasis on epistemology and metaphysics is a direct result of his own imposition of an Aristotelian approach onto Timon's text. We should not be led by it to believe that Pyrrho himself focused on such topics, especially in view of the fact that his main point—which he openly states—was precisely that we

[112] This is not really a problem for ordinary science—as long as one accepts the premise that science is strictly the study of phenomena—but it is a serious issue for metaphysics. Several of Timon's other comments indicate that Pyrrho was indifferent to "ordinary science" too, but considering that in his day science included metaphysics, one can understand his attitude.

[113] See Chapter Four.

should *not* be concerned with them. It is by being without such meaningless concerns that we can achieve peace.

Pyrrho's logic thus makes perfect sense "as is". No major higher textual or conceptual emendations are needed. His philosophy is also not fundamentally metaphysical, nor even epistemological, despite the claims to either effect by various scholars. The epistemology in the text of Timon recorded by Aristocles is clearly a byproduct of Pyrrho's own logical "declaration", which reveals the invalidity of traditional "dogmatic" philosophical analysis. His logical inference—that because, by definition of a differentia, *pragmata* 'ethical matters, affairs' are not themselves differentiated by differentiae, neither sense perceptions nor theories or views can tell us any ultimate truth *or* falsity about them—makes his thought fundamentally "Sceptical". He says that people should have "no views" and "not choose" between antilogies, thus adopting an attitude that is "uninclined" or neutral with respect to *pragmata*. As he showed by his own example, and as Timon tells us, those who did so would achieve passionlessness, and then undisturbedness. Since these are also the essential elements of Late Pyrrhonism, the ancient Sceptical tradition attested in the works of Sextus Empiricus, Pyrrho is the founder of Pyrrhonism in every significant sense of the word after all.

4. Pyrrho's Reception and Legacy

One would think that it was not any implication of Pyrrho's thought for epistemology and metaphysics, but rather its logical foundation, fortunately preserved for us in Aristocles' account and its parallels, which caused Pyrrhonism to be received with such opposition by Aristotelians such as Aristocles.[114] After all, logic is the topic on which Aristotle, one of the most brilliant thinkers of all time, wrote what are arguably his greatest and most influential works, and logic is the underpinning of many of his other works as well, in particular his *Metaphysics*. Yet Aristocles declares explicitly at the beginning of his chapter that the reason he presents the Pyrrhonians' views is to refute their *epistemology*. Although most scholars have paid little or no attention to the rest of

[114] Some Renaissance and Enlightenment philosophers in Western Europe, such as Hume, evidently saw Pyrrhonism as an attack (which it certainly was, in part) on Aristotelian dogmatism, and welcomed it.

Aristocles' chapter on Pyrrhonism (though it is quoted verbatim by Eusebius), it is manifestly the case that Aristocles had read at least two of Timon's own works, the *Silloi* and the *Pythō*, because amid his criticism of them he expresses considerable explicit knowledge of details about them *as physical texts*.[115] Why, then, did he ignore all other aspects of Pyrrho's teachings and focus more or less exclusively on epistemology, and to some extent on metaphysics? The main reason is surely that Pyrrho's powerful logical argument does undermine *Aristotelian* epistemology, and therefore also *Aristotelian* metaphysics.

However, Aristocles also says that Pyrrhonist scepticism "destroys the foundations of philosophy,"[116] suggesting that he partly misunderstood the thrust of Pyrrho's statements. While Pyrrho clearly had a low opinion of most of what passed for philosophy in his day, and his logical presentation does seem to be devastating to Aristotle (among others), the ancient accounts indicate that Pyrrho intended to destroy not philosophy per se, but only "dogmatism", which he thought was

[115] It has been argued convincingly that, by contrast, he clearly did *not* know Aenesidemus's *Outlines of Pyrrhonism* firsthand (Long and Sedley 1987: 2:6), though Bett (1994a: 179) contends we do not really know that for certain. In any case, it is hardly possible to deny that Aristocles' summary of Timon on Pyrrho is based on his reading of Timon's *Silloi* and *Pythō*; his comments about them indicate that he must have seen and read the actual works themselves, as noted by "most scholars" (Chiesara 2001: 126), including Bett (1994a: 173–174). Aristocles many times explicitly notes that his source is Timon, whom he quotes verbatim in the case of poems, at least, and several times mentions which of Timon's works was the source for his information. The idea that Aristocles based his treatment of Pyrrho on Aenesidemus (Chiesara 2001: 126–136), whom he explicitly cites as "saying" anything only one other time in his entire chapter on Pyrrhonism, is not believable. Bett (1994a; 2000; 2006) shows that Aristocles took uncommon care to get the best available information on the topics he wrote about, and also took care to quote or paraphrase them accurately. Why then would he take his knowledge instead from what seems to have been a defective epitome of Aenesidemus's late book? Chiesara also cites the *aphasia* in Aristocles' record of Timon's report as an example of Aenesidemus's influence, but as shown above, the original text of Aristocles, and its source—Timon—had *apatheia*. The mistake is late and cannot be blamed on either Aenesidemus or Aristocles. Moreover, since the comment "and Aenesidemus says *hēdonē*" cannot have been in the text of Timon that Aristocles has just given, it must have been added by Aristocles on the basis of his reading of *a different work*—probably Aenesidemus's *Outlines of Pyrrhonism*, which Aristocles cites by name in the chapter, or perhaps an account of Aenesidemus by someone else—which therefore could not be the source of Aristocles' copy of Timon's text.

[116] *Praep. evang.* XIV, 18:30; Chiesara (2001: 26).

illogical nonsense.[117] He clearly did think that other Greek philosophical traditions were at best worthless and at worst harmful, but a few thinkers whose ideas sometimes approached Pyrrho's are mentioned by Timon somewhat more favorably.[118]

The power of Pyrrhonism, with respect to epistemology and metaphysics, at least, comes from its attack on the very heart of dogmatic philosophy in general: in order to make any inferences it is necessary to be able to predicate *F* of *x*. For that to be meaningful, the criteria distinguishing *F* from *not-F*, as well as *x* from *not-x*, must also be specified, but in order to do so it is necessary to specify the criteria for distinguishing them; and so on.[119] As Brunschwig observes, Hellenistic philosophy as a whole was radically changed by Pyrrho:

> It is tempting to suppose that this reorientation was the effect of a radical questioning of the very possibility of knowledge, a questioning which first appears in the two chief versions of Hellenistic scepticism which go back to Pyrrho and to Arcesilaus (who was the younger by some fifty years).[120] After these men, the critical question ["Is there any knowledge?"] became the primary question to which every philosophical school had to provide an answer.[121] . . . The answer to the critical question usually took the form of a theory about the 'criterion of truth'.[122]

[117] Pyrrho nowhere says that *philosophy* is to be rejected. Plutarch (see Note 39) even cites him as saying that "reason and philosophy" can be used in "the struggle" against *pragmata*—matters conflicted with respect to their categorization as just or unjust, good or bad, etc. This suggests that he distinguished sharply between *philosophy* in general on the one hand, and on the other *doxai*, his regular term for 'theories, beliefs', including "dogmatic" schools of philosophy that emphasized metaphysics and similar subjects while also espousing fixed ideas on ethical concepts such as "the good", "the honorable", etc.

[118] Long and Sedley (1987: 1:22ff.; 1987: 2:13ff.).

[119] Diogenes Laertius IX, 94–95 gives an ancient presentation of the Problem of the Criterion: "The criterion has either been critically determined or not. If it has not, it is definitely untrustworthy, and in its purpose of distinguishing is no more true than false. If it has, it will belong to the class of particular judgements, so that one and the same thing determines and is determined, and the criterion which has determined will have to be determined by another, that other by another, and so on *ad infinitum*." See also Chapter 4.

[120] Brunschwig thus oddly mentions Pyrrho and Arcesilaus as equally innovative, even though he specifically remarks that Pyrrho was earlier by half a century.

[121] Brunschwig (1999: 230).

[122] Brunschwig (1999: 231), who adds, "either it was said that we have no access to the truth at all, that is that there is no such criterion; or else it was maintained that we do have one or more ways of discovering the truth, ways which must then be identified and described (this was the task to which, each in their own manner, the Epicureans and

By demonstrating the general *logical* invalidity of "dogmatic" philosophy—which claims that its attempts to make "ultimate" evaluations are built on logic—Pyrrho has shown there is also no way of demonstrating the "real existence" of anything, which appears to be "no more this than that", so "people do everything by custom and habit".[123]

To conclude, Pyrrho points out that because *pragmata* are by definition undifferentiated by differentiae, there is no logically valid, formal difference between "good" and "bad", "just" and "unjust", "true" and "false", and so forth. Therefore neither our sense perceptions nor our *doxai* 'views' can tell the truth or lie, as a consequence of which neither truth nor lying can "really" exist, nor is it possible to determine "in truth" whether anything exists. Therefore, we should not depend on our senses or theories to tell the "real" truth or lie about anything, because it is impossible for them to do it. Instead, we should be without views, both "uninclined" (toward any extreme) with respect to *pragmata*, and unwavering in this attitude about them, saying about every single one, "It no more is than it is not, or it both is and is not, or it neither is nor is not"—this formula being intended to show the invalidity of all dogmatic arguments.[124] What is left after maintaining this "attitude" is first *apatheia* 'passionlessness', and then *ataraxia* 'undisturbedness, calm'.

What is remarkable about Pyrrho's thought is that he saw the identification of this logical problem as a kind of salvation from the conflicts of *pragmata* 'conflicting questions, matters, events' and from the *pathē* 'passions, suffering' to which they can give rise. His teaching was thus about ethics above all, as Brunschwig has convincingly argued.[125] "His main, perhaps exclusive, interests were, again like Socrates, ethical . . . the scope of his scepticism is the fine and the disgraceful, the just and unjust."[126] But Pyrrho did not minimize his demonstration of the emptiness of dogmatic philosophy. He maximized it, and taught his followers to do the same, because by doing so they would achieve peace.

---

the Stoics dedicated themselves)." However, according to Pyrrhonism, the latter two schools are "dogmatic".

[123] Diogenes Laertius IX, 61.

[124] Bett (2000: 30); he discusses this and other interpretations at length.

[125] Brunschwig (1998; 1999); but as shown above, the nonzaniness of the crucial inference vitiates Brunschwig's theory about the text's alteration by Timon; cf. Notes 5 and 31. Ausland (1989) and others have also noted the ethical basis of Pyrrhonism.

[126] Hankinson (1995: 64).

Appendix B

ARE PYRRHONISM AND BUDDHISM BOTH GREEK IN ORIGIN?

Pyrrho taught a way to achieve "undisturbedness, calm". This sounds like the *telos* 'goal' of Democritus and numerous other Greek thinkers as well as that of the Buddha and other Eastern thinkers. Various scholars have argued that one or the other tradition or school of thought is the source of Pyrrho's thought, with Classicist scholars almost unanimously deciding in favor of "other Greek thinkers", except for minor details. That is, although they agree that Pyrrho did in fact go to India, nearly all of them reject any significant influence on Pyrrho's thought stemming from the experience, contending that the similarity of Pyrrho's thought to Indian thought is coincidental or irrelevant.[1] Three arguments for this view have been presented at some length.

One argument is that the Greeks did not know or could not learn foreign languages sufficiently well to be able to converse with the natives even after spending several years living in a foreign country.[2] It is no doubt true that Pyrrho and the other Greek and Macedonian courtiers did not know Persian, let alone Indian languages, when the army first crossed the Dardanelles into the East, but they were on

[1] The two significant exceptions in recent years are Kuzminski (2007), whose study is devoted to the theory, and Clayman (2009: 43), who concludes, "While it seems likely that Pyrrho developed his famous disposition in India, indeed, learned his Skepticism there, elaborately argued justifications for it were applied after the fact, first by Timon and later by others."

[2] Bett (2000: 176–178).

campaign in the Persian Empire for *ten years*, including *five years* in Central Asia and India. It would seem difficult to accept the idea that the Greeks and Macedonians of Alexander's army and court were so dense that they could not learn at least basic Persian or Gāndhārī after years among their speakers, many of whom had been attached to the court by Alexander himself. Moreover, while on campaign Alexander recruited or otherwise incorporated into his army many soldiers and courtiers of different origins—including local people (Persians, Central Asians, Indians, and others)—who of course must have been able to communicate with the Greeks. Nevertheless, much has been made about the necessity of communicating with the local people through bilingual traders or other uneducated interpreters, as Onesicritus claims (see below), such that the very idea they "would have been capable of communicating even a garbled account" of one of the philosophical points Bett discusses[3] "is simply too fantastic to entertain."[4] This is a very strong claim.[5] It is entertaining to imagine Alexander the Great and his men as mental weaklings who bumbled their way around Asia conquering a huge empire largely by accident, like Inspector Clouseau solving a case, but the court was in the territory of the Persian Empire for ten years, five of them in Persian-ruled Central Asia and India, and the ancient Greeks were hardly mental weaklings. After years of exposure many must have learned Persian at least, and some undoubtedly picked up other local languages, while the local people would have been powerfully motivated to learn Greek, the language of the invaders, and many local people in formerly Persian-ruled "India" knew at least some Persian.

This is not speculation. A number of impeccable sources contain references to bilingual speakers of Greek and of Persian (of both ancestries) and other languages mentioned in ancient Greek works.[6] Moreover, the

[3] The tetralemma (his "quadrilemma") has been argued by some to be an Indian import in Greek philosophy, but this is problematic. See the discussion in the Prologue and in Appendix A.

[4] Bett (2000: 178).

[5] Most scholars, not only Bett, have followed this view, which has not been seriously challenged.

[6] For a selection of such accounts—including that of Themistocles, who expected to take about a year to learn Persian, and evidently did so; of Peucestas, a member of

accounting records from Persepolis of emissaries to and from the Persian court from Central Asia and India reveal that there was already an entire class of functionaries who must necessarily have been at least bilingual within the Persian Empire before Alexander even set foot in it.[7] They necessarily included some who were bilingual in Persian and in Anatolian dialects of Greek, which was the language of a major region of the empire. Even if most of the Greeks, as the dominant people in the campaign, did not feel strongly compelled to learn the local languages, the local people certainly would have tried to learn Greek. The most important part of Pyrrho's basic teachings reported by Aristocles, his strikingly unusual declaration about the three characteristics of all things, is clearly his interpretation of the Buddha's statement of the *Trilakṣaṇa* 'three characteristics' of all dharmas. This fact indicates that one way or another Pyrrho did learn something from the people he met there—no doubt directly, not via interpreters, accounting for some of the differences in his presentation of the 'three characteristics'.

More to the problem at hand, Arrian's account of Alexander includes information about Calanus, a member of the Gymnetai sect from Taxila, in Gandhāra, who joined Alexander's court there and travelled with the Greeks to the West. When he became seriously ill in Pasargadae, in Persia, he committed suicide in public view by self-immolation. Just before he stepped onto the funeral pyre erected for him, he gave his horse to Lysimachus, "who had been one of his pupils in philosophy".[8] This tells us that Lysimachus was not the only one, but the text explicitly adds that Calanus distributed "among his followers" the "cups and rugs" Alexander had thrown on the pyre in honor of his friend. One way or another these men had managed to communicate with each other without serious problems. The much-overlooked comments of Arrian confirm what must have happened: a Greek court with a full complement of philosophers meets an Indian community of philosophers, one

Alexander's court who learned Persian and was appointed a satrap by him; and other such examples—and accounts of interpreters, see Kuhrt (2007: 2:844–848).

[7] Cf. the recently discovered Aramaic documents from Bactria dating to the period immediately before, during, and after Alexander's invasion (Naveh and Shaked 2012).

[8] Arrian, *Anabasis* VII, 3:3–4; translation by Robson (1933: 2:210–213); cf. Romm and Mensch (2005: 153), "he presented it to Lysimachus, one of his disciples."

of whom joins them and is highly favored by Alexander. How could they possibly have failed to learn something from him?[9]

This brings up the matter of Onesicritus.[10] He is widely suspected of having presented Cynical ideas as Indian ideas because he could not understand the Indians. He was accused of lying even in Antiquity. It is known that ancient Greek writers often accuse others of lying, even though the accusation may be demonstrably untrue, but there is reason to doubt Onesicritus in several instances. For example, according to Onesicritus's own report,[11] the Indian philosopher Mandanis (or Dandamis) told him that because they had to communicate via *three* interpreters he doubted the Greek would be able to understand anything useful about his philosophy.[12] The target languages were Greek and Gāndhārī. This account tells us that it was necessary for someone to translate from Greek to language *x*, then for someone else to translate language *x* to language *y*, then for someone else to translate language *y* to Gāndhārī. That comes to four languages in all, even though eastern Gandhāra (a region of "India" in the Greek view) had been a part of the Persian Empire for two centuries and was the immediate eastern neighbor of solidly Iranic-speaking Central Asia. Yet the instances where interpreters are recorded as having been used during the campaign always mention *only one*. Alexander evidently conversed with Taxiles via one interpreter, and "Nearchus had an interpreter among the Ichthyophagi".[13] Moreover, if the translators' understanding was as poor as Onesicritus pretends, it would have been impossible for him

[9] Romm and Mensch (2005: 153) comment, "The idea that an Indian ascetic would have had 'disciples' and 'followers' among Alexander's army is intriguing. Some scholars have suggested that developments of Greek philosophy at about this time, such as the evolution of the Cynic and Skeptic movements, were influenced by the Greco-Macedonian encounter with Indian religion."

[10] See the useful comments on him by Clayman (2006: 38–39).

[11] Preserved in Strabo XV, 1, 64.

[12] Radt (2009: 201–202) quotes "Brown . . . 42" (the volumes of Radt available to me contain *no* bibliographic references): "Mandanis' remark about the three interpreters is a curious one. Presumably, Onesicritus had brought them along, for had they been Indian sophists Mandanis would not have said that they 'knew no more than the rabble'. Onesicritus does well not to introduce them during the scene with Calanus, the liveliness of which would thus have been lessened."

[13] Arrian, *Anabasis* V ("Indica"), 28:5. Karttunen (1997: 61) notes that the sources typically do not mention interpreters, even when they must be assumed.

to have understood so accurately and eloquently what Mandanis presumably told him. The scenario Onesicritus reports is thus extremely unlikely. The account also assumes (no doubt correctly) his own ignorance even of Persian, but elsewhere he suggests (certainly falsely) that he knew Persian cuneiform writing.[14] Onesicritus's ignorance of languages is proverbial in the literature, and it is most unlikely that he introduced any serious Indian ideas to the Graecophone world. In short, the ancients were right: Onesicritus was a liar.

The mental weakness and untruthfulness of Onesicritus have unfortunately been extended to all Greeks, and used to argue against any Indian philosophical influence on the Greeks, including on Pyrrho.[15] This is an unsupportable assertion. Not only was Alexander's court with him in Central Asia and India for five years, the conqueror even introduced Persians and other local aristocrats into his entourage, actively encouraging the Greeks and Macedonians to fraternize with them, and some are explicitly said to have learned Persian, while some Persians learned Greek, and at least one Indian philosopher actually joined the court and taught philosophy to Greeks in the court. Pyrrho was still a student, and no doubt a young man. He was one of the greatest of the ancient Greek thinkers. Is it really possible to believe that in five years he could not learn Persian or Gāndhārī, which are similar to each other and related to Greek as well? Many young people who have visited the same regions in modern times have become fluent in several *months* without formal instruction, not to speak of several years.[16] Or was he so stupid that he alone could not learn anything from Calanus? The "Greek monoglot" theory must be laid to rest.

The second argument is that Pyrrhonism can all be explained on the basis of Greek thought. This is also highly problematic, and calls for closer examination.

[14] Strabo xv, 3, 7.

[15] Bett (2000: 176–178); cf. Clayman (2009: 39–40).

[16] I was in the region (what is now Afghanistan and northwestern Pakistan) when I was in my mid-twenties and in about four months there managed to learn two unrelated languages, one of which I had never studied at all, well enough that I could converse in them, tell stories, interpret for others, and so on (but sadly, no longer). I met others there who were far better at learning languages than I was, and I've met many more since then. For someone who is young and quick with languages, two years is enough to become quite fluent.

Most of the ancient sources on Pyrrho's philosophy—usually referred to as "testimonies"—have been treated quite cavalierly by scholars, perhaps as a result of their goal of finding a Greek origin for each of the elements of his strikingly unusual teachings. Yet by ancient accounts, Pyrrho's thought struck most Greeks as peculiar and inexplicable. The treatment by Aristocles of Messene, an Aristotelian who considered Pyrrho's thought bizarre, is typical of the general ancient reaction.[17] Why should the Greeks have thought it was so alien if it was thoroughly Greek? Why would they have paid any attention at all to a rehash of old Greek philosophy? The a priori assumption of an exclusively Greek source for his teachings—that "Pyrrho's thought can . . . plausibly be accounted for in purely Greek terms",[18] does not make sense.

Now, searching for a possible Greek origin of each individual aspect of his thought and practice is not necessarily a bad thing in itself,[19] but each particular point made in one or another fragment related to Pyrrho is analyzed essentially in isolation, and its putative source is identified in isolation too. The potential source can in practice be anything stated anywhere by anyone in the entire history of Greek philosophy—and it is by no means restricted to the period *before* Pyrrho's lifetime. Ancient Greek thought is very rich and varied, so that if one searches

[17] See Chiesara (2001). Perhaps because both Sextus Empiricus, a famous Pyrrhonian, and Diogenes Laertius, an important source for ancient Greek philosophy, are strongly pro-Pyrrhonist, and modern scholars have based much of their understanding of Pyrrhonism on these two works, the oddity—to the Greeks—of Pyrrho's teachings has been overlooked. One of the anonymous reviewers of the manuscript of this book objects to my remarks on how the Greeks viewed Pyrrho's thought as extraordinary: "But this does not mean that we have to postulate a non-Greek origin. The Cynics and Cyrenaics were also regarded as extraordinary, and this does not lead people to postulate non-Greek origins for their ideas." But of course, we *cannot rule out* a non-Greek origin, either, and the reviewer adds, "I do not mean to suggest that this puts into doubt Beckwith's claims about a substantial similarity between Pyrrho's thought and Buddhism."

[18] Quoted from the criticism of my approach here by one of the anonymous reviewers of the manuscript of this book who contends that Pyrrho himself followed a "smorgasbord approach" to the formation of his philosophical system, choosing various bits from different Greek philosophical traditions.

[19] Perhaps the best treatment of this kind is Bett (2000: 112–169), who methodically considers each potential Greek source. In particular, he devotes ten pages to thoughtful consideration of the hypothesis proposed by other scholars to the effect that Pyrrho's thought is fundamentally (or at least significantly) influenced by Indian thought. He concludes that it was not, though he does suggest that an Indian origin best explains Pyrrho's practice of yoga. This topic is discussed further in the Epilogue.

hard enough for almost any particular point, most likely one can indeed find it in the system of one or another thinker. Not only Democritus, but Antisthenes, Socrates, Plato, and many other thinkers have been cited as inspirations for elements of Pyrrho's teachings. Perhaps they did inspire him, but they cannot be shown to have taught a *system* even remotely like his, and that is, after all, the real problem.

With a very few exceptions, scholars have not attempted to first assemble the fragmentary testimonies of Pyrrho's ethical philosophy into a logical, internally consistent whole, and then try to discover what relationship it might have with some other way of thought. The few who have attempted anything like that have done so according to their own preconceptions, established on rather questionable grounds, and they have therefore ended up excluding known data relevant to the problem.[20] The smorgasbord approach to the history of religion or philosophy is thus very difficult to justify.

In fact, it is normally accepted without question that systems of thought must be understood and compared primarily *as systems*, that philosophies or religions should make some kind of sense on their own grounds, and that history of philosophy or religion (like history in general) ought to be based on careful examination of the sources, so we must begin by comparing whole systems, which have their own internal logic, goals, and origins. We must therefore attempt to determine the relationship of Pyrrho's teachings to other teachings *as whole systems* first, and continue to do so throughout the process. If we cannot find any system that is close to Pyrrho's, as a system, perhaps we would be justified in adopting the smorgasbord approach in order to explain his thought as a more or less purely Greek pastiche, but we are not permitted to pick and choose among the relevant data purely to satisfy our own preconceptions.

The smorgasbord approach is not, however, the only questionable approach that has been taken to the problem of the source of Pyrrho's teachings.

[20] I would like to emphasize that I fully understand the concerns of these scholars, and do see that many of the strands of Greek thought identified as sources or influences on Pyrrho's thought appear to make good sense on their own merits. But most make sense only if considered individually, with much argument; they do not fit together smoothly and seamlessly to form the logically and ethically coherent system that is Early Pyrrhonism.

The third argument, which has been proposed in one form or another by several scholars, is that Indian philosophy itself is Greek in origin, either in general or in selected details useful for the problem in question. The most recent representative of this view[21] concludes in essence that key elements of Indian thought are actually Greek in origin. This view is, in effect, an extreme version of the Classicist consensus, because if most Indian thought is "really" Greek, then Pyrrho's thought is ultimately Greek too, whether or not Pyrrho really was influenced by Indian thinkers. The idea is, however, built on highly fragmentary, contradictory, legendary, and in general *massively problematic* accounts of Greeks in "India" *centuries* before the invasion of Alexander.[22] It suggests that the people of ancient India were backward compared to the Greeks, who kindly provided them with proper philosophy, and it is unpleasantly Modern in too many other respects as well. Some *ancient* writers do of course argue that the Greeks invented *philosophia* (and everything else), but others considered *philosophia*—a combination of religion, science, and philosophy—to have originated among the *barbaroi* 'foreign peoples',[23] in particular, among the Persians, who were the *barbaroi* 'foreigners' par excellence for the Greeks. There is in fact a lot in favor of the latter view.

[21] McEvilley (2002).

[22] For a fairly thorough survey see Karttunen (1989); unfortunately, like other such works it depends heavily on material from Indic traditional sources, most of which is even more problematic, as is much of the scholarship on it.

[23] Diogenes Laertius (I, 1) says, "philosophy had its beginnings among the barbarians" (translation by Hicks 1972: 1:3). He subsequently argues against that view, saying that of course the Greeks invented philosophy (D.L. I, 3), but he seems to have deliberately given the "foreign origin" theory more prominence. It should be stressed that the ancient Greek word *barbaros* (plural *barbaroi*) does not mean exactly the same thing as the modern word "barbarian" and its analogues in other European languages. Already in Antiquity its semantics began developing in the direction of the modern word, and many Greeks did not like foreigners (*barbaroi*), but most ancient Greek writers still do not have anything like the modern pejorative sense of "barbarian" in mind when they say *barbaros*. For a lengthy discussion of the "problem of the barbarian", though it only scratches the surface and is far from perfect, see Beckwith (2009: 320–362).

Appendix C

ON THE EARLY INDIAN INSCRIPTIONS

The Major Inscriptions of the Mauryan period, which are explicitly and repeatedly declared to have been erected by a king known as Devānāṃpriya Priyadarśi,[1] are the very first inscriptions known to have been created in India. They are also the first datable examples of actual Indian writing.[2] The religious contents of these inscriptions are very important sources for the "popular" variety of Early Buddhism and are discussed at length in Chapter Three.

However, the Major Inscriptions are generally believed to be only a subset of a much larger set of well over two dozen Mauryan inscriptions, large and small, most of which are explicitly concerned with Buddhism—not Early Buddhism, but Normative Buddhism. Virtually *all* of them—that is to say, all inscriptions of any kind in early Brahmi script and Prakrit language, including the Major Inscriptions and the others—are now attributed not only to the Mauryan period, but specifically to a Mauryan ruler known from traditional Indian "histories" as Aśoka.[3] He is identified in these "histories" as the grandson of the

[1] However, the so-called Seventh Pillar Edict on the Delhi-Topra pillar is spurious. It is discussed at the end of this appendix.

[2] It remains uncertain if the Harappan inscriptions represent writing. Even if they do, they remain undeciphered and had no descendant in any later Indian writing system.

[3] E.g., Norman (2012), Salomon (1998), Falk (2006), Olivelle (2012), generally with a few extremely minor quibbles at most. The most significant exception is Falk (2006: 58), who concludes regarding the "Second Minor Rock Edict" (one of the synoptic, explicitly Buddhist edicts) that "analysis of its content . . . seems to indicate that it was not Aśoka who produced this text." (He takes the "First Minor Rock Edict" to be by Aśoka.) Olivelle (2012: 158), following and citing Falk, says that the Minor Rock Edicts "are problematic

dynasty's founder, Candragupta. All of the inscriptions are thus usually known today as the "Aśoka (or Aśokan) inscriptions".

Unfortunately, this determination is extremely problematic at best. Absolutely no careful scientific epigraphical or palaeographical study of the inscriptions themselves has ever been done in the century and a half since their first decipherment. No one knows what such a study would reveal. Careful *preliminary* examination indicates that the traditional view is partly or even wholly incorrect. It is thus necessary to determine why the inscriptions might have been erected, which among them are genuine Mauryan inscriptions, which (if any) were authored by "Aśoka", and when they were erected.

The Background of the Mauryan Inscriptions

There is unquestionable Old Persian influence on the Major Inscriptions, including language (Old Persian *ni-piš* "to write"); textual formulae—most notably the usual third-person introduction "King *x* says" followed by the king's proclamation in first person;[4] the Kharoṣṭhī alphabet (derived from Persian Imperial Aramaic script) used in the northwestern inscriptions, the area formerly under Achaemenid Persian rule; and the

in that they exist in many versions and were subjected to several editorial interventions in different places". He also questions whether all the texts had "the same author" or "multiple authors". Unfortunately he does not pursue these insights in any substantial way in his article, and actually treats all the inscriptions as being by Aśoka. Just about the only other hedges that have been expressed relate to a small number of short inscriptions, which have sometimes been ascribed to later authors. Aśoka's grandson Daśaratha is explicitly credited with the Nāgārjunī Hills inscriptions (Hultzsch 1925: xxviii; Salomon 1998: 76,n16; Falk 2006: 276, q.v. for the texts and translations), as already established by Prinsep in the nineteenth century (Salomon 1998: 208). Despite their extremely close connection to the Barābar Hill Cave inscriptions of "king Devānampiya" (Hultzsch 1925: xxvii), the latter are still generally attributed unquestioningly to Aśoka (e.g., Salomon 1998: 140; Falk 2006: 266–268), but Aśoka is actually never mentioned. Both probably belong to Daśaratha—whose historicity and chronology, however, depend wholly on the same pseudo-historical sources responsible for the questionable historicity and chronology of Aśoka. It is probable that he needs to be downdated along with Aśoka, as suggested below.

[4] Olivelle (2012: 166). This is also noted by others arguing that the Mauryan edicts were based on Persian models, e.g., Hultzsch (1925).

"Persepolitan" (Achaemenid Persian) style of the pillars and the capitals that graced them. All of this goes back to the period when "Sindhu and Gandhāra belonged to the Persian Empire."[5] One must add to these points the simple fact of creating monumental inscriptions at all, which was done for the first time in India, in blatantly Persian style, on both rocks and columns. They were erected along royal roads built and provided with rest houses, exactly as the early Achaemenids had done. On these roads Achaemenid royal emissaries made annual "tours of inspection"[6]—exactly as the Mauryans were to do, as we know from the Major Inscriptions themselves. Moreover, just as the inscriptions of Darius are a litany of praise and thanks to Ahura Mazda (God), the inscriptions of Devānāṃpriya Priyadarśi are a litany of praise and thanks—not to Brahma (God),[7] but to the Dharma.[8] This is one of the

[5] Hultzsch (1925: xlii). The Achaemenid Persian presence there is firmly established by the Persian royal inscriptions and by provincial travel reports to and from Gandhāra in the Persepolis Fortification Tablets, as noted in the Prologue, as well as by numerous Achaemenid sites in Sindh and Gandhāra (J. Choksy, p.c., 2013).

[6] Xenophon (*Cyropaedia* VIII, 6.16) says, "every year a progress of inspection is made by an officer at the head of an army, to help any satrap who may require aid, or bring the insolent to their senses . . ." (Meadows 2005: 185).

[7] The earliest information on the Indian Brahmanists' conception of God is given by Megasthenes, q.v. Chapter Two.

[8] Olivelle (2012: 174) says, "I propose that in the case of Aśoka's civil religion, the place of 'God' is taken by 'Dharma'." However, he then states that "like 'God', Dharma was a vacuous concept into which individuals and groups could read whatever content they desired." This is highly unlikely, as are his and other scholars' arguments in favor of Aśoka's view of Dharma as "civil religion". Against it may be mentioned the regular Greek translation of *dharma* as *eusebeia* "piety, holiness", which he cites (Olivelle 2012: 175). Interestingly, Dharma is translated into Aramaic once as *qšyṯʾ* (*qaššīṭā*) 'truth' in the Kandahar II/III Inscription (Itō, 1966), and Clement of Alexandria says that Buddhists (*Śramaṇas*) are those "who practiced the truth (*tēn alētheian askousi*)" (Parker 2012: 320). Significantly, 'my Dharma' is translated in the Aramaic inscription from Taxila (Parker 2012: 325n24) as *dty* 'my *dāta*', using the Old Persian word for 'divine law' used by Darius and others for the "Law of God". Olivelle (2012: 170–171) states flatly, "we can dismiss the early view that Asoka's Dharma was, in fact, the Buddhist Dharma, and we can agree fully with Romila Thapar . . . that 'Aśoka's *Dhamma* did not conform to the religious policy of any one of the existing religions of his time'." This claim is predicated upon the belief that the "religions of his time" are in fact well known, but that is not the case. The received view of "the existing religions of ['Aśoka's'] time" has hitherto been based exclusively on the Normative Buddhism of Saka-Kushan or later sources, which has been demonstrated to be, in large part, a development of those or later centuries.

strongest indications that the ruler's Dharma was, in fact, a form of Early Buddhism, in which the structural place for God is apparent, but it is unoccupied.

It is well known that some of these Persian-style pillars of the Mauryas were left uninscribed. It seems not to have been noticed, however, that those which were inscribed were done in a very curious fashion. Specifically, the pillar inscriptions are *not* inscribed around the cylindrical columns, as might perhaps be expected, but are instead placed in geographically oriented north, south, east, and west "faces".[9] Together it is clear that the pillars were erected first, uninscribed, and that the inscriptions were added later.

The so-called Seventh Pillar Edict on the Delhi-Topra pillar actually mentions the existence of blank pillars. The existence of uninscribed pillars has inexplicably been taken by Hultzsch, and evidently by subsequent scholars, to mean that the Buddhist Inscriptions—which are overtly Normative Buddhist—are *earlier* than the Major Inscriptions. The elaborate theory of Norman (2012) claims, among other things,

[9] Hultzsch (1925: xvi, 119–137); e.g., the Delhi-Topra pillar, Edicts I–VI. The so-called Seventh Pillar Edict, most of which is inscribed all around the circumference of the column, is found only on the Delhi-Topra column, and is in this and other respects a glaringly obvious later addition to the authentic synoptic edicts already inscribed on the stone. This is clearest in the rubbings in Hultzsch (1925), but is visible upon careful inspection of available photographs in Sircar (1957: the second plate between pages 24 and 25) and Falk (2006: 216 figure 4, 217 figure 6). Olivelle (2012: 160–161) says that on the Allahabad Pillar, "the inscriptions were carved in a circular manner while the pillar was erect; the same is true with regard to P[illar] E[dict] 7 at [Delhi-]Topra" (i.e., the pillar now in Delhi and known as the Delhi-Topra pillar). Unfortunately, neither the very poor photographs in Falk (2006) nor any posted online allow one to actually see very clearly how the Allahabad Pillar is inscribed, but close examination of the rubbing in Hultzsch (1925: 156) shows that the text does *not* in fact run circularly all around the column, though it does go partway around (how far is unclear). There is a space at the beginning and end of the lines in the rubbing, which shows that the lines do not continue in a continuous string the way the "Seventh Pillar Edict" on the Delhi-Topra column uniquely does. Salomon (1998: 139) remarks, "The Allahabad-Kosam pillar contains, in addition to the six principal edicts, two brief additional inscriptions", namely the "Queen's Edict" and "the so-called Schism Edict, addressed to the *mahāmātras* at Kosambi (Kauśāmbi), which refers to the punishment to be inflicted on monks or nuns who cause schisms within the Buddhist *saṃgha*." Examination of the rubbing in Hultzsch (1925) of the "Queen's Edict" on the same column clearly shows that it too was not written all the way around it, but in a panel with rather short lines.

that the Pillar Edicts were inscribed while horizontal, before erection; he does not mention the uninscribed pillars, nor the fact that such uninscribed pillars are actually mentioned explicitly in the "Seventh Pillar Edict" as still existing when that inscription was added to the Delhi-Topra column, nor that some still exist today. He also claims that the texts of all of the inscriptions were written out on perishable material in the capital, Pāṭaliputra and sent out to the provinces with "cover letters" that were supposedly "not meant to be published",[10] despite the fact that Megasthenes visited Pāṭaliputra in 305–304 BC and remarked that the Indians in that country did not know writing, and despite the fact that no "Aśokan Inscription" has ever been found there; the written texts were then translated into local dialects, or for the Pillar Edicts, copied verbatim.[11] While the closeness of the synoptic Pillar Edicts supports Norman's idea of a written exemplar, the synoptic Major Rock Edict inscriptions at least were undoubtedly memorized orally in sections (the "Edicts") and inscribed in the local dialect or language, thus accounting for most variations.

Now we must consider who first erected the pillars, and why, and who ordered some of them to be inscribed.

The absolutely unprecedented, specifically Persian character of the earliest Indian inscriptions,[12] as well as the complete failure of post-Mauryan Indians to erect inscriptions that are even remotely similar to them, as frequently noted by scholars, tells us that their creator must have been impressed by things Persian through firsthand experience. He must have *personally seen* monumental Persian inscriptions—which are mainly on cliff faces or stone slabs—and either read them or heard someone read aloud what they said.[13] It would therefore seem likeliest by far that the pillars themselves were *erected*, uninscribed, by the

[10] This is an ad hoc proposal based on speculation; the differences are surely there in many cases because the texts were recast by the inscribers, while some of them are clear forgeries.

[11] Norman (2012: 53; 56–57).

[12] This is obvious and unquestionable. See the excellent, careful overview in Falk (2006: 139–141), which is followed by a careful description of the pillars themselves, their materials, mode of production and erection, etc.

[13] If he had travelled from Gandhāra to Persepolis in the years before Alexander's invasion, he would have seen many impressive monuments.

dynastic founder Candragupta (in Greek, *Sandracottos*), who is known from Greek historical sources to have had direct personal and diplomatic contact of different kinds with the Greeks and Persians, and was undoubtedly influenced strongly by them, but they were *inscribed* by one of his successors.

Contradictions in the texts themselves indicate that all of the Mauryan inscriptions could not have been erected by the same person,[14] but it is clear—and explicit in those very texts—that all of the genuine Major Inscriptions were in fact erected by one and the same Mauryan ruler, Devānāṃpriya Priyadarśi. It is most plausible, on the basis of the chronology inferrable from the inscriptions' record of contemporaneous Hellenistic rulers' names, and on other historical grounds, that he is to be identified with Candragupta's son, Amitrochates (according to Greek sources) or Bindusāra (according to traditional Indian accounts). He actually proclaimed the authentic edicts of the Major Inscriptions on rocks and pillars and is responsible for the deeds recorded in them. Both Amitrochates ~ Bindusāra and his father had close political relations with the Greeks, as we know very well from Greek sources; both are historical and datable, if only somewhat roughly. The contents of these genuine, dated inscriptions are discussed in Chapter Three.

As for the minor monuments henceforth referred to as the "Buddhist Inscriptions", including the Minor Rock Edicts and Minor Pillar Edicts, a casual inspection of the inscriptional evidence and the scholarship on them might indicate that they were inscribed by Candragupta's grandson Aśoka, since the author of the First Minor Rock Edict is explicitly named "Devānāṃpriya Aśoka" in two copies of the text.[15] However, as shown below, they could not in fact have been inscribed until much later.[16]

Unfortunately, we do not have rich, reliable historical sources for the Mauryas. We have only extremely tenuous information about them—most of it about "Aśoka"—from very late Buddhist "histories", which are in large part fantasy-filled hagiographies having nothing to do with actual human events in the real world. Moreover, as Max Deeg

[14] Falk (2006: 58), on the Second Minor Rock Edict; Olivelle (2012: 158).

[15] Norman (2012: 41); see also the discussion by Falk (2006: 58).

[16] See below on this issue, and for which texts belong to which category.

has argued, not only did the inscriptions remain in public view for centuries, but their script and language remained legible to any literate person through the Kushan period (at least to ca. AD 250). This strongly suggests that the inscriptions influenced the legendary "histories" of Buddhism that began to develop at about that time.[17] That would explain why the story of Devānāṃpriya Priyadarśi's conquest of Kaliṅga, his subsequent remorse, and his turning to the Dharma is all repeated in the Buddhist "histories", though they attribute the events to "Aśoka", who is said to be the grandson of Candragupta.

Despite the deep learning and care many scholars have taken with the texts, some very striking irregularities in some of the inscriptions appear not to have been noticed. Hultzsch, author of the classic monumental edition of the inscriptions, rightly notes that the Seventh Pillar Edict on the Delhi-Topra column is "unique"[18] because unlike all the other Pillar Edicts, which (like the Major Rock Edicts) exist in synoptic copies, it is only found in a single exemplar. Salomon correctly remarks that it is "the longest of all the Aśokan edicts. For the most part, it summarizes and restates the contents of the other pillar edicts, and to some extent those of the major rock edicts as well."[19] Hultzsch says nothing at all about the inscription's date except to note that "the seventh pillar edict at Delhi-Topra was added in the next year" of Aśoka's reign after the inscription of the first six Pillar Edicts.[20] Norman similarly remarks, "The failure of this edict to reach other cities [than Topra] is one of the great unsolved mysteries of the Aśokan administration."[21]

Hultzsch's unquestioning acceptance of the "Seventh Pillar Edict" on the Delhi-Topra column is unlike his discussion of the Allahabad-Kosam Pillar, which he says has "four strata of literary records", of which the first consists of the "original inscriptions of Aśōka, viz.: (a) the first six edicts of the Delhi-Tōprā pillar; (b) the so-called 'Queen's edict' . . . ; [and] (c) the so-called 'Kauśāmbi edict' . . .".[22] He also mentions, "The Barābar Hill inscriptions record a grant of caves to the

[17] Deeg (2009); cf. Salomon (1998: 31).

[18] Hultzsch (1925: xvi).

[19] Salomon (1998: 139).

[20] Hultzsch (1925: xlviii).

[21] Quoted by Olivelle (2012: 180n8).

[22] Hultzsch (1925: xix).

Ājīvikas, but it is not absolutely certain whether the donor was identical to Aśōka."[23] Near the end of his chapter 4, "Asoka's Conversion", he says, "It must still be noted that the Calcutta-Bairāṭ rock-inscription[24] or 'letter to the *Saṃgha*' seems to be earlier than all the other rock and pillar edicts. The references to a few Buddhist tracts in this inscription suggest that after his visit to the *Saṃgha*, and before starting on tour, he was engaged in studying the sacred literature."[25]

Salomon comments that the unique text of the "Seventh Pillar Edict" is an "important early instance" of an inscription shedding "some light on the complex problems of the formation and history of the various Buddhist canons."[26] Although he notes—as others have before him—that the Nigālī Sāgar Inscription and the Lumbini Inscription "are different in content and character from Aśoka's other edicts", he ascribes this to the ruler's state of mind (much as is done by Hultzsch and nearly everyone else since). He notes that the former inscription "records the king's visit to the site and his expansion of the *stūpa* of the Buddha Konākamana there", while the latter "celebrates the site as the birthplace of the Buddha and commemorates the king's visit there."[27]

The latter inscriptions thus have been used, and continue to be used, as "proof" of this or that idea about "early" Buddhism, even by careful scholars such as Bareau,[28] but they have never been examined critically with respect to their dating, authenticity, or practically anything else. All has been accepted on belief right down to the present, and the false ideas embodied in them—at least as they are currently understood—have thus insinuated themselves into the publications of scholars whose work is otherwise very thoughtful.

[23] Hultzsch (1925: (xlixn1).

[24] Formerly also known as the "Bhābṛā" or "Bhābṛū" inscription.

[25] Hultzsch (1925: xlvii). These two sentences are more than usually astounding.

[26] Salomon (1998: 138, 241–242).

[27] Salomon (1998: 140).

[28] Bareau (1995: 216–218). He concludes with another remark about "the surprising rarity of canonical texts which locate the birth of the Blessed One at Lumbinī or which mention the Buddha Konākamana", and continues on about the diffusion of the legends recorded on the stones. The accuracy and usefulness of his otherwise insightful article has thus been negatively affected by the lamentable state of the field of Indian epigraphy. The same is true of his even more insightful article on the Buddha's supposed birth in Lumbini (Bareau 1987), q.v. below.

This is essentially the state of the field today, close to a century after Hultzsch's edition of the inscriptions was published. The archaeologist Anton Führer had already been publicly exposed as a forger and dealer in fake antiquities and expelled from his position in 1898,[29] so one might expect Hultzsch—and the legion of others who have written on the inscriptions since Führer's day—to have at least mentioned the possibility that one or more of the inscriptions that Führer "discovered" could be forgeries. But nothing of the kind has happened. Recent works on Indian epigraphy say not one word about this scandal, nor about its scholarly implications.[30] Yet even a cursory inspection of the Lumbini and Nigālī Sāgar Pillar Inscriptions—both of which were discovered by Führer, who was purportedly working on them when he was exposed—shows that the Lumbini Inscription repeats exactly much of the phraseology of the Nigālī Sāgar Pillar's text, but unlike the genuine "synoptic" Major Inscriptions, the phrases are not identical or closely parallel. That fact, plus the idea that an already divinized Buddha having been many times "reborn" could go back as far as the third century BC, or that anyone in the vicinity of Lumbini could have been given a *Sanskrit* epithet in the same period, centuries before Sanskrit is first attested in Indian inscriptions, ought to have at least aroused suspicion. Instead, scholars insist on the authenticity of all of the inscriptions, and also insist that they must all be ascribed to the ruler known from traditional—very late, fantasy-filled, pious, hagiographical—"histories", as well as from the Maski and Niṭṭūr Inscriptions, as "Aśoka".[31] Although the Maski Inscription and the Niṭṭūr Inscription are the only ones that support the view

[29] Phelps (2010).

[30] Major works on Mauryan period archaeology and Indian epigraphy usually mention Führer but do not cite his works in their bibliographies, with the partial exception of Falk (2006: 25).

[31] The name *Devānāṃpriya Aśoka* occurs only in the late Buddhist Inscriptions known as the Minor Rock Edicts, specifically the Maski Inscription and the recently discovered Niṭṭūr Inscription. According to Sircar (1975), the Gujarrā Inscription should be included with them, but it is extremely problematic, and seems to be a crude forgery, as discussed below. The rubbing of the Maski Inscription provided by Hultzsch (1925: 174) is very poor. Hultzsch reads *Asok*[*a*]*sa* 'of Aśoka' without comment or explanation of the bracketed "[*a*]", but in the rubbing the part that includes his *Asok*[*a*] is actually written very clearly [𑀤𑁂]𑀯𑁂𑀦[𑀁]𑀧𑀺𑀬𑀸𑀲𑀸𑀅𑀲𑁄𑀓𑁂𑀲𑀸 [*d*]*eva-na*[*ṃ*]*piyāsā Asokesā*, with the name in an eastern dialect form.

that any inscriptions in Mauryan Brahmi script are by a ruler named "Aśoka", the text is generally close to the other somewhat synoptic Buddhist Inscriptions,[32] so Hultzsch concludes on the entire authorship issue, "Every such doubt is now set to rest by the discovery of the Maski edict, in which the king calls himself Devānāṃpriya Aśōka".[33] But this is exactly the opposite of the logical conclusion: the Maski and Niṭṭūr Inscriptions confirm that the texts of the Major Inscriptions (which explicitly and repeatedly say they are by Devānāṃpriya *Priyadarśi*) on the one hand, and the Buddhist Inscriptions on the other, must have been promulgated by different rulers, and Devānāṃpriya Aśoka is of course responsible only for the Buddhist Inscriptions. It is time for Indologists to seriously consider the recent scholarship which suggests that some of the inscriptions are spurious.[34]

As Hultzsch himself notes, for *Devānāṃpriya* 'Beloved of the gods', some versions of the synoptic Major Inscriptions have *rājan* 'the king'. It is thus accepted that *Devānāṃpriya* is an epithet used as the equivalent of 'the King', or more appropriately, 'His Highness' or 'His Majesty'. As for *Priyadarśi* 'He who glances amiably', Hultzsch says that its Pali equivalents "occur repeatedly in the *Dīpavaṃsa*[35] as equivalents of

[32] Hultzsch (1925: 228–229).

[33] Hultzsch (1925: xxxi).

[34] See now Phelps (2010). Some have objected that the Lumbini pillar itself—the stone and its preparation—is unquestionably identical to the physical pillars used in the acknowledged Major Inscriptions. This is certainly the case. However, it is well known that there are a number of *blank* (uninscribed) pillars identical to pillars used in the Major Inscriptions, and the scholars who first saw the inscription on the Lumbini pillar remarked that it was remarkably clear, as if it had just been inscribed (Phelps 2010). Cf. the suspicious remarks of Schopen about the Lumbini Inscription (2004: 76–77). The inscription is also stunningly short. Even if the pillar was *not* recently inscribed by Führer, the text itself reveals that it belongs not to the authentic Major Inscriptions of *Devānāṃpriya Priyadarśi*, but to a much later period, no doubt exactly the period in which the legends about the Buddha's supposed birth in Lumbini were being created, as shown by Bareau (1987), who thus unknowingly—but brilliantly—demonstrates the lateness of the Lumbini Inscription. If he had even suspected that the Lumbini Inscription is spurious, his article would have made its case even more effectively than it does, and without the necessity of trying to explain what is patently an impossible historical background, as he actually shows very clearly. However, this topic requires much further specialized study.

[35] This is one of the most famous of the above-noted Buddhist hagiographical "histories". It is traditionally (and generously) dated to about the fourth century AD.

Aśōka, the name of the great *Maurya* king."[36] However, Hultzsch immediately points out, "A *limine*, another member of the Maurya dynasty might be meant as well; for, as stated above, the eighth rock-edict shows that the king's predecessors also bore the title *Devānāṃpriya*, and the *Mudrārākshasa* applies the epithet *Priyadarśana* to Chandragupta".[37] Moreover, as remarked above, Deeg notes that the inscriptions stood in the open for centuries after their erection, during which time anyone could have read them, so that the above very late literary works cited by Hultzsch, written as much as a millennium after the inscriptions were erected, were undoubtedly based on legends derived at least in part from the selfsame inscriptions. The only solution to this problem is to study the inscriptions *without* contaminating the data with material deriving from supposed Buddhist "historical" works such as those cited by Hultzsch.

If we set aside the "miscellaneous" inscriptions that have already been shown not to belong with the others,[38] as well as the Lumbini and Calcutta-Bairāṭ Inscriptions, which are spurious as Mauryan inscriptions and were inscribed long after the Maurya Dynasty, apparently in the Saka-Kushan period (see below), there would seem to be two distinct sets of inscriptions in Mauryan Brahmi script.

The earlier set consists of the monumental synoptic rock and pillar inscriptions, referred to herein as the "Major Inscriptions", including the "Major Rock Edicts" (Girnar, Kalsi, Shāhbāzgaṛhī, Mānsehrā, Dhauli, Jaugaḍa, Bombay-Sopārā) and the "Major Pillar Edicts" (Delhi-Topra I-VI, Delhi-Miraṭh, Lauṛiyā-Ararāj and Lauṛiyā-Nandargaṛh, Rāmpurvā, Allahabad-Kosam). These all appear to be genuine Mauryan inscriptions, and all are explicitly ascribed in the texts themselves to the same ruler, *Devānāṃpriya Priyadarśi*.

The other set, referred to henceforth as the "Buddhist Inscriptions", consists of all of the other inscriptions, which are later chronologically (in some cases explicitly), and are overtly Buddhist in content; most are also short and of very poor quality.

36 Hultzsch (1925: xxx).

37 Hultzsch (1925: xxx–xxxi).

38 These include the Barābar Hill cave inscriptions and several inscriptions in Mysore State (Hultzsch 1925: xxvi–xxvii, 175–181), which are (or perhaps should be) attributed to Aśōka's grandson Daśaratha (Hultzsch 1925: xxviii, 181–182).

The period of the Major Inscriptions is determinable on the basis of explicit information in the texts themselves on Hellenistic historical personages, whose common period of rule is 272–261 BC.[39] The Buddhist Inscriptions do not contain any foreign chronological references, but they do contain sufficient references to developed Normative Buddhism that they must be dated to one or more much later periods. In any case, there is absolutely no principled way to justify lumping all of the Mauryan Brahmi script inscriptions together as the work of a single author.

If we were to believe Hultzsch and many other scholars, the *Dīpavaṃsa*, a late Buddhist hagiographical "history", is a reliable historical work that can be trusted, so the author of the Major Inscriptions, who describes his remorse over his bloody war with the Kaliṅgas, must be identified with Aśoka. That would mean that the other set, the Later Inscriptions, which are sharply distinct in every respect, must be *unidentified* as to their author or authors, although unlike the Major Inscriptions they share the feature that they explicitly mention, and in most cases openly promote, Normative Buddhism. Moreover, one of the "Minor Rock Edicts"—preserved in two apparently genuine inscriptional copies—is clearly, explicitly said to be by *Devānāṃpriya Aśoka* 'His Majesty Aśoka'. Accordingly, "Aśoka" is the author of at least some of the later Buddhist Inscriptions, while other Buddhist inscriptions (most notably the Lumbini and Calcutta-Bairāṭ Inscriptions) were evidently composed and erected even later. But in any case, the positive identification of Aśoka as the author of the Maski and Niṭṭūr "Minor Rock Edict" inscriptions, which are radically different from any of the highly distinctive Major Inscriptions, makes it absolutely certain that "Devānāṃpriya Aśoka" *cannot* after all be the author of the Major Inscriptions, which explicitly and repeatedly say they are by Devānāṃpriya Priyadarśi 'His Majesty Priyadarśi'. Considering the fact that we have absolutely no reliable historical information on "Aśoka", and the fact noted by Deeg that the Major Inscriptions stood in open view for centuries after their erection

[39] Hultzsch (1925: xxxi–xxxvi) discusses this issue carefully and in some detail, but because of his belief that all of the inscriptions are by Aśoka, he has ended up tainting the evidence by use of medieval Buddhist literary "histories". The dates given here are based on the most conservative treatment of the Hellenistic references in the inscriptions.

and must have influenced the later writers of the Buddhist "histories" in question, it is most likely that "Aśoka" was not in fact a Mauryan ruler. We do not really know when or where he ruled, if he existed at all; we do not actually know that Daśaratha was the grandson of a *Mauryan* ruler named Aśoka; and so on.

In view of the above considerations, it is necessary to reorganize the inscriptions written in early Brahmi script into *three* groups:

1. The synoptic Major Inscriptions erected by the ruler called Devānāṃpriya Priyadarśi. These include the Major Rock Edicts and the Major Pillar Edicts. (But they exclude the nonsynoptic, later, and clearly spurious "Seventh Pillar Edict", q.v. below in this appendix.) Their contents relevant to the reconstruction of Early Buddhism are discussed in Chapter Three.
2. The Synoptic Buddhist Inscriptions erected by the ruler known simply as Devānāṃpriya, or in two instances (the Maski and Niṭṭūr Inscriptions), as Devānāṃpriya Aśoka, whose historical identity is unclear. His inscriptions pertain to Normative Buddhism, the mentioned elements of which are not attested to have come into existence until the Saka-Kushan period, over two centuries later. These inscriptions are discussed briefly in the following section.
3. A number of late, mostly spurious inscriptions that scholars have attributed to "Aśoka". The most significant of these are the inscriptions explicitly attributed to "Aśoka's" grandson Daśaratha; the "Seventh Pillar Edict"; the Lumbini Inscription; the Nigālī Sāgar Inscription; and the Calcutta-Bairāṭ Inscription. These texts are not usable as sources on religion in India during the Mauryan period and are not further discussed here, with the exception of the "Seventh Pillar Edict", the Lumbini Inscription, and the Calcutta-Bairāṭ Inscription, which have nevertheless been mistakenly used by many scholars as sources on Mauryan period Buddhism. They are discussed below.

The Synoptic Buddhist Inscriptions

The second group of inscriptions in Mauryan Brahmi script consists almost entirely[40] of the synoptic Buddhist Inscriptions.[41] These

[40] The exceptions are the dedications to the Ājīvikas, q.v. Falk (2006).

[41] A number of new inscriptional copies of texts belonging to this group have been found since Hultzsch's 1925 edition; see Salomon (1998: 138).

inscriptions, which mention the *Saṃgha*—the Normative Buddhist term for the organized community of monks—and give more detail about Buddhism, are all problematic *as Devānāṃpriya Priyadarśi inscriptions* for a number of other reasons, beginning with the significant, much-overlooked fact that none of them say they are proclaimed by Devānāṃpriya Priyadarśi, but by Devānāṃpriya or Devānāṃpriya Aśoka, as discussed above.

These inscriptions are synoptic versions of one short text[42] declaring that the Saṃgha should not be divided—thus telling us definitively that sectarian divisions had already happened. But once again their use of the term *Saṃgha* to refer to the Buddhists, instead of *Śramaṇa*, is a clear mark of a much later period, long after the Mauryas, when Buddhism became overwhelmingly monastic in character, namely the Saka-Kushan period.[43] These texts thus can only belong to Normative Buddhism.

The texts are also in general quite different in character from the Major Inscriptions, and have already been noted as calling for scholarly caution.[44] Most of the remaining Minor Pillar Inscriptions, including the Kauśāmbi Pillar Edict (on the Allahabad-Kosam Pillar), the Sāṃchi Pillar-Inscription, and the Sārnāth Pillar Inscription, as well as the Minor Rock Inscriptions—the Rūpnāth Rock Inscription, the Sahasram Rock Inscription, the Bairāṭ Rock Inscription (not to be confused with the Calcutta-Bairāṭ Inscription), the Maski Rock Inscription, and so on—are versions of the same short text on the progress of the author, Devānāṃpriya (*not* Devānāṃpriya Priyadarśi) 'His Majesty', as an *upāsaka* 'Buddhist lay worshipper'.[45] As noted, the Maski and Niṭṭūr Rock Inscriptions give the author's name as Devānāṃpriya Aśoka.[46] Therefore, these later and mostly much cruder Buddhist inscriptions were erected *not* by Devānāṃpriya *Priyadarśi*,[47] but by Devānāṃpriya *Aśoka.*

[42] As Hultzsch (1925) already recognized.

[43] For the linguistic and archaeological evidence, see Beckwith (2014).

[44] Norman (2012: 60), whose discussion mentions a number of points that suggest at least some of the inscriptions are spurious.

[45] For this latter group, see Hultzsch (1925: 228–230).

[46] Written *Devana[ṃ]priya Aśokesa*; the rest of the line is mostly damaged. Hultzsch (1925: 175) translates it "[A proclamation] of Devānāṃpriya Aśōka." The Niṭṭūr Inscription also mentions Aśoka, as noted above.

[47] The Gujarrā Inscription, according to the brief account of Falk (2006: 77), has "*devānāṃpiyasa piyadasino asāke rāja*", the last two words presumably "miswritten for *asoke rāja*". However, the many problems with this inscription noted by him (Falk 2006:

Who, then, really was Devānāṃpriya Aśoka? The evidence suggests at least two possibilities. One is that he was imagined by the Kushan period Normative Buddhists on the basis of their understanding of the monumental Major Inscriptions erected by the Mauryas—evidently by Amitrochates ~ Bindusāra. "Aśoka" was then projected back to the glorious Mauryan period as an ideal for good Kushan rulers to follow. A more likely possibility is that Aśoka was a historical ruler of Magadha in the Saka-Kushan period who was strongly pro-Buddhist, and sought to connect his lineage with the great Mauryan Dynasty, whose powerful rulers had left so many impressive monuments, including inscriptions, on the landscape of northern India. At any rate, the inscriptions of this Devānāṃpriya Aśoka, the apparent author of some of the Late Inscriptions, simply do not have anything in common with the Major Inscriptions of the Mauryas decreed by Devānāṃpriya Priyadarśi.

This very sketchy and preliminary study of the Buddhist Inscriptions indicates that they are much later than the Major Inscriptions—evidently centuries later—and thus do not belong to the Mauryan period and cultural milieu. They must be removed from the corpus of genuine Mauryan inscriptions. However, they are certainly of interest as relatively early monuments from ancient India, which tell us some interesting things about early Normative Buddhism. They deserve study in their own right.

All of the early Indian inscriptions in Mauryan Brahmi script need to be reexamined in detail in specialized studies intended to reveal what the texts actually do tell us, rather than to repeat what scholars have thought the texts *should* say.

---

77), including language, text ("*saṃpe* is miswritten for *saṃghe*"; "the beginning of this line is completely distorted"; "*upa* was misread as *ghā*"), palaeography ("*ḍha* or *ḍhi* . . . with missing inner coil"), and presentation ("the letters have not been incised very deeply"), indicate that it is a late, crude forgery by someone who did not know the Mauryan Brahmi script or Prakrit language very well. How could it be an edict by even a minor king, let alone one of the greatest rulers in Indian history? It is certainly not an authentic inscription of Devānāṃpriya Priyadarśi, or for that matter even an authentic inscription of Devānāṃpriya Aśoka (whenever he lived). It should be removed from the corpus entirely.

The Spurious Buddhist Inscriptions

According to the traditional analysis, the single most important putative "Aśoka" inscription for the history of Buddhism is the unique[48] "Third Minor Rock Edict" found at Bairāṭ, now known as the Calcutta-Bairāṭ Inscription,[49] in which "the king of Magadha, Piyadasa" addresses the "Saṃgha" (community of Buddhist monks) directly, and gives the names of a number of Buddhist sutras, saying, "I desire, Sirs, that many groups of monks and (many) nuns may repeatedly listen to these expositions of the *Dharma*, and may reflect (on them)."[50] The problems with the inscription are many. It begins with the otherwise unattested phrase "The Māgadha King Piyadasa",[51] *not* Devānāṃpriya Priyadarśi (or a Prakrit version of that name). The omission of the title Devānāṃpriya is nothing short of shocking. Moreover, it is the only inscription to even mention Magadha.[52] It is also undated, unlike the genuine Major Inscriptions, all of which are dated. In the text, the authorial voice declares "reverence and faith in the Buddha, the Dharma, (and) the Saṃgha".[53] This is the only occasion in all of the Mauryan inscriptions where the *Triratna* 'Three Jewels', the "refuge" formula well known from later devotional Buddhism, is mentioned. Most astonishingly, throughout the text the author repeatedly addresses the Buddhist monks humbly as *bhaṃte*, translated by Hultzsch as "reverend sirs". The text also contains a higher percentage of words that are found solely within it (i.e., not also found in some other inscription) than does any other inscription. From beginning to end, the Calcutta-Bairāṭ Inscription is simply incompatible with the undoubtedly genuine Major Inscriptions. It is also evidently incompatible with the other Buddhist inscriptions possibly attributable to a later ruler named Devānāṃpriya Aśoka.

[48] Unlike the synoptic "edicts", the text occurs only once, in this inscription.

[49] Also known as the Bhābrū Inscription, among other names.

[50] Hultzsch (1925: 174).

[51] In the rubbing reproduced by Hultzsch, what is visible is 𑀧𑀺𑀬𑀤𑀲𑀮[]𑀫𑀸𑀕𑀥𑁂 *piyadasa la*[ ] *māgadhe*, translated by Hultzsch as "the king (*lājā*, dial. for *rājā*) of Māgadha, Piyadasi" (Hultzsch 1925: 172–173).

[52] This is taken by Hultzsch (1925: xxx) as evidence that the author of the Major Inscriptions, Devānāṃpriya Priyadarśi, was a king of Magadha.

[53] Hultzsch (1925: 173).

However, because the inscription is also the only putative Aśokan inscription that mentions Buddhist texts, and even names seven of them explicitly, scholars are loath to remove it from the corpus. It therefore calls for a little more comment.

First, even if the Calcutta-Bairāṭ Inscription really is "old", it is certainly much younger than the genuine inscriptions of Devānāṃpriya Priyadarśi. If it dates to approximately the same epoch as the recently discovered Gāndhārī documents—the Saka-Kushan period, from about the late first century BC to the mid-third century AD—the same period when the Pali Canon, according to tradition, was collected, it should then not be surprising to find that the names of the texts mentioned in the inscription seem to accord with the contents of the latter collections of Normative Buddhist works, even though few, if any, of the texts (of which only the titles are given) can be identified with any certainty.[54]

Second, as noted above, specialists have pointed out that the script and Prakrit language of the Mauryan inscriptions continued to be used practically unchanged down through the Kushan period,[55] and though the style of the script changed somewhat in the following period, it was still legible for any literate person at least as late as the beginning of the Gupta period (fourth century AD),[56] so the inscriptions undoubtedly influenced the developing legends about the great Buddhist king, Aśoka.[57] Thus at least some of the events described in the Major Inscriptions, such as Devānāṃpriya Priyadarśi's conquest of Kaliṅga, subsequent remorse, and turning to the Dharma, were perfect candidates for ascription to Aśoka in the legends. In the absence of any historical source of any kind on Aśoka dating to a period close to the events—none of the datable Major Inscriptions mention Aśoka—it is impossible

[54] However, it must be borne in mind that the Trilakṣaṇa text discussed in Chapter One, though short, is by far the oldest known fragment of Buddhist text. It is thus possible that texts in the Pali Canon and the Gāndhārī documents that mention the Trilakṣaṇa might themselves be older than the other texts in the same corpora.

[55] Falk (1993: 328), cited in Deeg (2009: 117). Numerous short donative inscriptions in Brahmi script are dated (or archaeologically datable) to the end of the first millennium BC or first centuries AD, showing that the language and script of the Mauryan inscriptions continued to be used long after the dynasty fell (Michael Willis, p.c., 2012).

[56] At that time the script underwent substantial changes that soon made older forms of it unreadable.

[57] Deeg (2009: 117).

to rule out this possibility. The late Buddhist inscriptions, such as the Calcutta-Bairāṭ Inscription, may well have been written under the same influence.[58]

Third, because the Calcutta-Bairāṭ Inscription only mentions the *titles* of texts that have been identified—rather uncertainly in most cases—with the *titles* of texts in the Pali Canon, the actual texts referred to may have been quite different, or even totally different, from the presently attested ones. Because the earliest, or highest, possible date for the Pali Canon is in fact the Saka-Kushan period, the Calcutta-Bairāṭ Inscription and the texts it names cannot be much earlier.

The inscription's list of "passages of scripture" that "Priyadarśi, King of Magadha" has selected to be frequently listened to by the monks so that "the True Dharma will be of long duration" is translated by Hultzsch as "the *Vinaya-Samukasa*, the *Aliya-vasas*, the *Anāgata-bhayas*, the *Muni-gāthās*, the *Moneya-sūta*, the *Upatisa-pasina*, and the *Lāghulovāda* which was spoken by the blessed Buddha concerning falsehood."[59] Among the texts considered to be identified are the *Vinaya-samukasa* and the *Muni-gāthā*.

The *Vinaya-samukasa* has been identified with the *Vinaya-samukase* 'Innate Principles of the Vinaya', a short text in the *Mahāvagga* of the Pali Canon. After a brief introduction, the Buddha tells the monks what is permitted and what is not.

Vinaya-Samukase

> Now at that time uncertainty arose in the monks with regard to this and that item: "Now what is allowed by the Blessed One? What is not allowed?" They told this matter to the Blessed One, (who said):
>
> "Bhikkhus, whatever I have not objected to, saying, 'This is not allowable,' if it fits in with what is not allowable, if it goes against what is allowable, this is not allowable for you.

[58] It is possible that the Maski and Niṭṭūr Inscriptions, in which Aśoka is mentioned by name, were written at the same time, following the model of the other roughly synoptic Buddhist Inscriptions.

[59] Hultzsch (1925: 173–174). The rubbing reads (with my added punctuation and capitalization), "*Vinaya-samukase, Aliya-vasāṇi, Anāgata-bhayāni, Muni-gāthā, Moneya-sute, Upatisa-pasine,* e cā *Lāghulovāde* . . .".

> "Whatever I have not objected to, saying, 'This is not allowable,' if it fits in with what is allowable, if it goes against what is not allowable, this is allowable for you.
>
> "And whatever I have not permitted, saying, 'This is allowable,' if it fits in with what is not allowable, if it goes against what is allowable, this is not allowable for you.
>
> "And whatever I have not permitted, saying, 'This is allowable,' if it fits in with what is allowable, if it goes against what is not allowable, this is allowable for you."[60]

Although the Buddha's own speech in this text is structured as a tetralemma, which was fashionable in the fourth and third centuries BC,[61] it must also be noted that the tetralemma is a dominant feature of the earliest Madhyamika texts, those by Nāgārjuna, who is traditionally dated to approximately the second century AD. But the problems with the inscription are much deeper than this. The Vinaya per se cannot be dated back to the time of the Buddha (as the text intends), nor to the time of Aśoka; it cannot be dated even to the Saka-Kushan period. All fully attested Vinaya texts are actually dated, either explicitly or implicitly, to the Gupta period, specifically to the *fifth* century AD: "In most cases, we can place the *vinayas* we have securely in time: the *Sarvāstivāda-vinaya* that we know was translated into Chinese at the beginning of the fifth century (404–405 C.E.). So were the *Vinayas* of the Dharmaguptakas (408), the Mahīśāsakas (423–424), and the Mahāsaṃghikas (416). The *Mūlasarvāstivāda-vinaya* was translated into both Chinese and Tibetan still later, and the actual contents of the Pali Vinaya are only knowable from Buddhaghosa's fifth century commentaries."[62] As Schopen has shown in many magisterial works, the Vinayas are layered texts, so they undoubtedly contain material

[60] Mv. [Mahāvagga] VI 40.1. From "That the True Dhamma Might Last a Long Time: Readings Selected by King Aśoka", selected and translated by Thanissaro Bhikkhu, *Access to Insight*, June 7, 2009, http://www.accesstoinsight.org/lib/authors/thanissaro/Aśoka.html (punctuation modified to fit the style of the present book).

[61] See Appendix A.

[62] Schopen (2004: 94), who adds, "Although we do not know anything definite about any hypothetical earlier versions of these *vinayas*, we do know that all of the *vinayas* as we have them fall squarely into what might unimaginatively be called the Middle Period of Indian Buddhism, the period between the beginning of the Common Era and the year 500 C.E."

earlier than the fifth century, but even the earliest layers of the Vinaya texts cannot be earlier than Normative Buddhism, which is datable to the Saka-Kushan period. It thus would require rather more than the usual amount of credulity to project the ancestors of the cited texts back another half millennium or more to the time of the Buddha.

The *Muni-gāthā* 'Discourses on the Sage' has been identified with the *Muni Sutta* in the *Sutta Nipāta.* Its emphasis on the Forest-dwelling sage certainly might support an argument for a relatively early date. However, it could also support an argument in favor of identifying the text with early Mahayana, a school of Buddhism thought to be contemporary with Nāgārjuna, which also insists on the superiority of the Forest-dwelling *śramaṇa.*[63]

Note that the inscription does not mention *reading* the sutras.

As for other well-known but evidently spurious "Aśokan" inscriptions, note that the "Minor Pillar Inscription" at Lumbini not only mentions "Buddha" (as does, otherwise uniquely, the Calcutta-Bairāṭ Inscription), it explicitly calls him *Śākyamuni* 'the Sage of the Scythians (Sakas)',[64] who it says was born in Lumbini.[65] The use of the Sanskrit form of his epithet, *Śākyamuni*, rather than the Prakrit form, *Sakamuni*, is astounding and otherwise unattested until the late Gāndhārī documents; that fact alone rules out ascription to such an early period. But it is doubly astounding because this Sanskritism occurs in a text otherwise written completely in Mauryan Prakrit and Brahmi script. What is a Sanskrit form doing there? Sanskrit is not attested in any inscriptions or manuscripts until the Common Era or at most a few decades before it.[66] Significantly, the inscription also notes that the village of Lumbini is exempted from tax and has to pay less in kind as well, yet not one of the other Mauryan inscriptions includes such "benefice" information.

[63] See Boucher (2008). The *Muni Sutta* reads strikingly like a passage from the *Tao Te Ching* or the *Chuangtzu* (or vice versa). It appears that no one has ever done a scholarly comparison of these Indian and Chinese texts.

[64] The Lumbini Inscription, line 3, has *Budhe jate Sakyamuni ti* "the Buddha *Śākyamuni* was born here" (Hultzsch 1925: 164).

[65] See the discussion of this and other related issues in Phelps (2008).

[66] Bronkhorst (2011: 46, 50), who cites Salomon (1998:86) on the existence of four inscriptions ascribed by some, including Salomon, to the first century BC; otherwise the earliest inscriptions in Sanskrit are from Mathurā in the first and second centuries AD (Salomon 1998: 87).

It is incredible that an avowedly Buddhist Inscription bestows imperial largesse on a village (though the village of Lumbini has been shown not to have existed yet in Mauryan times) rather than on a Buddhist institution.[67] Perhaps most telling of all, the inscription is uniquely written in ordinary third person (not royal third person) and is in the past tense. That means the text is narrated by some unknown person and does not even pretend to have been proclaimed by its putative sponsor Devānāṃpriya Priyadarśi, the king who authored the synoptic Major Inscriptions (nor of course by Devānāṃpriya Aśoka, who may have authored the synoptic Buddhist Inscriptions). It says that it records events that supposedly happened at some time in the past, but those events have been shown to be fictitious.[68] The inscription is strikingly unlike the unquestionably authentic Major Inscriptions in general, and based on its contents is much later in date than it evidently pretends to be. It is a spurious inscription.[69]

Finally, the Delhi-Topra pillar includes a good version of the six synoptic Pillar Edicts, which are genuine Major Inscriptions, but it is followed by what is known as the "Seventh Pillar Edict". This is a section that occurs only on this particular monument—not on any of the six other synoptic Pillar Edict monuments. It is "the longest of all the Aśokan edicts. For the most part, it summarizes and restates the contents of the other pillar edicts, and to some extent those of the major rock edicts as well."[70] In fact, as Salomon suggests, it is a hodgepodge of the authentic inscriptions. It seems not to have been observed that such a mélange could not have been compiled without someone going from stone to stone to collect passages from different inscriptions, and this presumably must have involved transmission in writing, unlike with the Major Rock Edict inscriptions, which were clearly dictated orally to scribes from each region of India, who then wrote down the texts in their own local dialects—and in some cases, their own local

[67] I am indebted to M. L. Walter (p.c., 2013) for this observation, which had escaped me; cf. Schopen (2007: 61) and Bronkhorst (2011: 18). For a discussion of some nonreligious functions of later Buddhist monasteries, see Schopen (2006).

[68] Bareau (1987).

[69] The only question now is to determine when it was created—probably late in the Saka-Kushan period, but see Phelps (2008).

[70] Salomon (1998: 139).

script or language; knowledge of writing would seem to be required for that, but not actual written texts.[71] For the Delhi-Topra pillar addition, someone made copies of the texts and produced the unique "Seventh Pillar Edict".[72]

Why would anyone go to so much trouble? The answer is to be found in the salient new information found in the text itself. It mentions a category of *mahāmātra* officers unmentioned anywhere else,[73] saying that they are in charge of the different sects: it names the *Saṃgha* 'Buddhists' and the Brāḥmaṇas 'Brahmanists', but also (uniquely) the Ājīvikas and Nirgranthas (Jains), and "various other sects" who are unnamed.[74] Most incredibly, the Buddhists are called the "Saṃgha" in *this section alone*, but it is a Normative Buddhist term; the Early Buddhist term is *Śramaṇa*, attested in the genuine Major Inscriptions. Throughout the rest of the "Seventh Pillar Edict" Buddhists are called *Śramaṇas*, as expected in texts copied from genuine Mauryan inscriptions. There can be no doubt that this great pastiche was created for

[71] Norman (2012: 56) notes that the Major Pillar Edicts, which are dated to a later period of the reign of the king, are in the same dialect and are virtually identical, indicating that they were copied from a written exemplar, but on the following page he shows (unintentionally) that the texts must have been oral. Further study is needed.

[72] The bilingual Aramaic and Prakrit (both in Aramaic script) fragment from Kandahar known as Kandahar II or Kandahar III, which is written in an extremely odd fashion (Falk 2006: 246), has been identified as representing a portion of the "Seventh Pillar Edict" (Norman 2012: 43), but strong doubts remain about the reading of the text (Falk 2006: 246). It is also by no means exactly like the "Seventh Pillar Edict", not to speak of the peculiar presentation of text and translation. In fact, it looks like a student exercise. It is very similar to the content of the Taxila Inscription and the two Laghmān Inscriptions, both of which are also highly problematic, q.v. Falk's (2006: 253) conclusion: "There is no clear evidence for an Aśokan influence on this text [the Taxila Inscription]. Like the two Laghmān 'edicts' this text as well could be of a rather profane nature, mentioning Aśoka as king just in passing." However, Falk (2006: 241) also says of Kandahar II/III that "Asoka must have ordered to bring his words to the public unchanged regarding their sound and content. Presenting this text in two languages using one script for both is a remarkable thought, aimed at avoiding flaws in the translation." This is an unlikely speculation. Finally, the "Seventh Pillar Edict" shares some of the peculiarities of the other minor inscriptions from Afghanistan. (I.e., they are to be distinguished from the genuine fragments of a Greek translation of the Twelfth and Thirteenth Rock Edicts, found at Kandahar, q.v. Halkias 2014.) C.f. Ito (1996), a study of the Greek and Aramaic bilingual inscription from Kandahar. These texts all await detailed, serious study.

[73] As noted by Senart in "(IA, 18. 305)," according to Hultzsch (1925: 136n5).

[74] Hultzsch (1925: 136).

a single purpose: to acquire "grandfathered" legal protection for two sects—the Ājīvikas and Jains—which were perhaps under pressure by the government of the day. Which government might that have been? One imagines the Kushans, under whom Normative Buddhism developed and flourished.[75]

Yet it is not only the contents of the text that are a problem. It has been accepted as an authentic Mauryan inscription, but no one has even noted that there is anything *formally* different about it from the other six edicts on the same pillar. At least a few words must therefore be said about this problem.

The "Seventh Pillar Edict" is palaeographically distinct from the text it has been appended to. It is obvious at first glance. The physical differences between the text of the "Seventh Pillar Edict", as compared even to the immediately preceding text of the Sixth Pillar Edict on the East Face, virtually leap out at one. The style of the script,[76] the size and spacing of the letters, the poor control over consistency of style from one letter to the next,[77] and the many hastily written, even scribbled, letters are all remarkable. These characteristics seem not to have been mentioned by the many scholars who have worked on the Mauryan inscriptions.

The text begins as an addition to the synoptic Sixth Pillar Edict, which occupies only part of the East Face "panel". After filling out the available space for text on the East Face, the new text incredibly continues *around* the pillar, that is, ignoring the four different "faces" already established by the earlier, genuine edicts. This circum-pillar format is unique among all the genuine Mauryan pillar inscriptions.[78]

Another remarkable difference with respect to the genuine Major Inscriptions *on pillars* is that the latter are concerned almost exclusively with Devānāṃpriya Priyadarśi's Dharma, but do not mention either

[75] In the total absence of any studies at all on the problems of this text, or any other significant issues involving it, little more can be said at present.

[76] For an obvious example, compare the different shape of the syllable form 𑀠𑀺 *ḍhi* in the First Pillar Edict (line 6) on the Delhi-Topra column and in the "Seventh Pillar Edict" (lines 13 and 14) on the same column.

[77] Note the many shapes of the letter 𑀚 (*ja*), including some that look like Greek ϵ (e.g., line 26).

[78] See Note 9 in this appendix for previous scholars' discussion of the circum-pillar format.

the *Śramaṇas* 'Buddhists' or the *Brāḥmaṇas* 'Brahmanists' by name. This is strikingly unlike the Major Inscriptions on rocks, which mention them repeatedly in many of the edicts. In other words, though the Pillar Edicts are all dated later than the Rock Edicts, for some reason (perhaps their brevity), Devānāṃpriya Priyadarśi does not mention the *Śramaṇas* or the *Brāḥmaṇas* in them. The "Seventh Pillar Edict" is thus unique in that it *does* mention the Buddhists (*Śramaṇas*) and Brahmanists (*Brāḥmaṇas*) by name, but the reoccurrence of the names in what claims to be the last of Devānāṃpriya Priyadarśi's edicts suggests that the text is not just spurious, it is probably a deliberate forgery. This conclusion is further supported by the above-noted unique passage in the inscription in which the Buddhists are referred to as the "*Saṃgha*". This term occurs in the later Buddhist Inscriptions too, but it is problematic because it is otherwise unknown before well into the Saka-Kushan period.[79]

The one really significant thing the text does is to add the claim that Devānāṃpriya Priyadarśi supported not only the Buddhists and the Brahmanists but also the Ājīvikas and Jains. However, all of the Jain holy texts are uncontestedly very late (long after the Mauryan period). The very mention of the sect in the same breath as the others is alone sufficient to cast severe doubt on the text's authenticity.[80]

The "Seventh Pillar Edict" claims that it was inscribed when Devānāṃpriya Priyadarśi had been enthroned for twenty-seven years, that is, only one year after the preceding text (the sixth of the synoptic Pillar Edicts), which says it was inscribed when Devānāṃpriya Priyadarśi had been enthroned for twenty-six years. The "Seventh Pillar Edict" text consists of passages taken from many of the Major Inscriptions, both Rock and Pillar Edicts, in which the points mentioned are typically dated to one or another year after the ruler's coronation, but in the "Seventh Pillar Edict" the events are effectively dated to the same year. Most puzzling of all, why would the king add such an evidently important edict to *only a single one* of the otherwise completely synoptic pillar inscriptions?[81]

[79] This is one of the many reasons for dating all of the Buddhist Inscriptions to the Saka-Kushan period at the earliest.

[80] See the discussion in the Preface.

[81] Cf. Norman (2012).

Perhaps even more damning is the fact that in the text itself the very same passages are often repeated verbatim, sometimes (as near the beginning) immediately after they have just been stated, like mechanical dittoisms. Repetition is a known feature of Indian literary texts, but the way it occurs in the "Seventh Pillar Edict" is not attested in the authentic Major Inscriptions. Moreover, as Olivelle has noted, the text repeats the standard opening formula or "introductory refrain" many times; that is, "King Priyadarśin, Beloved of the Gods, says"[82] is repeated verbatim nine times, with an additional shorter tenth repetition. "In all of the other edicts this refrain occurs only once and at the beginning. Such repetitions of the refrain which state that these are the words of the king are found in Persian inscriptions. However, this is quite unusual for Aśoka."[83] In fact, this arrangement betrays the actual author's misunderstanding of the division of the authentic Major Inscriptions into "Edicts", and his or her consequent false imitation of them using repetitions of the Edict-initial formula throughout the text in an attempt to duplicate the appearance of the authentic full, multi-"Edict" inscriptions on rocks and pillars.

In short, based on its arrangement, palaeography, style, and contents, the "Seventh Pillar Edict" cannot be accepted as a genuine inscription of Devānāṃpriya Priyadarśi. The text was added to the pillar much later than it claims and is an obvious forgery from a later historical period. These factors require that the "Seventh Pillar Edict" be removed from the corpus of authentic inscriptions of Devānāṃpriya Priyadarśi.

The Calcutta-Bairāṭ Inscription, the Lumbini Inscription, and the "Seventh Pillar Edict" of the Delhi-Topra pillar thus do not belong with either the authentic Major Inscriptions of Devānāṃpriya Priyadarśi or the possibly authentic inscriptions of Devānāṃpriya Aśoka.[84 xiv]

[82] Olivelle (2012: 166), Norman (2012: 45).

[83] Olivelle (2012: 180n8).

[84] The next task is for scholars to study the spurious inscriptions to see when exactly each was inscribed, and in some cases why, so as to be able to attribute the information in them to approximately correct historical periods. See also Endnote xiv.

Endnotes

i. His fate upon returning to Scythia is not certainly known (Kindstrand 1981: 11), but the fact that Herodotus could not find anyone in Olbia who had heard of him does not mean that Anacharsis never actually existed, as Kindstrand (1981: 16) concludes—especially considering that Kindstrand cites copious evidence against this view throughout his own book. Although Herodotus's story of the fate of the half-Greek Scythian prince Skyles and that of Anacharsis are very similar (Kindstrand 1981: 15), as Herodotus himself suggests, Szemerényi (1980) conclusively shows that the name *Skyles* is actually just another form of the name *Scythes* 'Scythian'; both derive from Old North Iranic *skuða 'archer'. As a half-Greek who was nevertheless a Scythian prince, Anacharsis would inevitably have been equated with a prince called Skyles "the Scythian", who was also half-Greek. There is no reason to believe the story Herodotus tells of the death of Anacharsis (the lone point of biographical similarity between the two, other than the fact that both are said to have been half-Greek). Since the Scythians were at the time not literate, it is hardly likely that they would have remembered a long-ago Scythian who had left Scythia for a time and then came back. If he actually was killed almost upon arrival, it was undoubtedly for political reasons, as he would have been seen as a potential contender for the throne.

ii. Bronkhorst (2007; 2011) also argues that Brahmanism was either unknown or uninfluential in Gandhāra and Magadha during the time of the Buddha. While this seems undoubtedly correct for Magadha, the eye-witness testimony of Megasthenes in 305–304 BC shows that Early Brahmanism (not, of course, Late Brahmanism, which had not developed yet) was known by his time in eastern Gandhāra at least. Bronkhorst (2007) further contends that the ideas of karma and rebirth, which are unknown in the Rig Veda, appear in Indian thought at the time of the Buddha because he lived in the area of "Greater Magadha" (essentially, the Ganges basin), where the ideas were native to the region. However, he does not explain why such ideas should have appeared in that region or have been native to it in the first place, and much of his argument is based on accepting the traditional Indian projection of great teachers, such as Mahāvīra, back to the time of the Buddha (e.g., Bronkhorst 2011: 130) or earlier. His argument that the ideas of rebirth and karma are fundamental to Buddhism also forces him to argue the highly improbable position that the Buddha's basic teaching of *anātman*, "no (inherent) self (-identity)", does not *really* deny the "self" (Bronkhorst 2009: 22–25; 2011: 6–8). His theory also does not account for the pervasive rejection of antilogies (absolute opposites such as Truth and Falsehood, Good and Bad) in Early Buddhism.

iii. The fragment of Timon's panegyrical poem has some textual problems, but it is attested in several sources and is certainly authentic: "You alone lead humans in the manner of the god / Who revolves back and forth around the whole earth / Showing the flaming circle of his well-turned sphere." Translation of Bett (2000: 71), q.v. for the sources and discussion of the textual issues; cf. Clayman (2009) for identification of the reconstitution, context, and significance of the fragments, which have not been properly understood in their literary context. It is conceivable, if perhaps unlikely, that Timon's comparison could reflect the Pre–Pure Land school of Buddhism partially described by Megasthenes (see Chapter Two), because one of the very earliest Buddhist texts translated into Chinese, the *Pratyutpanna Samādhi Sūtra*, is a fully developed Pure Land work in which the Buddha Amitābha is, in effect, the Sun God dwelling in a radiant Heaven. For discussion of this long controversial topic, see Halkias (2013a: 20–24).

iv. An account of Nicolaus Damascenus reported by Strabo says that an Indian envoy to the Roman emperor Augustus (63 BC–AD 14) burnt himself to death in Athens, and an epitaph was inscribed on a memorial stone there, reading, Ζαρμανοχηγὰς Ἰνδὸς ἀπὸ Βαργόσης κατὰ τὰ πάτρια Ἰνδῶν ἔθη ἑαυτὸν ἀπαθανατίσας κεῖται. "Here lies Zarmanochēgas the Indian from Barygaza, having immortalized himself following the customs of the Indians" (Strabo XV, 1, 73; text from Radt 2005: 4:226). However, the supposed name *Zarmanochegas* is spelled *Zarmarus* in Cassius Dio 54, 9, 8–10 (cited in Karttunen 1997: 64n270). There is no reason to fantasize that Zarmanochegas was a Śramaṇa, as Radt (2009: 195, 208) and many others claim, without any basis in the ancient sources. Some have drawn this conclusion based solely on a vague resemblance of the word to the man's name, without taking into consideration the fact that the spelling of uncommon foreign names in the received (late medieval) text of Strabo is erratic and hardly a reliable basis for such ideas, some of which have been repeated for nearly two centuries now, e.g., the translation of Strabo by de La Porte du Theil et al. (1805–1819), cited by Radt (2009: 195) and others. Such approval usually is accompanied by acceptance of the doubtful idea that the Gymnosophists were probably Jains. Although criticized briefly by Karttunen (1997: 65), who says that for Jains "religious suicide was not rare, but the only permitted means was fasting to death", he does not criticize it on the basis of any genuinely early Indian sources on them. See further below in Chapter Two.

v. It has long been thought that the Pramnae, described later in Strabo on the basis of unnamed "writers" (obviously not Megasthenes; Strabo's source or sources for this are otherwise unnamed), are a subvariety of the Brahmanists (cf. the βραμεναι in the following note), despite the fact that the account explicitly opposes them to the Brachmanes. It is possible that they were a distinct regional subsect of the Brāḥmaṇas, but it is more likely that this is a pastiche taken from other writers Strabo used as sources. In any case, the account clearly mixes up several different sects that are distinguished by Megasthenes, so it is of little use for the present study.

vi. The point is recognized already in the edition and translation of McCrindle (1889: 98, note). The variants with and without the *-r-* reflect ancient Indian dialects—examples of both can be seen in the Mauryan inscriptions, the texts of which were evidently dictated orally and written down from memory in each location according to the local dialect of the time, and in some cases edited to reflect sensitivity to local conditions. The fragmentary beginning of a Greek version of the Thirteenth Rock Edict has been found in Alexandria in Arachosia (what is now Kandahar in Afghanistan), the westernmost region of the Mauryan realm. In it the word is written σραμεναι *Sramenai* "Śramaṇas", while "Brāḥmaṇas" is written, similarly, βραμεναι (q.v. the previous note). For a study of the Greek inscriptions that puts them in the context of religious history, see Halkias (2013b).

vii. Specifically it comes from Josephus's *Bellum Iudaicum* VII, 8.352–357, as pointed out by the editors of Porphyry's *De abstinentia*, Patillon and Segonds (1995: xxxviii–xlii; cf. 1995: 30n270), with discussion and references to the extensive scholarship on it. Deeg and Gardner (2009) do not mention this textual problem and were evidently unaware of it. The section of Porphyry that they give is taken from Winter (1999), who is also clearly unaware of the extensive literature on the identification of this passage as having been taken verbatim from Josephus. That Josephus is the source of the section is mentioned also briefly by Clark (2000: 190n649), who used the Budé edition by Patillon and Segonds (Clark 2000: 22), but nevertheless—like nearly all other translators of this popular work—adds "the Samaneans" into this section of Porphyry's text, thus misleading the unsuspecting reader into thinking that the section mentions *śramaṇas* and has something to do with them. But the word *Samanaioi* "Samaneans" is *completely absent* from this third section, which has been solidly demonstrated by Patillon and Segonds as originally having had nothing to do with the second section.

viii. An anonymous reviewer of the manuscript of this book objects, "The traditional Greek conception of gods and of the soul does not line up very well with the Zoroastrian ideas against which Buddha, or the Christian ideas against which Hume, are reacting; Greek religion does not have a clear heaven, and the soul does not outlive the body in any significant sense. Pyrrho may be reacting against absolutist *philosophical* views of one kind or another (e.g., Plato's), which would include ideas about God, heaven and the soul that would fit much better with the Zoroastrian and Christian ones; but I see no reason to think that these topics were central to his thinking. This seems to be a case where Pyrrho is being assumed to go along with Buddhist thought, even when the evidence for this is not there." However, after ten years in Alexander's "philosophical court" it would be unreasonable to think that Pyrrho did not have a very good idea about the many Greek *philosophoi* 'philosophical-religious teachers' who promoted belief in a creator God, including Plato. In my opinion, the traditional "old gods" of the Greeks are a red herring. Nevertheless, the implied reaction against theism in Pyrrho's system seems to me an artifact of his having taken over Early Buddhist ideas. See the detailed discussion in Chapter Four.

ix. I am indebted to E. Bruce Brooks for his discussion of textual layering throughout the *Chuangtzu*: "I . . . don't see a warrant for assuming that the narrative voice is mistaken, any more than it is mistaken in the early, discursive parts of the chapter. The narrative voice is presumably expressing the text's view. The text then seems to be saying that there must be some distinction between Jou [Chou] (note the third person form) and the butterfly; it ends by giving a name to the difference, or to the way of properly regarding the difference: 此之謂物化。. . . I think there is a sort of generic similarity between the positions that Jwang Jou [Chuang Chou] holds, or is perplexed about, or . . . makes mistakes in, throughout the Jwangdz [*Chuangtzu*] text. And that these positions have similarities to the positions in anecdotes where Jwangdz appears as the articulator of the text's view. What I see in this is a group of people who adopted Jwang Jou as their spokesman for a certain view, and then grew beyond that view, while retaining Jwangdz (though now portrayed as erroneous) as still holding a recognizable version of that view. The text grows, but Jwangdz, at least in some chapters, does not grow with it, but remains identified with positions he was previously portrayed as articulating. In this [as] in every textual enterprise I can imagine, I think we need to read the whole text, but we also need to avoid assuming that it will say the same thing at every point." (E. Bruce Brooks, April 8, 2012, Warring States Workshop list posting, quoted by permission.)

x. It has been argued from time to time that in early Antiquity not only did things Indian make their way to China, and things Chinese make their way to India, via perilous trails through the high mountains and gorges separating the northeastern Indian subcontinent from southwestern China, known in the twentieth century as "the Hump", the trade also included influential ideas (e.g., Brooks and Brooks 2015). The theory cannot be ruled out because just such a trade route is thought to have existed no later than the visit of Chang Ch'ien to Bactria in 128 BC. Nevertheless, Chang and the other Chinese of his time had never even thought of trying such a route, which they had never heard of. When Chang did hear of it—to his great surprise—the subsequent Chinese efforts to reach India that way failed, so they continued using the Central Asian route. The once important trade route that went from Szechuan via the Tsaidam Basin in northeastern Tibet to western Kansu and along the "southern" route through the Tarim Basin is most likely the one referred to by Chang Ch'ien's informants, who were after all in Bactria, the center of which in his time was to the north of both routes.

xi. The "Advertisement" on page A2 of the 1777 edition of the *Enquiry* contains a comment on this by Hume himself, who says,

> Most of the principles and reasonings, contained in this volume, were published in a work in three volumes, called *A Treatise of Human Nature*: A work which the Author had projected before he left College, and which he wrote and published not long after. But not finding it successful, he was sensible of his error in going to the press too early, and he cast the whole anew in the following pieces, where some negligences in his former reasoning and more in the expression, are, he hopes, corrected. Yet several writers, who have honoured the Author's Philosophy with answers, have taken care to direct all their batteries against that juvenile work,

which the Author never acknowledged, and have affected to triumph in any advantages, which, they imagined, they had obtained over it: A practice very contrary to all rules of candour and fair-dealing, and a strong instance of those polemical artifices, which a bigotted zeal thinks itself authorised to employ. Henceforth, the Author desires, that the following Pieces may alone be regarded as containing his philosophical sentiments and principles.

xii. Much has been written attempting to identify putative ancient Indian "Sceptics" sometimes called "eel-wrigglers" with the Greek Sceptics. For example, Clayman (2009: 41) says, "Of particular note is the school of Sanjaya, a contemporary of the Buddha who espoused complete skepticism on all issues." She compares this school to Pyrrho's thought. However, this variant of the "smorgasbord" approach to identifying sources of Pyrrhonism, as discussed in Appendix B, is vitiated by the fact that the sources for this supposed "contemporary" of the Buddha and other putative Indian sect founders are stories composed in Late Antiquity, the Middle Ages, or even later. There is no source material on them that is remotely close chronologically to that which we have for Early Buddhism and Early Brahmanism. These teachers and their sects cannot possibly be projected back to the Buddha's own time, or even to the first few centuries afterward. The same is true for some scholars' comparisons with Madhyamika or even Hindu uses of the tetralemma, also based on medieval texts (e.g., Frenkian, cited in Clayman 2009: 42).

xiii. Soudavar (2010: 125–126) adds, "the monotheistic reverence of Darius and Zoroaster for Ahura Mazdā stemmed from an ideology that must have been popular among a small group of Iranians, and it is likely that some of Darius' fellow conspirators, if not all, belonged to that group. Indeed, both Herodotus and Bisotun [the Behistun Inscription] agree that the usurper magus, Gaumata, was in control of the army and harshly suppressed any opposition. . . . It therefore seems logical . . . that the conspirators needed to trust each other. Their trust was probably based on common religious beliefs or affiliations." Soudavar's scenario is solidly confirmed by the Silver Plaque of Otanes, on which see below in the Epilogue.

xiv. After the present book was already in page proofs, I learned (courtesy of Michael L. Walter) of the existence of a book on spurious Achaemenid inscriptions, a topic of direct relevance to this Appendix. I therefore take advantage of the available space on this page to give the reference: Schmitt, Rüdiger 2007. *Pseudo-altpersische Inschriften: Inschriftenfälschungen und moderne Nachbildungen in altpersischer Keilschrift*. Vienna: Österreichischen Akademie der Wissenschaften.

References

Abdi, Kamyar 2010. The Passing of the Throne from Xerxes to Artaxerxes I, or How an Archaeological Observation Can Be a Potential Contribution to Achaemenid Historiography. *In*: John Curtis and St. John Simpson, eds., *The World of Achaemenid Persia: History, Art and Society in Iran and the Ancient Near East*. London: I.B. Tauris, 275–284.

Adams, Douglas Q. 1999. *A Dictionary of Tocharian B*. Amsterdam: Rodopi.

Aiken, Charles Francis 1910. Jainism. *In*: *The Catholic Encyclopedia*, Vol. 8. New York: Robert Appleton. http://www.newadvent.org/cathen/08269b.htm.

Alekseyev, A. Yu 2005. Scythian Kings and "Royal" Burial-Mounds of the Fifth and Fourth Centuries BC. *In:* David Braund, ed., *Scythians and Greeks*. Exeter: University of Exeter Press, 39–55.

Aristotle, *Metaphysics*. *See* Tredennick 1933–1935.

Ausland, H. 1989. On the Moral Origin of the Pyrrhonian Philosophy. *Elenchos* 10: 359–434.

Babbitt, Frank Cole, ed. and trans. 1927. *Plutarch: Moralia*. Vol. 1. London: William Heinemann.

Bareau, André 1963. *Recherches sur la biographie de Buddha dans les Sūtrapiṭaka et les Vinayapiṭaka anciens: De la quête de l'éveil à la conversion de Maudgalyāyana*. Paris: École Française d'Extrême-Orient (Publications de l'École Française d'Extrême-Orient, LIII).

——— 1979. La composition et les étapes de la formation progressive du *Mahāparinirvāṇasūtra* ancien. *Bulletin de l'École Française d'Extrême-Orient* 66: 45–103.

——— 1987. Lumbinī et la naissance du futur Buddha. *Bulletin de l'École Française d'Extrême-Orient* 76: 69–81.

——— 1995. Some Considerations Concerning the Problem Posed by the Date of the Buddha's Parinirvāṇa. *In*: Heinz Bechert, ed., *When Did the Buddha Live? The Controversy on the Dating of the Historical Buddha*. Delhi: Sri Satguru Publications, 211–219.

Baums, Stefan. 2009. A Gāndhārī Commentary on Early Buddhist Verses: British Library Kharoṣṭhī Fragments 7, 9, 13 and 18. PhD dissertation, University of Washington.

Baums, Stefan and Andrew Glass 2010. *A Dictionary of Gāndhārī*. Berkeley and Seattle, October 27, 2010. http://Gāndhārī.org/a_dictionary.php.

Baxter, William H. 1992. *A Handbook of Old Chinese Phonology*. Berlin: Mouton de Gruyter.

Bayle, Pierre 1740. *Dictionnaire historique et critique. 5e édition.* Amsterdam: P. Brunel.

Beckwith, Christopher I. 1984. Aspects of the Early History of the Central Asian Guard Corps in Islam. *Archivum Eurasiae Medii Aevi* 4: 29–43.

——— 1987. *The Tibetan Empire in Central Asia: A History of the Struggle for Great Power among Tibetans, Turks, Arabs, and Chinese during the Early Middle Ages.* Princeton: Princeton University Press. Rev. ed. 1993.

——— 2004. *Koguryo, the Language of Japan's Continental Relatives: An Introduction to the Historical-Comparative Study of the Japanese-Koguryoic Languages, with a Preliminary Description of Archaic Northeastern Middle Chinese.* Leiden: Brill. 2nd ed. 2007.

——— 2006. Old Tibetan and the dialects and periodization of Old Chinese. *In:* C. I. Beckwith, ed., *Medieval Tibeto-Burman Languages II.* Leiden: Brill, 179–200.

——— 2007a. On the Proto-Indo-European Obstruent System. *Historische Sprachforschung* 120: 1–19.

——— 2007b. *Phoronyms: Classifiers, Class Nouns, and the Pseudopartitive Construction.* New York: Peter Lang.

——— 2008. Old Chinese Loans in Tibetan and the Non-uniqueness of "Sino-Tibetan". *In*: C. I. Beckwith, ed., *Medieval Tibeto-Burman Languages III.* Halle: IITBS GmbH, 161–201.

——— 2009. *Empires of the Silk Road: A History of Central Eurasia from the Bronze Age to the Present.* Princeton: Princeton University Press. Rev. ed. 2011.

——— 2010a. A Note on the Heavenly Kings of Ancient Central Eurasia. *Archivum Eurasiae Medii Aevi* 17: 7–10.

——— 2010b. Old Chinese Loanwords in Korean. *In*: Sang-Oak Lee, ed., *Contemporary Korean Linguistics: International Perspectives.* Seoul: Thaehaksa, 1–22.

——— 2011a. The Central Eurasian Culture Complex in the Tibetan Empire: The Imperial Cult and Early Buddhism. *In*: Ruth Erken, ed., *1000 Jahre asiatisch-europäische Begegnung.* Frankfurt: Peter Lang, 221–238.

——— 2011b. Pyrrho's Logic. *Elenchos* 32.2: 287–327.

——— 2012a. On Zhangzhung and Bon. *In*: Henk Blezer, ed., *Emerging Bon.* Halle: IITBS GmbH, 164–184.

——— 2012b. The Origin of the Avesta and the Spread of Mazdaism in the "Axial Age". Paper presented at the conference "The Influence of Central Eurasian Religious Beliefs on the Cultures of the Periphery", Ruhr-Universität, Bochum, April 25.

——— 2012c. *Warriors of the Cloisters: The Central Asian Origins of Science in the Medieval World.* Princeton: Princeton University Press.

——— 2013. Sources of the Axial Age: Western Old Indic Elements in Old Persian and Their Influence on China and Korea. Lecture 3. Seoul: AKS Lecture Series of World Distinguished Scholars, 80–94.

——— 2014. The Aramaic Source of the East Asian Word for "Buddhist Monastery": On the Spread of Central Asian Monasticism in the Kushan Period. *Journal Asiatique* 302.1: 109–136.

——— Forthcoming-a. Forest Śramaṇas and Town Śramaṇas: On the Lifestyles of Early Buddhist Ascetics. *In*: Nikolas Jaspert and Reinhard F. Glei, eds., *Locating Religions.* Leiden: Brill.

——— Forthcoming-b. Old Chinese "Boat." *Warring States Papers* 2.

Beckwith, Christopher I. and Michael L. Walter 2010. On the Meaning of Old Tibetan *rje-blon* during the Tibetan Empire Period. *Journal Asiatique* 298.2: 535–548.

Benveniste, Émile, et al. 1958. Une bilingue gréco-araméenne d'Asoka. *Journal Asiatique* 246: 1–48.

Bett, Richard 1994a. Aristocles on Timon on Pyrrho: The Text, Its Logic and Its Credibility. *Oxford Studies in Ancient Philosophy* 12: 137–181.

——— 1994b. What Did Pyrrho Think about "The Nature of the Divine and the Good"? *Phronesis* 39.3: 303–337.

Bett, Richard, trans. 1997. *Sextus Empiricus, Against the Ethicists*. Oxford: Clarendon.

——— 1999. On the Pre-history of Pyrrhonism. *Proceedings of the Boston Area Colloquium in Ancient Philosophy* 15: 137–166.

——— 2000. *Pyrrho, His Antecedents, and His Legacy*. Oxford: Oxford University Press.

——— 2005. *See* Sextus Empiricus 2005.

——— 2006. Pyrrho. *In:* E. Zalta, ed., *Stanford Encyclopedia of Philosophy*. www.plato.stanford.edu/entries/pyrrho/.

——— ed., 2010a. *The Cambridge Companion to Ancient Scepticism*. Cambridge: Cambridge University Press.

——— 2010b. Introduction. *In:* R. Bett, ed., *The Cambridge Companion to Ancient Scepticism*. Cambridge: Cambridge University Press, 1–10.

Böhtlingk, Otto 1928. *Sanskrit-Wörterbuch in kürzerer Fassung* (St. Petersburg 1879–1889) with *Nachträge zum Sanskrit-Wörterbuch* by Richard Schmidt (Leipzig 1928), from *Cologne Digital Sanskrit Dictionaries* online. http://www.sanskrit-lexicon.uni-koeln.de/scans/PWScan/disp2/.

Bosworth, A. B. 1988. *Conquest and Empire: The Reign of Alexander the Great*. Cambridge: Cambridge University Press.

Boucher, Daniel 2008. *Bodhisattvas of the Forest and the Formation of the Mahāyāna: A Study and Translation of the Rāṣṭrapālaparipṛcchā-sūtra*. Honolulu: University of Hawaii Press.

Boyce, Mary 1979. *Zoroastrians: Their Religious Beliefs and Practices*. London: Routledge & Kegan Paul.

Boyce, Mary and Frantz Grenet 1991. *A History of Zoroastrianism*. Vol. 3. Leiden: Brill.

Braarvig, Jens and Fredrik Liland, eds. 2010. *Traces of Gandhāran Buddhism: An Exhibition of Ancient Buddhist Manuscripts in the Schøyen Collection*. Oslo: Hermes.

Bretfeld, Sven 2003. Visuelle Repräsentation im sogenannten "buddhistischen Yogalehrbuch" aus Qïzïl. *Veröffentlichungen der Societas Uralo-Altaica* 61 (Indien und Zentralasien: Sprach-und Kulturkontakt): 168–205.

Briant, Pierre 1996. *Histoire de l'Empire perse: de Cyrus à Alexandre*. Paris: Fayard.

Bronkhorst, Johannes 1986. *The Two Traditions of Meditation in Ancient India*. Stuttgart: Franz Steiner Verlag Wiesbaden.

——— 2007. *Greater Magadha: Studies in the Culture of Early India*. Leiden: Brill.

——— 2009. *Buddhist Teaching in India*. Boston: Wisdom.

——— 2011. *Buddhism in the Shadow of Brahmanism*. Leiden: Brill.

Brooks, E. Bruce 2010. The Formation of the Dàu/Dv́ Jīng. *Warring States Papers* 1: 143–147.

Brooks, E. Bruce and A. Taeko Brooks 2007. An Overview of Selected Classical Chinese Texts. May 12, 2013. http://www.umass.edu/wsp/resources/overview.html#04c.

——— 2015. *The Emergence of China: From Confucius to the Empire*. Amherst: Warring States Project.

Brunschwig, Jacques 1992. Pyrrhon et Philista. *In:* M.-O. Goulet-Cazé, G. Madec, and D. O'Brien, eds., *Chercheurs de sagesse: Hommage à Jean Pépin*. Paris: Institut d'Études Augustiniennes, 133–146.

——— 1994. *Papers in Hellenistic Philosophy*. Cambridge: Cambridge University Press.

——— 1997. L'aphasie pyrrhonienne. *In:* C. Lévy and L. Pernot, eds., *Dire l'évidence (Philosophie et rhétorique antiques)*. Paris: L'Harmattan, 297–320.

——— 1998. Pyrrho. *In*: E. Craig, ed., *Routledge Encyclopedia of Philosophy*. London: Routledge. www.rep.routledge.com/article/A101.

——— 1999. Introduction: The Beginnings of Hellenistic Philosophy. *In:* Keimpe Algra et al., eds., *The Cambridge History of Hellenistic Philosophy*. Cambridge: Cambridge University Press, 229–259.

Bury, R. G., ed. and trans. 1933. *Sextus Empiricus*. Vols. I–IX. Cambridge, Massachusetts: Harvard University Press.

Castagnoli, L. 2002. Review of *Pyrrho: His Antecedents and His Legacy* (Oxford: Oxford University Press, 2000) by R. Bett. *Ancient Philosophy* 22: 443–457.

Cawthorne, Nigel 2004. *Alexander the Great*. London: Haus.

Chiesara, M. L. 2001. *Aristocles of Messene: Testimonia and Fragments*. Oxford: Oxford University Press.

Choksy, Jamsheed K. 2007. Reassessing the Material Contexts of Ritual Fires in Ancient Iran. *Iranica Antiqua* 42: 229–269.

Clark, Gillian, trans. 2000. *Porphyry: On Abstinence from Killing Animals*. London: Duckworth.

Clayman, Dee L. 2009. *Timon of Phlius: Pyrrhonism into Poetry*. Berlin: Walter de Gruyter.

Clement of Alexandria. *See* Stählin 1906.

Conche, Marcel 1994. *Pyrrhon, ou l'apparence*. Paris: Press universitaires de France.

Curtis, John E. and Shahrokh Razmjou 2005. The Palace. *In:* John E. Curtis and Nigel Tallis, eds., *Forgotten Empire: The World of Ancient Persia*. Berkeley: University of California Press, 50–103.

Curtis, John and St. John Simpson, eds. 2010. *The World of Achaemenid Persia: History, Art and Society in Iran and the Ancient Near East*. London: I.B. Tauris.

Curtis, John E. and Nigel Tallis, eds. 2005. *Forgotten Empire: The World of Ancient Persia*. Berkeley: University of California Press.

D'Amato, Mario 2009. Why the Buddha Never Uttered a Word. *In*: Mario D'Amato, Jay L. Garfield, and Tom J. F. Tillemans, eds., *Pointing at the Moon: Buddhism, Logic, Analytic Philosophy*. Oxford: Oxford University Press, 41–55.

Dandamayev, Muhammad A. 1993. Cyrus II the Great. *Encyclopaedia Iranica* 6.5: 516–521.

Decleva Caizzi, Fernanda 1981. *Pirrone: Testimonianze*. Naples: Bibliopolis.

Deeg, Max 2009. From the Iron-Wheel to Bodhisattvahood: Aśoka in Buddhist Culture and Memory. *In:* Patrick Olivelle, ed., *Aśoka: In History and Historical Memory*. Delhi: Motilal Banarsidass, 109–144.

Deeg, Max and Iain Gardner 2009. Indian Influence on Mani Reconsidered: The Case of Jainism. *International Journal of Jaina Studies* 5.2: 1–30.

de Jong, Albert 2010. Ahura Mazdā the Creator. *In:* John Curtis and St. John Simpson, eds., *The World of Achaemenid Persia: History, Art and Society in Iran and the Ancient Near East.* London: I.B. Tauris, 85–89.

de La Porte du Theil, F.J.G., D. Coray (Korais [Adamantios Koraēs]), A. J. Letronne, and P.G.J. Gosselin, trans. 1805–1819. *Géographie de Strabon.* Paris: L'Imprimerie impériale.

Dihle, A. 1964. Indische Philosophen bei Clemens Alexandrinus. *In:* Alfred Stuiber and Alfred Hermann, eds., *Mullus: Festschrift Theodor Klauser.* Münster: Aschendorff, 60–70.

Diogenes Laertius, *Lives of Eminent Philosophers. See* Hicks 1925.

Dutt, Sukumar 1962. *Buddhist Monks and Monasteries of India.* London: George Allen and Unwin.

Eichner, H. 1970. *Friedrich Schlegel.* New York: Twayne.

Eusebius 1983. *Praeparatio Evangelica.* Ed. K. Mras, *Eusebius Werke*, Achter Band: Die *Praeparatio Evangelica*, Zweiter Teil: Die Bucher XI bis XV, Register. Berlin: Akademie-Verlag.

Falk, Harry 1993. *Schrift im alten Indien—Ein Forschungsbericht mit Anmerkungen.* Tübingen: Gunter Narr Verlag.

——— 2006. *Aśokan Sites and Artefacts: A Source-book with Bibliography.* Mainz: Philipp Von Zabern.

——— 2009. The Diverse Degrees of Authenticity of Aśokan Texts. *In:* Patrick Olivelle, ed., *Aśoka in History and Historical Memory.* Delhi: Motilal Banarsidass, 5–17.

Freiberger, Oliver, ed. 2006. *Asceticism and Its Critics: Historical Accounts and Comparative Perspectives.* Oxford: Oxford University Press.

Frye, Richard N. 2010. Cyrus the Mede and Darius the Achaemenid? *In:* John Curtis and St. John Simpson, eds., *The World of Achaemenid Persia: History, Art and Society in Iran and the Ancient Near East.* London: I.B. Tauris, 17–19.

Gethin, Rupert 1998. *The Foundations of Buddhism.* Oxford: Oxford University Press.

Ghosh, A., ed. 1990. *An Encyclopaedia of Indian Archaeology.* 2 vols. Leiden: Brill.

Gifford, Edwin H., trans. 1903. *Preparation for the Gospel.* Vols. 1–2. Oxford: Clarendon. Reprinted, Eugene: Wipf and Stock, 2002.

Godley, A. D., ed. and trans. 1926. *Herodotus.* London: W. Heinemann. Perseus online ed.

Gombrich, Richard 1996. *How Buddhism Began: The Conditioned Genesis of the Early Teachings.* London: Athlone Press.

Gómez, Luis O. 1976. Proto-Mādhyamika in the Pāli Canon. *Philosophy East and West* 26.2: 137–165.

Graham, A. C. 1981. *Chuang-tzu: The Seven Inner Chapters and Other Writings from the Book "Chuang-tzu".* London: George Allen and Unwin.

Griffith, Mark 2013. *Aristophanes'* Frogs. Oxford: Oxford University Press.

Halbfass, Wilhelm 1995. Early Indian References to the Greeks and the First Encounters between Buddhism and the West. *In:* Heinz Bechert, ed., *When Did the Buddha Live? The Controversy on the Dating of the Historical Buddha.* Delhi: Sri Satguru Publications, 195–209.

Halkias, Georgios 2012. *Luminous Bliss: A Religious History of Pure Land Literature in Tibet.* Honolulu: University of Hawaii Press.

——— 2013. When the Greeks Converted the Buddha: Asymmetrical Transfers of Knowledge in Indo-Greek Cultures. *In*: Peter Wick and Volker Rabens, eds., *Religions and Trade: Religious Formation, Transformation and Cross-Cultural Exchange between East and West*. Leiden: Brill, 65–115.

Hamilton, Sue 2000. *Early Buddhism: A New Approach*. Richmond, Surrey: Curzon.

Hankinson, R. J. 1995. *The Sceptics*. London: Routledge.

Harrison, Paul 1998. *The Pratyutpanna Samādhi Sūtra, Translated by Lokakṣema, Translated from the Chinese (Taishō Volume 13. Number 418)*. BDK English Tripitaka 25–II, 1–116. Berkeley: Numata Center for Buddhist Translation and Research.

Härtel, Herbert 1995. Archaeological Research on Ancient Buddhist Sites. *In*: Heinz Bechert, ed., *When Did the Buddha Live? The Controversy on the Dating of the Historical Buddha*. Delhi: Sri Satguru Publications, 141–159.

Henderson, Jeffrey 2002. *Aristophanes: Frogs, Assemblywomen, Wealth*. Cambridge, Massachusetts: Harvard University Press.

Henricks, Robert G. 2006. *Lao Tzu's Tao Te Ching: A Translation of the Startling New Documents Found at Guodian*. New York: Columbia University Press.

Herodotus. *See* Godley 1926.

Hicks, R.D., ed. and trans. 1925. *Diogenes Laertius: Lives of Eminent Philosophers*. Cambridge, Massachusetts: Harvard University Press. Reprinted 1991.

Hirzel, Rudolf 1883. *Untersuchungen zu Ciceros philosophischen Schriften*. Vol. 3. Leipzig: S. Hirzel.

Holt, Frank Lee 1989. *Alexander the Great and Bactria: The Formation of a Greek Frontier in Central Asia*. Leiden: Brill.

Hultzsch, E. 1925. *Corpus Inscriptionum Indicarum, Vol. I: Inscriptions of Asoka*. New ed. Oxford: Clarendon.

Hume, David 1758. *An Enquiry Concerning Human Understanding*. *In*: David Hume, *Essays and Treatises on Several Subjects. A New Edition* [Vol. 1, *Essays, Moral, Political, and Literary*. Vol. 2, *An Enquiry Concerning Human Understanding. A Dissertation on the Passions. An Enquiry Concerning the Principles of Morals. The Natural History of Religion*]. London: Printed for A. Millar; Edinburgh: A. Kincaid and A. Donaldson. Reprinted in 1760, 1764, 1767, 1768, 1770, and 1772 for A. Millar or his successor, T. Cadell, in the Strand, London; and A. Kincaid, and A. Donaldson, at Edinburgh.

Itō, Gikyō (伊藤義教) 1966. 阿育王のアラム語碑について (Aiku-ō no Aramugo hi ni tsuite, On the Aramaic Inscriptions of Aśoka). オリエント (Oriento), Bulletin of the Society for Near Eastern Studies in Japan 8: 1–24.

Jaspers, Karl 1949. *Vom Ursprung und Ziel der Geschichte*. Zürich: Artemis. Translated into English as *The Origin and Goal of History*. New Haven: Yale University Press, 1953.

Jones, Horace Leonard 1930. *Strabo: Geography*, Books 15–16. London: William Heinemann.

Jones, W.H.S., ed. and trans. 1917. *Pausanias: Description of Greece*. Vol. 3. London: William Heinemann.

Karlgren, Bernhard 1957. *Grammata Serica recensa*. Stockholm: Museum of Far Eastern Antiquities. Reprinted from *Bulletin of the Museum of Far Eastern Antiquities* 29, 1972.

Karttunen, Klaus 1989. *India in Early Greek Literature*. Helsinki: Finnish Oriental Society.

——— 1997. *India and the Hellenistic World.* Helsinki: Finnish Oriental Society.

Keown, Damien 1996. Buddhism and Suicide: The Case of Channa. *Journal of Buddhist Ethics* 3: 8–31.

Kindstrand, Jan Fredrik 1981. *Anacharsis, the Legend and the Apophthegmata*. Uppsala: Acta Universitatis upsaliensis.

Kleine, Christoph 2006. The Epitome of the Ascetic Life: The Controversy over Self-Mortification and Ritual Suicide as Ascetic Practices in East Asian Buddhism. *In:* Oliver Freiberger, ed., *Asceticism and Its Critics: Historical Accounts and Comparative Perspectives*. Oxford: Oxford University Press, 153–177.

Korais. *See* de La Porte du Theil et al.

Kuhrt, Amélie 2007. *The Persian Empire: A Corpus of Sources from the Achaemenid Period*. 2 vols. London: Routledge.

Kuzminski, Adrian 2007. Pyrrhonism and the Mādhyamaka. *Philosophy East & West* 57.4: 482–511.

——— 2010. *Pyrrhonism: How the Ancient Greeks Reinvented Buddhism*. Lanham, MD: Lexington Books.

Lammenranta, Markus 2009. Epistemic Circularity. *In: Internet Encyclopedia of Philosophy*, May 20, 2009. http://www.iep.utm.edu/ep-circ/#H5.

Lamotte, Etienne 1988. *History of Indian Buddhism: From the Origins to the Saka Era*. Louvain-la-Neuve: Université catholique de Louvain, Institut Orientaliste.

Landesman, Charles 2002. *Skepticism: The Central Issues*. Oxford: Blackwell.

Laycock, Henry 2010. Object. *In:* Edward N. Zalta, ed., *The Stanford Encyclopedia of Philosophy*, Winter 2011 ed. http://plato.stanford.edu/archives/win2011/entries/object/.

Lee, Mi-Kyoung 2010. Antecedents in Early Greek Philosophy. *In:* R. Bett, ed., *The Cambridge Companion to Ancient Scepticism*. Cambridge: Cambridge University Press, 13–35.

Lennon, Thomas M. and Michael Hickson 2013. Pierre Bayle. *In:* Edward N. Zalta, ed., *The Stanford Encyclopedia of Philosophy*, Winter 2013 ed. http://plato.stanford.edu/archives/win2013/entries/bayle/.

Liddell, H., R. Scott, and H. Jones 1968. *Greek-English Lexicon*. 9th ed. Oxford: Clarendon.

Long, A. A. and D. N. Sedley 1987. *The Hellenistic Philosophers*. 2 vols. Cambridge: Cambridge University Press.

Lubac, H. 1952. *La rencontre du bouddhisme et de l'Occident*. Paris: Aubier.

Magee, Peter and Cameron A. Petrie 2010. West of the Indus—East of the Empire: The Archaeology of the Pre-Achaemenid and Achaemenid Periods in Baluchistan and the North-West Frontier Province, Pakistan. *In:* John Curtis and St. John Simpson, eds., *The World of Achaemenid Persia: History, Art and Society in Iran and the Ancient Near East*. London: I.B. Tauris, 503–522.

Mair, Victor 1990a. [*The*] *File* [*on the Cosmic*] *Track* [*and Individual*] *Dough*[*tiness*]: Introduction and Notes for a Translation of the Ma-wang-tui Manuscripts of the *Lao Tzu* [*Old Master*]. Philadelphia: University of Pennsylvania (Sino-Platonic Papers No. 20).

——— 1990b. *Tao te ching: The Classic Book of Integrity and the Way, by Lao Tzu*. New York: Bantam.

Malandra, W.W. 2009. Zoroaster ii. General Survey. *In: Encyclopaedia Iranica.* http://www.iranicaonline.org/articles/zoroaster-ii-general-survey.
Marshall, John Hubert 1951. *Taxila: An Illustrated Account of Archaeological Excavations Carried Out under the Orders of the Government of India between the Years 1913 and 1934.* Cambridge: Cambridge University Press.
Mattos, Gilbert L. 1998. Notes on a Warring States Period Jade Inscription: The Xíng Qì Yù Inscription 行氣玉銘. Handout, Warring States Working Group 10, April 25, 1998.
——— Forthcoming. The Xing Qi Jade Inscription. *Warring States Papers* 2.
Mayrhofer, Manfred 1976. *Kurzgefaßtes etymologisches Wörterbuch des Altindischen.* Vol. 3. Heidelberg: Winter Verlag.
McCrindle, J. W. 1877. *Ancient India as Described by Megasthenês and Arrian.* Calcutta: Thacker, Spink.
McEvilley, Thomas 2002. *The Shape of Ancient Thought: Comparative Studies in Greek and Indian Philosophies.* New York: Allworth Press.
McNabb, J. W. 2009. Review of *The Riddle of Hume's Treatise: Skepticism, Naturalism, and Irreligion* (New York: Oxford University Press, 2008) by Paul Russell. *Eighteenth-Century Fiction* 22.1: 151–154.
Meadows, Andrew R. 2005. The Administration of the Achaemenid Empire. *In:* John E. Curtis and Nigel Tallis, eds., *Forgotten Empire: The World of Ancient Persia.* Berkeley: University of California Press, 181–209.
Mette, Adalheid 1995. The Synchronism of the Buddha and the Jina Mahāvīra. *In:* Heinz Bechert, ed., *When Did the Buddha Live? The Controversy on the Dating of the Historical Buddha.* Delhi: Sri Satguru Publications, 179–183.
Minon, Sophie 2007. *Les inscriptions éléennes dialectales (vi^{e}-iie siècle avant J.-C.).* 2 vols. Geneva: Librairie Droz.
Mitchell, Donald W. 2008. *Buddhism: Introducing the Buddhist Experience.* 2nd ed. New York: Oxford University Press.
Monier-Williams, Monier 1899. *A Sanskrit-English Dictionary.* New ed. Reprinted, Delhi: Motilal Banarsidass, 1988.
Morris, William Edward and Charlotte R. Brown 2014. David Hume. *In:* Edward N. Zalta, ed., *Stanford Encyclopedia of Philosophy*, Summer 2014 ed. http://plato.stanford.edu/archives/sum2014/entries/hume/.
Nattier, Jan 2008. *A Guide to the Earliest Chinese Buddhist Translations: Texts from the Eastern Han* 東漢 *and Three Kingdoms* 三國 *Periods.* Tokyo: International Research Institute for Advanced Buddhology.
Naveh, Joseph and Shaul Shaked 2012. *Aramaic Documents from Ancient Bactria (Fourth Century* BCE*) from the Khalili Collections.* London: Khalili Family Trust.
Nöldeke, Th. 1898. *Kurzgefasste syrische Grammatik.* Leipzig: Tauchnitz.
Norman, K. R. 1987. Aśoka's "Schism" Edict. *Bukkyōgaku seminā* 46: 1–34.
——— 1993. Review of *The Oldest Pāli Manuscript. Four Folios of the Vinaya-Piṭaka from the National Archives, Kathmandu* (Untersuchungen zur Sprachgeschichte und Handschriftenkunde des Pāli II) by Oskar von Hinüber. *Journal of the Royal Asiatic Society*, Third Series 3.2: 281–284.
——— 2012. The Languages of the Composition and Transmission of the Aśokan Inscriptions. *In:* Patrick Olivelle, Janice Leoshko, and Himanshu Prabha Ray, eds. *Reimagining Aśoka: Memory and History.* Oxford: Oxford University Press, 38–62.

Norton, David F. 2009. An Introduction to Hume's Thought. *In*: David F. Norton and Jacqueline Taylor, eds., *The Cambridge Companion to Hume*, 2nd ed. Cambridge: Cambridge University Press, 1–39.

Norton, David F. and Jacqueline Taylor, eds. 2009. *The Cambridge Companion to Hume*. 2nd ed. Cambridge: Cambridge University Press.

O'Keefe, Tim 2006. Anaxarchus (c. 380–c. 320 BC). *In: Internet Encyclopedia of Philosophy*. http://www.iep.utm.edu/anaxarch/.

Olivelle, Patrick, ed. 2009. *Aśoka in History and Historical Memory*. Delhi: Motilal Banarsidass.

——— 2012. Aśoka's inscriptions as text and ideology. *In*: Patrick Olivelle, Janice Leoshko, and Himanshu Prabha Ray, eds., *Reimagining Aśoka: Memory and History*. Oxford: Oxford University Press, 157–183.

Olivelle, Patrick, Janice Leoshko, and Himanshu Prabha Ray, eds. 2012. *Reimagining Aśoka: Memory and History*. Oxford: Oxford University Press.

Olson, S. Douglas 2008. *Athenaeus: The Learned Banqueters*. Bks. 6–7. Cambridge, Massachusetts: Harvard University Press.

Pai Yü-lan 白於藍 2012. 戰國秦漢簡帛古書通假字彙纂 *Zhanguo Qinhan jianbo gushu tongjiazi huizuan*. Fu-chou: Fu-chien jen-min ch'u-pan-she.

Parker, Grant 2008. *The Making of Roman India*. Cambridge: Cambridge University Press.

——— 2012. Aśoka the Greek, converted and translated. *In*: Patrick Olivelle, Janice Leoshko, and Himanshu Prabha Ray, eds., *Reimagining Aśoka: Memory and History*. Oxford: Oxford University Press, 310–326.

Patillon, Michel and Alain Ph. Segonds 1995. *Porphyre: De l'abstinence. Tome III, Livre IV. Texte établi, traduit et annoté*. Paris: Les belles lettres.

Pausanias. *See* Spiro 1903 and Jones 1917.

Phelps, T. A. 2010. *The Lumbini and Piprahwa Deceptions & the Identification of the Real Sites of the Buddha's Birth and Death*. N.p.: Terence Phelps (= T. A. Phelps, *Lumbini on Trial: The Untold Story*, 2008). http://www.lumkap.org.uk/Lumbini%20On%20Trial.htm#ref38.

Plato. *See* Shorey 1937.

Plutarch, *Moralia*. *See* Babbitt 1927.

Popkin, Richard H. 1951. David Hume: His Pyrrhonism and His Critique of Pyrrhonism. *Philosophical Quarterly* 1.5: 385–407.

Popper, Karl R. 1965. *Conjectures and Refutations: The Growth of Scientific Knowledge*. Rev. ed. New York: Basic Books.

Porphyry. *See* Patillon and Segonds 1995.

Poucha, Pavel 1955. *Thesaurus linguae Tocharicae dialecti A*. Prague: Státni Pedagogické Nakladatatelství.

Pulleyblank, Edwin G. 1991. *Lexicon of Reconstructed Pronunciation in Early Middle Chinese, Late Middle Chinese, and Early Mandarin*. Vancouver: UBC Press.

Radt, Stefan 2005. *Strabons Geographika, Band 4. Buch XIV–XVII: Text und Übersetzung*. Göttingen: Vandenhoek & Ruprecht.

——— 2009. *Strabons Geographika, Band 4. Buch XIV–XVII: Kommentar*. Göttingen: Vandenhoek & Ruprecht.

Razmjou, Shahrokh 2005. Religion and Burial Customs. *In:* John E. Curtis and Nigel Tallis, eds., *Forgotten Empire: The World of Ancient Persia*. Berkeley: University of California Press, 150–180.

Reale, G. 1981. Ipotesi per una rilettura della filosofia di Pirrone di Elide. *In:* G. Giannantoni, ed., *Lo scetticismo antico*. Naples: Bibliopolis, 245–336.

Robins, Dan, Forthcoming. The Theme of Uselessness in the Jwāngdž. *Warring States Papers* 2.

Robson, E. Iliff 1929–1933. *Arrian*. 2 Vols. London: Heinemann.

Romm, James and Pamela Mensch 2005. *Alexander the Great: Selections from Arrian, Diodorus, Plutarch, and Quintus Curtius*. Indianapolis: Hackett.

Ross, W. D. and J. A. Smith 1908. *The Works of Aristotle*. 12 vols. Vol. 3, *Meteorologica; De mundo; De anima; Parva naturalia; De spiritu*. Oxford: Clarendon.

Russell, Paul 2008. *The Riddle of Hume's Treatise: Skepticism, Naturalism, and Irreligion*. New York: Oxford University Press, 2008.

——— 2012. Hume on Religion. *In: The Stanford Encyclopedia of Philosophy, Spring 2012 ed.* http://plato.stanford.edu/archives/spr2012/entries/hume-religion/.

Salomon, Richard 1998. *Indian Epigraphy: A Guide to the Study of Inscriptions in Sanskrit, Prakrit, and the Other Indo-Aryan Languages*. New York: Oxford University Press.

Schlingloff, Dieter 2006. *Ein buddhistisches Yogalehrbuch*. Unveränderter Nachdruck der Ausgabe von 1964 unter Beigabe aller seither bekannt gewordenen Fragmente Herausgegeben von Jens-Uwe Hartmann und Josef Röllicke. Düsseldorf: Haus der Japanischen Kultur (EKO).

Schopen, Gregory 1987. Burial ad Sanctos and the Physical Presence of the Buddha in Early Indian Buddhism: A Study in the Archaeology of Religions. *Religion* 17: 193–225. Reprinted in Schopen 1997: 114–147.

——— 1997. *Bones, Stones, and Buddhist Monks: Collected Papers on the Archaeology, Epigraphy, and Texts of Monastic Buddhism in India*. Honolulu: University of Hawaii Press.

——— 2004. *Buddhist Monks and Business Matters: Still More Papers on Monastic Buddhism in India*. Honolulu: University of Hawaii Press.

——— 2005. *Figments and Fragments of Mahāyāna Buddhism in India: More Collected Papers*. Honolulu: University of Hawaii Press.

——— 2006. The Buddhist "Monastery" and the Indian Garden: Aesthetics, Assimilations, and the Siting of Monastic Establishments. *Journal of the American Oriental Society* 126.4: 487–505.

——— 2007. Cross-Dressing with the Dead. *In:* Bryan J. Cuevas and Jacqueline Ilyse Stone, eds., *The Buddhist Dead: Practices, Discourses, Representations*. Honolulu: University of Hawaii Press, 60–104.

Searle, John R. 1983. The Word Turned Upside Down. *New York Review of Books*. October 27, 1983.

——— 1995. *The Construction of Social Reality*. New York: Free Press.

Senart, Émile 1891. The Inscriptions of Piyadasi. Chapter IV. The Author and the Language of the Inscriptions, trans. G. A. Grierson. *Indian Antiquary* 20: 229–266.

Sextus Empiricus. *See* Bury 1933.

Sextus Empiricus 2005. *Adversus mathematicos*, trans. Richard Bett: *Sextus Empiricus: Against the Logicians*. Cambridge: Cambridge University Press, 2005.

Shahbazi, Shapur A. 2012. Darius I the Great. *Encyclopaedia Iranica* 7.1 (1994): 41–50, updated online edition.

Shih chi. *See*: Ssu-ma Ch'ien.

Shorey, Paul, ed. and trans. 1937. *Plato: The Republic*. London: William Heinemann.

Sims-Williams, N. 2010. A Bactrian Buddhist Manuscript. *In*: Jens Braarvig and Fredrik Liland, eds., *Traces of Gandhāran Buddhism: An Exhibition of Ancient Buddhist Manuscripts in the Schøyen Collection*. Oslo: Hermes, 72–73.

Sircar, D. C. 1975. *Inscriptions of Aśoka*. 3rd ed. New Delhi: Publications Division, Ministry of Information and Broadcasting, Government of India.

Soudavar, Abolala 2010. The Formation of Achaemenid Imperial Ideology and Its Impact on the *Avesta*. *In*: John Curtis and St. John Simpson, eds., *The World of Achaemenid Persia: History, Art and Society in Iran and the Ancient Near East*. London: I.B. Tauris, 111–138.

Speicht, Allen 2011. Friedrich Schlegel. *In:* Edward N. Zalta, ed., *Stanford Encyclopedia of Philosophy*, Winter 2011 ed. http://plato.stanford.edu/archives/win2011/entries/schlegel/.

Spiro, Fridericus, ed. 1903. *Pausaniae Graeciae descriptio*. Leipzig: Teubner.

Ssu-ma Ch'ien 1963. *Shih chi*. 10 vols. Peking: Chung-hua shu-chü.

Stählin, Otto, ed. 1906. *Clemens Alexandrinus, zweiter Band,* Stromata *Buch I–VI*. Leipzig: J.C. Heinrichs'sche Buchhandlung (Die Griechischen Christlichen Schriftsteller der ersten drei Jahrhunderte, herausgegeben von der Kirchenväter-commission der Königl. Preussischen Akademie der Wissenschaften, Band 15).

Starostin, Sergei A. 1989. Реконструкция древнекитайской фонологической системы. Moscow: Nauka.

Stein, Otto. 1931. Megasthenes. *Paulys Real-Encyclopädie der classischen Altertumswissenschaft: neue Bearbeitung*. Band XV, Halbband 29: 230–326.

Stopper, M. R. 1983. Schizzi Pirroniani. *Phronesis* 28: 265–297.

Strabo, *Geography*. *See* Radt 2005, 2009 and Jones 1930.

Svavarsson, Svavar Hrafn 2010. Pyrrho and Early Pyrrhonism. *In:* R. Bett, ed., *The Cambridge Companion to Ancient Scepticism*. Cambridge: Cambridge University Press, 36–57.

Szemerényi, Oswald 1980. *Four Old Iranian Ethnic Names: Scythian–Skudra–Sogdian–Saka*. Vienna: Österreichischen Akademie der Wissenschaften.

Tambiah, Stanley J. 1984. *The Buddhist Saints of the Forest and the Cult of the Amulet*. Cambridge: Cambridge University Press.

Thorsrud, Harald 2009. *Ancient Scepticism*. Berkeley: University of California Press.

Tredennick, Hugh, ed. and trans. 1933–1935. *Aristotle: Metaphysics*. London: William Heinemann. Perseus online ed.

Tugendhat, Ernst 1982. *Traditional and Analytical Philosophy: Lectures on the Philosophy of Language*. Cambridge: Cambridge University Press.

Van Bladel, Kevin 2010. The Bactrian Background of the Barmakids. *In:* Anna Akasoy, Charles Burnett, and Ronit Yoeli-Tlalim, eds., *Islam and Tibet: Interactions along the Musk Routes*. Farnham: Ashgate, 43–88.

Vickers, John 2010. The Problem of Induction. *In: Stanford Encyclopedia of Philosophy*, Online ed. http://plato.stanford.edu/entries/induction-problem/.

von Fritz, Kurt 1963. Pyrrhon. *Paulys Realencyclopädie der classischen Altertumswissenschaft* 47: 89–106.

Wachsmuth, Curt and Otto Hense, eds. 1884. *Ioannis Stobaei Anthologium*, Bd. 1 (Books I–II). Berlin: Weidmann.

Walter, Michael L. 2013. All That Glitters *Is* Gold: The Place of the Yellow Metal in the Brahmanic, Scythian, and Early Buddhist Traditions. *In: Nepalica-Tibetica: Festgabe for Christoph Cüppers*. Andiast: International Institute for Tibetan and Buddhist Studies, 2: 283–298.

Waters, Matt 2010. Cyrus and the Medes. *In*: John Curtis and St. John Simpson, eds., *The World of Achaemenid Persia: History, Art and Society in Iran and the Ancient Near East*. London: I.B. Tauris, 63–71.

Watkins, Calvert 2000. *The American Heritage Dictionary of Indo-European Roots*. 2nd ed. Boston: Houghton Mifflin.

Watson, Burton 1968. *The Complete Works of Chuang Tzu*. New York: Columbia University Press.

Wilhelm, Helmut 1948. Eine Chou-Inschrift über Atemtechnik. *Monumenta Serica* 13: 385–388.

Willemen, Charles, Bart Dessein, and Collett Cox 1998. *Sarvāstivāda Buddhist Scholasticism*. Leiden: Brill.

Winter, Franz 1999. *Bardesanes von Edessa über Indien: Ein früher syrischer Theologe schreibt über ein fremdes Land*. Thaur: Druck- und Verlagshaus Thaur.

Wu, Xin 2010. Enemies of Empire: A Historical Reconstruction of Political Conflicts between Central Asia and the Persian Empire. *In*: John Curtis and St. John Simpson, eds., *The World of Achaemenid Persia: History, Art and Society in Iran and the Ancient Near East*. London: I.B. Tauris, 545–563.

Wynne, Alexander 2005. The Historical Authenticity of Early Buddhist Literature: A Critical Evaluation. *Wiener Zeitschrift für die Kunde Südasiens* 49: 35–70.

Index

Note: Inclusively-numbered pages include all relevant footnotes on those pages. Endnotes are numbered with lower case Roman numerals attached to their page numbers, as in the text. Frequently cited authors or works, when cited strictly as sources, are not indexed.